ALFRED LOISY

THE ORIGINS OF THE NEW TESTAMENT

(*Les Origines du Nouveau Testament*)

AUTHORIZED TRANSLATION FROM THE FRENCH

BY

L. P. JACKS

THE ORIGINS OF THE NEW TESTAMENT

Alfred Loisy

Translated from the French by

L. P. Jacks

THE BOOK TREE
San Diego, California

This English edition originally published
1950
George Allen & Unwin, Ltd.
London

New material & revision
© The Book Tree 2018

ISBN 978-1-58509-391-5

Cover art
Opening page to St. Mark's Gospel:
the Evangelist Page
from the Harley Golden Gospels
produced circa 800-825 AD, Germany
(text written entirely in gold)
Currently located at The British Library

Cover layout
Paul Tice

Published by
The Book Tree
P O Box 16476
San Diego, CA 92176

www.thebooktree.com

We provide fascinating and educational products to help awaken the public to new ideas and information that would not be available otherwise.
Call 1 (800) 700-8733 for our FREE BOOK TREE CATALOG.

INTRODUCTION

This modest essay on the origins of the New Testament is an explanatory complement to the volume published in 1933 under the title: *La Naissance du Christianisme*—the Birth of the Christian Religion.[1] We propose to resume the examination, as a whole and with greater precision in detail, of documents born in a realm almost outside that of history and written without any care for historical truth as it is now understood. A long-established Christian tradition would exclude these documents from control by scientific and historical research, at least as to the substance of their contents, treating it as almost beyond the scope of such researches and in the main defying appreciation by their method. There are still some who would so exclude them entirely.

A preliminary question which we have not directly attacked in our former publications and which creed-bound interests tend naturally to keep alive, whether consciously or not, the question namely of the supernatural quality in the Bible, must first be probed to the bottom, in order that the rights of criticism in this field may be established without other restriction than that of the rules proper to itself. The question turns on an idea which may be taken in two senses—the idea of the supernatural—and involves a real equivocation. We are well aware that criticism is not capable of solving every problem; but neither are we ignorant that the investigations of the critic cannot have, ought not to have and, in fact, have not any limits save those of its own natural resources. No authority has the right to impose conclusions upon the critic in anything that falls within the field of his experience, the field namely of everything susceptible of methodical observation in the system of universal reality.

When the question of the supernatural has been clearly answered the field will be open for the discussion of the essential theme of this book, namely the progressive evolution of the Christian teaching, or catechesis, in all the variety of its forms. These include: (1) the Gospel or Message of Jesus and the primitive teaching about "the last things," or eschatological catechesis,

---

[1] Two earlier complements are: *Le Mandéisme et les origines Chrétiennes* (1934); and *Remarques sur la littérature épistolaire du Nouveau Testament* (1935).

as developed in Christian apocalyptic; (2) the testimony, said to be traditional, concerning the origin of the canonical Gospels; (3) study of the internal evidence afforded by these books, in respect of the Gospel according to Mark, the Gospel according to Matthew, the twin-born books to Theophilus, which afterwards became the Gospel according to Luke and the Acts of the Apostles; the Gospel according to John; (4) the contribution of the Epistle-literature to the elaboration of the primitive catechesis of the Last Things, and the testimony rendered by this literature to the preparation and the fixation of the collection known as the Canon of the New Testament.

Finally it will behove us to crown this long analysis by a general synthesis and interpretation of the conclusions to which we have been led. In this we shall see clearly how the formation of the literature, to which the name "New Testament" is given, was conditioned by the evolution of Christian propaganda and became, so to say, stabilized at the very time when the Church called catholic was constituted and declared the guardian of what it had resolved to uphold as the authentic tradition of Christianity, a tradition which it opposed to the spreading floods of *gnosis*, thenceforth to be condemned as heresy. A great achievement of humanity was here, and not a chain of miracles; an upsurge of spiritual life, but defective in its manifestations, as all things human are. But, being spiritual in origin and essence, it brought the supernatural to light in the only sense in which we of this age are able to conceive the supernatural and to regard it as playing a real part in history.

Doubtless there are some who will judge such a work to be singularly inopportune in present circumstances. The same has been said of some of the author's earlier works which were highly unwelcome to a good many people. Perhaps this book will be equally unwelcome. Whoever has enough goodwill to see in it, before all else, a rather new programme for the research that is needed in this field, and is far from being completed, will exactly discern the intention of its author. As to those who would deem it superfluous, superficial and preposterous, we shall content ourselves with supposing that they have not yet found leisure to consider the true character and infinite complexity of the subject under treatment.

CONTENTS

CHAPTER		PAGE
	AUTHOR'S INTRODUCTION	5
I.	*The Bible as Supernatural*	9
II.	*Eschatological Catechesis the First Form of Christian Teaching*	33
III.	*The Evidence of Tradition concerning the Gospels*	56
IV.	*Analysis of the Gospel Catechesis in Mark*	77
V.	*Analysis of the Gospel Catechesis: The Gospel According to Matthew*	111
VI.	*Analysis of the Writings attributed to Luke*	141
VII.	*The Gospel According to John*	193
VIII.	*The Epistles and the Catechesis*	239
IX.	*Conclusions*	286
	Index	331

Chapter I

THE BIBLE AS SUPERNATURAL

ORTHODOX defenders of Scripture, especially its Catholic defenders, are wont to charge independent critics with lacking intuitive perception of the supernatural which, according to their accusers, shines out in the Scriptures, especially in the New Testament, thus creating a privileged position for the books sacred to Christians and clothing them with authority beyond the range of discussion. These, they say, are divine books alike by their origin and character, replete with truth for all time; records of clearly miraculous events, by which God, from the beginning of time, showed forth the salvation of humanity in signs, prepared it, and at last made it effectual.

In all this, a double meaning, an equivocation, is clearly apparent, of which both the orthodox apologist and the over-confident critic seem alike to be the victims. There are two "supernaturals." The one, which we shall designate as magical, is found existing in all religions and mythologies, as well as in fairy tales; in this kind of supernatural the Jewish and Christian Scriptures have their full share, both in their content and in the orthodox tradition which interprets them. The other, which we shall designate as moral and spiritual, is manifested by the religions of humanity in marvellous outbursts of spiritual life, more notable in some religions, less in others, but outstandingly intense in Judaism and Christianity and conferring on these two an eminent place in the moral evolution of mankind. This supernatural reality is overlooked by those extremists who can see in religion, and in its beliefs and practice, nothing more than the transmission of time-honoured and oppressive absurdities. But this supernatural, while not a miracle in the vulgar sense of the word, belongs to a higher realm than the miraculous. It is the only supernatural worthy of the name and the only kind whose real existence can be confidently affirmed. And theologians who, thinking to defend it, confuse it with miraculous magic, understand it but ill and serve it no better.

THE ORIGINS OF THE NEW TESTAMENT

DIVINE AUTHORSHIP

The idea of books entirely God-made, but written in the languages of men, in the native dialects of particular peoples and in the idiom of given times, an idea widely spread in the ancient world and retained in Christian orthodoxy, is inconsistent and self-contradictory. Professional authors are relatively newcomers in the history of our race. But even if they were more ancient than they are, we can hardly imagine anything more indiscreet, not to say more flagrantly impious, than to put God among these worthies, where he has to be furnished with assistants, as though he could not dispense with them, to write down what he would say and attend to the publication of his works. Theologians tax their wits to explain how God can be, in any real sense, the author of books which he has neither written himself nor dictated word by word. Their explanation is that he *suggested* them. How do they know that? Do they really understand what they are saying?

Had they taken the pains to look into the matter, without thought of axes to be ground, they would have seen that the books themselves make not the slightest claim to the divine origin attributed to them by the theologians, but are in fact made up, in the human manner, of tradition and teaching; of rules political, social and ritual; of liturgical chants; of oracles deemed prophetic (not uncommon in the ancient world, and of which we should be hard put to it to find the fulfilment); of collections of moral precepts such as we find among all nations; and of a group of myths, clearly recognizable as such, to account for the origin of the world and of mankind. All of which has undergone an age-long process of glossing and amalgamation clearly due to human initiative, and not even to be thought of as proceeding from God's initiative in any part or stage of it. What anthropomorphism could be more naïve than that which counts the authorship of books among the attributes of God?

These remarks, it will be said, apply to the Old Testament only. They apply equally to the New. A long, slow process brought the Gospels to their present form without any sign of divine initiative at the beginning or the end or at any point between the two; at a given time they were selected, from among many, by the Church authorities and the text of their content finally determined. The same is true of the Acts of the Apostles. It is well worthy of note that the author of the third Gospel and of Acts, who wrote the prologues to Theophilus, assumes full responsibility for his work, for his method and for the object he has in view. The apostolic Epistles, authentic or not, are personal works called forth by particular occasions. Moreover a considerable part of them are forgeries, for which it would be unseemly enough to make God directly responsible. And what of the Book of Revelation—the Apocalypse of John? The best that can be said of it is that for centuries men have taxed their wits to find in it a meaning which is *not* there, for the simple reason that the meaning which *is* there was immediately contradicted by the course of events. Alas, this glowing prophecy was not fulfilled. Who can believe that it came entire from God? In short, the idea of God as author of books is a myth, if ever there was one, and a myth redolent of magic. A book written by the hand of man and filled throughout with the light of God is as inconceivable as a square circle. The books reputed all divine are simply not filled with truth from beginning to end—far from it! They contain as many errors as books of their kind, written when they were, could be made to hold.

To this notion of divine authorship, so artificial and fragile, the Church committed her future and compromised it in so doing. Persuaded that her sacred books were filled with truth for all time she has not hesitated to oppose them to the scientific movement of our age. We know what has come of that. Everyone has heard of Galileo's adventure and knows what it meant. Meanwhile the Church continues to equivocate; even on the affair of Galileo which, nevertheless, is transparently clear. She is still convinced, and would have it believed, that her sacred books contain nothing contrary to truth about the order of the universe, and that the Bible, though knowing nothing about the matter, does not contradict it, but only uses the common language of mankind which speaks of things as they seem to be. Can she really believe that by a subterfuge of this kind, which amounts to charging the Scriptures with ignorance, she is really safeguarding their divine authority? Is there any denying that the first chapters of Genesis profess to give a true account of the creation of the world, the origin of humanity up to the Deluge and the genealogy of the peoples? All that is unadulterated myth, the babblings of humanity's childhood, but not unmingled with sublimity. If God is the responsible author of the story he must have been ignorant of the constitution of the universe which, on the orthodox hypothesis, he had created, and equally ignorant of the long and confused pre-history of the race which he had brought into being and established on the earth to serve him.

Not only at this starting point, but along the whole line of historical and literary criticism, the traditional doctrine is in complete collapse. To begin with, consider the question which concerns the authenticity of the documents. Since God is their author the divine guarantee covers their attribution to the particular scribes whose names they carry. What an embarrassment is thereby erected by the Pentateuch alone! The attribution of this collection to Moses is attested by Jewish tradition, but equally, it would seem, by the New Testament and by the authority of the Christ himself who, in a certain passage of the fourth Gospel (John v, 46), declares that Moses wrote concerning him. And yet it is the almost unanimous verdict of critics that the oldest sources from which the compilation is derived go no further back than the time of the Israelite monarchy, while the bulk of the cultural legislation contained in it is later than the Babylonian captivity. Not a page, one might even say not a line, can be traced to him whom the tradition of Israel and of the Christian Church regards as the founder of Jewish religion. To explain the divinity of the sources the Papal Commission of Biblical Study declared, in a memorable decree, that Moses had secretaries. The secretaries of Moses! A brilliant discovery, to be sure! But we have nothing to do with them since, if these interesting persons ever existed, we should have to admit that not a trace of their work has come down to us.

This, far from being a solitary case, is only one of the more conspicuous and significant. The case of Isaiah is also worth recalling. The book named after Isaiah as it appears in the Bible contains much besides the authentic oracles of the prophet who was contemporary with Ezechias. Notably one whole section, the last twenty-four chapters, were written, as all the evidence shows, either in presence of the conquest of Babylon by Cyrus or shortly afterwards. None the less they were reputed the work of Isaiah for the sole reason that in the process of copying the manuscript they were attached to the roll that had Isaiah's name on it. Speaking generally we may say that the oracles of the ancient prophets have been systematically completed and interpolated in the process of coming down to us. Has the veracity of God nothing to do with the false attribution of these additions to the authors of the original oracles?

The question assumes a more difficult aspect, if that be possible, when we turn to the books of the New Testament. Here all the writings have human authors who either name themselves or are expressly indicated by tradition. Everyone knows that the Church recognized and retained four Gospels respectively attributed to the apostle Matthew, to Mark (reputed a disciple of Peter), to Luke, who was a disciple of Paul, and to the apostle John. Now it is morally certain, and admitted by the majority even of moderate critics, that these attributions are, to say the least, approximative, the books not having been written all at one time by single hands nor given their present canonical form from the beginning. Many, moreover, are of the opinion that not one of the Gospels is the work of the apostolic person whose name it bears, and that the apostle John, in particular, had nothing whatever to do with writing the Gospel attributed to him. But, if God is their guarantee, his veracity demands that each of them be integrally the work of the author assigned by tradition. We shall return to these Gospels later on to find that their contents, no less than their presumed authenticity, are replete with difficulties for the apologists in question.

We have already mentioned the Acts of the Apostles, a book which, like the third Gospel, presents conditions somewhat peculiar. Alone among New Testament writings these two carry a dedication, of a well-known type in Greco-Roman antiquity. Luke was not the author of the dedications to Theophilus, the general prologue (Luke i, 1–4) forbidding us to include the author of it in the first Christian generation. Furthermore, the part of the prologue to Acts which has been preserved implies that the former book to Theophilus did not contain the birth stories and related only the *ministry* of the Christ up to the time of his death. Finally all the evidence shows that the second part of the original prologue to Acts, n which the proper object of the book was stated by the original author, has been mutilated by a writer who understood that object in a different manner from the author to Theophilus and who, in consequence, had to reconstruct his book from beginning to end as, in fact, he has done. All this later writer has conserved of Luke's work is certain fragments of his memoirs of which the original author to Theophilus had made a fuller use. It follows that Luke wrote neither the third Gospel nor Acts. He wrote only certain passages of the latter book, and we are compelled to recognize at least two stages in the composition of both books. It would seem, however, that the veracity of God forbids us to observe and record such things, and obliges us to maintain that both books, in their canonical edition, are from the hand of Luke.

According to tradition Paul wrote fourteen Epistles and the veracity of God demands the belief that all are truly his. But the Epistle to the Hebrews is positively not from him; the second to Thessalonians is almost certainly apocryphal; so is the Epistle to the Ephesians; many hold that the Epistles to Timothy and to Titus, in their main contents, cannot be his. And we have already pointed out in another work[1] that there is much to be said against the full authenticity of the Epistles to the Romans, to the Corinthians, to the Galatians, to the Colossians. Here is a group of questions which the veracity of God forbids us even to raise.

As to the Catholic Epistles, there is strong reason to think that the Church deemed it necessary to include in the Canon, as pendant to Paul's Epistles, a number of others bearing the names of reputed apostolic persons other than he, notably Peter, John and the two "brothers of the Lord" James and Jude. Not one of these Epistles goes back to the first Christian age. Pseudo-James launches discreet polemic against the theory in Romans of justification by faith alone; pseudo-Jude crosses swords with the gnostics; pseudo-Peter, in the second Epistle, repeats the diatribe of pseudo-Jude and cites a collection of Paul's Epistles of which heretics are making wrong use—not as natural a proceeding as defenders of tradition would make out. For there is not a doubt that he was aiming at Marcion towards the middle of the second

[1] In *The Birth of the Christian Religion.*

century. Add to this that the author, at the beginning of the same Epistle, refers implicitly to the Apocalypse of Peter, composed towards the year 135; a supreme instance of false attribution, though the writing was held in credit by some of the Churches to the end of the second century. The second Epistle of Peter is a barefaced forgery. The first Epistle is not more authentic; it depends on the Pauline group and cannot be earlier than the second third of the second century. The three Epistles attributed to John were composed in the course of the same century to accompany the fourth Gospel when its claims were being pressed among the Asiatic Churches. They are no more the work of the apostle John than is the Gospel itself. But the veracity of God would give us no alternative to believing that all these apocryphal productions come from the persons whose names they bear. Need we add that the Book of Revelation is the work of a certain John who was not John the apostle?

We abstain from the cruelty of further insistence. He compromises God who makes him the author of written books.

MIRACULOUS MAGIC AS AN OPERATING CAUSE OF EVENTS

The compromising effect on traditional belief, due to confounding the supernatural with magic, is equally apparent when we consider the particular events for which magic is made responsible. We limit our remarks to a few essential points in the two Testaments.

The myth of creation in the first chapter of Genesis need not delay us for long. The creation, by the spoken word, of the different parts of the universe, childishly conceived as cut up into separate compartments, is an act of divine magic, which all the goodwill of its apologists will never succeed in bringing into harmony with the known facts of cosmic and terrestrial evolution. The wonder-story of Eden, with the creation of the first human pair and the commission of the first sin, older than the cosmic myth both in conception and structure, is also an obvious myth, a scene from the realm of enchantment where the imagination of adolescent mankind, just beginning to reflect, finds its playground. Whence comes death? is the question then asked. Imagination answers, surely death is something that need not have been; the first man and the first woman ate a strange fruit which their creator had forbidden them to eat. Among good tales here is one finely told. But nothing more.

Another such, mythological and purely pagan, is the story of the intercourse of the sons of God, the angels, with the daughters of men, of which were born the giants whose abominable conduct brought on the Deluge, a story no more worthy of belief when found in the Bible than when found in the old fables of Greece about the union of gods with mortal women, but adopted as true in both Epistles of Peter and in the Epistle of Jude.

As to the Deluge itself, it is beyond dispute that the myth was created in Lower Mesopotamia. The prototype of the Bible story has been found in the bricks of Nineveh and the priority of the Accadian text admits not the slightest doubt: another old fable which Israelite tradition has borrowed from ancient Mesopotamia and has little enough to do with the true history of mankind.

Then the Tower of Babel and the miraculous confusion of tongues, a miracle on the grand scale intended to explain the diversity of peoples, but pure fiction, explaining nothing. A genealogy of the nations which traces their descent from Adam through Noah is little more than a fantasy to smile at, whose sole historical interest lies in a crude chart, or something like it, of the peoples inhabiting the Eastern shore of the Mediterranean at the time the chart was made. Another instance of the mythological fiction to which all these prodigies are reducible.

Turning next to the origin of the Israelites we are not surprised, after what has gone before, to learn that this people also is descended from a single couple, Abraham and his wife Sarah, emigrants from Mesopotamia. Abraham and Sarah produced Isaac who had twin sons, Esau and Jacob, by his wife Rebecca, Esau or Edom, ancestor of the Idumeans; Jacob, finally called Israel, who begat of four wives twelve sons, fathers of the twelve tribes of Israel; the eleventh of these sons is sold by his brothers and carried off into Egypt where he became Pharaoh's chief-minister, in so much that on famine breaking out in Canaan, Jacob and his family migrate to the fertile lands of

Egypt, where they have various experiences; on arrival they are seventy in number; after several generations they become a great people multiplying at such a rate that the Egyptians become alarmed; the Pharaoh of the time who, we are told, knew not Joseph, gives orders to destroy all the Hebrew males as soon as born; but God, who has called Abraham out of Mesopotamia and promised the land of Canaan to his posterity, brings it to pass that the child of a certain Amram, of the tribe of Levi, is found by Pharaoh's daughter exposed in a wicker cradle on the Nile and brought up; this child is Moses; his brilliant career then follows; his flight into Midian and return into Egypt; his unloosing of plagues on Egypt by raising his magic wand which changes into a serpent; departure from Egypt of the chosen people under Moses and his brother Aaron; passage of the Red Sea which divides its waters to let the Israelites pass over and closes them again on Pharaoh's army. Then come forty years in the desert and the feeding of the people with manna and quails, and with water made by Moses to gush from the rock, ending with the departure of the host from the desert for the conquest of Canaan and the death of Moses on Mount Pisgah, whence he can see the land where Israel is to settle. Then comes the passage of the Jordan whose bed becomes dry for the march of the Israelites, and the capture of Jericho whose walls collapse at the sound of Israel's trumpets; the battle of Gibeon where Joshua makes the sun stand still that Israel may have time to complete the enemy's overthrow. After which Joshua proceeds at leisure to parcel out the conquered land among the tribes.

A splendid epic, from which, alas, history can glean hardly a particle of solid matter. Clearly enough its construction of Israel's genealogy is artificial. Peoples are not born in that way. The names, Abraham, Isaac, Jacob-Israel, certainly existed and each of these vocables must have originally corresponded to somebody or to something, but to whom, or to what, is not easily determined. Jacob, as everyone knows, won his name of Israel in a strange combat in which he got the better of God himself. His twelve sons are not simple individuals but types of heroes, divine or tribal. The patriarchal myths figure a peaceful occupation of Canaan and these are doubled, so to say, by myths of a conquest which, taken as they stand, are hardly less imaginative than the former. The adventures of Joseph make a noble story linking the two series of myths together, but nothing of it can be retained by the historian. That relations existed of old between the tribes and Egypt is beyond doubt, but what is here narrated of them never happened. It is to be noted that the legend cannot even give the name of the Pharaoh who exalted Joseph and welcomed his family, and is equally ignorant of the name of the Pharaoh who turned oppressor. Commentators are still cudgelling their brains to discover these names; they may continue to cudgel them to the end of the world but will never find what they seek. The Moses legend is a counterpart to the myth of the oppression and miraculous flight, which the different sources of the Pentateuch have adorned with prodigies enough and to spare. The least uncertain point of the Moses legend is its attachment to the sanctuary of Kadesh. If Moses ever existed it was at Kadesh that he gave out the law, near to the fountain of Judgment, and manipulated the casting of lots (*urim* and *thummim*) which seems to have traditionally belonged to Levi. The Book of the Covenant was not his work, but belongs to the time of the monarchy; neither was Deuteronomy which dates from the reign of Josias, if not from the first years of the captivity; nor the legislation known as Levitical which is less ancient than Deuteronomy. And not only is the authorship of these books none of his; it is improbable that he had any part in the migration of the tribes towards the land of Canaan. This movement had a character very different from that of a conquest achieved by one sweeping stroke. When exactly it began we cannot say and it was not completed before the establishment of the monarchy. Various movements of penetration have to be distinguished; one, from the South by the tribes of Judah, Simeon and Levi, of which that of Judah alone succeeded, the tribes of Simeon and Levi becoming exhausted in the course of it, while another thrust, by the Northern tribes, was made to the East and, in course of time, with more success. It is possible that Joshua played a leading part in the early battles, and that is all we can claim to know about him. Few persons nowadays can seriously believe that he caused the sun to stand still over Gibeon, which some chronicler inferred from what he read in a collection of heroic songs, the *Jashar* (Joshua x, 13). This chronicler, whether understanding or misunderstanding what he read, was clearly the dupe of his gift as a storyteller.[1]

Of the other Old Testament miracles we pause but for a moment over that of Jonah shut up for three days and three nights in the belly of a great fish, and while there even composing a hymn to the glory of the Lord. To question the historicity of this splendid story is doubtless impermissible, but belief in it is not easy. From the historical point of view it has the same guarantees as the adventures of Puss-in-boots or of Hop-o'-my-thumb.

We hasten on to the New Testament which is hardly less penetrated by magic than the Old. On the very threshold we meet an undeniable proof in the stories of the miraculous birth. Two genealogies confront us: the first in Matthew (i, 1–17) comes down from Abraham to Jesus; the second in Luke (iii, 23–38) goes up from Jesus to Adam. (As to the latter we have only to think for a moment on the degree of impossibility involved, in a genealogy of any individual belonging to the human race, which takes its departure from the origin of that race itself. For that reason alone the bare idea of such a list of ancestors belongs unquestionably to the realm of magic.) In the generations covered by both lists they disagree, and will never agree in spite of all the forced and ridiculous conjectures of their interpreters. Moreover—and this is the chief point to be noted—it is clear to all who open their eyes that they were invented to show that Jesus was descended from David through his father Joseph, the last name on the list. This, their original aim, is completely upset

---

[1] It seems probable that the original citation ended with the distich given in verse 12:

> Sun stand thou still over Gibeon
> And thou, Moon, over the valley of Ajalon,

the object of the apostrophe being different from what the writer of *Joshua* takes it to be. In the Greek version of 1 Kings viii, 53 we find a similar citation, with the reference, which seems to have alone preserved the complete text, as spoken by Solomon about the Temple. Reconstructed from the Greek text their meaning would be:

> "Jehovah has fixed the Sun's place in the heavens;
> He bade the Sun take his stand beyond the darkness;
> I have built thee a house for thy habitation
> In which thou shalt dwell month by month."

This refers to the passage of the sun through the signs of the Zodiac and is borrowed from a creation-poem. It was easy in the time when *Joshua* was written to make the sun stand still. Cf. *Iliad*, ii, 411; *Odyssey*, xxiii, 243.

by the introduction of the idea of the virgin conception at a later stage in the development of the story.

That is not all. The two stories, in their main features, have independent origins. That in the third Gospel seems to be a counterpart to a legend of John the Baptist, to which it has been joined on. It presents the parents of Jesus, already espoused, in their home in Nazareth when the angel Gabriel appeared on the scene—and need we say that the proceedings of angels do not impress the modern historian as very solidly guaranteed? Gabriel informs Mary, whose fiancé Joseph is said to belong to the house of David, that she will give birth to a son who will be the Messiah; as guarantee that the promise will be fulfilled he cites the case of Elisabeth whose miraculous pregnancy may well serve for testimony. Here comes a surcharge on the original text in the two verses which announce the virgin conception (Luke i, 34-35). Passing over the marvels which immediately follow and adorn the story, we come to the circumstance which brings Joseph and Mary from their home in Nazareth to Bethlehem, the city of David, in order that Jesus may be born there—the census for taxation ordered by Quirinius. Now the census of Quirinius did not take place before the year 6 of our era, and we are told that the whole affair happened in the time of Herod who died four years before our era began; whence results a difference of at least ten years between the birth of Jesus and the census of Quirinius. To this our hagiographer has paid no heed, and the exegetes labour in vain to put the matter right. We have no heart to dwell on the intervention of angels on the memorable birth-night to guide the shepherds to the cradle. Eight days afterwards the child is circumcised, at the end of forty taken to Jerusalem to be ransomed as a first-born; the aged Simeon prophesies concerning him; the venerable Anna likewise, and the parents return quietly to their home town of Nazareth. The legend is a work of art, and of next to no value as a record of historical happenings.

Luke's story, moreover, flatly contradicts the legend in Matthew, which is no less artificially constructed and no better founded than the other. In this Gospel the home of Joseph and Mary is not Nazareth, but Bethlehem, where they are living as an espoused couple, and it is at Bethlehem that the miraculous conception takes place, an angel explaining the matter to Joseph and quieting the misgivings which such an announcement could hardly fail to arouse. All this happens, so the hagiographer informs us, as the fulfilment of an oracle in Isaiah vii, 14, on which he puts a forced meaning—a point we shall not dwell upon, since a meaning, more or less forced, is put on all the Old Testament texts alleged to have their fulfilment in the New, a proceeding well in keeping with supernatural magic by forcing into texts meanings not naturally theirs. After this the legend becomes solemn and tragic: astrologers (Magi) arrive from the East at Jerusalem to adore the King of the Jews about to be born there —they have seen the rising of his star. Disturbed by the news Herod assembles his wise men who declare that the Messiah must be born in Bethlehem, for so, they say, the prophet Micah has foretold. The astrologers accordingly take the road to Bethlehem, Herod requesting them to return to Jerusalem to report. The star reappears, and guides them to the house where the child is laid; they enter, adore, offer their gifts, and, a premonitory dream warning them not to see Herod again, they return to their country by a different road. Another angel commands Joseph to fly into Egypt with the child and his mother, to escape from Herod's inquisition. So to Egypt they depart, thereby accomplishing an oracle of Hosea (xi, 1)—which refers to the Israelite people. Follows the massacre of children in Bethlehem and the region round about, according to a prophecy of Jeremiah (xxxi, 15)—forced like the others into the service. At last the cruel Herod dies; an angel bids Joseph return to Judea, to Bethlehem; but this he dares not do and betakes himself instead to Galilee, to Nazareth, thereby fulfilling a saying of prophecy concerning the Christ: "he shall be called a Nazarene." But the exegetes have been unable to discover where the prophecy is to be found.

The important point to note is that Matthew's legend is incompatible with Luke's from beginning to end: the two are equally full of marvels and magic; but neither is inwardly consistent and the two cancel each other out. In their mythology and magic they belong to the history of the growth of belief and throw not a ray of light on the historical origin of Jesus.

Supernaturalism of the same type, a mixture of magic and mythology, colours the main body of the Gospel narrative to a lesser degree, but it is far from being absent. Moreover it is clear from the outset that the account of the public career of Jesus, from his baptism by John to his death and entry into immortal life, though having a certain resemblance in all the four Gospels, is understood by the fourth, as to its principal features, in a sense quite different from that given to it by the first three.

In the first three, a figure, to all seeming that of a human being, presents himself for John's baptism and receives it under miraculous conditions, in which he is invested with the Messianic dignity of the Holy Spirit. This Spirit is henceforth to possess him, having first appointed him Son of God. Setting aside the secondary variants in the three Gospels this scene clearly represents the consecration of Jesus as Messiah and is at the same time the prototype of Christian baptism, in other words it is the first and principal stage in the formation of the myth of the Christ and of the institution of baptism. Though Jesus was probably baptized by John it was not under these conditions. In this we see that the synoptic account does not begin as an historical record of Jesus the teacher. It begins as doctrinal instruction, as a catechesis, by presenting a doctrine to the Christian initiate. All that follows up to the end is in keeping with the beginning.

As we shall later study in detail the growth of the Gospel catechesis, we confine attention for the present to its general features. It is certain that all the materials of the Gospel catechesis, various and ill-ordered as they are, are intended to show that the teaching was wonder-working. Jesus is the Messiah announced by the miracle of his baptism. To this point of view everything is systematically adjusted. The aim is the instruction of Christians, not at presenting the real course of Jesus' ministry which, for all who have eyes to see, consisted in the announcement of the imminent Kingdom of God; in this the rôle of miracle-worker can have had but a very small place. The number of miracles of which a *detailed* description is given is not considerable, and it is worthy of note that whenever a miracle is described in detail the meaning of it lies in the saving work accomplished by Jesus; its mystic significance as a work of salvation always outweighs the importance of the material facts. With regard to these latter the Gospel narratives are completely indifferent, witness the facility with which different evangelists change the setting, modifying at will the order and connection of events and circumstances, and not hesitating, by way of making the proof more convincing, to introduce what we may call *editorial* miracles to heighten the *mise en scène* or to make a discourse more impressive. Offensive as such proceedings may be to modern standards, they are valuable to the critic by revealing the ground on which the Gospel stories are constructed, the ground namely of doctrinal teaching and pious legend, and not the ground of history. We shall enter later into fuller detail; note only, as typical examples, the *bloc* of miracles which Jesus, in Mark iii, 10–12, performs, before proceeding to the mission of the apostles; the miraculous cure of the two blind men (ix, 27–33) in which Matthew doubles the cure of Bartimeus at Jericho, and the cure of the deaf mute brought in at the same point (ix, 32–34), both to provide ground for the answer Jesus will presently give to John's messengers; in like manner the raising of the young man at Nain (Luke vii, 11–17), which a reviser of the third Gospel improvises for the same purpose and on the same occasion, to say nothing of the miscellaneous collection of miraculous cures which he inserts so oddly (vii, 21) in the middle of the dialogue between Jesus and the messengers. By these proceedings the evangelists themselves invite us to rate such miracles at their proper worth. They are piled up to satiety and without more scruple than if they were metaphors.

The second part of the synoptic catechism, introduced by Peter's confession at Caesarea Philippi, has a perspective leading up to its dominating feature in the saving death of Jesus, which he is represented as predicting on various occasions for the instruction of his disciples. Fundamentally this part of the catechism is intended to explain the mystery of the Communion Supper along with that of the Christian Easter, celebrated on Sunday. We know that the observation of Easter on this particular day of the week was adopted by the majority of the Churches, beginning with the Roman Church, in the course of the second century. Needless to say it was not the primitive custom. It is certain that the earliest believers were in the habit of celebrating their Passover on the movable day when the Jews celebrated theirs, and it was only when the idea of a distinctively Christian method of salvation had been elaborated that it was deemed expedient to separate from Jewish practice by celebrating on a fixed day, as the culminating point of the divine epiphany and saving work of Jesus. This was his resurrection, and Sunday, which had already become the Lord's Day, that is the day consecrated to the immortal Christ, was obviously the day on which the resurrection must be supposed to have taken place. Here again we are on doctrinal ground, the ground even of gnosis and mystery, not on that of history or attested fact.

But even at this point the Gospel narratives are far from reflecting a consistent and homogeneous tradition. The stories of the Passion and of the Resurrection are loaded with other matter and full of incoherencies. In Mark the last meal of Jesus, which was not a paschal meal in the earliest version of it, has been doubled in the story of the Anointing (xiv, 3–9), the intention apparently being to arrange a kind of holy week, in which the institution of the Supper was commemorated on Thursday evening, when Jesus himself was said to have celebrated the Passover; the Passion would then be assigned to Friday. Passing over the flagrant impossibility of Jesus being arrested and tried by the Sanhedrin on the holy night of the Passover, we find that he remains in the tomb for the whole of the Sabbath (Saturday) and is raised up just before the dawn on Sunday morning. Such is the underlying myth which supports the ritual commemoration on Sunday.

We know how the authentic version of Mark ends abruptly with the discovery of the empty tomb by the women who flee in panic without telling any man of the miracle they have seen. At a yet older stage in the formation of the Gospel it would seem to have concluded with the centurion's confession of faith (xv, 39), the moment of Jesus' death being considered as also the moment of his resurrection to glory and immortal life. But this simple conception of his resurrection, which was certainly held by the first believers, was presently deemed insufficient. The discovery of the empty tomb was then imagined to provide a material proof, the resurrection being now conceived under the idea that the dead body of Jesus must have been re-animated and delivered up *from a tomb* in which it had been immured for some time. This materialized conception of the matter is pursued in the other Gospels to the point of extravagance and in self-contradictory forms, the material body of Jesus being endowed with the immaterial quality of spirit, while the Christ is represented (in Luke and Acts) even as taking part in the meals of the disciples. In addition to this self-contradiction, Luke flatly contradicts the stories in Matthew and Mark who place the first apparition of the risen Jesus in Galilee. From all this the conclusion follows that what we have here is not a historical tradition of a factual resurrection which, after all, is not an observable fact of the physical order, but an assertion of faith. The stories of imagined apparitions are, for the most part, apologetic constructions for buttressing belief by clothing it in material form. Whence it follows in this crucial case, as in that of miracles in general, that the only history we can glean from stories of supernatural magic is the history of belief.

THE CHRIST OF THE FOURTH GOSPEL

The primary difference between the point of view of the fourth Gospel and that of the Synopsis is that the Christ it presents is not a human being raised above humanity by a Spirit emanating from God, but a divine being *from the outset*, a hypostasis, an original emanation, the transcendent Son, the Logos of God. This Son or Logos is made manifest in the flesh that he may gather believers, who, by true faith in him whom God has sent, will themselves become God's children. The Son has neither father nor mother in this world. Nevertheless, in his earthly manifestation, he appears as the member of a family, is reputed son of Joseph and has a mother and brothers. But the book, *in the form in which it has come down to us*, seems to attribute to the Christ an existence completely human, assigning him a real birth followed by an integral human life up to the age of thirty after which his ministry, as divine revealer of a mystery, begins and lasts for about three years. Not only is this in violent and consciously intended contradiction to the Synopsis but is an addition and a contradiction to the fundamental idea of the fourth Gospel itself, the idea namely of a divine incarnation for the manifestation and fulfilment of human salvation, the said manifestation having no need to pass through preparatory stages while concealed under a developing human envelope.

It remains to add that, while the Johannine Christ is presented as revealing and instituting the religion of spirit, he fulfils that function exclusively by means of two revealing images, light and life, which after all are sensible symbols, and by "signs" which are not merely symbols but miracles, prodigies effected by supernatural magic, intensified in narration to enhance the spiritual lesson, which, on its side, tends to compromise the material reality of the facts in the story. But their material reality is none the less intended by the narrator. Thus: the Christ is the Light of the world; proof, the miraculous cure of the man born blind: the Christ is resurrection and life; proof, the raising of Lazarus after four days in the grave. Both these marvels are presented as factually occurring, and as leading up to the spiritual dénouement. The same method is applied in the presentation of the other miracles.

The stories of the Passion and of the Resurrection are constructed on a like principle. Although they have been retouched to soften their profound and significant difference from the synoptic presentation, the Johannine stories of these events were originally written and still remain, under all that has been added, in harmony with the primitive Easter observance, known as quartodeciman, the Christ being deemed to have died on the 14 Nizan, on the day and at the very hour when the paschal lamb was sacrificed. The contradiction of the Synoptics on this essential cannot be resolved. Nor could the conflict as to the two observances, which went on during the second century.

The divergence shows that both dates are commemorative. Neither can pretend to indicate the chronological place of the Passion. They are ritual conventions, not history. Both being symbolic, and the one no more historical than the other, the historian is under no obligation to choose between them. They are mutually destructive.

Note further, on account of its importance, the incident of the lance-thrust. This incident, though secondary, fictitious and a late insertion into the story, is full of meaning. Not only is it presented as the fulfilment of two prophecies, but the water and blood that flow from the pierced side of Jesus are figures of the sacraments of Christian initiation, baptism and the Supper, and of the double witness of the Spirit, emitted in the last breath of the

Crucified. To find in the natural decomposition of blood an explanation of a miracle and symbol so finely conceived, as some would do, is an exercise of ingenuity in which only a blind exegesis could indulge itself (John xix, 30-37; cf. vii, 37-39; 1 John v, 6-8).

The Johannine stories of the resurrection, which have been worked over in successive revisions of the Gospel, are incoherent and self-contradictory. They are out of harmony with the underlying principle of the Gospel itself, according to which the Christ returns to his eternal life, which had been interrupted, as it were, by his temporal incarnation, with the last utterance of his expiring breath. Incoherently with this spiritual conception, tradition introduced a proof of material resurrection by proclaiming the discovery of the empty tomb. Incoherently again, the Christ, entering through closed doors as an *immaterial* spirit, proceeds to show the disciples his *material* body scarred by the nails and the lance, and the scene is repeated a second time to convince the sceptical Thomas. Here is miraculous magic enough: but there is more to come. A supplementary chapter (xxi) is given up to an apparition in Galilee, doubtless derived from the oldest tradition of the post-resurrection visions, in which the risen Jesus mingles for a time in the daily life of his followers. But the end of the story shows that the whole episode has been introduced for the purpose of creating some sort of link between the glorious memory of Peter, head-shepherd of the Christ's sheep, with that of the beloved disciple of Jesus whom the churches of Asia venerated as their supposed founder, the true and truthful author of the Gospel in which these great marvels are reported. But the Johannine Gospel, like the others, is so full of such marvels, and in a sense fuller of fiction than they, that we cannot bind the historian to accept all these operations of miraculous magic, as real events irrefragably attested. They are constructed for a purpose.

THE TRUE SUPERNATURAL

It would be idle to press further our proof of the presence in the Bible, even in the New Testament, and in the Gospels, of a supernatural magic unthinkable by contemporary intelligence. In the supernatural so understood we have here no part or lot, for the plain reason that it is untrue, that it crumbles to pieces, save so far as it is held together by the ignorance of the believing masses, and by the wilful blindness of the theologians who refuse to see what is before them; nor can the suspicion be avoided that these theologians sometimes play a part which ranges them with opportunists, apologetic politicians, exegetical strategists, rather than with those who really and personally believe in this false supernaturalism, which they seem determined to impose as a perpetual burden on the religious mind. We beg to tell them, and to say it once for all, that their pretensions are preposterous and their assumption of infallibility an unpermitted revolt against exact knowledge. In the measure to which they condemn themselves to follow their principle they deprive their works of all claim to scientific value.

Let those who seek edification in such proceedings find the edification they seek. Our own task is to establish the real position of the biblical problem in our time, and to show the place that remains for the true supernatural when the false supernatural of magic and myth has been dismissed.

The problem before us is that of ascertaining, without exaggeration and without reticence, the true place of Christianity in the scale of religious values, taking full account of the development in our time of the natural sciences, of our knowledge of the universe, of anthropology, of human palaeontology, of historical and pre-historical archaeology, of general history and the philosophy of history, and of the knowledge of man himself. With an urgency which no words can fully express we invite the theologians of all the Christian confessions, and believers of every religion in the world, to ponder the infinite perspectives which now open before us on all sides and in presence of which all the cosmogonies, all the mythologies, nay, all the theologies bequeathed to us by antiquity vanish like the dreams of childhood.

Consider the immensity of the universe and the harmony of its laws as now revealed to us; the mystery of infinite worlds moving eternally on their way in the unfathomable depths of space; consider the mystery of the atom, of the infinitely little, each one a world and yet hardly perceptible to our senses, enshrining in itself the mystery of the great universe, as it confronts us in the life of every star and of all the stars in their totality. In the presence of that what becomes of all the ancient mythologies, including the biblical? In strictness of speech they come to nothing. To be sure, the mystery of the universe does not suppress the mystery of God, but intensifies it beyond measure and shifts it to regions where all the old definitions of God vanish like bursting bubbles. The idea of a completed and simultaneous creation of all things—what now becomes of that? What madman in our days would dare to write down the age of the universe in arithmetical figures? In the ages when the religions of the world were born and their sacred books indited, barely a suspicion had arisen of the mystery of the universe and the mystery of God as they now confront us. An important fact in itself and in its consequences.

That is not all. There is another mystery equally ignored by all the religions in their sacred books, the mystery of man. On this, as on the other, all they have to offer is fable, the work of the imagination. Into the slow and painful ascent of man as he rose from the animal condition to a growing consciousness of his humanity, our vision now begins to penetrate, even to the countless millenniums of his pre-history; even on the origins of history a new light now begins everywhere to fall, and chiefly on the ancient history of the neighbouring East where the religion of Israel and the Christian religion had their birth. Of this mystery, gradually disclosing itself to our astonished gaze, the Bible, in truth, knows next to nothing. Israel and its God, who became the Christian God, are late comers into human history and into that of the Eastern Mediterranean; their sacred legend is relatively recent, and, being a legend, cannot be fitted in with the history, as now reconstructed, of the second millennium before the Christian era and with that of the two or three preceding millenia. Still less can it be fitted with the incalculable millenia before history began, of which the legend knows nothing whatever. In regard to the remote past of the human race, and to the mysterious past of the universe, the legend hangs in air without connection. It is no more a final revelation of the mystery of man than of the mystery, unknown to it, of the universe, but goes on its way without a suspicion of where the human mystery lies.

In the relations to both these mysteries the biblical legend is the work of that fable-making faculty whose activities M. Bergson has lately described with so much perspicacity, though without sufficiently insisting on the fact that fable-making is not dead, but is still at work in all religions, and even plays a part, up to a certain point, in the construction of all the philosophic systems.

Need we add that Judaism and Christianity, originally as limited in their outlook towards the future as in their consideration of the past, cannot be accepted as a revelation, and a perpetually valid and sufficient rule, of that religious and moral ideal towards which humanity has never ceased to press forward through all its many illusions and fallings away? The messianic expectations in which Christianity had its birth were, so to say, a short-term revolution of limited range alike in the world and the social order. Here again we encounter an element of that false supernaturalism from which neither Judaism nor Christianity felt any need to shake itself free, although neither religion could grow, or even hold its own, without progressively enlarging the scope of its aspirations and hopes, as in fact they were constrained to do.

Contemplate these stupendous facts. Are they not enough, is not their certitude sufficiently established, to justify the impartial observer, who is also a man of goodwill, but intent on the truth before and above all else, in asserting that the religious phenomenon of Judaism and Christianity is not an absolutely unique and incomparable fact of history, nor a primordial fact of history, nor a fact fully realized in history, needing nothing to be added, till our race, after an indefinite future, comes to its end? May he not affirm that here is no revelation for all time given to humanity in its cradle, fully complete at the outset and never since then falling short of its plentitude, destined, in virtue of its initial force, to guide humanity to the end of its evolution, an end which none can foresee and is undisclosed by the revelation itself? Be it said, quite simply, that Judaism and Christianity, taken together, are not the revelation they have professed to be, but an outstanding manifestation of religion, probably the most remarkable humanity has produced.

Deeply considered, the real economy of the universe, of which we now begin to get glimpses, is more marvellous than all the old cosmogonies; and the real history of man is a revelation of wonders greater than all the mythical schemes of salvation.

Does this imply that religion must now be imagined as having no future on our planet? By no means. What has perished for ever is the dominance, in the concept of religion, of the false supernatural. In a sense, the Christian ideal has never been more necessary, never more immediately applicable, than it is to the movement of civilization in our time. What then is the Christian ideal? It is expressed in the notion of the reign of justice, realized or realizable by the law of love, the noblest ideal our minds are capable of grasping, but presented in the Gospel, thanks to its eschatological form, in Utopian colours and to be realized by magic. It is expressed again in the notion of inward peace, product of faith in the profound value of the regenerated soul, of spiritual life under the law of justice and love, a notion found in the writings attributed to Paul, but there presented in a form not less mythical than in the heretical gnoses. Lastly it finds expression in the vision of a universal society of believers, the true Catholic Church, the common fatherland of souls, united in the practice of justice under the law of love, the confident conviction and clear consciousness that they are being born to a higher life through the working of this sublime law; of all which traditional catholicism, with an imposed orthodoxy, a ruling hierarchy and a papacy blindly imperialist, while professing to be a true representation, is but a caricature.

The essence of Christianity may be found in this ideal, unrealized though it has been at any period of Christian history; nay, it is the essence of the religion of humanity, advancing to perfection, with ever increasing promise, in a future to which no limit can be assigned. But to look for a clear conception or express formulation of it in the New Testament would be the most childish of anachronisms. We find it there only in germ, embedded in supernatural magic. But the germ was alive; there was already in it a large measure of spiritual life, that is, of the true supernatural, which must either grow and expand in the individual soul and in society, or humanity will perish.

Just as the Christianity of old, in adapting its message to the conditions of the Mediterranean world, impressed itself on that age by bringing to it a human ideal far superior to that of the pagan religions and the speculations of Greek wisdom, so it behoves the followers of the gleam in our time, to free Christianity from traditional fetters, to enlarge it to the dimensions of the rightful aspirations and needs of civilization, to raise speculation to the height of true science in all its findings, welcoming the light from whatsoever quarter it may come. Above all the travail of humanity, in the midst of which we are living, let the children of the light proclaim on high the divine principle of love, of devoted love, to the end that a religion may arise, crown of the Christian religion and of every other, all taken up into one, and concentrated on the perfecting of humanity in the life of the spirit, that is, in communion with God.

Chapter II

THE ESCHATOLOGICAL CATECHESIS

CHRISTIANITY was not founded on a revelation contained in a book peculiar to itself; nor, in strictness of speech, on the Jewish Bible, though this was its only sacred book when the Christian message was first proclaimed, and so remained for a long time, even after it had begun to produce its own religious literature. Nor was its departure taken from any abstract dogma or lofty mysticism. It rested on a popular and uncriticized belief which Jesus embraced with all the ardour of an unquestioning faith, and with a perfect trust in the God who watched over Israel and guided the destinies of all mankind. The central affirmation of this faith, the theme of it, was the imminent coming of the Reign of God. The same theme, enhanced by faith in Jesus, now raised from the dead and waiting to return in glory as the Christ, was also the central affirmation of the preaching we call apostolic, and it was carried further in the literature of Christian apocalyptic, more or less expanded and enriched with additions, some even foreign.

THE FIRST CATECHISM

As far as we can judge in the extreme poverty of documentary evidence bearing on the point, a poverty far greater than has hitherto been generally admitted, the message of Jesus, so far as it consisted in teaching, was of the greatest simplicity imaginable. It was summed up in the formula "Repent! for the Reign of God is at hand." John, surnamed the Baptizer, had proclaimed the same message before Jesus took it up. Neither John nor Jesus was the founder of a school; nor was John a hair-splitting theologian, nor a man profoundly versed in the Scriptures. He was a prophet by intensity of conviction, the prophet of a single oracle, and Jesus, after him, lifted up his voice in the self-same trumpet-call.

It is true that John, as his surname indicates, was a prophet with a rite. This rite was baptism, which was no common ablution, nor a substitute for the purifications prescribed by the Law, but a total immersion, understood as a sacrament of repentance, a token of moral cleansing and a passport into the Kingdom of God. This rite, to which we can hardly doubt that Jesus submitted, was taken up and continued by Christianity, Jesus himself having conformed to it. By the Christians, as by John, baptism was originally practised in close connection with the announcement that the Kingdom was at hand.

Like John again, Jesus, during the short time his ministry seems to have lasted, was given a surname the meaning of which, though less clear than the surname carried by John, must be closely analogous if not almost identical. As John was called *the Baptizer*, so Jesus was called *the Nazorean*. "Nazoreans" was also the name of his followers, called so after him (cf. Acts xxiv, 5). It was a sect-name. It was not as originating from Nazareth that he acquired the name. On the contrary, it was because he was a Nazorean and recognized as such that the supposition grew up later of his Nazareth origin, with the afterthought, probably conscious, of causing the real meaning of the name to be forgotten. Now the orthography of this word excludes as impossible the sense of "consecrated" or "under a vow" (the *nazir* of Jewish tradition; cf. p. 21) and points distinctly to that of "observer of a rite" (*nôtzer*), the rite "observed" being unquestionably that practised by John and his disciples, to wit, baptism. There is certainly no disparagement of Christianity in recognizing that its followers were a baptist sect at the birth of the religion, for that is what they really were and what Christians have remained ever since.

The Reign of God announced by John and Jesus implies that a judgment will be held at the outset, a severe judgment of God. In that we see an unmistakable feature of the prophetic tradition. The general judgment is, as it were, the preliminary condition and natural introduction of the divine government. Hence it is that the exhortation to repent precedes the announcement of the Kingdom; hence it is that baptism, the sacrament of cleansing, is the mystic certificate of innocence wherewith to face the Judge. All that holds together well and demands no great effort of mind to understand. For us, no doubt, the idea of a judgment of all mankind is not quite the simple idea that it was for those who first announced it; but that need not detain us. The great difficulty that criticism has to overcome in these matters lies in the way our creed-bound exegetes have of twisting or overlooking facts which are not in harmony with their own religious feelings, and in the way more independent minds fail to grasp the true nature of these facts when they offend their sense of what is reasonable—habits intelligible enough but difficult to cope with.

As examples, take the following. To that age the idea of the Kingdom of God was just as simple as the idea of a general judgment, but no more capable of becoming realized in the conditions imagined for it by those who announced its immediate coming. What were these conditions? As the dead were to be judged along with the living, a general resurrection of all the dead must naturally precede the general judgment—a condition which a moment's reflection will show to be quite unrealizable at any point of history: none the less the idea was accepted without the need to criticize it being felt either by the prophet or by his audience. Then again, the wicked were to be separated from the righteous, excluded from the Kingdom and punished as they deserved—a thing clearly impossible in the normal current of human life on our planet. Along with this, the righteous dead who have been raised and the righteous who are still living will enjoy happiness without alloy in the land promised to Abraham, Isaac and Jacob. Who that knows anything of the natural conditions of human life can imagine the establishment of such a society? But our prophets, John and Jesus, were unconcerned with natural conditions, and their faith, in consequence, was entirely untouched by the crowding objections which assail the modern mind in the presence of these ideas. This, however, affords no reason for changing the thought of Jesus by distilling his simple hope of the Kingdom into some fine essence more intelligible to our age, or seemingly so.

Another condition attached to this reign of justice and happiness was its *immediate* realization: it was *at hand*. This condition was self-evident: it was impossible to conceive that a miracle so great and so ardently desired would be indefinitely postponed. God was coming, and God is not a lingerer. So, too, with the urgent call to sinners—repent, and lose not a moment about it, for the Judge is at the very doors! To say that all that is unbelievable is to say nothing to the purpose, for the fact is that it was believed, and believed with a faith which had no turn for the critical discussion of its object; nor was it believable otherwise. And so firmly was it believed that the contradiction it continued to receive from the course of events availed but very slowly to damp the ardour of the faith and that, even to-day, in Christian communions most emancipated from tradition, the outlook is more or less still dominated by the vision, far off, of the Great Event.

It seems, then, that no essential difference is to be remarked between the teaching of Jesus and the teaching of John. The deliberate subordination of John to Jesus, more or less plainly avowed, in which the Gospel teaching would place him, does not belong to history. It seems certain also that the distinction made between the two baptisms, which represents the baptism of John as simple baptism in water and the Christian rite as baptism in spirit, was imagined in Christian tradition long after both prophets had perished, with the object of marking the difference of the two sects and of enhancing the value of the Christian sacrament. It may be affirmed without the least hesitation that John could never have professed, nor even conceived, the subordination assigned him by the evangelists. That being so, it must not be taken for granted that John, the herald of the Great Judgment, announced himself at the same time as the precursor of the Messiah.

A comparative estimate of the two masters, formulated after their disappearance and inserted into the Gospel catechesis, invites us to suppose that there existed between them a difference of temper and attitude. It runs (Matthew xi, 18–19; Luke vii, 33–34):

> John came neither eating nor drinking,
>   and they say: "he has a demon."
> The Son of Man came eating and drinking,
>   and they say: "a glutton and wine drinker,
>   friend of publicans and sinners."

It would seem that, essentially, both played the same part, John with a more decided turn to asceticism and Jesus with a more liberal address and a gentler way with sinners. None the less it is said, in another passage (Mark xi, 30–32), that the baptism of John was "from heaven," and the Jewish authorities are severely blamed for not having sought it while publicans and harlots were eager to be baptized (Matthew xxi, 31-32; cf. Luke vii, 29-30).

It is obvious that so simple a faith did not need elaborate explanation. But one point it specially behoves us to note, because so many deliberately shut their eyes to it: the faith proclaimed by the two prophets *was subversive of established authority and, in essence, revolutionary*. The Kingdom of God was no metaphor; it was a real Kingdom and excluded that of Caesar. Hence the speedy coming of God to reign on earth meant also the speedy overthrow of Roman power, at least in Judea, and the disappearance of the petty Herodian prince who reigned in Galilee. True, neither John nor Jesus advocated armed revolt against the rulers of this world; but this made little difference in view of the essential fact that both prophets announced their immediate destruction. Is it likely that the authorities would regard the popularity of such teaching as politically harmless? The point is of importance as showing that the preaching careers of John and of Jesus could not be, and were not, of long duration. We are bound to regard them as soon suppressed, even though our texts do not give us clear statements to that effect.

In all this are we laying down too narrow a base to support the Christian religion? Are we not overlooking some sublime element that would justify the eager reception accorded the message by a significant portion of so religious a nation as the Jews? Must it not be that Jesus reveals a religion destined to become universal and to last for ever?

All these questions are unanswerable because, in the reality of the matter, they have no existence. This is not the place to show that the Gospel of Jesus and the Christianity that came after it are, in reality, a single movement, outstanding among all others, produced by that mysterious force which operates through all religions and urges humanity forward on the highway of spiritual progress. That we hold to be proved, because it is a fact of history. The question whether the Gospel of Jesus, as we have just described it, is too narrow and fragile a base for the many forms of Christianity which have issued from it in the course of ages, and are still issuing, affords no matter for discussion. When something has happened and is a fact, the question of its possibility no longer exists.

Some of our Christologists take too much upon themselves when they imagine they can explain the origin of Christianity by giving Jesus the honour of having formally taught the essence of their own religion. No essence of religion expressible in abstract forms was proclaimed by Jesus. He spoke to his fellow countrymen of things in which they were interested and in language they could understand. Our doctors of divinity are unaware that they are constructing a Christ in their own image, nor do they perceive that such a Christ, if he had lived in the time of Pontius Pilate would not have found two men to follow him nor one to be his enemy. Learned discourse on the methodology of New Testament criticism is as irrelevant to our present business as are the special pleadings for supernatural magic, or the baseless conjectures of those who deny the historicity of Jesus.

The sole point we have here to make good lies in the question whether the Gospel of Jesus, as we describe it, accounts for the response, somewhat limited, that his preaching evoked in his lifetime, and whether that Gospel presents itself naturally and intelligibly as the initiating cause of the Christian movement. Here there is no difficulty, since we know that Jesus preached the imminence of the Kingdom, and that disciples survived him who integrated their new faith in him as the Christ risen from the dead with their former faith in the speedy coming of the Kingdom as announced by him.

The idea of the Reign of God was widely spread in the region where, and at the time when, Jesus appeared on the scene: this explains why he was able to gather disciples around him. The idea was not the property of learned men or theologians; still less of politicians. It was the form of a popular faith, and a faith intense enough to provoke outbreaks of violence. Judas the Galilean who made himself notorious at the time when Quirinius carried out his census was a frenzied devotee of the Kingdom, his principle being that the people of Israel had not, and ought never to have, other Master upon earth than God. This was also the principle of the fanatical instigators of the war which led to the ruin of the Temple of Jerusalem in the year 70, and the same war-cry inspires the revolt of the Messiah Barkochba in the time of Hadrian, which completed the ruin of Jewish nationalism. Between these furious zealots and prophets of the

Kingdom such as John and Jesus there was only one difference, but a difference that went to the root of the matter. The zealots believed that they were able, and under the duty, to promote the Coming of God by force of arms: John and Jesus left the fulfilment of God's promise entirely to God. The faith was the same, but with John the Baptist and Jesus the Nazorean it has a colour of spirituality lacking to the others. On the one side as on the other there was the same confidence in the speedy annihilation of Roman rule.

If that be considered, it is not only evident but cannot fail to be evident, that the Gospel of Jesus was not conceived by himself under the form of absolute religion destined to become the universal religion of humanity *in saecula saeculorum*. Never did he propose to institute a religion; he announced that the great hope of Israel's religion was on the point of fulfilment. Never did he dream of sending out propaganda all over the world; he said that the Reign of God was about to be set up in Judea. Never did he behold the long centuries of the world's history stretching away into the future; for him, history, the story of man's wandering from God, would come to an end immediately with God's arrival on the scene. The speculations of modern Christologists who fancy they are discovering the essence of Christianity were foreign to Jesus. Most assuredly he was neither a Roman Catholic, nor an orthodox Protestant nor a liberal Protestant of any denomination: in all that his share was nothing and could not be anything, for he was a man of his time. Had he possessed the faintest conception of what was in store for humanity in the centuries to come, his message of the coming Kingdom would have been impossible and, needless to say, he would not have risked his life proclaiming it.

Christian believers in all the Confessions are naturally loath to admit that the Christ, the object of men's faith and worship, can have been in some degree the victim of illusion. This, from the earliest times, they have never been willing to recognize, and that is precisely why the original Gospel message has been progressively changed, diluted and doctored, a process which still goes on in the efforts of contemporary interpreters to palliate the reality by any means available, taxing their wits to foist upon the Christ their own notions of his work. But Jesus was rather the victim of his human environment than of an illusion peculiar to himself, his illusion, such as it was, being one widely shared by his countrymen and in his time. In itself it was a generous illusion and helpful in raising humanity from its low estate. And what more would you have to the glory of him who lived for the illusion and died for it? But was there no germ of life beneath it? Doubtless there was, and who denies it save those who would substitute for his illusion an abstraction out of their own workshop or their own illusion of some mechanism falsely named supernatural?

THE GOSPEL STORY NO PART OF THE EARLIEST CHRISTIAN TEACHING

That the death of Jesus was not the end of his life is proved by the fact that he lived on afterwards. In history proper his life covers space of the smallest: but he has lived on outside history or, if you will, above it. It is a frequent saying that Christianity was born in history. The assertion is true, though often understood in a sense far beyond what historical testimony is available to warrant. But nothing could be more incontestable as an historical fact than the appearance of Jesus in the time of the Emperor Tiberius and the procurator Pontius Pilate. In point of fact, our sure knowledge of the circumstances in which he finished his message and met his death amounts almost to nothing; nor is our knowledge greater of the process which brought his first disciples to believe in his resurrection and to proclaim it abroad. As to the Gospel, or message of Jesus, which we have just explained, it was conceived almost outside human history, and as its *terminus ad quem*. He who preached it and they who accepted it had no suspicion that it would be told as a story for the edification of generations to come. For that reason there has never been a history of it in the proper sense of the word; and there never will be. Still less are we able to find any sure historical tradition concerning the resurrection of Jesus and his exaltation as the Christ to come. These were matters of faith; in no sense or degree were they facts attested by the historical records of external proof; faith called unto faith in proclaiming them. Had the mentality of the disciples been of the kind that believes only on material proof, they would have had nothing to believe. For those proofs did not exist when their belief was born; they were only imagined later on to meet objections by the story of a miraculous resurrection of the material body, operated by magic. The first believers had no conception of any such phenomenon.

Paul's Summary of the Primitive Teaching

Here are the terms in which Paul sums up his own catechesis (Romans x, 9–10).

> If you confess with your mouth that Jesus is Lord and believe in your heart that God has raised him from the dead, you will be saved. For by the heart we believe to gain righteousness and by the mouth we confess to gain salvation.

What is the "salvation" here spoken of? Simply admission to the Kingdom of God which the Lord Jesus is about to bring in. From this we see that the teaching, which we may regard as the primitive catechesis, announced the speedy coming of the Kingdom, as did the gospel of Jesus. Like that gospel it demanded repentance for sin and it practised baptism as a guarantee that sin was remitted. Beyond that it presented the risen Jesus as *Lord*, exalted in his immortality to the right hand of God. This profession of faith was all gathered up as it were in one word, *Maranatha*—"the Lord comes," is on the point of coming (cf. 1 Corinthians xvi, 22). From First Corinthians (i, 12–15) it results quite clearly that the above profession of faith in Romans, in which the earliest catechetical teaching was summarized, was the profession required of catechumens at baptism, early administered in the name of Jesus Christ. And since Paul thus baptized in the name of Jesus Christ we may well believe that the practice was started by the missionaries of Antioch, who had come to the decision, before Paul, to receive pagans to baptism without imposing circumcision.

The custom of conferring baptism in the name of Jesus Christ was doubtless not universal at the very beginning. It is quite possible that the earliest group of disciples in Jerusalem continued to confer it after the manner of John, accompanied with a profession of faith in Jesus risen from the dead; and it would be the same with some propagandists outside Judea. This would explain the case of Apollos who had been touched by the faith in his native country of Alexandria and who, while well informed of the things concerning Jesus, was ignorant of other baptism than that of John (Acts xviii, 24–25), the statement which follows (xix, 1–7) about the disciples who knew only the baptism of John, and whom Paul baptized in the name of the Lord Jesus, probably referring to converts made by Apollos, though what then follows about the Holy Spirit coming upon them and their speaking with tongues is obviously the writer's embroidery. It is conceivable that the Antioch missionaries, including Paul, made use in their catechetical teachings of an express formula containing the principle of salvation for all men by faith in the Christ as risen from the dead, nothing else being required and the necessity of legal observances thereby repudiated. In that they would be repeating, with John the Baptist, that descent from Abraham according to the flesh availed nothing, and that God could raise up posterity to Abraham from the stones on the highway (Matthew iii, 9)—a posterity according to spirit, to faith.

On this point let us hear the testimony of Paul, an unimpeachable witness, in his letter to the Romans (iv, 13, 16):

> The promise made to Abraham and his posterity that they should inherit the world did not come to him through the Law but through the righteousness of faith. . . . It is through faith, that it may be through grace, so as to guarantee the promise for the whole of posterity, and not only to that part of it which comes by way of the Law, but to that which comes through Abraham's faith, for he is the father of us all.

This passage demands the most thorough consideration; it is an authentic expression of the Christian faith in the earliest period of its diffusion in the Roman world. A promise was given by God to Abraham as a man of faith and to his faithful posterity. The faithful posterity in question are those who are now persuaded that God has raised Lord Jesus from the dead. Now the resurrection of Jesus guarantees the promise to Abraham that he and his posterity are to be "heirs of the world." But the heritage of the world is not a blessed eternity in heaven: it is the happiness of the faithful, made righteous by their faith, *on this earth* under the Reign of God—the Kingdom. The saying "my Kingdom is not of this world" (John xviii, 36) was not attributed to the Christ by Paul.

THE ESCHATOLOGICAL CATECHESIS

There is therefore no difficulty in obtaining a clear idea of Christian catechetical teaching in its primitive form. The career and ministry of Jesus had no place in it; the coming of the Great Kingdom dominated the outlook; Jesus, raised from death as Christ the Lord, was about to bring it in; let every man prepare for it by repenting of his sins, of which baptism will give him remission. A catechesis at once moral and eschatological.

While the first form of the catechesis is thus clearly defined, documentary evidence is defective as to the detail of its evolution to the form which followed. It seems, however, that a considerable time elapsed before it included any record of the personal action and teaching of Jesus in the course of his mortal life. We have two proofs of this; first, in the book known as *The Teaching of the Apostles*, the *Didache* (*circa* 100); and second, in an indication furnished by the Epistle to the Hebrews (110-130) concerning the common form of Christian instruction at the time and in the circle to which the book belongs. We consider them in turn.

Evidence from the "Didache" and the Epistle to the Hebrews

The *Didache* in the form in which it has come down to us contains elements of relatively late date, for example, the formula of baptism "in the name of the Father, the Son and the Holy Spirit" and the text of the Lord's Prayer, which has been taken from Matthew's Gospel, but in its original substance and general tendency it represents a type of catechesis current in certain Christian churches of the East, probably the Syrian, between the years 100 to 130. The gist of the moral instruction preliminary to baptism consists in the doctrine of the "two ways," in which a Jewish book of morals is adapted to Christianity; following this are summary rules for baptism and the communion supper, and the whole is crowned by monitions appropriate to the coming of the Lord. So here again we have a type of Christian catechetical teaching still dominated by the expectation of the Second Coming and marked by a complete absence of any reference to the earthly life of Jesus and any defined notion of Christology.

The Epistle to the Hebrews sets out to teach a Christological gnosis which it sharply distinguishes from the teaching common to all Christians, that is, from the theme of the baptismal catechesis, as follows (Hebrews vi, 1-2):

> Leaving behind us the elementary theme of the Christ, let us raise our minds to the perfect theme (that of gnostic initiation) instead of laying the foundation over again, which foundation is repentance from dead works, faith in God, the doctrine of baptisms, imposition of hands, the resurrection of the dead and eternal judgment.

These last are what the author a little earlier has described (v, 12) as "the rudiments of divine revelation." The indication is the more significant inasmuch as this author desires above all to recommend his gnosis and, by way of contrast, incidentally calls to mind the common catechesis in which he sees the rudiment only of saving truth. To repeat this rudiment would be useless, he says, in the case of those who have gravely violated the moral rules laid down in it, since no further relief or remission of sin is available after baptism (vi, 4-7):

> For it is impossible that those who, once illuminated, have tasted the heavenly gift, participated in the Holy Spirit, tasted the good word of God and the power of the world to come, and then fallen—it is impossible that these people be renewed unto repentance a second time, since they crucify the Son of God, so far as the Son of God is in them, and put him to public shame. For the land that absorbs the rain that often falls upon it, shares the blessing of God, but that which produces thorns and thistles is condemned and under a curse (Genesis iii, 17); its end is to be burnt.

This commentary completely explains the object of the common catechesis as practised in the author's time, and shows that it had received by then some additions to the first form described above. "The elementary theme of the Christ," "the rudiments of divine revelation" are now called "illumination," though they mostly consist of moral and eschatological instruction; the moral instruction teaches the virtues to be practised, the sins and vices to be avoided, what of the past has to be deplored and what must be repented of before receiving the baptism which purifies the penitent. Express mention is made of faith in God, which shows that Christian propaganda is now being addressed either to recruits who come direct from polytheism or even to those tainted by heresies, which now (110-130) had wandered far from the true faith in regard to the Godhead. What the author means by the "doctrine of baptisms" is somewhat obscure. Does the plural indicate a complication of the ritual? Clearly the rite is less simple than in the time of Paul, the chief new elements being revealed in what the writer says about "imposition of hands," "the heavenly gift" and "participation in the Holy Spirit." Moreover, since "doctrine" is the writer's theme, we are invited to suppose that he is here discriminating among the baptismal rites then practised with a view to defining the normal type of the sacrament. "The imposition of hands" and "participation in the Holy Spirit" are certainly connected, and constitute a rite that goes with baptismal immersion, but is distinct from it. In "the heavenly gift" and "the power of the world to come" we can hardly fail to detect a mystic interpretation of the Supper. "The good word of God" is the divine guarantee of salvation, which the whole of this conveys. It is to be noted that there is a complete absence of any special reference to Christology, though the whole may be regarded as "the elementary theme of the Christ," a theme, however, which, elementary though it be, remains as it was in the earlier form and has its climax in the resurrection from the dead and the judgment to come. But the mystical sense of the Christ's death is not absent, since the Christian sinner is said to crucify the Christ anew "so far as the Christ is in him." But this last statement is probably the author's commentary.

To what extent and in what manner did teaching deemed to be that of Jesus in his earthly life enter into this catechesis? We cannot say. In one passage (ii, 1–14) the author alludes to the preaching of Jesus, and traces, so to speak, an apostolic chain from the Gospel onwards. After describing the superiority of the Christ over the angels he concludes as follows:

> We must therefore pay the more attention to what we have heard, for fear that we perish. For if the word spoken by angels (the revelation of the Old Testament and especially of the Law) held good, and all transgressions and disobedience received due punishment, how shall we escape if we neglect so great a salvation which, proclaimed at the beginning by the Lord, was confirmed to us by those who heard him, God acting with them by signs, prodigies, divine miracles and distributions of Spirit according to his will?

From this we learn that the author knows, or thinks, that salvation was first announced by Jesus himself, but there is nothing to indicate whether, in his understanding of the matter, the announcement includes much more than the promise of the Reign of God. On the other hand it is overwhelmingly clear that the earliest age of Christianity is seen by him as far off and enveloped in the mists of legend. He himself does not belong to the age called apostolic but is distant from it by more than one generation. Moreover his conception of the passion and the resurrection is not that of the Gospel story. For him the resurrection means the entry of the Christ on his immortal life. In like manner, while he is quite firm in asserting the real existence of Jesus and his rôle as the announcer of the Gospel, there is not the slightest ground for maintaining that he makes what we now call the Gospel tradition any part whatsoever either of the elementary Christian teaching of which he summarizes the content, or of the gnosis which he develops in his Epistle.

As to the Passion of the Christ, what is said about it in the Epistle has no direct relation to the Gospel story. The theme proper of the Epistle, the gnosis it sets out to develop, is the priesthood of Jesus, and it is in connection with this that we read as follows (v, 7–10):

> He who, in his days of the flesh, having offered to Him who was able to save him from death prayer and supplication, with strong crying and tears, and being answered in his anguish, learnt, though a Son, obedience by the things he suffered and who, made perfect (initiated by death into his high priesthood), became, for those who obey him, the author of eternal salvation, having been proclaimed by God high priest after the order of Melchizedek.

This passage, taken as a whole, relates to the mystic gnosis of the Epistle, but has a relation to it also in the detail of the prayer that was answered. For this allusion does not refer, in reality, to the prayer which the Synoptics place in Gethsemane on the eve of the Passion, nor to the cries or prayers which the same Gospels attribute to Jesus on the cross. The author views the whole redemptive action of the Christ, from his humiliation in suffering to his final exaltation, as prefigured in Psalm xxii, which is also the source from which the evangelists have drawn the scene in Gethsemane and the cry of Calvary. Our author therefore is not

THE ESCHATOLOGICAL CATECHESIS

referring to the tradition called evangelical, nor does he depend upon it. He is making use, for the dramatization of his mystery, of the same texts which, in the Synoptics, we find converted into narrative.

TEACHINGS OF THE RISEN CHRIST RECEIVED IN VISION

That sayings attributed to the *Lord* Jesus were introduced into the primitive catechesis of the Last Things, while it was still the only form of teaching extant, is not an impossibility; but there is a probability, amounting almost to certainty, that a goodly part of the teachings collected in the canonical Gospels, even those incorporated in the public preaching of Jesus, began as teachings of the Risen Christ, of Christ the Spirit, believed to have been received by his organs, the Christian prophets.

The apparition of the Risen Christ in Matthew xxviii, 16-20, together with the discourse there attributed to Jesus, was privately accorded to the eleven disciples, but contains nevertheless the formal institution of the apostolate to all nations, we might even say the institution of the Church, and the promise of the continued presence of the immortal Christ "until the consummation of the age," that is, of the then present age of the world. Here we must recall that these eleven "disciples," or the Twelve, were never in reality apostles to all nations, nor strictly speaking apostles at all (see *The Birth of the Christian Religion*, 137-140). This conclusion of Matthew, therefore, cannot be earlier than a date well advanced in the second century. In the teaching it attributes to the Risen Christ it echoes a relatively old tradition of which we have many other witnesses.

The deuterocanonical ending of Mark (xvi, 9-20) belongs to the same class. A little later, as finally revised, than the ending of Matthew, it is conceived in the same spirit, and contains an instruction to the Eleven to employ the time before the Second Coming in "preaching the Gospel to every creature," with an assurance that abounding miracles would reward their faith. Matthew and the Epistle to the Hebrews present the same legendary conception of the primitive apostolate. In the same way the fourth Gospel represents the apostolic mission as instituted, with power to forgive sins, by the Christ after his resurrection (xx, 21-23).

In the supplement to this Gospel (xxi) the miraculous draught of fishes is a symbolic representation of the apostolate to the whole world, and Peter, whose martyrdom is predicted, is appointed shepherd of the entire Christian flock. Here we have the débris of a wider tradition, evoked at this point to further the entry of the Johannine version of the Gospel into the current of the catechetical teaching then become common.

But the most explicit testimony to the post-resurrection character of this later catechesis is to be found, as to certain aspects, in the Third Gospel and the Book of Acts. In the Gospel (xxiv, 13-53) it is the Risen Christ who makes clear, first to the disciples at Emmaus, and then to all the disciples assembled, that what has happened to Jesus was announced in the ancient Scriptures. (From this we may infer that the practice of building the Gospel narrative on Old Testament prophecies was believed to derive from instructions given to that effect by the Risen Christ.) It is also the Risen Christ who sends them out "to preach repentance and the forgiveness of sins to every nation, beginning at Jerusalem." The same theme is resumed in the opening of Acts (i, 1-12), unquestionably by the same editor of the original document, but in an expanded setting. Here the time of the Christ's manifestation to his followers after his rising from the dead is enlarged to forty days. (This time-scheme, designed to fit in with the story of Pentecost, is an accessory contrivance, like the whole development of the theme. What we find in it replaces the second part of the original prologue, suppressed by the editor along with everything the writer to Theophilus had to say about the circumstances in which the disciples became convinced that Jesus was risen.) The Risen One, we are told, speaks to his followers about the Reign of God. The disciples ask him whether he is about to re-establish the Kingdom of Israel here and now, and are told in reply that the Day of this restoration is God's secret, and that the disciples of Jesus, while waiting for his return, must serve him as witnesses "in Jerusalem, in all Judea, in Samaria and to the ends of the earth." (This is the actual order of Acts, but with different indications from those of the analogous statement in the source exploited by the editor.) Thereupon Jesus is carried up to heaven in a cloud, and two angels inform the disciples that he will return in like array. In conclusion we learn that the scene took place on the Mount of Olives. A point to be kept in mind, not only because the place is messianic, but because we shall find it again in the Apocalypse of Peter, which seems to have had the same setting as the source document made use of by the editor of Acts in summarizing it into the passage before us, the whole forming a revelation of the Last Things ending in the exaltation of Jesus Christ in heaven.

Evidence of the Apocalypse of John

We turn to the Book of Revelation, the Apocalypse of John. This, as we can recognize at the outset, is not merely an instruction of the Risen Christ; it is a complete book addressed by Jesus to the faithful, with one of his prophets for intermediary. The case is not solitary but assuredly one of the most considerable. Here we find the immortal Christ delivering his oracles more than sixty years after his resurrection, and it is a noteworthy fact that, in this long prophecy of the Last Things, the Christ recalls neither the preaching nor the miracles attributed to him in the Gospel. His teaching here is purely eschatological. But his eschatology shows signs of erudition; it is almost an eschatological textbook.

Certain parts of this compendium have a meaning which awakes curiosity to the uttermost: to begin with, the letters addressed to the seven churches which introduce the great revelation. Why did the immortal Christ dictate these letters to his amanuensis? It was not the amanuensis, assuredly, who began the practice of corresponding with churches. Clearly he is here adopting a method practised by writers who, in those times, were in the habit of inditing letters to churches or, more exactly, the method practised by one writer in particular, whose Epistles were then making a stir in that part of Asia where the Apocalypse saw the light. The letters to the seven churches make a violent attack on Paul's Epistles and on those who uphold them. It may be said without paradox that the seven letters to the Asiatic churches would never have been written if Paul's Epistles had not existed before them. The entire book is an affirmation and defence of eschatology; but the author would not have been so absolute in his assertion that the end was at hand, nor so vehement against Paul and his literature, had he not felt that eschatology was already menaced. It was menaced by the gnostic movement then taking shape and by the gnosis, or the gnoses, which were beginning to find their way into the Epistles. And there was a further menace from the delay of the Second Coming, which menace, as time went on, became ever more deeply felt and disquieting; it was the void created by this delay that he set himself to fill by his series of plagues adjusted in order. These, at bottom, are all variations on a single theme, dominated by the outlook to the predicted end, which seemed to be ever fading into the distance.

But the prophet himself is not exempt from gnosis. Independently of his borrowings from astral mythology, which he makes perhaps unknowingly, since he found them already made in his source, notably the myth of the heavenly woman and her son carried up to heaven as soon as born that he may escape from the dragon (xii, 1–6), and independently of this, the symbolic name "the Lamb," under which the Christ is usually designated in the body of the book, show him familiar with the Christian symbol of the Christ as the paschal victim. He is therefore nearer than he thinks to the Pauline gnosis which he condemns in the prelude to his great vision. We might even suppose that he had been initiated into the sublime gnoses of the fourth Gospel since, in one passage (xix, 13), he mentions incidentally that the name of the triumphing Christ is "the Word of God." But this must have been added later in order to create a link between the Apocalypse and the Gospel, at the time when it was decided to attribute the two books to the same author—the apostle John.

For this attribution to the apostle the author himself is not responsible. An important feature characteristic of the Christian prophecy now before us is its complete authenticity, in the sense that the author never makes claim to any other status than that which he assumes in presenting his revelation to the churches. This status is indicated thrice over in the following passages. First the title of the book (i, 1–2):

> Revelation of Jesus Christ,
>   which God gave him,
> To reveal to his servants
>   What must soon happen,
> And made clear by a messenger, his angel,
>   to his servant John,

THE ESCHATOLOGICAL CATECHESIS

> Who attests it as the word of God,
> > and the witness of Jesus Christ,
> > Even all that he has seen.

Next, in the address (i, 4–6):

> John,
> > to the seven churches in Asia
> > Grace to you and peace, etc.

Next, in the introduction (i, 9–11):

> I, John, your brother and companion
> > in the tribulation, the Kingdom and the waiting for Jesus,
> Was in the isle called Patmos
> > for the word of God
> > and the testimony of Jesus.
> I was in the spirit, on the Lord's Day,
> > and I heard behind me a great voice,
> > as of a trumpet, which said:
> What thou seest, write in a book,
> > and send it to the seven churches,
> > to Ephesus and to Smyrna, etc.

On his own showing the author is a simple believer named John, an ordinary prophet of the churches in Asia to which he addresses himself, with special attachment to Ephesus, just as the good Hermas, a little later, was an ordinary prophet of the church in Rome; for the time being he is confined to the island of Patmos and there he has his vision. He makes no pretence to be an immediate disciple of Jesus, still less to be one of the Twelve. He knows of the Twelve in the legend which has made them "apostles of the Lamb," and their names are graven on the foundation stones of the wall of the eternal Jerusalem (xxi, 14). He has no suspicion that one day, and soon, he will be counted as one of those Twelve. Thus the Apocalypse is, in itself, an authentic book, nay, an honest book, and the more valuable for that reason as throwing light on our present subject. For it proves beyond gainsaying that Christian prophets continued for a long time to deliver oracles in the name of the immortal Christ, and did so without evoking the teachings which Jesus is supposed to have given before his death.

Unfortunately it remains to be added that our Apocalypse, with its honest writer, was very soon promoted to apostolic dignity by the conscious and interested fraud of others. That, too, is a fact and one which helps us to understand the practice of authors who, unlike John, wrote Apocalypses purporting to contain teachings of the Risen Christ, under false names deliberately assumed. That was the case with the Apocalypse of Peter, to which we now proceed.

Evidence from the Apocalypse of Peter

As this Apocalypse did not succeed in finding its way into the Canon (or rather in remaining there) nobody in our time finds it worth while to defend its authenticity as the work of Peter. But the document is none the less important for the student, since it reveals the same preoccupation as the Apocalypse of John, that, namely, of satisfying and reassuring those who were anxiously waiting for the Second Coming. This it does by explaining the delay as in the order of providential designs, and, further, by making use of events already happened or of legends already formed in the author's time.

There can be no question that the Apocalypse of Peter, like the other writings falsely attributed to this apostle, the two epistles to begin with (both of which succeeded in getting into the Canon and remaining there), was published in Peter's honour, with the object of enhancing his personality, already become legendary, and for the consecration of the legend. But the intention was, also, to carry on the tradition of teachings given by the Risen Christ, by that time well established. What makes this eschatological compilation of peculiar interest is that, in addition to precise information about the legend of Peter, it contains considerable elements which the Gospels antedate and transpose to the earthly ministry of Jesus.

Elsewhere we have made a detailed analysis of this Apocalypse (see *The Birth of the Christian Religion*, pp. 35–39). Here we note the following points:

(1) Dependent on the Apocalypse, composed about the year 135, are, with high probability, the first Epistle of Peter and, with certainty, the second Epistle, which, moreover, is not earlier than 170.

(2) In all it professes to predict about the martyrdom of Peter, the Apocalypse does not depend on the fourth Gospel (xxi, 18–19,

and previously in terms more veiled, xiii, 36), but the Gospel rather depends on the Apocalypse or on the legendary tradition on which the Apocalypse depends.

(3) A similar relation exists between the Apocalypse and what may be read in the last chapter of Luke and the first of Acts, concerning the teachings of the Risen Christ, his instructions about the end of the world and his ascension into heaven (see above, p. 48); that is to say, in the writings named after Luke the view of these things is analogous to that of the Apocalypse, though less balanced and somewhat incoherent, so that here also these writings, if not dependent on the Apocalypse itself, depend on a document analogous or identical with its source.

(4) Lastly, the Apocalypse, which might seem to have transformed the scene of the Transfiguration in the Synoptics into the story of the ascent into heaven, on the contrary presents that story in its proper place and original setting. From which the presumption clearly follows that the discourses on the Last Things in the Synoptics and the parable of the barren fig-tree in Luke (xiii, 6–9), were first conceived as teachings of the Risen Christ.

Taking it all in all, the so-called Apocalypse of Peter is a dramatization suggested by the primitive eschatological catechesis which we may regard as summed up in the declaration attributed to Peter in his discourse after Pentecost (Acts ii, 36):

> Let all the house of Israel know of a surety that this Jesus whom ye crucified God has made Lord and Christ.

The Ethiopian version of the Apocalypse, it is true, contains certain features which might have led us to suppose that it depends on the Gospel story of the Transfiguration. But Second Peter took the leading feature from the Apocalypse, the voice from on high (2 Peter i, 17): "This is my beloved Son in whom I am well pleased." What is improbable, and must result from a surcharge on the original, is that the author should have written the words we first read in the Ethiopian version after the description of the happiness of the elect:

> "I rejoiced, I believed and took confidence, and I understood the words that are written in the book of my Lord Jesus Christ. And I

said to him: 'Desirest thou that I build here three tents, one for thee, one for Moses, one for Elijah?' Then he answered me in anger: 'Satan is making war on thee, he troubles thy thought. There is only one tent, etc.'"

All that, beginning with the inept reference to Gospel literature, is a paraphrase of the synoptic story of the Transfiguration and of the rebuke undergone by Peter, in Mark and Matthew, after the messianic confession. But the whole passage has all the marks of an interpolation, the original text of the Apocalypse resuming its course in the words which follow: "And suddenly there came a voice from heaven, etc." That granted, the conclusion remains, as was conjectured long ago, that the transfiguration scene in the Synoptics is an antedating to the earthly life of Jesus of what, in the eschatological teaching, was the assumption of the Christ into heaven before the eyes of the disciples on the Mount of Olives. But this has a much wider bearing than has been commonly supposed.

The antedating of this scene was done deliberately with the object of transposing a passing vision of the Christ's glory into his career on earth, and of putting the messianic stamp on that part of the Gospel story which is consecrated to the death of Jesus. This part begins with Peter's confession at Caesarea Philippi, equally antedated from the story of the Transfiguration and co-ordinated with it, but so arranged that Peter appears in it to his disadvantage, understanding nothing (at least in Mark, but with a contradiction in Matthew) of the mystery of salvation, of the death that is necessary and of the glory of which he has been given a glimpse. In reality, Peter did not confess Jesus as the Christ until he had acquired his faith in the resurrection. Moreover, the anticipation betrays itself in the prohibition which forbids the disciples to proclaim Jesus as the Christ before his death, and in the command to the witnesses of the Transfiguration to keep silence about it until Jesus has risen from the dead. All that is profoundly significant. And there is more to the same effect.

Other Evidence of Antedating

Another instance of antedating is to be found in the story of the baptism of Jesus (Mark i, 11; Matthew iii, 17; Luke iii, 22), in which the heavenly voice utters the same words. The object of this is, again, to put the messianic stamp on what was for long the Gospel catechesis—the activity of Jesus from the baptism of John until his death and assumption into heaven (Mark: cf. *supra* p. 23; Acts i, 1–2, except for the surcharge which introduces the interpolated verses that follow).

The stories of the miraculous birth in Matthew and Luke are anticipations of a different order from the preceding. But it may be said, without falling too far into paradox, that what is offered as the Gospel tradition has no proper base of its own, the Gospel catechesis being, for the main part, an antedating and duplication of the Last Things—the primitive eschatological catechesis. It remains for us to see under what conditions this transposition was carried out.[1] Needless to add that the fourth Gospel, the latest of the canonicals, is conceived from beginning to end as the story of a divine epiphany. It is obvious that these conclusions must find their confirmation in our coming discussion and analysis of the Gospel catechesis, to which we shall proceed in due course.

[1] On the antedatings here mentioned see Bacon, *Studies in Matthew* (1930), 145–164.

Chapter III

THE EVIDENCE OF TRADITION CONCERNING THE GOSPELS

WE shall presently describe the birth and growth of the evangelical teaching, or catechesis, as far as it is possible to do so, that is, by means of near and reasonable conjecture. But before proceeding to this it is necessary to examine thoroughly the external evidence, known as the evidence of tradition, concerning the documents which contain the catechesis, that is, the Gospels. Of the external evidence at our disposal the most striking is that which Irenaeus attributes, in regard to the fourth Gospel, to the "Elders" who had known John. This evidence about the fourth Gospel, as we shall see, is bound up, in the utmost possible closeness, with the sayings of Papias about the Gospels of Mark and Matthew, making a unity of the two testimonies; there is nothing of equal antiquity concerning the Gospel of Luke. The result is, that if the united testimony of Irenaeus and Papias should turn out to be worthless, no resource, or nearly none, will be left to the historian of the pretended tradition save that of a conscientious analysis of the *internal* evidence in the texts themselves. In addition we shall find that the Gospel of Luke and the Book of Acts contain an attestation about themselves the meaning and bearing of which will need to be disengaged.

IRENAEUS

To begin with, let us see how Irenaeus commends the fourth Gospel to honour among Christians. In *Heresies* (ii, 22, 5), speaking of the gnostics, he writes of them as follows:

> Under pretext that "the year of the Lord's favour," of which the prophet speaks (Isaiah lxi, 2), support their chimera, they pretend that the Lord preached only for one year, and that he died in the twelfth month of that year.

Irenaeus would here seem to be charging only gnostics with error. In reality, he is attacking the common perspective of the first three Gospels, where the events and teaching of Jesus' ministry are assembled in a way which gives them the appearance of occupying a short time, ending with the Passover which brought him to Jerusalem, where he met his death. The third Gospel, in fact, specifies the providential year as the fifteenth of Tiberius (Luke iii, 1), and is at pains to give in full the text of Isaiah, relating to this "year of grace," in the discourse attributed to Jesus by which he inaugurated his public preaching at Nazareth, "where he had been brought up." It would seem, then, that the opinion of the gnostics had been originally professed, and that publicly, by Jesus himself.

Let us now see how Irenaeus accommodated the statement in Luke to the chronology which he claims to be that of the fourth Gospel:

> They suppress the period in the Lord's life which was the most important and the most honourable, that of his complete maturity when his teaching won for him universal respect. How can he have had disciples if he had not taught? And how can he have taught if he had not reached the age of a master?

Strange reasoning; especially when we remember that, in the view of his Person taken by the fourth Gospel, the Incarnate Logos, the Son of God had no need to graduate, before he could speak with authority. But this is a case of propping up a thesis, in which the interest to be defended determines the quality of the argument brought forward to support it.

> For at the time he presented himself for baptism, he had not yet reached the age of thirty, and was only entering on his thirtieth year.

This at least is how Irenaeus understands the somewhat confused statement in Luke iii, 23. But immediately following there is a notice in the text which contradicts the sense of the whole passage and can only be a clumsy interpolation:

> Beginning from his baptism he preached for one year only and died at the end of his thirtieth year, still young and before attaining a ripe age.

If this sentence be authentic it can only be an "indignant exclamation" of Irenaeus against the holders of an opinion judged by him to be preposterous. More probably it is, as Turmel maintains,[1] the work of an interpolator who "shamelessly makes

---
[1] *Histoire des Dogmes*, i, 319, note 1.

nonsense of the thought of Irenaeus." In any case the most careless of critics would hardly make Irenaeus say, in the quoted sentence, that the Elders support the opinion which the same Elders and Irenaeus have vigorously combated in the whole course of the argument. But he proceeds:

> Now thirty years is the age of youth which, as all men agree, continues to forty years. Between forty and fifty begins the age of maturity, at which our Lord gave his teaching, as the (fourth) Gospel attests; and all the Elders who in Asia were in contact with John, the disciple of the Lord, declare that they hold that from John, who remained with them to the time of Trajan.

We shall presently see how the fourth Gospel corroborates the testimony of the Elders. The Elders had good ground for knowing the corroboration and we can make a shrewd guess as to why they knew it. From what follows it results that this "John, disciple of the Lord" was also an apostle. The designation is somewhat loose, but tends to support the opinion now called traditional, namely, that the fourth Gospel is of apostolic origin. As it was then well known that the Gospel in question had but lately come into being, pains were taken to put on record that John had lived to a great old age—"till the time of Trajan" (98–117). These Elders who had conversed with John would have heard him in the early years of the second century. If we go by the Johannine chronology, this John would have been much younger than Jesus, but even so he would have been of a ripe old age at the beginning of the second century. In addition, those who drew up the appendix to the fourth Gospel (xxi) have also been at pains to inform us that "the brethren believed he would not die" (23), and have not failed to add that it was this disciple, so old, so unusually old, who wrote the Gospel and that they knew, yes, *they* knew, that his witness was true (24). All of which very plainly comes from the same workshop and serves the same cause.

Unfortunately for their efforts, John, the son of Zebedee, never set foot in Asia and cannot have died of old age, having perished, along with his brother James, at the hand of Agrippa I, in the year 44, long before the idea occurred to anybody of making him the author of the Apocalypse or of the fourth Gospel. The Gospel of Mark (x, 37–40) is here an unimpeachable authority. It represents the two brothers, John and James, asking Jesus to give them the two chief seats by his side in the Kingdom:

> And Jesus said to them: "Ye know not what ye ask. Are ye able to drink the cup I have to drink or to be baptized with the baptism wherewith I must be baptized?" They said to him: "We are able." But Jesus said to them: "The cup that I have to drink ye shall drink, and with the baptism wherewith I have to be baptized, ye shall be baptized. As to sitting on my right hand and my left, that is not mine to give: it is for those for whom it has been prepared."

This scene was conceived independently of the Ephesian legend about John and long before it gained credit in the churches. Whoever described it (whether he invented it or not matters little) knew or believed he knew for a certainty that John and James had suffered martyrdom, probably on the same occasion. James was put to death by order of Agrippa I in the spring of 44, and the clumsiness of the formula used by the editor of the Acts in recording the matter (xii, 2) gives ground for thinking that the execution of John, mentioned in the source document before that of James, was afterwards suppressed out of consideration for the Ephesus legend which by that time had become established. A jealous care for this legend is perceptible in other passages in Acts and even in the third Gospel, from which the above story of Mark (x, 35–40) has been deliberately omitted. The critic has other grounds for affirming as a certainty that neither the Apocalypse nor the fourth Gospel is the work of John the son of Zebedee and one of Jesus' first disciples. But, though fictitious, the testimony of the "Elders who had known John" gives abundant food for thought.

Irenaeus continues:

> But some of them saw not only John but other apostles, and heard the same things from them, attesting a similar story.

So we are to believe that all the apostles met together in Asia. Polycrates of Ephesus in his letter to Pope Victor mentions only Philip, and mistakes him for another, for the Philip of whom he speaks was he whom Acts presents as one of the Seven, a companion of Stephen. Irenaeus amplifies the evidence. Finally he returns to the argument furnished by the fourth Gospel concerning the age of the Christ:

> Moreover the Jews themselves who then disputed with the Lord Jesus Christ make the matter clear. When the Lord told them that their father Abraham had desired to see his day, they answered him: "Thou art not yet fifty years old and thou hast seen Abraham!" (John viii, 56–57). Now this saying has no sense except as addressed to one who was over forty, is not yet fifty, but not far short of it.

Nothing could be clearer, and Irenaeus might have strengthened his case by quoting another passage of the Gospel connected with the foregoing. After the expulsion of the traders from the Temple the Jews say to Jesus (John ii, 18–22):

> "What sign showest thou, that thou hast done this thing?" And he answered them and said: "Destroy this temple and in three days I will raise it up." The Jews then said: "Forty-six years was this temple in building, and thou, wilt thou raise it up in three days?" But he, he spoke of the temple of his body. When therefore he was raised from the dead his disciples remembered that he had said this, and they believed the Scripture, and the word that Jesus has spoken.

All the elements of this picture are taken from the Synopsis, but with a different marking of time and place, and with nothing new except the interpretation. The variation "destroy this temple" renders inoffensive, and full of mystic meaning, the saying brought up in evidence against Jesus at the trial which ended in his condemnation: "I will destroy this temple and rebuild it in three days." In that form of the saying would lie the proof of his messianic pretension. Here the same pretension is implied, but with a totally different meaning. The temple, we are plainly told, is now the body of the Christ; the Jews are challenged to destroy it by putting him to death, and Jesus undertakes to restore it by raising it from the dead. But this conversation does not belong to the realm of historical fact; it is a mystic vision, a kind of enigma, to which the key is not to be found in anything we can learn from history about the building of the Temple. Commentators, therefore, walk blindly into a trap when they attempt, as many have done, to explain the forty-six years by connecting them, as the old interpreters did, with the time occupied by the building of Solomon's Temple, or with its reconstruction by Zerubbabel, while many of the moderns, with a candour wholly scientific, imagine they have found the key in the reconstruction begun by Herod in the year of Rome 734–5 (29–19 B.C.) and finished about 63–64. The forty-six years would bring us to 27–28 of our era. Is not that a marvellous coincidence? But more marvellous still than the pretended coincidence is that our learned exegetes, speculating on this conversation as though it had really taken place in the circumstances indicated, should have overlooked the fact that the redactors of the fourth Gospel, who between 125 and 135 arranged the story, were little concerned with Herod and his temple building, and the further fact that, while they found the forty-six years somewhere, it was certainly not in personal recollections, of which they had none, nor in Josephus, whom they had not consulted, but in some passage of Scripture which they had opportunely dug out to serve as base for their chronological arrangement of the age of Jesus—the passage which the disciples are said to have believed later. This text exists: it is the passage in Daniel (ix, 24–27) where the angel discourses about the seventy week-years which are to elapse before the messianic age. The seven weeks which pseudo-Daniel sets apart in this prophecy were to be understood as covering the temple of Zerubbabel and the age of the Christ, and the half-week, which is distinguished from them, as referring to the duration of his ministry. In this way Jesus would be about fifty years old when he died (John viii, 57) and exactly *forty-six* when, shortly after the beginning of his ministry, he drove the traffickers out of the Temple. This explanation of the forty-six years was given long ago by the author of the treatise *de Montibus Sina et Sion*, a treatise preserved among the works of St. Cyprian (*edition*, Hartel, iii, 108). This is the only explanation that fits the mystical character of the story. So explained, we are not surprised on reading (ii, 22) that the disciples did not understand the mystery until after the resurrection, and that then "they believed the Scripture and the word that Jesus had spoken," having by that time perceived the meaning of Daniel's prediction and of the Christ's declaration about the temple destroyed by the Jews and raised again after three days. All that balances perfectly, if we place ourselves outside history, as the authors of the story did, and inside the realm of mythical fiction.

It follows that Irenaeus, and the Elders before him "who had known John," were not deceived in saying that their assertions concerning the Christ's age were authorized by the Gospel; they are indeed to be found there either logically implied or plainly announced. It appears, moreover, that this edifying concert of "Elders" and Gospel cannot have been fortuitous, the nature of the case making that impossible, and that both the construction of the testimony of the Elders who had seen not only John but other apostles, and the introduction into the Gospel of the passages where we read indications of the Christ's age, are, at all points, the work of one and the same group. Who were these persons? They were the very men who edited the Gospel and first presented it to the Christian public, and at the same time constructed the testimony of the "Elders who had seen John and other apostles." Gospel and testimony are the offspring of one and the same fiction, of which the object was to guarantee the apostolic origin of the book, so as to assure its acceptance by the churches. In the end the fiction took hold, and it is no exaggeration to say that modern criticism has not escaped from its grip, though it seldom has the hardihood to maintain that Jesus at the time of his death was approaching his fiftieth year.

Be it noted, however, that when we here speak of the Gospel we have in mind the book as it was first presented to the churches of Asia, without prejudging the greater part of the elements which entered into the composition. Some of these elements are later than this first publication, having been added to procure the acceptance of the book, alongside the Synoptics, by the whole body of Christian churches, and not only by those of Asia. In the other direction, the first version of the book embraced elements of older date than itself. But these considerations belong to the history of what is commonly called evangelical tradition, for which we prefer the exacter name of evangelical catechesis. Our task has been to examine the so-called traditional witness to the fourth Gospel, and our conclusion is that no such witness exists, what claims to be such being in truth a colossal fiction, one of the most noteworthy in the entire history of the New Testament and one of the easiest to verify (cf. *Remarques*, 172, n. 1).

THE EVIDENCE OF TRADITION CONCERNING THE GOSPELS

THE TESTIMONY OF PAPIAS

The common opinion has hitherto been that the testimony of Papias of Hierapolis in the name of John the Elder concerning the Gospels of Mark and Matthew has no connection with the testimony of the Elders, who claimed to have known John, in regard to the fourth Gospel. We have just seen that the latter testimony was aimed at the Synopsis or, more exactly, against all Gospels of the synoptic type with the object of assuring a greater, if not an exclusive, authority to the Johannine type. Now it may well be that the sayings of Papias are, in their origin and primary intention, co-ordinated with the pleading in favour of John, in which case we shall be led to attach no more historical weight to them than we have found due to the Elders who claimed John's authority. Let us see, then, how the matter stands with these sayings of Papias, on which there has been endless dissertation among exegetes, but perhaps without perception of their real significance.

Papias wrote in five books an *Explanation of the sentences of the Lord* which has not been preserved. Eusebius calls attention to it in his *Ecclesiastical History* (iii, 39), gives some extracts and at the end reproduces "the tradition which Papias has passed down to us concerning Mark who wrote the Gospel." It is therefore a fragment taken out of the context that Eusebius offers to the consideration of his readers. It runs as follows:

> And the Elder said this: "Mark, having become Peter's interpreter, wrote accurately, but not in order, all that he remembered, of the sayings and doings of the Lord. For he had not heard the Lord nor been of his company, but later, as I have said (he accompanied) Peter. Peter gave the teaching, as the need arose, but without arranging the sayings of the Lord in their order, so that Mark was not mistaken in thus writing down certain things as he remembered them; for his only care was to omit nothing of what he had heard and to insert nothing false."

Such, then, is what Papias has to tell us about Mark. And here is what he says about Matthew:

> "Matthew made a collection of sentences in the Hebrew tongue, but everyone translated them as he could."

It is to be noted that, in another passage quoted earlier, Papias says that he had questioned those who had seen Andrew, Peter,

Philip, Thomas, James, John, Matthew, and was also informed of what was said by "John the Elder and Aristion, disciples of the Lord." Clearly then he distinguishes two Johns, the Apostle and the Elder, as Eusebius remarks. In addition Eusebius affirms that Papias has been in direct contact with John the Elder and with Aristion, though this is not deducible from the texts he quotes. In any case the distinction between the two Johns is important, and for Papias it is John the Elder alone who came into Asia. Thus it is clear that "the Elders who had known John" have passed off John the Elder as the Apostle John.

A further point of importance is that Papias is *paraphrasing* the sayings of John the Elder about Mark. Plainly it is he who explains and excuses what John the Elder denounces in Mark's lack of order. But the Mark of Papias is a legendary figure, as John the Elder's Mark already was: he is the Mark of the first Epistle of Peter (v, 13)—which is not authentic—whom this Epistle, in all probability, would discreetly commend as an evangelist for the good reason that the Gospel of Mark had been in existence for some time when the Epistle was written. The information furnished about him by the Elders and by Papias may well be less dependable and go back less far into the past than is commonly believed, since it belongs to the same family, as we shall presently perceive more clearly, with the information about the fourth Gospel furnished by the Elders who had known John, the value of which we have already assessed. The praise of Mark's accuracy comes only from Papias, who was in no position to verify it, but whose intention was to paraphrase the assertion of the Elder in a manner favourable to Mark. All that we have to examine is this assertion; the intentions of those who formulated it in the name of the Elder may well have been less disingenuous than those of Papias.

About the notice concerning Matthew interpreters are divided, some maintaining that it comes from the Elder, others that Papias alone is responsible for it. The latter opinion is improbable. On his own responsibility the good Papias would never have depreciated the Gospel of Matthew (which he certainly knew) as this notice does. There is no doubt that he failed to catch what the Elder's assertion was aiming at and so reproduced it without commentary. But the two statements about Mark and

THE EVIDENCE OF TRADITION CONCERNING THE GOSPELS

Matthew run parallel, and aim, together, at putting a measure of disqualification on two Gospels, widely used by the churches, in comparison with another Gospel, doubtless regarded by their author as superior to the other two.

Nor have we to search far to find the Gospel more unquestionably apostolic, better ordered than Mark and more reliable than the translations of Matthew. This incomparable Gospel is assuredly the fourth, said to come from an immediate disciple of Jesus; the Gospel with the admirable chronology, whose merits are praised by the Elders who had known John, and which, moreover, reproduces the Lord's discourses as the beloved disciple of the Christ had heard and collected them, that disciple of whom the Elders themselves emphatically attest that his "witness is true" (John xxi, 24; xix, 35). The conclusion is that the sayings of the Elder about the Gospels of Mark and Matthew, transmitted to us by Papias, and the sayings of the Elders, piously preserved by Irenaeus, about the fourth Gospel, the duration of the Christ's earthly life of fifty years and the length of his ministry, issue from one and the same source.

With all this before us there is no need to engage in controversy on secondary points, for example whether the Gospel of Mark, to which the Elders and Papias refer, was identical with that of Christian tradition; or whether the "sentences" or "oracles" of Matthew are a source only of the first Gospel, that from which the discourses of the Christ have been taken and which may really come from the apostle Matthew. What imports before all else is the value of the evidence as such, and this, being nothing at all, discussion of these details is superfluous. As to Mark, the reference is certainly to our second Gospel, but from what we are told about it nothing can be deduced as to the stage to which the drafting of it had arrived in the time of John the Elder (that is, at the time of those who put words in his mouth) or in the time of Papias. The judgment before us refers to the Gospel as a whole, an erroneous judgment as we shall presently see, but which, even if it held together, would not permit us to prejudge the re-arrangements, retouches and additions undergone by Mark from the time of its first drafting to the time when the fixing of the canon of the four Gospels determined also the fixation of their text.

As to the notice about Matthew, it also certainly points to our first Gospel, and not to one of its sources. Neither the Elder nor Papias had any acquaintance with the theory, formulated by modern critics, of the two sources of Matthew—Mark and the *Logia*. If they speak in particular of the Lord's discourses, it is because these discourses formed, in their eyes, the distinctive matter of the Gospel, apart from what it had in common with Mark. What their purpose required them to say about them is what they tell us, namely, that they were first given out in the Aramean language, of which we have only the untrustworthy translations into Greek. As to the stories in Matthew, neither the Elder nor Papias was concerned to know whether they came from Mark or from another source; but these stories shared in the defect attributed to Mark, which is also represented as originally a translation of information which must have been received in Aramean from Peter. These testimonies taken as a whole are marked, by their very character, as insusceptible of the discussion proper to documentation truly traditional and historical. Their evidence is tendentious, constructed for a purpose and non-historical.

That this is the real character of the evidence results from the way in which it is presented, which rules out the possibility of assigning it a very early date. It treats the Gospels as catechism, and this is important, since the catechism in question, the manual of Christian initiation, is presented as a narrative of the earthly career of the Christ up to the climax of his death and resurrection. They tell the story of a divine epiphany, which forms an introduction to the mystery of salvation. Without a doubt the Gospels are precisely such a catechesis and not a history of Jesus. But neither can there be any doubt that this conception and form of catechesis are not primitive in any sense, since the original instruction of converts at the so-called apostolic age was essentially moral and eschatological, and so remained for a considerable time afterwards. Now the evidence we have been considering reveals a complete and radical transformation of the original catechesis, which has become, at the date of the evidence, not only *the* Gospel or evangelical message, but is now fixed in written Gospel*s*, of which there are already a goodly number. Plainly Mark and Matthew are supposed to be earlier than John, which is now being put forward to supplant them. This carries us far, very far, from Gospel origins. Nor do our witnesses show signs of having even a suspicion of the evolution which produced the books whose merits they discuss and whose comparative values they assess.

Considered from this point of view, the information they profess to give us is amazingly puerile. In the notice relating to Mark it is implied that Peter was a kind of universal missionary, which he never was, except in a legend of late origin. But this active missionary, who would seem to have made the round of the known world (he is supposed to have come to Rome, as the two Epistles of Peter make out), could probably express himself only in Aramean, no small drawback for an apostle to the world at large, even were his ministry limited to the Jews dispersed about the world, as our texts in no wise indicate that it was. Peter, so the evidence runs, not knowing Greek, would teach his hearers in Aramean; but he had Mark for interpreter; what he taught his hearers was what Mark the interpreter has reproduced in his Greek Gospel; and Mark, though accurate, has put no more order into his book than Peter put into his preaching. Let us attend carefully to what this is meant to convey. Certainly it does not mean that Peter, in his preaching, would sometimes place the passion of the Christ before his baptism; what it is intended to convey, and to convey nothing else, is that Peter's catechizing, reproduced by Mark, does not give a correct picture of the Christ's career. And that is why we are to think that Mark is not the best catechism for the initiation of Christians; the true catechism, and the only true, is that of John. This, for a wilfully contrived anachronism, is cleverly done; but it was contrived at the moment when the Gospel ascribed to John was a newcomer in process of being introduced to the Christian public, while the Gospel attributed to Mark was an old-timer, possessed and used by many churches. Moreover, as our coming analysis will soon show, the Gospel of Mark is very far from being a translation of apostolic teaching, Peter's or another's.

The Gospel of Matthew, whatever else it may be, was not translated from Aramean any more than that of Mark was. It was imagined to be so because, just as the apostle Peter spoke in Aramean, so the apostle Matthew must have written in the same language. The difference was that Matthew, unlike Peter, had no disciple to act as his translator into Greek; the first-comers undertook the operation without further credentials. To risk this statement the authors of it had no need to be acquainted with the different versions of the first Gospel. The idea of translation had suggested itself spontaneously and was found useful for disqualifying Matthew, as well as Mark, in favour of the Johannine Gospel. The only historical fact to be got out of the statement is that the first Gospel was known to the churches of Asia, and attributed to the apostle Matthew, at the time the statement was made. That this or that element in Mark or in Matthew was first written in Aramean is probable enough; but that is not the question now before us. The same may be said about the sources of the fourth Gospel.

The fiction on which all this evidence rests is concerned with the Gospel of John. It implies that Gospels of the synoptic type were in existence and held in credit, and we can name two of them without hesitation—Mark and Matthew, reserving the case of Luke for the time being. The two Gospels are discreetly denounced as not having known the real duration of the earthly life of Jesus and of his public ministry, or at least for not rendering them correctly. Moreover, it is certain that the Elders did not fix the duration in question in accordance with any historical tradition, but were moved only by considerations of theological fitness according to a typology constructed for a purpose, in which the concept of a Christ purely divine was combined with that of a teaching Christ, a Christ come to earth and in the flesh, to live for a time among men and teach them the secrets of God in a mystery. This framework for the life and activity of the incarnate Logos, presented as though it were historical, is manifestly the work of a gnosis which the Gospel has incorporated into itself. It follows that the elaboration of the Gospel, as such, is, in large measure, the work of the very persons who invented the fiction by which they commend it as superior to the others already in use. Thus the Johannine Gospel is proclaimed by its own showing to be later than the Gospels of synoptic type, in comparison with which its champions exalted its value as a Gospel book, a catechism transcendently exact; the one, therefore, to be preferred above all the rest.

THE EVIDENCE OF TRADITION CONCERNING THE GOSPELS

The name John guarantees nothing, for the apostle John is out of the question; nor is there ground for supposing that John the Elder played any part in the fiction which takes him as its point of departure. Speaking strictly, "John" is no more than a date or a label affixed to the monumental fraud which commended the fourth Gospel to the high consideration of the Christian churches. Fundamentally, John the Elder has as little to do with the fourth Gospel as with the Apocalypse. His person and his name, deliberately identified with the person and name of the apostle John, were exploited by those whom we may politely describe as the author-editors of the Johannine library.

But what dates are to be assigned to the birth and evolution of the Gospel catechesis? For the moment, when our concern is less with the catechesis itself than with the external evidences regarding it, we note that the work of John the Elder in the churches of Asia was finished about the year 110. A point is made of telling us that he died at a great age, having lived to the time of Trajan; and this may be true. At the other end of the chain of evidence is Papias. We cannot state precisely the age in which Papias wrote his *Explanation of the Lord's sayings*, seeing that this excellent but rather limited man (according to Eusebius who had read the book) was somewhat behind his times. But he must have written long before Irenaeus. If he wrote after the outbreak of Marcionism we can hardly suppose that so great an explosion of heresy would have left him untouched. Let us then suppose that he wrote about 140. The launching of the Johannine group of books was not much earlier than this date. But it is improbable that Papias had personally known John the Elder; he merely repeats what has been told him. There is nothing, therefore, to prevent us placing the first publication of the Johannine Gospel, and the attribution of the Apocalypse to the same author as the Gospel, towards the years 130–135. The way in which the Gospel was offered to the churches proves that Mark and Matthew were known previously, not indeed in the rigorously fixed form of the canon, but with their traditional attributions. Matthew therefore would be earlier than 130, and Mark, on whom Matthew certainly depends for the framework of his story, would go still further back. Thus the existence of these two Gospel catechisms, with attributions of authorship either apostolic or equivalently so, is almost certainly guaranteed by the first third of the second century.

Since these attributions of authorship are false, there are no signs to carry us further back. It is noteworthy that so late as 140 Basilides was putting out a Gospel under the name of Glaucias a disciple of Peter—probably following the example of Mark—and that Valentinus who, about the same time, perhaps a little earlier and before Marcion, had published his, set his "Gospel of the Truth" under the authority of Theodas, a supposed disciple of Paul. It is possible, even probable, that some first drafts of the Gospel catechesis, with no author's name attached, may have existed before the year 100; but it must be confessed that we know nothing about them.

The conclusions to which we have come will not be accepted by scholars who defend the authenticity of the letter of Ignatius of Antioch, who place the letter of Polycarp to the Philippians about 110, carrying back the letter of Clement to the Corinthians to 95 and the Epistle to the Hebrews to about 80. We have given elsewhere[1] the weighty reasons which tell against that opinion. The letters named after Ignatius of Antioch are, in their first form, apocryphal; they are the work of the Marcionist bishop, probably named Theophorus, who wrote about the year 170; they were interpolated in the catholic interest about 200, and the Epistle of Polycarp to the Philippians, written about 150–160, was interpolated to give them weight. The letter of Clement of Rome to the Corinthians is by the Clement named in the Shepherd of Hermas (*Vision*, iii) about 130–140, and we have already seen the date of the Epistle to the Hebrews. The values and the dates commonly assigned to these documents are highly convenient for building up an apologetic system. We have abandoned them because they seemed to us, on examination, to be wholly false and incompatible with the real evolution of primitive Christianity.

THE THIRD GOSPEL

The reader will probably be asking why, in the preceding discussion, no mention has been made of the writings ascribed

---

[1] *Remarques sur la Littérature Epistolaire du Nouveau Testament*, 103–105, 113, 147–169.

to Luke, namely the third Gospel and the Acts of the Apostles. The answer is that our witnesses, the Elders and Papias, say nothing about them. Beginning with Irenaeus, ecclesiastical authors proclaim with one voice that both books are the work of Luke, a disciple of Paul, the Gospel of Luke having the same relation with Paul as that of Mark with Peter. But when Irenaeus affirms (*Heresies*, i, 1, 1) that "Luke, the companion of Paul, put into a book the Gospel preached by him," the assertion is as groundless and false as the Elders' presentation of Mark as a translation into Greek of Peter's teaching. Before Irenaeus, Justin seems to have counted Luke among the "Memoirs of the Apostles"; and before Justin there was Marcion whose Gospel was regarded by Irenaeus, Tertullian, and other writers who knew it, as a mutilated Luke.

In Marcion, it was simply *"the* Gospel" without the addition of an author's name. The book of *Antitheses,* in which Marcion explained his system and justified his biblical canon, not having been preserved, we are ignorant how Marcion understood the relation of his own Gospel book to that which the great Church guarded under the name of Luke. It is in the highest degree improbable, not to put it more strongly, that the Church received a Gospel hitherto unknown to it from the hand of Marcion,[1] and equally probable, on the contrary, that, among the various types of catechesis current in the great Church, Marcion would choose for his own use that one among them which he judged to have the best credentials, lacking only adaptation to his doctrine; it was, indeed, a moral necessity of his situation that he should do so. On the other hand we should probably be wrong in thinking that Marcion found the Gospel of Luke exactly in the form in which the canonical version preserved it, and that this version contains no line added to it after Marcion's time. But it cannot be admitted for a moment that Marcion is responsible for having, in any sense, created the Christian catechesis and that the whole Gospel literature proceeds, in any way, from him. It is impossible to make Mark depend on Marcion, for it is Luke, in Marcion's version, as in the others, which depends on Mark. To be sure, Marcion complicates the problem of the

[1] Thesis of P. L. Couchond in *The Hibbert Journal,* January 1936, pp. 265–277; *Is Marcion's Gospel one of the Synoptics?* refuted by the author of the present book in the same Review, April 1936, pp. 378–387, *Marcion's Gospel.*

Gospel catechesis, but he does not suppress it. Nor is it easy to see how, from this anonymous book, there could have arisen the twin books, the Gospel according to Luke and the Acts of the Apostles, together with the prefaces connecting the one with the other. In reading the Marcionite Gospel, so far as known to us, it is easy to see how Marcion has, so to say, rubbed down preexisting Gospel materials to prevent them contradicting his doctrine; but he does not invent them. Moreover, the total invention of such a book, in the conditions in which he is supposed to have achieved it, is quite inconceivable. We conclude that Marcion was not the founder of Gospel catechesis. He took it up at a given point in its development in a given type, that of the third Gospel, which, in the part common to the two writings, was not very different from the canonical text.

The opening of Marcion's Gospel shows that his most drastic cuts were made at the beginning. It opens as follows with a combination of Luke iii, 1a, and iv, 31–32:

> The fifteenth year of Tiberius, in the time of Pilate, Jesus descended at Capernaum and taught in the Synagogue. And they were all astonished at his doctrine for he spoke with authority.

The cure of the demoniac (iv, 33–35) immediately follows; then, considerably contracted, comes the previous scene of the preaching at Nazareth, with the conclusion (iv, 28–30) fully retained; next, the story resumes its thread from Capernaum (iv, 40–43); next, the calling of the four chief disciples and the miraculous draught of fishes. All that compared with our Luke gives the impression of abridgment and arbitrary re-arrangement. From the omissions at the beginning of chapter iii we gather that Marcion decided not to preserve the baptism by John, the genealogy and the temptation in the wilderness. As to the omitted stories of the miraculous birth, it is impossible to say whether Marcion omitted them deliberately or whether the copy he had before him did not contain them. But what he has preserved shows that Marcion was working on a text already in existence as he did, in another book, with Paul's Epistles.

One would give much to know why Papias had nothing to say about the third Gospel. But had he nothing to say? If we begin by supposing that he must have known it we shall have to conclude either that he said nothing or that Eusebius thought his remarks about it might be neglected as of no interest. But these are not precisely the terms in which the question ought to be faced. What most concerns us to know is why the "Elders" who knew John did not bring the third Gospel under a condemnation similar to that which they passed on Mark and Matthew. For it is evident that, if they had passed any such judgment on Luke, Papias would not have failed to reproduce it, nor Eusebius to call attention to it. From which we may infer that the patrons of the fourth Gospel refrained from judging Luke. Was it that they did not know it, because the Gospel according to Luke had no circulation among their Asiatic churches? Or, on the contrary, did they know the Gospel and prudently keep silence about it because it was held in honour among their people at the time when they were laying plans to make their pretended Gospel of John prevail over the others?

Since they knew Mark and Matthew it is hardly probable that they knew nothing of Luke, whose original area of diffusion seems to have been Rome and Greece proper, besides some points of contact with the Syrian Orient implied by the birth-legend and the Book of Acts. We know, moreover, that the Gospel named after John was not the oldest Gospel catechism; "the Elders who had known John" make that clear enough. In their time, as we have shown, the catechism had become *evangelical*, in the sense that it was understood as being, naturally and necessarily, a presentation of the doings and teachings which had characterized the messianic career of Jesus, these doings and teachings forming henceforward the authentic manual for instructing the Christian initiate. Under these conditions is there any serious objection to the conjecture that the Gospel called Luke's was the very Gospel most widely authorized in the Asiatic churches before the introduction of the Gospel named after John? If this hypothesis be admitted we can understand why our worthy Elders did not risk an open attack on the text in use, among their churches, for initiation into the Christian cult.

There is, indeed, one serious objection that can be brought against the above hypothesis. It is that Luke contradicts the Easter usage adopted, at least to the end of the second century, by the Asiatic churches. These churches celebrated Easter on the variable day of the week when the Jews celebrated the Passover, while Luke, in its canonical form, like Mark and Matthew, authorizes celebration on Sunday only. To resolve this difficulty we must briefly examine the exact position revealed, by the prologues to Theophilus (Luke i, 1–4, and Acts i, 1–2), as the position of the third Gospel in the evolution of evangelical catechesis.

Later on we shall undertake a more thorough discussion of the writings ascribed to Luke, but the two prologues to Theophilus interest us, at this point, as witnesses to the history of the Christian catechesis, because they permit us to determine the character, the purpose and the age of the first book to Theophilus, which tradition made later into the Gospel according to Luke. Now what does the first prologue tell us (Luke i, 1–4)? It tells us that "many having undertaken to compose a narrative of the acts accomplished (among believers) according as they have been handed down by those who were from the beginning witnesses of the word, it has seemed good (to the author, after serious and long observation of the matter) to write in continuous sequence (the matter needed) for the sound instruction of the catechumen."

The man who wrote this did not belong, and was far from belonging, to the very first age of Christianity. Gospels have been written before his; Mark certainly and others probably, such as the primitive form of Matthew, or various versions of the original eschatological teaching which might have been considered as narratives of the first origin of Christianity (such as the Apocalypse of Peter). The writer, like many in our own day, has no suspicion that the primitive teaching was an exclusively *eschatological* catechesis; he thinks that it has always been *evangelical*, and a story told by the first witnesses of Jesus. Papias and the "Elders who had known John" thought the same; our author cannot be much earlier than they. Let us place him, without hesitation, at the beginning of the second century, and with no insistence on the first years of it. At length he has decided that he, too, will write "exactly and in order," late as it is! This is not a man of the first Christian generation, nor even of the second; we need not hesitate to place him in the third or the fourth; therefore, he is not Luke.

Whoever he was, and for us he is anonymous, he decided, when he came to write the prologue to the second book, to follow good usage by summarizing what he had put into the first. Let us listen to what he says and reflect on it:

> I composed the first book, to Theophilus, about all that Jesus did and taught from the beginning (of his ministry), until the day when he was carried up (to God).

What follows after the first part of the prologue to Acts (i, 1–2) is merely a clumsy surcharge intended to bring in, by hook or crook, the long interpolation substituted for the second part of the prologue, in which the original author states what he proposes to put into this, his second book, destined to become later the Acts of the Apostles. Enough that we know what he purposed to present in his first book, namely, "the doings and sayings" which had given its character to the messianic ministry of Jesus. Note that our author uses terms similar to those of Papias; but note further, and especially, that the stories of the miraculous birth are not included in his summary description of the content of his Gospel, but rather excluded. No doubt there were many other differences between the first book addressed to Theophilus and the canonical Gospel of Luke. Whence it follows that Marcion, before he came to Rome, and while still in his own country of Asia Minor, may have known a version of Luke from which the birth-stories were absent.

And we have to remark also, and in the first place, that, as we shall later prove, the story of the Last Supper in the canonical edition of Luke is evidently founded on an original version in which the last meal was not the Passover meal, and that this original has been altered after the event, and additions made to it so as to bring the story into line with the observance of Easter on Sunday only.

The internal evolution of our author's first book to Theophilus would, then, lead us to conclude that, in its original form, it corresponded with the usage of the quartodecimans as preached in the Asiatic churches. The same may be said with equal truth of Mark, in which it is generally agreed to recognize the presence of an ancient Roman Gospel. Thus we see that the evolution of the Gospel catechesis is linked with the general evolution of

Christian belief as was also, from the first, the substitution of the Gospel catechesis for the eschatological. All this, taken together, was a unitary movement, the reality of which is not to be contested, but which we must avoid the mistake of over-simplifying. And all this we offer as prelude to our investigation of the Gospel catechesis in the Gospel books. It is possible, indeed rather probable, that the churches of Asia, before accepting the Gospel named after John as their regular manual of Christian initiation, had made use of another Gospel in harmony with their quartodeciman celebration of Easter and that this Gospel was a pre-canonical form of Luke. Certain points of contact between the third Gospel and the fourth would thus be explained, but this is not the place to discuss the matter. We have now to analyse the books representing the Gospel catechesis, in detail and with all possible precision.

Chapter IV

ANALYSIS OF THE GOSPEL CATECHESIS

THE GOSPEL ACCORDING TO MARK

THE catechesis we have called evangelical, though officially certified by names deemed to be apostolic, does not go back to the earliest age of Christianity and is far from such antiquity. First and foremost it is a *catechesis*. True it is that the majority of modern critics, in our time, obstinately regard it as a collection of memories, more or less authentic, of the life of Jesus. It is, however, nothing else than a manual of Christian initiation, as the eschatological catechesis was before it, but with this difference, that whereas the latter presented the *risen* Christ, glorious with God and on the point of coming to set up the Great Kingdom, the evangelical catechesis presents the Christ, the Kingdom and the Good News in quite another light. In the eschatological teaching the epiphany of the Messiah has yet to come; in the gospel teaching this epiphany is antedated, and considered as already effected in and by the earthly life of its hero; this earthly epiphany, coming to its climax in the death and resurrection of Jesus, is what the evangelical catechesis now offers. This anticipation corresponds to a general move forward in belief, to the need of defending the faith, and to the transformation of the primitive Gospel into a mystery of salvation incorporated, so to say, with the present life.

Under the light of these observations we now venture upon an analysis of the four evangelical books, beginning with that which all probabilities indicate as the oldest, that is, the Gospel according to Mark.

THE FIRST PHASE OF THE MARCAN CATECHESIS

An unprejudiced reader of our second Gospel could not fail to recognize that it contains, beneath a certain superficial unity, a conglomerate of incoherent materials which ill disguise the additions made to an original form or the transformations it has undergone, and this in cases where the material is of most importance. We may, without much difficulty, distinguish two parts in the Gospel; one may be called the baptismal catechesis, in which the epiphany of the Christ is begun in the baptism of Jesus by John; the second, which may be called the catechesis of the Communion Supper, or of the saving death, may be said to open with the confession of Peter and to be completed on the discovery of the empty tomb, offered as material proof that Jesus rose from the dead. It is obvious that here we must confine ourselves to pointing out the features that are most striking and the contradictions most evident.

First of all, that the epiphany of the Christ, and the catechesis, are strictly confined to his *public* life. Accordingly, the messianic consecration of Jesus is effected, or seems to be, by his baptism, or on the occasion of it. The presentation of John the Baptist (Mark i, 1–8) serves as the needed preamble to this baptism, a preamble embarrassed by the fact that the covering prophecy, quoted as coming entirely from Isaiah (xl, 3) comes, as to its first part, from Malachi (iii, 1), thereby betraying the overlapping text from Malachi as a surcharge. The account of John the Baptist is obviously intended to present him as a forerunner subordinate to the Christ, and his baptism as an empty sacrament, prelude to Christian baptism in the Holy Spirit—a distinction imagined after the event and ill concealing the original identity of the two rites. Moreover, Matthew (iii, 7–12) and Luke (iii, 7–9; 16–18) having here a more extended text, original in relation to Mark, the presumption is that Mark depends on their source; in other words, that the account of John the Baptist is a later addition in Mark's catechesis. In like manner the story of the temptation in the wilderness gives the impression of being a shorter account original in relation to Matthew (iv, 1–11; cf. Luke iv, 1–13). All the features in this picture of Jesus presented as Messiah at his baptism betray the antedating of the messianic consecration, which the earlier eschatological catechesis reserved for the *risen* Jesus. At this stage of the catechesis it is at his *baptism* that God says to him: "Thou art my beloved son; in thee I am well pleased" and not, as in the Apocalypse of Peter, after his resurrection (cf. *supra*, p. 52).

Looking closely into the matter, it is perfectly natural that, in the early rudiments of the Gospel catechesis, Jesus should be represented as making his first appearance at the moment when his public ministry began, and that afterwards the feeling should arise that this was also the right moment to explain the initial relations between John and Jesus, between John's baptism and Christian baptism by interpreting John's providential mission as preliminary to the higher messianic mission of Jesus. Moreover, the descent of the Spirit into Jesus seems to be understood, not as a simple operation of the Spirit, but as the realization of an immanence of the Spirit which, in Jesus, was itself his higher being, the very person, we might say, of the Son of Man, of Christ the Saviour. The description of the descent as "like a dove" marks the perceptible individuality of this Spirit.

Next in order comes the calling of the first disciples (i, 16–20) whom Jesus is deemed to have intended for apostles. Another anticipation. We shall have many occasions to remark that the apostolate was originally understood as instituted by Jesus when risen from the dead, and in place of its institution after his death we shall find the myth of the miraculous draught of fishes during his lifetime.

Mark appears to be specially interested in the thaumaturgic activity of Jesus, and chiefly with the cure of the demoniacs, whose evil spirits recognize the messianic quality of their exorcist. It is no part of our purpose to discuss these cases from the pathologist's point of view, nor their relation to the real history of the Galilean prophet, a history which the documents withhold from our grasp and which it is not their object to narrate. Whoso will may believe that Jesus cured many of these madmen, exorcising their evil spirits, who loudly proclaimed him the Messiah, in spite of the constant injunction laid on them to keep silence, lest he should be recognized. The systematic intention of these stories is quite clear. In Mark i, 24 the man with an unclean spirit says to Jesus: "What is there in common between us and thee, Jesus of Nazareth? Thou art come to destroy us! I know who thou art, the Holy One from God." The cures of the demoniacs are offered as proofs of Jesus' supernatural powers, confessed by the demons themselves. The fourth Gospel, as we know, drops the argument and omits all these demoniac-cures. The importance attached to them by the Synoptic catechesis is all the more significant. Note that the cure of the Capernaum demoniac (i, 23–

26, 27*b*) is superimposed on the scene of the preaching in the synagogue (i, 21–22, 27*a*, 28) and belongs, therefore, to a secondary layer of editorial deposits (as also i, 34*b* and the last words of 39). Thus we may conclude that this earliest form of Gospel catechesis was not completed *currente calamo* by a single author. On the contrary it was a long time on the anvil.

To commentators in search of its historical explanation much embarrassment has been caused, more or less everywhere, by the *silence* which Jesus enjoined on the cured demoniacs, on the sick whom he healed (i, 32–34), on individual witnesses of his miracles and sometimes on his disciples, a silence which the Gospel editors declare to have been actually kept in regard to some of the events they have just recorded. But the explanation is quite easy, not indeed by any circumstances attending the ministry of Jesus, but by those of the Gospel catechesis in the process of its formation. Our Gospel catechesis was first drawn up with an eye to the eschatological catechesis, already in being, in which Jesus was exalted to Messiahship when he ascended to God, and not till then. From the moment his epiphany as Messiah was thrown back into his public ministry on earth an explanation became necessary of these marvellous novelties, now heard of for the first time as belonging to the activity of the Christ *before* his saving death. The silence repeatedly enjoined on these occasions was the explanation, naïve enough, but indispensable, of why they had not been heard of before.

It is not surprising, then, that Jesus has to withdraw himself from the crowds of sick folk flowing into Capernaum. He resolves to preach elsewhere, his mission being essentially that of a teacher (i, 35–39). This is required because moral instruction must have its place in the catechesis under elaboration. Hence the place assigned to it beside the miracles.

The healing of the leper (i, 40–45) takes place in a setting of Jewish legalism and under injunction to keep silent; the story, as arranged by its editor, is clearly that of the day at Capernaum told over again in another form, and with the same deep significance—the ministry of salvation brought by the Christ to the Jews.

There follows a series of anecdotes in which Jesus is shown in conflict with the Pharisees, a conflict whose real background consists of certain later points of friction with Jewish legalism, and belongs to a time when the Christian sect was already separated from the main stock of Judaism. The paralytic of Capernaum is the first case (ii, 1–12), editorially constructed as a miracle of healing, on which has been grafted a declaration addressed by Jesus to the Pharisees concerning the power "of the Son of Man to forgive sins on the earth" (ii, 5*b*–10). In Mark's Gospel the Son of Man is identified with the Christ of mystery, who by his death has paid the penalty of human sin; a conception which corresponds to an important stage in the growth of the Gospel catechesis, though perhaps not the earliest.

The second case is the association of Jesus with publicans and sinners (ii, 15–17); these are they who need salvation; it justifies the mission to the Gentiles. The third is the question of fasting (ii, 18–22); the answer of Jesus inclines to allegory; his disciples will have their fast-days in commemoration of his death (19–20) —a touch which dates the invention of the incident. The following sentences present Jewish legalism as outworn, another mark indicating an origin long after the age called apostolic. The fourth case presents two anecdotes about the Sabbath aimed at rabbinical casuistry; the first is the story of the ears of corn, in which the disciples are defended by the example of David and by the rational aphorism: "The Sabbath was made for man," etc., capped by the saying not in line with the preceding: "So that the Son of Man is Lord even of the Sabbath," meaning that the Christ of mystery can dispense his followers from a sabbatical observance. The second sabbath-story presents a miraculous cure (iii, 1–6) justified by the right and duty of everyone to do good at all times. Our catechesis is here attacking official Judaism on the highest ground. But note how this whole *bloc* of stories is concluded (iii, 6): the Pharisees take counsel with the Herodians how they might destroy Jesus. All the cases we have been considering are grouped from a point of view which looks back on the death of the Christ as a past event. In its first stage the Gospel catechesis did not place them as far away from that termination as they are in the passages now before us.

In the chapters that follow we find a good deal of matter that is, in truth, little more than padding. First come two short scenes, of which one presents the beneficent activity of the

Christ (iii, 7–12) and the other the choice of the Twelve (13–19). In the actual arrangement of the stories, the first seems to prepare the way for the dispute about the exorcisms here placed after the intervening choice of the apostles. Matthew and Luke use it as preamble to the great discourse which appears in Matthew as the Sermon on the Mount. Obviously a piece of no historic significance which the Gospel draughtsmen could insert wherever they found it convenient. The choice of the Twelve, which is represented as taking place "on the mountain," was not made at the very beginning, as here depicted. The Twelve, who we are here told were chosen as apostles at the side of Christ during his lifetime, were not so elected even after his death. They were the leaders of the first believing group in Jerusalem, and were only transformed into apostles by a later legend which at first opposed them to Paul and put them above him. In other parts of Mark's Gospel we shall find their importance deliberately belittled. Whence the presumption that the two short scenes now in question are additions of later date to the catechesis named after Mark.

The dispute about the exorcisms makes an unnatural breach in the story of the attempt by the family of Jesus to bring him back into the house (iii, 20–21 and 31–35). The disputants are nascent Christianity and Jewish doctrine, and their dispute turns on the probative value of Christian exorcisms. If the move made by the family be taken as historical, it reflects no honour on his kindred, whom Jesus himself is made to repudiate on the spot. The story may be taken as relatively an old one. But may it not be intended as a figure of the Jewish attitude towards Jesus, who has found outside official Judaism a new family in his faithful believers? None the less this group of sayings, motived by ill-will, has been carefully put together. As it has no attachments to what precedes or follows it must have been placed where it is for amplification of the narrative.

A point of difficulty not to be passed over in silence is the mention of sin against the Spirit, which is said to be the only sin that is unforgivable (iii, 28–30). This declaration is in keeping with a particular conception of the Spirit, and of its rôle in the Church, of which no explanation is given in our texts. Although the editors of Mark have tried to integrate it with the dispute about exorcism, its presence there is adventitious. Luke (xii, 10) gives it as an isolated saying among others concerning the action of the Spirit. Matthew (xii, 31–32) attaches it, like Mark, to the dispute about exorcism, but gives it rather different form, identical, in the main, with the reading in Luke. While Mark distinguishes blasphemy against the Spirit, alone punishable, from blasphemy in general, Matthew and Luke declare "a word against the Son of Man" to be a pardonable offence, in contrast to blasphemy against the Spirit, for which there is no pardon. There is no proof of any kind that Mark's reading is primitive in relation to Matthew's and Luke's, of which it is rather a deliberate attenuation. What we need to know is how the difference between blasphemy against the Son of Man and blasphemy against the Spirit can have been conceived. There is no reason to have recourse to Montanism for the explanation of this singular feature. It was in opposition to the "spiritual men" of gnostic theory that the Church declared itself the depository and dispenser of the Spirit (cf. Acts viii, 18–24), and sin against the Spirit is committed by him who denies the Church that privilege. The saying thus fits in with the notion of the Spirit as replacing the Christ in the guidance of the Church. We must therefore regard it as an element of secondary origin and a relatively late addition to the Synoptic catechesis (cf. *supra*, p. 44).

Another conglomerate, of which the elements are more or less erratic, consists of parabolic discourses (iv, 1–34). Here the drafting seems to have passed through several stages. A first edition had assembled certain parables as a specimen of Jesus' teaching, that of the Sower and that of the Seed, with a preamble and appropriate conclusion (iv, 1–9; 21–29, 33). A second has inserted, after the parable of the Sower, an aside addressed by Jesus to the disciples in explanation of the parable (iv, 10, 13–20) and perhaps the parable of the Mustard Seed and other sentences (iv, 21–25; 30–32), taken from the collection of Jesus' oracles which must be assumed as a common source of the three Synoptics. Between the demand for explanation and the commentary on the Sower, a final edition has lodged a reflection on the object of parables in general, which is said to be that of causing the blindness of the Jews predicted by Isaiah (vi, 9–10), while it is "given" to the disciples alone to "understand the mystery of the

Kingdom of God." This mystical interpretation of the parables, along with "the mystery" in which we are to look for their inner meaning, is a belated final touch. The parabolic mode of utterance, which was common among the rabbis of the time, has nothing in it to cause blindness, and the parable of the Sower is to be commended for the ease with which it can be applied to the results of Gospel preaching. But it is in regard to the mystery of salvation by the death of the Christ that parables are deemed to have become a cause of blindness "to them that are without"—meaning, no doubt, the Jews in particular and unbelievers in general. In other passages of Mark we find that the Galilean disciples themselves are not immune to this blindness. Perhaps that is the reason why the request for explanation (iv, 10) is so strangely attributed to the people who were about Jesus "with the disciples."

The discourse in parables is followed by four miracles, appeasement of the tempest (iv, 35–41), cure of the madman at Gerasa (v, 1–20), raising of Jairus' daughter and cure of the woman with an issue of blood (v, 21–43). These form a group the members of which are apparently bound together, though the group as a whole stands isolated in the compilation. The stories are full of life, but of life given to them by the faith and imagination of the narrator rather than by the precision of real memories or by intimate connection between the parts of the action. That they are not, in some degree, legendary reproductions of incidents that really happened cannot be rigorously demonstrated; still less can it be disproved that they are largely constructed, according to pre-existing types, to the glory of the Christ; the first of them giving pre-eminence to power over the elements presented under the figure of his rôle as Saviour, and especially his presence with the Church in the days to come; the second, power over the demons and their master, in conditions which symbolize the conversion of the pagans; while the third, in its double recording (cleansing of a woman affected with perpetual impurity and raising of a dead girl to life), presents the Saviour's rôle which, by faith, procures both pardon and immortality for mankind.

It cannot be said that this symbolism is a gratuitous supposition on our part. For the evangelist and for his first readers the chief interest of these stories lay precisely in the symbolism.

There, too, is the only reasonable explanation and the only possible justification of two indisputable facts which force themselves upon us in spite of ourselves: the extreme poverty of the evangelical legend in narratives considered as such, and the not less extreme incoherence, together with the artificial and arbitrary character of the literary construction. The two things that mattered most to the success of the catechesis in the attainment of its object were moral instruction and the education of faith. With this end in view the evangelists were able to find, or to put into their more or less fictitious narratives, the depth of meaning which they had discovered or introduced with the parables. No complicated method is needed to understand it, and it can be proved without endless research.

The four miracles are followed by a series of incidents still worse adjusted each to other than their predecessors. First comes the fruitless preaching of Jesus "in his own country" (vi, 1–6), a repetition in some respects of his preaching at Capernaum (i, 21–22; 27a–28), but here turned so as to figure the failure of Christian propaganda among the Jews; it probably contains nothing to guarantee historical tradition except the indications about the family of Jesus. The mission of the apostles (vi, 7–13) duplicates that previously mentioned (iii, 13–15), but in the present context, with an abridgment of the discourse which Matthew and Luke (x, 1–16) give *in extenso*, it figures Christian propaganda among the Gentiles. The story of John the Baptist's death (vi, 17–29) is legendary throughout. Introduced most unnaturally by statements put into the mouth of Antipas (vi, 15–16, an enlargement of viii, 28) and violently wedged in between the mission of the Twelve and their return, it might seem to be wholly without purpose. But, for the Gospel editor who inserts such a passage, the object in view would be, not to record the death of John as a matter of interest belonging to the narrative, but to hint that his burial was the end of him, a rather summary way of disowning any relation of Jesus and Christianity with John and the sect which survived him.

The first multiplication of loaves, for which the return of the disciples prepares the ground, is a symbolic miracle if ever there was one, and we are repeatedly told that the disciples understood nothing of its meaning (vi, 52; viii, 21). It represents the oldest myth of the institution of the Christian communion meal, not yet arrived at the eucharistic theory in which the saving death of the Christ was mystically signified in breaking the bread-body and distributing the wine-blood of Jesus, but at the earlier stage when the Father was praised for the life and knowledge which "he has made known by his servant" Jesus, as in the *Didache* (ix, 2 and x, 2).

Welded on, as best might be, to what goes before, comes the miracle of walking on the water. The symbolism is analogous to that of the calmed tempest (iv, 35–41) which it duplicates, the construction showing influence from the first stories of so-called tradition about apparitions of Jesus after his resurrection. In that respect it antedates material which belonged originally to the eschatological catechesis, images of the invisible presence of the Christ among the faithful as they waited for his second coming.

The next passage, relating to the coming of Jesus to Gennasar, or Gennesareth (vi, 53–56), is a transition piece, an interlude loaded with miracle, which betrays the editorial hand but has no significance peculiar to itself. It forms a natural introduction to the anecdote of the Syro-phenician woman (vii, 24–30) from which it is cut off by the dispute about the washing of hands. This dispute is a fragment of anti-Jewish polemic for which this was probably thought to be the best place. Like the discourse in parables, it is built up on some sayings attributed to the Christ (vii, 9–12; 14–15), the last of them imparting moral instruction in terms rather gross. This has been overlaid with a gloss (vii, 3–4), a prophetic quotation (6–8) and an admonitory explanation, the whole tending to make Jesus proclaim the futility of Jewish prohibitions and scruples about food.

The miracle of a cure operated at a distance, in response to the mother's prayer, on a girl possessed by a devil, the mother being a woman of the country and said to be Syro-phenician, forms a counterpart to the story of the Roman centurion in the other two Synoptics (Matthew viii, 5–13; Luke vii, 1–10) and signifies in like manner that nations never visited by Jesus, as the Jews have been visited, will be saved by him. The cure of the deaf-mute in the country of the Decapolis is a miracle operated for symbolic reasons in pagan territory, which are also the reasons for the utterly unintelligible itinerary which the narrative makes Jesus follow between the two miracles of multiplied loaves. This cure of the deaf-mute, peculiar to Mark, is counterpart to that of the blind man at Bethsaida (viii, 22–26), the two being cut out on the same model. Both must be attributed to an editor of Mark who may have freely exploited some deposit of written or oral tradition, or may himself have constructed the two stories with a view to the lesson to be drawn from them, on the lines of other Gospel narratives or of the practice commonly followed by exorcist-healers in those times.

No argument is needed to prove that the second miracle of multiplication is a duplicate of the first. It may have been imagined to figure the initiation of the Gentiles into the Christian mystery; or it may be that another version of the first miracle has been utilized for that purpose. At all events it is not by chance that in the first multiplication twelve baskets full of fragments are left over, twelve being the cypher for Israel, and corresponding to the Twelve who first governed the community of Aramean-speaking believers in Jerusalem, while in the second miracle there are seven baskets, the cypher for the Gentiles, corresponding to the Seven presiding over the group of hellenist believers whose dispersion after the death of Stephen set on foot the propagation of the Gospel outside Palestine and among the pagans. It is noteworthy that the second multiplication does not occur in the third Gospel, and that the stories are omitted which Mark has lodged between the first and the confession of Peter: whence we may infer that this long section of Mark (vi, 45 to viii, 26) belongs to a late stage in the development of our Gospel.

As though to explain and justify the future reprobation of the mass of the Jews the evangelist has introduced, after a second multiplication of loaves, a sentence about the Pharisees asking for signs, in which Jesus refuses the sign demanded (viii, 11–12). This trait comes from a source known to Matthew (xii, 38–40; cf. xvi, 4) and to Luke (xi, 29–30). But in the source the sign mentioned is the sign of Jonah. Did our evangelist reflect that the sign of Jonah, that is the sign of the resurrection, did not take place for the Jews? It is more probable that the sign of Jonah, which was made much of at the first, soon became embarrassing with its three days and three nights, which could not be fitted into the liturgical framework adopted by most churches in the second century for commemoration of the Passion and the Resurrection. The liturgical framework being interpreted as a chronology in which Jesus rose the third day after his death it was difficult to see how he could have spent three days and three nights in the tomb, like Jonah in the belly of the fish.

Thinking it appropriate to follow this up by a reflexion of his own, on the first disciples' lack of understanding in presence of the mystery of salvation, our editor attaches it to a saying about the leaven of the Pharisees, which the collection of *logia* places in another context (cf. Luke xii, 1*b*), his object being to make Jesus unsuccessfully hint to the disciples that the two multiplications signify the inexhaustible gift of salvation: whereas the disciples were thinking only of food to put into their mouths. As an historical record it is of no value. But the indication it gives of ill-will towards the Galilean disciples is important and should be kept in mind.

The cure of the blind man at Bethsaida (viii, 22–26) has also a symbolic value, but falls into another current. It serves as introduction to Peter's confession and seems intended to figure the progressive education of the first disciples, their adhesion to the messianic faith and the origin of the Jewish-Christian community. If we refer to the third Gospel, where Peter's confession follows on immediately after the multiplication of loaves (Luke ix, 10–21), it would seem that the version of Mark which the writer to Theophilus has reproduced presented the two events in the same close succession, and localized both the miracle and the confession at Bethsaida. A complete misunderstanding of the character and origin of our documents is shown by those critics who explain the relation between Mark and Luke, in this part of the two Gospels, by supposing that Luke was making use of an accidentally mutilated copy of Mark. Is it, then, so natural that Mark, in its earliest form, had the multiplication of loaves and the calming of the tempest, etc., twice over? In these matters the simplest hypotheses are not always the best. To be sure, canonical Mark is a very slender document; nevertheless it shows no lack of duplications, re-shapings, overlays and editorial superfluities.

SECOND PHASE OF THE MARCAN CATECHESIS

With the confession of Peter (viii, 27–30) we enter on the second part of the Gospel catechesis, the cycle of the Last Supper, and encounter at the outset an almost certain antedating of an element fundamental in the eschatological catechesis, namely Peter's faith in Jesus-Messiah, in Jesus-Christ. No account need be taken of the preamble (viii, 27–28) which has already served to introduce the legend of John the Baptist (vi, 14–16). The essential element is the messianic confession of Simon: "Thou art the Christ." As in all similar cases, the imposition of silence on the disciples (viii, 30) is a sure sign that material of post-resurrection origin is being thrown back into the record of Jesus' ministry on earth. Whatever the historical preparation may have been for Peter's faith in Jesus as the Christ, his first *affirmation* of that faith was not made until, in his belief, Jesus was already risen as the Christ. That granted, we may be sure that the natural sequel, and probably the original sequel, to Peter's confession is to be found in the declaration of Jesus (ix, 1), with all restriction removed, "Those who are here shall see the coming of God's kingdom," intimating that the Great Event is at hand. Attached to this is the disciples' question about the preliminary coming of Elijah, with the answer given by Jesus (ix, 11–13): "Elijah indeed is already come, and they have done to him what they would, as it is written of him," to be understood of the ministry of John conceived as preliminary, not to the earthly ministry of Jesus, but to the advent of Jesus-Messiah in the Kingdom of God. The insertions in the text between these two eschatological utterances belong to the development of the Gospel catechesis. Let us now consider these in turn.

The first insertion (viii, 31–38) opens with the first announcement of the passion and resurrection of the Son of Man, and we are told that the announcement was made publicly, in contrast to what just before has been indicated concerning the Messiahship of Jesus. Now the Son of Man is constantly, in our Gospel, the Messiah who redeems mankind from sin by his saving *death*; he is the Christ of the salvation-mystery as presented in the gnosis of the Epistle to the Romans. There follows, on the announcement, a vigorous protest from Peter, who has understood nothing of the mystery's economy, with the yet more vigorous reprimand of Jesus: "Get thee gone, Satan!" etc. (viii, 31–33). This episode, plainly to Peter's discredit, falls into the current of mystical gnosis and is in line with the invectives launched in the Pauline Epistle against the old disciples, reputed apostles and treated as Judaizers. After this comes a general call to renunciation as a normal condition of salvation (viii, 34–38); this is a gloss of the evangelist on sayings taken from the collection of *logia*, an oracle of some Christian prophet speaking in the name of Jesus (cf. x, 38–39; 32–33). Taken by themselves these sayings in the *logia* already implied the obligation laid upon the believer to become united mystically and morally with the risen Christ, if he would be recognized by Jesus when he came in his glory.

The second insertion (ix, 2–10) is the miracle of the Transfiguration, an antedating of the exaltation of Jesus as the Christ, of his assumption into glory, as taught in the eschatological catechesis. Here the final exaltation is reduced to a provisory miracle, prelude to the final glory. The antedating is again betrayed by the charge to keep silence, which we are told was kept by the three witnesses of the miracle. These witnesses were chosen with a purpose in view; because this abbreviated miracle could not be conveniently presented as a public spectacle, and also because it was designed to exhibit the three disciples as witnesses who did not understand what they saw, aiming especially at Peter, who is credited with the absurd notion of domiciling Jesus, Moses and Elijah on the mountain by building three tents for them to live in (cf. *supra*, pp. 53-4).

The miracle of the epileptic (ix, 17–29), artificially co-ordinated with the miracle of the Transfiguration, is a common case of exorcism, but strongly dramatized, with a view to emphasizing the power of true faith, in presence of the mighty and beneficent Christ, the incredulity of the Jews and the impotence of the disciples. The mention of a journey *incognito* across Galilee serves to bring in a second prediction of the Passion (ix, 31–32), presented as not understood by the disciples, and for the same reason.

There follows a series of lessons the interconnection of which is not easily grasped; they must have been taken from the collection of *logia*, and compose a catechesis mainly ethical, which the

Gospel editors have framed in their usual manner. First comes the lesson of apostolic service, conceived as having been provoked by the preposterous claims of the disciples—another point not intended to enhance their glory—and combined with instruction on the obligation to receive the least of the Christ's people, and the advantage that follows from receiving him as one who is the Christ himself and God in the Christ (ix, 36–37). Next, the saying: "Who is not against us is with us," strange counterpart to "who is not with me is against me" in the collection of *logia* (Matthew xii, 30; Luke xi, 23) here brought in as conclusion to the anecdote about the unqualified exorcist (ix, 38–40), together with the saying about the cup of water given in the name of the Christ (ix, 41; cf. Matthew x, 42)—the whole permeated by the spirit of mystical gnosis. Next, propositions about scandal and the punishment in store for him who causes it (ix, 42), and on scandal already experienced, which must not continue, on pain of Gehenna. Finally, the metaphor of the savourless salt with the appropriate lesson (ix, 49–50).

From this example, one of many others, we are able to see that the Gospel editors proceeded in their work as if the sayings they utilized were teachings whose sense was not very clearly defined, and whose connections of time and place in the life of Jesus could be laid down at will, for the simple reason that nothing whatever was known about the matter. We have already remarked how they operated in the same way with the facts adorning their narratives. By these proceedings they were able to construct and fill out a legend, astonishingly poor in real memories, into the artless mosaic before us, whose incoherence is ill-disguised by the manifold devices of the editors to provide it with a containing frame.

The itinerary of the journey to Judea is vague enough, and the editor, in search of matter to garnish it, found to hand the question of divorce (x, 1–12), the saying about children, with whose simplicity men should accept the announcement of the Kingdom (x, 13–16), and the case of the rich young man (x, 17–22), into which are brought the sayings about the difficulty of salvation for the rich (x, 23–27) and the reward in store for those who have left all for Christ (x, 28–31). The reprobation of divorce is a characteristic feature of early Christianity. We are given the biblical ground for condemning divorce (x, 2–9), the origin of which has still to be explained. The biblical argument is some fragment of controversy on the subject; the reprobation is taken from the collection of *logia* (cf. Matthew v, 32; Luke xvi, 18); the setting is artificial (cf. 1 Corinthians vii, 10, where the reprobation seems derived from Christian mysticism). The story of the children is the original version in relation to the version which doubles it in ix, 36, but seems to have been conceived to enforce the duty of receiving the announcement of the Kingdom with unquestioning simplicity.

Though not otherwise dated or localized, the anecdote of the rich young man is more circumstantial, but, in spite of this, is tybical rather than historical. Even the saying: "Why callest thou me good? None is good save God" is a mystic subtilty rather than a living trait; the command to follow Jesus seems to carry, not a literal sense, but the moral sense of initiation into the Christ and entry into the community of the believers, while the reflections on the difficulty of salvation for the rich are made to fit in with corresponding features in the narrative. Entirely second-hand and artificial is the promise of double reward, in this world and the next, to those who have followed Jesus, that is, to believers (x, 28–31). The source, derived perhaps from the eschatological catechesis, probably contained the promise of thrones to the twelve disciples, as arranged in the tradition which glorified them (Matthew xix, 28; cf. Luke xxii, 30): the outlook toward the messianic triumph has been replaced by the promise of reward for renunciation and by a clear and detailed prophecy of the Passion (x, 33–34).

Judging by the preamble to it (x, 32) and by the context of it (x, 32–34) this prediction seems intended to introduce the Jerusalem cycle of the Gospel legend; taken as a whole and in connection with what follows (the request of James and John and the lesson of service, 35–45), it would seem to be constructed on the idea of the messianic triumph, as we have just seen, but so as to push it back in order to mark the conditions to be fulfilled before the Great Event. After the two earlier prophecies of the Passion, the point made prominent is the lack of understanding on the part of the disciples, especially on Peter's. Here this lack of understanding is fixed upon James and John, and figured by their claim to the two highest thrones on the right and left of the Christ. Jesus answers by announcing their coming martyrdom and throwing back upon God the distribution of places in the Kingdom; after which he turns to the disciples in a body and gives them the lesson of service, of which all are supposed to be in need, supporting it with the authority of his own example: "The Son of Man is come to serve and to give his life as a ransom for many." Both the pretensions of the disciples and the lesson of service have been anticipated in the preceding cycle (ix, 33–35). This repetition and expansion of a lesson already given is yet another witness to the poverty of the tradition. As we have just seen, the lesson of service corresponds to the mystical conception of salvation by the death of the Christ and to the age when the Christian community was organized. Its insertion into the legend of Jesus is, therefore, artificially contrived.

The miracle at Jericho (x, 46–52) is presented under the same conditions as the chief miracles in Galilee. It is a symbol and figure of salvation, of the light given to faith. It is fittingly placed at the threshold of the great mystery and may have been originally conceived as a fulfilment of prophecy (Isaiah xxxv, 5). The story is otherwise isolated, and the narrator has not thought of making it contribute to the coming outburst of enthusiasm on the Mount of Olives. All the incidents in the Passion cycle of the Gospel are presented as independent one of another, the reason being that they are not a sequence of memories but are deduced, more or less, from biblical texts.

Clearly, also, the messianic triumph on the Mount of Olives (xi, 1–10) has been constructed on certain Old Testament texts (cf. Zechariah ix, 9; Psalm cxviii, 26; Genesis xlix, 11). The localization of the incident is in like manner related to a text in prophecy (Zechariah xiv, 4). Have we not already seen the Mount of Olives chosen for the messianic exaltation (*supra*, p. 54)? The invention of the preliminaries in Mark is a masterpiece of childlike invention (xi, 1–6).

In what follows an artificial time-order is constructed to serve as frame for the events narrated and the teachings recorded. This time-order may well be in direct relation with the ritual commemoration of the events described, which are presented in their mystical meaning and value, and not in the order of their real historical sequence, so far as they can be said to belong to that order at all.

The cursing of the fig tree (xi, 12–14) and its effect (xi, 20–21), separated the one from the other, sit awkwardly astride on the expulsion of the traders, an independent story, conceived as a fulfilment of prophecy (Malachi iii, 1; Zechariah xiv, 21), like the messianic triumph, with which it is logically co-ordinate. The miracle of the fig tree is a symbolic act, conceived in the same spirit as the parable of the fig tree (Luke xiii, 6–9), if not constructed upon it, to represent the Christ's futile visit to Israel and placed, with that intention, in connection with the arrival of Jesus in the temple. But, with a view to amplifying the teaching of Jesus in Jerusalem, this fiction is joined by the editors to the lesson of faith (xi, 22–23), taken from the collection of *logia* (cf. Matthew xvii, 20), which they have exploited in the story of the epileptic (ix, 23–24; *supra*, p. 90). To this are added some words on the certainty of an answer to prayer and on the need to pardon one's neighbour in order to obtain pardon from God (xi, 24–26; cf. Matthew vii, 11; xviii, 19; Luke xi, 5–13; xviii, 1–8).

By an editorial combination the question of the priests (xi, 27–33) seems to be related to the expulsion of the traders, as the latter is more or less attached to the messianic triumph (xi, 12–14 makes a place for the cursing of the fig tree before the expulsion of the traders, while xi, 18–19 is a general remark originally conceived as the conclusion of the Jerusalem stories). In answer to the priests' demand for the authority on which he claimed to act, Jesus is made to pose an embarrassing question about the baptism of John. To discuss its historical probability would be wasted time; it bears witness to the link which originally existed between Christianity and the sect founded by John, to the advantage which Christian apologetic sought to derive from it and to the purely rabbinical subtilty of the argument when first started. Originally the incident must have figured among the sayings about John the Baptist, of which the main body is preserved in Matthew xi, 2–19 and Luke vii, 19–35.

The natural conclusion of this story would be the retreat of the questioners (xii, 12: "And leaving him they departed"), who thereupon send some of the Pharisees to trap him over the question of tribute. Between the anecdote and this conclusion someone has intercalated the parable of the Wicked Husbandmen (xii, 1–11), a short apocalypse which turns on the fall of Jerusalem, the evangelization of the pagans and of the assumption of Jesus into glory; a fragment of apologetic in the style of the discourses attributed in Acts to the first Christian preachers, and even ending with the usual quotation of the apologists (Psalm cxviii, 22–23). This must be the work of some Christian prophet, utilized at first as the conclusion of the Jerusalem ministry (note the correspondence of xii, 12a with xiv, 1–2) before being replaced for that purpose by the great apocalyptic discourse (xiii).

The question and answer about tribute to Caesar is intended to prove that the Christ was not a rebel against Roman authority. It was composed to prevent the Christians being classed with the Jewish Zealots, in revolt against the empire. No such question arose for Jesus and the believers of the first generation; but, when hopes of the Second Coming began to waver, the timeliness of thus defining the principle involved is not hard to understand.

Just as the question about tribute was conceived, for the setting of the scene, as posed by the Pharisees in league with the Herodians, so the question about the resurrection (xii, 14–27) is raised by the Saduccees, people "who say there is no resurrection," but here presented in a body, whereas in the preceding case the precaution had been taken of bringing to the front only "*some* of the Pharisees and Herodians." The intention evidently was to show Jesus in conflict at close quarters with the principal Jewish sects. And yet no two things could belong to regions further apart than this question and that of the tribute, since the point raised about the resurrection is treated as a dispute of the schools, while the greater part of the passage, both question and answer, might have been borrowed, just as it stands, from Jewish scholastic. Nevertheless there are two elements in Jesus' answer: a direct argument drawn from the actual conditions in the Kingdom of God, and an argument derived from a mystical and spiritual conception of immortality, which is the more remarkable in this passage by reason of its incompatibility with the vulgar notion of the resurrection retained in the *corpus* of the anecdote, and which we shall presently see applied to the Christ himself.

Immediately following comes the Great Precept of love to God and man, brought in, like its predecessors, without natural connection. Taking the anecdote literally we should conclude that this principle, in which many in our time have gone out of their way to find the essence of the Gospel, was not announced by Jesus until he had to answer an academical question posed for him by a scribe who wished to test the soundness of his judgment. Comparing Mark's account of the incident with Luke xii, 25–28, it seems that the story was first constructed without any indication of place, and that the questioner himself found the good answer to his question, Jesus merely praising him for answering so well. This the tradition of Mark has transposed to the Jerusalem ministry, and it is evident that the canonical version of the Gospel has been arranged so as to put the first announcement of the great commandments in the mouth of Jesus. At least it is clear that the Gospel editors were not thinking about "the essence of Christianity."

The whole group of these arguments is wound up by the saying: "No man dared to ask him any more questions." The perspective is conventional; for, between the announcement of the Kingdom and Jewish authority, there was nothing to debate in matters of casuistry, morals or even chronology. But our Gospel goes further. It exhibits Jesus as taking the offensive and publicly raising the problem of the Christ (xii, 35–37). The scribes say that the Christ is the son of David; but are not the scribes under deception, seeing that David himself, in a text inspired by God (Psalm cx, 1), addressed him as his Lord? Tradition has here picked up, probably without understanding, some story born in Christian circles in which the authority of Scripture was invoked to get rid of the Messiah's Davidic descent, and profession made that the Lord Christ had no need of descent from an earthly king, if indeed he was humanly descended at all. So, once more, what we have before us is an anticipation, in which Jesus himself is made to bring to light the text which Christian tradition soon pitched upon as meaning that he was Lord Christ, not by filiation to David, but became so by resurrection from the dead.

ANALYSIS OF THE GOSPEL CATECHESIS IN MARK

The tradition of Mark has borrowed from the collection of *logia* an abridgment of invectives against the Pharisees (xii, 38–40) just as it borrowed from the same source an abridgment of the discourse on the apostolic mission (this collection seems originally to have consisted in the main of moral precepts and of anti-Jewish polemic, in keeping with the eschatological catechesis). If, in these cases, more was not taken from the source, the reason is that Mark's tradition makes no pretence to replace it, but rather indicates it by way of reference.

The story of the widow and her gift of two farthings (xii, 41–44) comes we know not whence. This story, which is of mediocre import, was probably constructed on a theme previously known, and inserted here for the simple reason that the compiler was in search of something more to say. It attaches to nothing in the context, and has no analogy with the other incidents grouped together as appropriate to the Jerusalem ministry.

Finally comes the great apocalyptic discourse (xiii) of which a detailed analysis would here be superfluous. Critics freely admit that it is based on a short Jewish apocalypse earlier than the capture of Jerusalem and the destruction of the Temple by Titus in 70: we may even assume that it goes back to the time of Caligula. This Jewish apocalypse, adopted by the Christians, has been filled out at various points, as much to enrich its moral significance as to show that Jesus himself had revealed to his disciples that many things must happen before the Great Event, by him announced as near at hand. Needless to say the apocalypse in its Christian form is later than the year 70, and that it was not elaborated all at once; the three Synoptics give it in three different versions. All three attach the main prophecy to a special prediction about the destruction of the Temple (Mark xiii, 1–2; cf. Matthew xxiv, 1–2, Luke xxi, 5–6). But Mark's tradition has a significant peculiarity in that it makes Jesus address the discourse in private, as a secret, to the four leading disciples—a proof that the Gospel catechesis at first knew nothing of the discourse as forming part of Jesus' teaching at Jerusalem. It is yet another fragment of the eschatological catechesis antedated in the evangelical.

The summary impression left by the above analyses is to the following effect. While the legend of the Galilean ministry, critically speaking, is extremely thin and artificially constructed, the story of the Jerusalem ministry, in spite of all these readjustments and additions, is even thinner and more artificial. Of the latter legend almost nothing is matter of fact save the very point which tradition has done its utmost to disguise, namely that Jesus came to Jerusalem as the herald of the Great Event, fully confident that he would succeed, through the intervention of God, in rooting out the rule of the foreigner and all the abuses rampant in Israel. This is what he expected. What met him was the wooden stake of crucifixion, unaccompanied by the extraordinary actions, discussions and discourses recorded in the story before us.

They waste their labour who search in the realm of historical reality for the solution of a problem that belongs to the realm of mystical speculation and religious myth-making. Such is the problem presented to exegetes by the contradiction between the Gospels as to the day on which Jesus suffered the death-penalty. According to the fourth Gospel it was the very day on which the Jews sacrificed the paschal lamb: according to the first three it was the next day, Jesus having eaten the Passover with his disciples on the day before (cf. *supra*, pp. 23–24). Critical exegetes up to now have been slow to recognize that this disagreement has nothing to do with the true day on which the Passion took place as an historical event, a day unknown to both sides, but corresponds to two divergent Easter observances between which the Christian churches were divided in the second century, those of Asia, which kept Easter on the same day as that on which the Jews kept the Passover, and the other, which celebrated theirs on the following Sunday, the fourth Gospel being in line with the Asiatic usage, called quartodeciman, while the Synoptics were in line with the celebration on Sunday. It is intelligible, on general grounds, that the first Christians should keep Easter on the same day as that on which the Jews kept the Passover. It is also intelligible that very soon they began to find in their Easter festival a sense peculiar to Christianity, in which the Jewish commemoration, at the Passover, of Israel's liberation gave place to commemorating the gift of salvation by Jesus Christ. Thus, for the churches of Asia, Easter celebrated the saving and triumphant death of the Lamb, the Lamb-Christ, the Lamb of God. Nevertheless the custom established itself elsewhere, and gradually spread, of transferring the Passion, now become the Christian Easter, to the Sunday, the Lord's day, the day of the *risen* Christ, adopted as the day of *resurrection* on which the work of salvation came to its crowning point, rather than on the day of *death*, the commemoration of which was now attached to the preceding Friday, while the institution of the eucharist, now become a mystic symbol of the saving death, remained attached to the last meal of Jesus, understood as the paschal meal. Thus the Gospel catechesis, in its two forms, canonized the quartodeciman observance on the one side and the Sunday observance on the other. On neither side was there any concern to fix the historical day on which Jesus suffered. We do not even know the precise year of the Passion; little wonder then that we are ignorant of the day. But let us first consider how Passion Week is presented in Mark.

The Passion in Mark

According to our Gospel (xiv, 1-2) two days before "the Passover and the feast of Unleavened Bread"—this, in the language of Mark and Matthew, might mean the previous day, that is, 13 Nizan, but including in it what would be for us the evening of 12th—"the high priests and scribes" decided to make an end of Jesus, but to avoid arresting him during the festival, which might have provoked a tumult among the people. The matter in hand, then, was to get the affair over before 14 Nizan, the day of the feast. This preamble, which seems of ancient date in its present place, does not agree with what follows. It naturally introduces, and should be followed by, the plot hatched between the high priests and Judas for the secret arrest of Jesus (xiv, 10-11). But between the two there has been intercalated the scene of anointing at Bethany (3-9), lodged precisely in the place occupied by the last meal of Jesus—the evening on which 13 Nizan began. The writer having delayed this last meal in order to identify it with the Jewish Passover—the evening on which 14 Nizan began—has put another meal in place of that originally indicated as the last; but, just as he introduces into the last meal the symbolism of the saving death along with the institution of the mystic Supper, so he introduces it into his duplicate of the last, making use perhaps of some story in which a sinful woman pours ointment on Jesus (cf. Luke vii, 36–50). The inventor of the scene in Mark was no admirer of the disciples who are here represented as railing at the woman for wasting her money, while Jesus has to explain to them the mystic sense of what she has done. It is interesting to note that the statements of Jesus about "the Gospel preached throughout the whole world" presupposes that the Gospel catechesis, to which the writer assigns a place in the scene just constructed, has already taken a constituted form.

Follows the bargain struck between the high priests and Judas for the betrayal of Jesus (xiv, 10–11). The question may well be asked whether the rôle assigned to Judas is not fictitious from beginning to end, a symbol of Judaism as the villain of the piece. The truth is, as we shall see, that the Judas-legend underwent continuous enlargement in Christian tradition, and that Judas (if he ever existed) cannot have been one of the Twelve, since the college of the Twelve was not instituted by Jesus. He is also an embarrassment in the legend of the Twelve, which was first formed with no knowledge of Judas. We have already called attention (*supra*, p. 92) to the saying about "the twelve thrones" reserved in the Kingdom for Jesus' companions (Matthew xix, 28): are we then to suppose that Judas was to occupy one of them? A traitor being needed for the elaboration of the drama, imagination invented the rôle of Judas and biblical texts were duly found to give authority to the legend.

The story of the last meal comes between the traitor's compact and the arrest of Jesus (xiv, 12–31). The preliminary story (12–17) of the finding of the guest chamber is a writer's fiction equally artless and cut to the same pattern as that of the tied colt which introduces the messianic triumph on the Mount of Olives (xi, 1–6). It was deemed appropriate to make Jesus, as the meal proceeded, announce the coming treachery of which he was to be the victim, the circumstances and form of the prediction showing that the writer had in mind the text of Psalm xli, 9 (expressly quoted in John xiii, 18), while the threat aimed at the traitor suggests that the evangelist was already acquainted with some sombre legend about Judas, such as that in Matthew xxvii, 3–8 and Acts i, 16–19.

ANALYSIS OF THE GOSPEL CATECHESIS IN MARK

The essential point of the meal lies in its mystical relation with the Christian Supper, of which it is the prototype. But two different conceptions of the Supper are present in the story, one superimposed on the other. According to the earlier conception it was imagined that Jesus, in the course of this his last meal, which was not the paschal meal, after pronouncing the customary benediction on the bread and the cup, announced to the disciples that their next meal together would be in the Kingdom of God (xiv, 25). In this type the Supper was understood as anticipating the fellowship of the elect with the Christ in his Kingdom, an anticipation in which memory of Jesus' death and resurrection is implied only. Upon this primitive and eschatological meaning of the Supper, already figured in the miracle of the multiplied loaves, the editing hand has grafted (xiv, 22–24) the conception of the mystic Supper, according to which the bread becomes symbolically the body of the Christ, and the wine his blood, the Supper being now understood as a rite of holy communion with Jesus, redeemer of mankind by his death, as announced in 1 Corinthians xi, 23–25. Note that, in this conception, the Christ is the paschal lamb of the Christians, and that this was not the precise point of departure for fixing Easter on Sunday. This in passing; what we have here to point out is the editorial artifice of the superposition. The artifice is clearly perceptible in Mark (xiv, 23–25):

> And taking the cup, after giving thanks, he gave it to them, and they all drank of it. And he said to them: "This is my blood of the covenant, shed for many. Verily I say unto you, I will drink no more of the product of the vine until that day when I shall drink it new in the Kingdom of God."

When the disciples had drunk the wine, the time was past for saying "this is my blood," which is here made to follow the drinking. The natural sequence after "they all drank of it" is "I will drink of it no more," etc. This was the order in the basis-story: it spoke *only* of the bread that he would eat no more and of the wine that he would drink no more till they ate and drank together in the Kingdom of God. The institution of the mystic Supper ("this is my blood," etc.) is a highly distinct afterthought in the development of the Gospel catechesis.

The meal over, the company withdraws to the Mount of

Olives, and Jesus announces the defection of all the disciples conformably to the prophecy in Zechariah xiii, 7, a prediction of early date in the tradition, as is also the discovery of the suitable text. But what follows (xiv, 28): "But after my resurrection I will go before you into Galilee" is a palpable surcharge to bring in the discovery of the emptied tomb, a fiction whose adventitious and later character is thus plainly indicated. Another prediction is that of Peter's denial (xiv, 29–31). It is obvious that the denial, if it really happened (or even if it did not), and the defection or flight of the disciples must have formed part of the tradition before it was deemed advisable to make the Christ predict them. But, in view of the ill-will to the original Galilean disciples, and especially to Peter, which characterizes one of the currents in Mark, it is permissible, in the one case as in the other, not only to suspect, but to affirm, that even the story of the denial has been invented at all points in the tradition of Mark, although it seems to have been retouched on the last revision which attenuated Peter's cowardice by his repentance (xiv, 72). After all, the blow hits Peter no harder than the story of his protest at the first prediction of the Passion, or that of his obstinate slumber during the threefold prayer in Gethsemane, in which the offence is also thrice repeated. Indeed, the whole scene in Gethsemane, the agony of the Christ in the Olive Garden, seems, when probed to its base, to rest entirely on Psalm xxii (cf. Hebrews v, 7, a witness independent of our Gospels, but not pointing to the scene in Gethsemane; cf. p. 46). In the Gospel before us the whole story (xiv, 32–42) is given a turn which brings out the stupidity of the three leading disciples in presence of the mystery of the redeeming death. At the last moment (xiv, 42) another prediction, that of his coming arrest to follow the betrayal of Judas, is attributed to Jesus.

A rabble, recruited by the Sanhedrim in the middle of the night and guided by the traitor, now lays hands on Jesus after brief resistance by the disciples, in which a servant of the high priest has an ear cut off, the evangelist giving prominence to the kiss of Judas, the sign agreed between him and his following, and to Jesus' declaration that all has been providentially arranged (xiv, 24–50)—the dramatic presentation of an event of which the real conditions are unknown to us. Then comes the conclusion, which is primitive in relation to the rest: the disciples take to flight in a body, abandoning Jesus to his fate; which contradicts what is to be told us a little later on about Peter's proceedings and his denial.

A trait peculiar to our Gospel which the others have not retained, doubtless thinking it insignificant, is the incident of a certain young follower in the crowd who fled naked, leaving in the hands of his assailants the cloth that covered him (51–52). Certain exegetes believe that this unknown and mysterious youth can be identified with Mark in person. Far more probably the incident is intended to fulfil a line of prophecy, "the courageous among the mighty shall flee away naked in that day" (Amos ii, 16). It has been said that such an application would be forced. Doubtless it would, but it is no less likely for that reason. Can any application of prophecy be found hereabouts which is not forced?

The crucifixion of Jesus is explicable on one ground only: he was sentenced to death and executed by the Roman authority as a sower of sedition against itself, and simply so. The efforts of the traditional legend have been concentrated on transferring responsibility for his death to the Jews, and on doing this in such a way as to make it appear that the death sentence was extorted from Pilate, or imposed upon him, while he, for his part, acknowledged the perfect innocence of the accused. In pursuit of this purpose a sentence by the Sanhedrim was imagined, and condemnation pronounced on the ground that Jesus laid claim to be Son of God, that is, to the divine character which belonged to him in the faith which accepted the Christian mystery. In this there is a double anachronism: first, in view of the fact that the Sanhedrim, in the time of the procurators, had retained full powers over the Palestinian Jews, except in matters political; and, second, that Jesus, as all four evangelists are compelled to admit, was condemned to death by Pilate on political ground as "King of the Jews," that is, to use equivalent terms, as a messianic agitator laying claim to some kind of royalty in Israel subversive of the imperial government. Historically the case of Jesus is intelligible only if we admit from the outset that he was sentenced to death by Pilate alone, acting as representative of Roman authority. Need we repeat once more that our texts are in no way concerned with history in the strict sense of the term? Their object is catechetical and, in a minor degree, apologetic.

The fictitious account of the trial before the Sanhedrim (xiv, 55–65) is oddly entangled with Peter's denial (53–72) of which a beginning is made in 53–54 and the rest of the story, given in 66–72. But, of the two stories, that of the denial is the added one. The trial scene is constructed of three elements easily distinguished: first, the evidence of the witnesses (55–59) which agrees with the saying about the temple, which Jesus was accused of boasting he would destroy and rebuild in three days, a saying which seems to have caused considerable embarrassment in Christian tradition and which, if really spoken, may have been brought up in evidence before Pilate as proof of messianic pretensions; second, the declaration of Jesus affirming his character as Son of God (60–64), brought in at that point to correct the impression given by the condemnation of the pretended King of the Jews, and to account for this condemnation by the blind fanaticism of the Jewish authorities in the presence of the Christ of mystery, divine saviour of mankind; lastly, the scenes of outrage (65) introduced for the accomplishment of prophecy, especially Isaiah l, 6; liii, 3 (Septuagint). Peter's denial, in Mark's account of it, is complicated by a *double* cock-crow. We get a glimpse of a simpler story behind it in which the crowing of the cock was not a narrative detail, but an indication that it was the third hour of the night (according to Roman usage) when the triple denial was finished (cf. xiii, 35).

The morning session of the Sanhedrim, held before Jesus is led away to Pilate's court (xv, 1), now duplicates the nocturnal session at which he was condemned. Originally, in the tradition of the second Gospel, this may have been the meeting at which the accusers concerted the charge to be brought before Pilate. In the trial before the procurator nothing has real consistence save the charge—that of pretending to messianic royalty. Our Gospel (xv, 2–5) places the interrogation of the accused before the accusation, in presence of which Jesus keeps silence, as he had done before the witnesses of Caiaphas, and for the same reason—the fulfilment of Isaiah liii, 7. Pilate's astonishment at his attitude is made to prepare the incident of Barabbas (6–15). Whatever may be the source of this fiction, which defies all probability, the aim of it is to relieve Pilate's responsibility, while establishing the innocence of Jesus. Only at the last moment does the procurator concede the order for execution which he is represented in like manner as not being able to refuse in law, the verdict of the Sanhedrim having been given according to rule.[1] Before handing Jesus over to the Jews, Pilate has him scourged, after which there follows a scene of mockery in the pretorium, of comic royalty, probably in imitation of the ancient carnivals which ended in the execution, sometimes pretended and sometimes real, of the carnival king. But here probabilities are all against the reality of a scene which is conceived in a fulfilment of a prophecy (Isaiah liii, 3–7) prefiguring the glory awaiting Jesus as celestial King (cf. Hebrews ii, 9).

Finally the soldiers, after divesting Jesus of his mock purple, give him back his own clothes and lead him off to crucifixion (xv, 20); to carry the cross, they lay hold of a bystander, Simon, a Cyrenian, "father of Alexander and Rufus" (21). So precise a detail in a story otherwise lacking in signs of clear memory, is somewhat surprising. The precision may be affected, like the name of Jairus in the resurrection miracle or that of Bar-Timaeus at Jericho. But the detail was not invented to signify that the believer must carry the cross as he follows Jesus, since it is not under compulsion, as here, that the cross must be carried: the object was rather to spare Jesus the humiliation of carrying it. The sad procession goes on its way and finally comes to a halt at a place called Golgotha, that is, Calvary (xv, 22), which was probably the usual place for execution by this method.

It seems likely that, in the story at the base of all this, mention of crucifixion (24*a*) followed immediately on the arrival at Golgotha, and that what is said further on about the inscription on the cross (26) followed the fixation of the body. The incidents of the aromatic wine (23) and the division of the garments (24*b*) mark the fulfilment of prophecies; the indication of the hour (25) belongs to the writer's systematic time-scheme which proceeds to divide the day of the Passion into four parts, the judgment of Pilate taking place in the first quarter and the fixing to the cross in the second—details connected with the ritual commemoration

---

[1] The situation in which Pilate is thus placed is not without analogy to that of certain Roman magistrates who, *in the time of the Antonines*, found themselves compelled to sentence Christians to death against their own conscience.

rather than memories. The offering of aromatic wine may be the first form under which the fulfilment of Psalm lxix, 21 was represented: "They gave me gall for meat and vinegar to slake my thirst"; while the refusal by Jesus was possibly suggested by verse 22 of the same Psalm. The clothes of the executed criminal were the perquisite of his executioners, but the evangelists mention it only as marking the fulfilment of Psalm xxii, 18. The inscription bearing the charge is a detail of Roman usage; it is mentioned by the evangelists in order that the cross may have above it the idea of messianic royalty, and they have worded it accordingly. "The King of the Jews" is the simple wording of our Gospel. The two thieves crucified with Jesus (27) are mentioned to signify the fulfilment of Isaiah liii, 12, expressly cited in the common text of Mark, though not in the oldest manuscripts. The incident was suggested by the text. The passers-by who wag their heads in derision come from Psalm xxii, 7; the insults of the Sanhedrim, who we might think had moved in a body to Golgotha (31–32), adding themselves to those of the crowd (they seem to be a late addition) are aimed at the Christ of faith, Saviour and Son of God (cf. Psalm xxii, 8; Matthew xxvii, 43); while the reproaches of the two thieves (32) are a climax to the ignominy, and complete the fulfilment of the Psalm (xxii, 7).

Dense darkness envelops the scene and lasts for three hours, from the sixth to the ninth. The darkness is an addition in Mark's version; it comes from Amos viii, 9–10 (connect with the trait mentioned above, p. 103). At the ninth hour Jesus cries with a loud voice in Aramean: "My God, my God, why hast thou abandoned me?" Such a cry of distress, say some of our modern critics, perhaps a little innocently, no one would ever have dared to put into the mouth of Jesus had he not really uttered it. They are the first words of Psalm xxii, which may be said to have guided the whole construction of the Passion, and it is natural enough that the idea of putting the first words of the Psalm on the lips of the dying Christ should occur at once to the evangelists, not indeed as attributing to him any feeling of despair (!) but the better to bring out the full realization of the Psalm, both in the incidents of the Passion and in the mind of the Christ. The appeal to God (Eli) provokes a paltry jest from a bystander about the name Elias, followed by the offering of vinegar (another fulfilment of Psalm lxix, 21 *supra cit.*; cf. Psalm xxii, 16). Then Jesus, after emitting a great cry, breathes his last (37). In the fundamental document this cry, which is inarticulate but of superhuman violence, was the only cry mentioned, the quotation of Psalm xxii and what followed it being added in the course of the Gospels formation. At the moment of death the temple veil is rent from top to bottom and the centurion on guard cries out: "This man was the Son of God." The rending of the veil has the meaning of Hebrews vi, 19–20; x, 19–20. It signifies the rupture of the "veil which was his visible flesh" and the liberation of the Christ for his entry into the heavenly sanctuary, there to make oblation of his blood and open the way for believers into Eternal Life.

The centurion's profession of faith is the evangelist's; the witness also which the Gentiles render to Christ the divine. At the beginning, and for some time afterwards, this must have been the conclusion of the Gospel legend. Admirable conclusion and of high significance when rightly understood! It means that the Christ, freed from his earthly covering of flesh, enters immediately into the glory of his eternal life. His resurrection is spiritual; it coincides with the moment of death; death and resurrection may be commemorated simultaneously: the glorious death that saves mankind, the last sigh of Jesus and the exaltation of the Lamb; the three coincident. And this, clearly understood, will help us greatly to put the right value on the next stage of the Gospel revision.

What we now go on to read (xv, 40–xvi, 8) corresponds, in general, to the later concept of a material resurrection of the body verified the third day after the death of Christ. It would seem that there were present on Calvary certain women, their existence unsuspected hitherto, who had ministered to Jesus in Galilee and followed him to Jerusalem; we are told their names (xv, 40–41).[1] According to our Gospel these women it was who established the fact of the resurrection. But in order that a material resurrection may take place a tomb must be indicated and suitable conditions provided. Legend has provided them.

So it happened that a certain Joseph of Arimathaea, a new-

---

[1] The rôle assigned to these women in the service of the Christ and his companions is that of the widows who, in the earliest times, ministered to the wants of the Christian communities.

comer on the scene and as unexpected as the women, a distinguished member of the Sanhedrim who awaited the Kingdom of God and was for that reason interested in the fate of Jesus, though we are not told that he was his disciple—that this Joseph had the courage to beg permission from Pilate to bury the remains of the crucified. Before granting it, Pilate sends for a centurión and gets assurance that Jesus is really dead. This is to rule out the theory that the body had been carried away, a question disputed between Jews and Christians, neither of whom knew anything of what had really happened. The permission granted, Joseph purchases a winding sheet, which must be a new one for the Christ, wraps the body in it and lays it in a sepulchral cave, the evangelist forgetting to tell us how the cave came to be at Joseph's disposal. The tomb is said to have been hewn out of a rock, doubtless in reference to prophecy (Isaiah xxii, 16; xxxiii, 16); the great stone closing the entrance is to enhance the coming miracle. Finally the Galilean women, who have been brought to Calvary for the purpose, take note of the exact spot in the cave where the body has been laid. And all that takes place in the last minutes of "the preparation," that is, at the moment when Friday's sun is setting and the Sabbath about to begin (xv, 42–47).

In this way the story is given a form which makes Jesus remain in the tomb for the entire length of the Sabbath day, *plus* the first hours of the following night. As he will leave the tomb on Sunday morning, the theft of the body could hardly be effected without violation of the Sabbath, of which the disciples are supposed incapable. Moreover the chief advantage of the arrangement is that it assigns the resurrection to the Day of the Sun, the Lord's Day, the Day of the Risen Christ, chosen as necessarily the Day of Resurrection. It is with this aim in view that the crucifixion is fixed on Friday, the Sabbath offering all the advantages needed for the duration of the period in the tomb, alike for apologetic, as we have just seen, and for symbolism, the repose of the Sabbath day providing a fitting conception of the kind of interval that death would cause in the existence of the Christ. Nevertheless the time arrangement is somewhat mechanical, though this accords with the materialized conception of the resurrection it is intended to serve. We may add incidentally that a relation exists between this ritual and symbolical time-scheme and the arrangement of the fêtes of Adonis, which comprised a first day of feasting for the marriage of Adonis, followed by his death, then a day of mourning and, on the third day, the mystical fête of the resurrection. This relation cannot be fortuitous, since the text in Hosea (vi, 2–3) which was held to announce the resurrection of Jesus, seems to contain an allusion to the fêtes of Adonis.[1]

The Sabbath ended, three women, Mary of Magdala, Mary the mother of James, and Salome, buy spices to embalm the dead body, and, Sunday morning come, arrive at the tomb just after the sun has risen. We are to suppose that Jesus had risen from the tomb as the sun rose, for the great stone is rolled to one side, the tomb is empty and a man in white, that is an angel, tells the women that Jesus the Nazarene[2] is risen and bids them inform the disciples and Peter to go into Galilee, where they will find him, as he foretold (xiv, 28; *supra*, p. 34). The frightened women then take to flight and "say nothing to any man."

So ends the authentic text of the Gospel named after Mark. The discovery of the empty tomb is held to be guaranteed by the experience of these women whom fear has prevented from speaking of it. The Gospel editor, a simple and well-intentioned man, says no more, the reason being that he is conscious of stating a fact, a pretended fact, of which nobody has heard until he here discloses it. Moreover he knew well enough that, according to a tradition from which he had not the least intention of departing, the disciples' faith in the resurrection was formed in Galilee. And, further, he probably felt himself incapable of relating the later manifestations of the risen Christ, or thought he might abstain from doing so. We may well believe that his powers of invention had already been exercised to a point which made him think it advisable to call a halt. The silence he attributes to the women is to be explained in the same way as are the injunctions to say nothing imposed on all the anticipations of Jesus' Messiahship during his earthly career.

The evangelist did not suspect that his story would soon be

---

[1] Cf. Glotz, *Les fêtes d'Adonis sous Ptolémée*, ii, in *Revue des Etudes grecques*, xxxiii, 12, April–June, 1920.
[2] A form substituted for "Nazorean" to mean more surely "from Nazareth"; cf. *supra*, p. 34.

judged unsatisfactory. But, before that feeling arose, other revisions of the Gospel catechesis had supplanted his in the usage of the churches. The conclusion known as deuterocanonical, the addition of which was deemed necessary, served simply to put his Gospel more or less in accord, for the Christian reader, with the other forms of the catechesis. Some of our exegetes discourse learnedly about the lost end of Mark—one of the problems for which no solution can be found for the simple reason that they have no real existence. We have already said a word (p. 69) about the approximate date of Mark.

Chapter V

ANALYSIS OF THE GOSPEL CATECHESIS

(continued)

THE GOSPEL ACCORDING TO MATTHEW

THE other witnesses to the Gospel catechesis must now be examined. The Gospel named after Matthew, in view of its close dependence on Mark, will be taken first; the writings ascribed to Luke and the Gospel named after John, which require special examination, will be considered later.

MARK FOLLOWED BY MATTHEW

The sketch of the legend of Jesus Christ as presented by Mark is meagre enough; but, meagre as it is, the Gospels rest upon it, especially Matthew, and Luke also, while John, who would correct it, has no other. In this we have conclusive proof of the initial poverty of what we are wont to call the Gospel tradition. In Mark it consists more of invention and of compiler's arrangement than of tradition in the strict sense. The same is true of the others, and of Matthew in the first place, which has, moreover, even more distinctly than Mark, the character of a compilation. The evidence is unmistakable that the latest revision of Mark has been absorbed, almost entire, into Matthew, though not without a partial dislocation of the material; numerous discourses, largely common to Matthew and Luke, have been inserted; and just as the construction of Mark reveals a long process of editorial operations, so the collection or collections of these discourses are progressively constructed compilations, while some of the discourses embodied in the compilation are themselves compiled. From this and from what our previous study of the Gospel catechesis and our analysis of Mark have taught us, we may safely conclude that the elements of moral instruction, with which the discourses in Matthew are almost exclusively occupied, represent, in their totality, the moral part of the eschatological catechesis, both in the elements which were simply borrowed from Jewish tradition and in those which, at first, were directly attributed to the *risen* Christ.

Before proceeding to relate the public ministry of Jesus, for which our Gospel borrows the sketchy frame given it by Mark, it presents a kind of pre-history, parallel to what we read in Luke, but so completely different as to leave no sign that the two disparate but equally fictitious stories are closely related by dependence on a common source, though we may say that they answered the same demand of the Christian consciousness. In our Gospel this pre-history comprises a genealogy of Jesus, his miraculous conception and early infancy (i–ii). Having next described the preliminaries of the Gospel preaching (iii–iv, 22) parallel to Mark (i, 1–20), the writer announces the two-fold activity he attributes to Jesus, the chief object of most of the book: "to preach the Gospel of the Kingdom and to heal all manner of disease and all manner of sickness among the peoples." We find, accordingly, all through the book, that the teaching function takes precedence of the healing activity, each main section beginning with a great discourse, or compilation of sayings, followed by a series of narrated events. These sections are as follows:

(1) The discourse known as the Sermon on the Mount (v–vii), a veritable summary of the Christian Law expressly confronted with the Jewish Law, followed by ten miracles (viii–ix, 26) freely selected from those which Mark recounts before the death of John the Baptist. (2) The discourse on the apostolic mission (ix, 35–x) which brings in a succession of precepts intermixed with some fragments of Mark omitted from the preceding selection. (3) The discourse in parables (xiii, 1–52), dominating the rest of the Galilean ministry (xiii, 53–xvii) in which the directing hand follows the order laid down in Mark. (4) A less extensive discourse (xviii) but important for the evangelist as bearing on the organization of the churches; this introduces the departure from Judea and the stories of the Jerusalem ministry (xxi–xxii). (5) The discourse against the Pharisees (xxiii) and the great apocalyptic discourse (xxiv–xxv), which close the preaching of Jesus and bring on the stories of the Passion and of the resurrection (xxvi–xxviii). In all probability the distribution of this book of initiation to the mystery of the Christ into five

ANALYSIS OF THE GOSPEL CATECHESIS IN MATTHEW

sections—it may equally be called the book of the Christian Law—was conceived with an eye to the five books of the Jewish Law. In virtue of the influences it has undergone and the preoccupations it reveals, the Gospel according to Matthew can be described as Jewish Christian. Beyond doubt it is of Syrian origin; but it does not seem to be of great antiquity.

Genealogy and Birth Story

The Christian catechesis, at the beginning, knew very little about the life of Jesus prior to his public preaching; it knew, in fact, next to nothing. When curiosity arose as to these antecedents it led, not to investigation of the real facts of his earlier life—it was probably too late to make useful inquiries into that—but to imagination of what ought to have happened. The early stories in Matthew, no less than those in Luke, are adhesions to the main body of the Gospel of which they constitute the preamble, and the part whose mythical character is most obvious; they are fables built up on biblical texts in fulfilment of prophecies. Their character as fabulous is easiest to verify in Matthew because most of the texts in the writer's mind are expressly cited. The material of the stories may have been partly borrowed, consciously or not, from ancient mythologies of Eastern origin, and then worked up with an eye to Old Testament texts deemed to be prophetic.

The material begins (i, 1–17) with a genealogical list from Abraham to Joseph. Of Joseph we are told, not without some embarrassment,[1] that he was only the putative father of Jesus, espoused to the Virgin Mary, of whom was born Jesus. Evidently the evangelist found ready to his hand a list at first constructed to show how Jesus, through his father Joseph, was the authentic descendant of the patriarch Abraham, father of the faithful, recipient of the divine promises, and of King David from whom the Scriptures declared—or so it was believed—the Messiah was to issue. To prove the genealogy entirely fictitious would be

[1] Embarrassment is shown by the variation in the ancient readings, notably by the reading of the Syrian *Codex Sinaiticus*: "Jacob begat Joseph; Joseph, to whom the Virgin Mary was betrothed, begat Jesus who is called Christ." It is vain to contend that this cannot be true reading when compared with the equally awkward reading of the canonical version: "Joseph, espoused to Mary, of whom was born Jesus," etc., which deprives the genealogy of all meaning. The true reading, *pre-evangelical*, is surely: "Joseph begat Jesus, called Christ."

waste of argument; it is even doubly so; first, because its fundamental datum, the biblical point of departure, the patriarchal legend namely, does not hold together and, second, because the dates corresponding to the monarchy and to the later times are inexact or simply imagined. Three series, of fourteen names each, were aimed at, which ought to give a total of forty-two ancestors from Abraham to Joseph (or to Mary); actually there are only forty, since that was the number wanted; doubtless then David must be counted twice over as last of the first series and first of the second, and the same with Josiah, chosen for no reason, as last of the second and first of the third. A mystical number-play intended to show that Jesus was the Messiah promised to Israel.

The symbolic fiction of the genealogy was in currency before the stories of the miraculous birth, no less fabulous and symbolic, were elaborated. The two fictions were co-ordinated. First comes the story of the virgin conception (i, 18-25) forming a commentary on the prophecy in Isaiah (vii, 14) with the names of Joseph and Mary, furnished by tradition as the parents of Jesus. In the Septuagint translation[1] Isaiah speaks of a virgin who would conceive; this our story understands of a virgin who would conceive without intercourse with a man; which is not what the text in Isaiah was intended to convey. Mary is presented as betrothed to Joseph and impregnate by the action of the Holy Spirit, that is, by God himself. This causes perplexity to Joseph who, observing Mary's condition, plans to repudiate her privately; whereupon an angel intervenes in a dream and informs Joseph of the miracle, Mary's husband thus becoming the guarantor of his wife's virginity. This artless fable, though modelled on the text in Isaiah, may have been invented as an answer to some sally of Jewish wit about the virgin conception of Jesus—for example, the slanderous legend preserved in rabbinic tradition—at the time when the idea of it first saw the light among Christian circles in the East. The text in Isaiah would not have sufficed, by itself, to produce the belief; this was suggested quite simply by ancient mythology. The story as it originally stood in Luke, also

---

[1] Moreover it is not certain that the word virgin (*parthenos*) which appears in the original translation is equivalent of the Hebrew *alma*. It may have been substituted by a Christian hand for the more exact translation "young woman" (*neanis*). The detail is unimportant for our subject.

founded on the text, had nothing to say about the virgin conception.

Our evangelist, believing that he had warrant in the prophet Micah (v, 2) for the birth of the Messiah at Bethlehem, supposes it to have been the home of Joseph and Mary. He gives no account of the actual birth of Jesus but illustrates it by a fantastic tale. As became a Son of God, Jesus had his star, and certain wise men from the East who were expecting the appearance of the star, because Balaam, one of their ancestors, had predicted it (Numbers xxiv, 17), set out to pay homage to the newly born King of the Jews. Arrived at Jerusalem, they inform Herod of the place where his birth is due to happen; this causes a great commotion; the learned men are summoned to council; yes, Bethlehem is the place, for Micah has said it. To Bethlehem the magi accordingly go, and there the star reappears to show them the house where the Christ is laid; they enter, adore and present their gifts, as announced in Psalm lxxii, 10–15 and Isaiah lx, 6. The lore of fairyland has no tale more marvellous.

The life of the infant Christ is now to be threatened by the wicked Herod. We are told that the magi, warned by a dream, did not return to Jerusalem to report as the King had ordered, while Joseph, on his part equally warned by a heavenly messenger in a dream, took flight into Egypt with the mother and child. But the tyrant, in his rage, makes a futile slaughter of all the children in Bethlehem and the neighbouring region, and succeeds only in procuring the fulfilment of an oracle of Jeremiah (xxxi, 15) concerning the sorrows of Rachel (ii, 13–18). The text in Jeremiah refers to certain events of the Captivity; the legend was conceived independently of the text and is, in the last analysis, the myth of the divine child, a solar deity, whom the dragon of darkness would devour at his birth. We find this myth again in the Apocalypse (xii) applied to the Son of the Heavenly Virgin, the Christ, and almost in its native form. The Gospel transports the myth from heaven to earth, where it has no more reality than in heaven.

The sojourn in Egypt was suggested by historical types (Abraham and Moses) and our evangelist has the hardihood to apply to the infant Christ a text of Hosea (xi, 1) which refers to the Jewish people. His next task was to manage the coming of the holy family into Galilee, where tradition located the manifestation of Jesus. So, on the death of Herod, another angel comes in a dream to Joseph with the order to return. But Bethlehem of Judea is too dangerous for a place of abode, since a son of Herod, Archelaus, is now reigning in that province. A new dream, accordingly, guides them towards Galilee—our evangelist being apparently unaware that another son of Herod (Antipas) is reigning there—and Joseph settles down at Nazareth, thereby fulfilling the saying of prophets: "He shall be called a Nazorean." Which of the prophets said this, and where it is to be found, the commentators have had some difficulty in discovering. The name "Nazorean" is intended by the evangelist to mean "belonging to Nazareth." But mention of Nazareth is made nowhere in the Old Testament. The pretended prophecy rests on a play of words, and probably refers to what is said in the Book of Judges (xiii, 5) about Samson and the "nazir." We have seen above (p. 34) what seems to have been the original meaning of "Nazorean."

The whole of this birth legend thus resolves itself, on analysis, into a phantasmagory of myth and symbol. But let us never forget that what was always held to be the main theme of the Gospel was the doctrine of salvation, and not the legend by which it was conveyed. This remark covers our whole study of the evangelical legend.

The Baptism and Temptation

The baptism of John, the baptism of Jesus and the temptation in the desert serve as introduction, in Matthew as in Mark, to the main theme of the catechesis, to which they are preliminary. A transition of the most artificial kind, and inaccurate into the bargain, here attaches the account of John to the birth stories— "in those days" (iii, 1). It was not at the time of the Christ's birth, and probably not for many years afterwards, that John appeared on the banks of the Jordan. For the account it gives of John (iii, 1–12) our Gospel made use of Mark and of the source from which Mark borrowed what he chose to take from the discourse there tatributed to John. The account has been arranged so as to allow for the usual introduction by a prophecy (Isaiah xl, 3). The writer is also mistaken in making John address

ANALYSIS OF THE GOSPEL CATECHESIS IN MATTHEW

his allocution "to the Pharisees and Sadducees," for it was not among them but from the common people that John gathered his following. The discourse is edited from the Christian point of view which subordinates John to Jesus. And a difficulty is created by what is said about baptism "in holy Spirit and fire." At the end of the discourse (iii, 12) the fire is that of eternal punishment, which is hardly to be associated with the Spirit in the baptismal formula. It would seem that in the common source of the three Synoptics there was no mention of baptism with the Spirit but only of baptism with fire; that Mark, in substituting Spirit for fire, in that part of the discourse to which he gives a Christian turn, has radically changed the meaning of the statement attributed to John; that Matthew and Luke have followed Mark by combining his reading with that of the source-document, and by taking "fire" as here the symbolic accompaniment of baptism (recall the "tongues of fire" in the miracle of Pentecost); and, finally, that the document behind it all originated in the Baptist's sect and that, in it, John was represented as the precursor of God (rather than of Messiah) in the coming judgment. "Fire," in the two passages where it is mentioned, would thus refer to the fire of judgment and punishment. It remains to add that John, having adopted the rôle of Elijah, would clothe himself accordingly, or be said to do so.

It has already been pointed out that the baptism of Jesus by John in the Gospel catechesis is the institution of Christian baptism mythically presented and the antedating of his messianic consecration when risen from the dead. The editors of our Gospel, in which Jesus is born of the Spirit and so consecrated Messiah at the moment of his conception, were therefore bound to explain in some way why Jesus wished to be baptized by John, and for this purpose an imaginary interplay of dialogue is introduced between John, who would refuse to baptize him by whom he, John, ought rather to be baptized, and Jesus, who overcomes the reluctance of his precursor by alleging the obligation on both of them to fulfil "all righteousness." Thus the baptism of Jesus acquires for all believers the authority of a great example, while remaining, as before and always, the moment of Messiah's epiphany, clearly signified by the descent of the Spirit and the voice of the Father proclaiming his well-beloved Son (iii, 13–17).

The story of the baptism, though mythical, has some historical foundation in the relations of the Christian sect and, at first, of Jesus himself, with John the Baptist. In distinction from this, the story of the temptation is purely mythical. It reflects speculations which arose in early Christianity about the great trial through which Jesus passed in order to prove his obedience to God. Originally the great ordeal lay in the death he voluntarily accepted; it is shown forth in advance, as we have already seen and shall see again, in the agony of Gethsemane connected with the imminent reality of the redeemer's death. The scene of the temptation in the desert is another anticipation, but bears a different sense. It is here the personal trial of the Messiah as such, led by the Spirit itself into the wilderness, there to be assaulted by the prince of this world, "Satan" in Matthew, "the devil" in Luke, who appears in the story to have earthly royalty in the present age, and all its splendour, at his sovereign disposition, or thinks that he has. Two myths seem to be combined in the Christian version: that of the man of God retiring into the desert for initiation before entering on his providential mission, and that of the combat between God's agent and the Power of Evil, who tries to give him a fall or to win him over to his own service. Without entering into minute details of exegesis we may observe that the three assaults, or passages of arms, are, to judge by the blows exchanged, theological contests in which the weapons are biblical texts, as in rabbinical arguments, and that the first two temptations solicit Jesus to work miracles of supernatural magic, by turning stones into bread to satisfy his hunger, or by flinging himself from a pinnacle of the temple to prove that God is with him—miracles which, in themselves, are not so very different from those attributed to Jesus in the Gospels, but with a different significance; and, lastly, that the third solicitation, that of obtaining the kingdoms of this world by an act of homage to its prince, has a distinctly moral character—the betrayal of God to the advantage of Satan in order to usurp the power of divine authority which God alone can confer on his agent. In other words, the Christ cannot, ought not and will not be a conjurer as, for example, Simon Magus is said to be, nor a spurious Lord, invested by Satan with authority falsely called divine such as are the Roman empire and its emperor, Rome's Caesar, the

Beast of the Apocalypse, whom we are not surprised to find linked in the myth before us with Simon the Magician. The whole picture has a profound meaning which can hardly have been put into form before the years 120–130. It may be added that the vague outline of the scene in which the action is set attests the mythical character of the subject. The mountain, for example, from which all the kingdoms of the world can be viewed, is not to be found on any map.

Jesus Begins to Preach

Mark brings Jesus directly from the desert to the Sea of Galilee by way of the Jordan (i, 14–15); Matthew, on the other hand (iv, 12–13), supposes that Jesus, having learnt of John's imprisonment (effected during the sojourn in the desert), withdrew from Judea to Nazareth and afterwards made his way to Capernaum, to the land of Zebulun and Naphtali, because a prophecy of Isaiah (viii, 22–ix, 1) required him so to do. There is no need to linger over the situation beyond saying that it is in the manner of our evangelist, who has a turn for situations which he thinks prophetic. Arrived at the lake-side Jesus begins to preach, saying: "Repent, for the reign of Heaven is at hand." Matthew constantly uses the phrase "the reign (or kingdom) of Heaven" in passages when the other Synoptics say "the reign of God." The two phrases are synonymous; but Matthew conforms to the rabbinical usage which employs the word "Heaven" in order to avoid naming God. Whether the evangelist chose the word on his own account or found it in the source, or sources, from which he took the discourses of the Lord, the point is interesting as attesting a relation between our Gospel and the Jewish Christianity of Palestinian Syria.

In the calling of the first four disciples (iv, 18–22) Matthew follows Mark exactly (i, 16–20). But immediately afterwards, omitting the preaching scene at Capernaum, he constructs his introduction to the Discourse on the Mountain (iv, 23–v, 2), where he reproduces Mark's setting of the omitted scene (i, 28, 39; iii, 7–8, 10–13) of the preaching at Capernaum, and of the calling of the Twelve, stories not preserved by the editors of Matthew. It is another illustration of the truth that what our

Gospels are concerned with is the symbolic presentation of their topics while unconcerned with their historical accuracy.

The Discourse on the Mountain

The common source of the Sermon or Discourse on the Mountain (v, 3–viii), which has its parallel in Luke (vi, 20–49), where it takes place in a plain, seems to have contained the Beatitudes (Luke vi, 20–23) as an isolated exordium; the antithetical comparison of the Law and the Gospel (the principal theme of Matthew v, 17–48); the comparison (Luke vi, 43–45) of the good and the evil tree; the warning to those who give Jesus lip-service without observing his precepts (Matthew vii, 21–23); the parable of the two houses (Matthew vii, 24–49) illustrating the contrast of the diligent and the negligent hearer of his word. This shows that, already in the source, the Discourse was a compilation of detached sayings, a discourse, therefore, never delivered. None the less it has a preamble suggesting delivery, which Mark himself has used for another occasion, the calling of the Twelve, and in which we find again the gathering of crowds, numerous cures and even the mountain, which has nothing to do with the matter in hand.

Originally the Beatitudes (v, 3–12) were four in number (as in Luke vi, 20–23), eschatological in meaning and reflecting the situation of persecuted believers. They are the outpouring of some Christian prophet, selected as a kind of exordium for the discourse before us. Either our evangelist, or the version he has chosen for reproduction, has given the Beatitudes a moral turn by paraphrases and by addition, making the real poor into "the poor in spirit," the hungry into "those who hunger for righteousness," and adding to them "the gentle," "the merciful," "the pure in heart" and "the peacemakers." Before coming to the parallel between Law and Gospel he inserts the similes of "salt" (v, 13) and "the lamp" (v, 14–16), applying them to the disciples and pointing to the Good Example (cf. Mark ix, 49–50; iv, 21; Luke xiv, 34–35; xi, 33).

The long instruction on the relations of Gospel and Law (v, 17–48) is addressed to Christian communities already formed outside Judaism. The moral sayings of which it is composed were originally independent, but the work of bringing it to its present form as a collection must have been earlier than the compilation of our first Gospel. The dominant idea, expressed in the preamble (v, 17–18) was that the Law subsists as an integral element, but completed, in the Gospel; the idea of a spiritual and moral realization of the Law, more perfect than the literal fulfilment of prescriptions by the Pharisees, is superimposed upon it (v, 17, 20). The antithetic presentation of the two moralities is not carried through without considered design in the arrangement. The first example (v, 21–22) opposes the Mosaic prohibition of murder to the Christian prohibition of anger and insult; but, while the Law forbids murder, that is not with a view to permitting or commending outrageous language. Before passing to the second antithesis the writer inserts two counsels of practical wisdom; the first, on reconciliation (v, 23–24) which alludes to the temple cult, is, in all probability, a precept of Jewish morality; the other, on the drawbacks of litigation (v, 25–26) is a counsel of common prudence, awkwardly applied, by suggestion, to the question of salvation. Such various proceedings make it plain that we are here in the presence of a compilation of moral precepts, not of an ethical treatise logically constructed, still less of a discourse continuously spoken.

The second antithesis, which bears on adultery and evil desires, is more forced than the first, since evil desires are forbidden by the Law no less than by the Gospel, which shows this play of antitheses to be an exercise in academic debate, as malevolent as it is uncalled-for. To the second antithesis the Gospel editors have judged it opportune to annex an injunction against yielding to the involuntary suggestion of the senses in general, which Mark had found in a collection of sayings on "causing to stumble" (ix, 42–48).

The third antithesis (v, 31–32) brings out the Christian reprobation of divorce which the Law allows: it is derivative in relation to Mark x, 2–9. An exception is introduced into the prohibition by Matthew: "save in case of fornication," which upsets the balance of the antithesis and weakens its effect.

The fourth antithesis (v, 33–37) is directed against oath-taking which the Law allows while forbidding perjury. The entire piece, a discussion in rabbinical casuistry, may well be a personal contribution of the compiler who drew up this whole series of oppositions.

In the fifth antithesis (v, 38–42) a subtle contrast is drawn between the legal rule of an eye for an eye and the teaching of long-suffering and renunciation, a lesson which must originally have stood alone.

The same applies to the sixth antithesis (v, 43–47) in which the lesson on loving enemies is opposed, quite improperly, to the legal precept "thou shalt love thy neighbour" interpreted as though it meant "thou shalt hate thy enemy," which the Law says nowhere, and which the evangelist has no right to make it say. Thus we are bound to conclude that the famous parallel between Law and Gospel, which dominates the Discourse on the Mountain, is far from deserving the admiration bestowed upon it by commentators.

Complete in itself and composed in very accurate rhythm, the teaching of the three works of piety, almsgiving and fasting (vi, 1–6, 16–18), which is found only in Matthew, has been introduced into the Discourse by an editorial combination. This lesson, also, is addressed to Christians already separated from Judaism, whose essential practice it preserves, while forbidding practice after the manner of the "hypocrites," by which no doubt we are to understand the Pharisees, who are supposed to do these works less to please God than to win applause from men. In the second paragraph, relating to prayer, the Gospel editors have thought it fitting to introduce the Lord's Prayer with a didactic preamble (vi, 7–8) and a complementary lesson on the need to pardon men their offences if we wish to be ourselves pardoned by God (vi, 14–15). Luke (xi, 1–4) gives the same prayer in a shorter form and in a different connection, from which it would seem that the prayer itself, of which the core is Jewish, was not worded at first in the traditional form as given in Matthew. While it goes back to the earliest times of Christianity, there is no certainty that it was enjoined by Jesus himself.

The special lessons which now follow (vi, 19–30) are found dispersed in Luke but are here gathered together by Matthew to give more body to the Discourse: treasures to be amassed in heaven, not on earth (vi, 19–21; Luke xii, 33–34), a saying in harmony with the spirit of the earliest Christian community and doubtless also with that of Jesus, but possibly borrowed from Jewish wisdom; simile of the eye, light of the body (vi, 22–23; Luke xi, 34–36), a *dictum* of uncertain application with a slight rabbinical flavour, which somehow found its way into Christian tradition; impossibility of serving two masters, God and money, at the same time (vi, 24; Luke xvi, 13), another proverb of which the moral application may not have been confined to Christians; exhortation against worry about food and raiment, because God provides them (vi, 25–33; Luke xii, 22–31), a lesson on the same note and probably of the same origin as the preceding but with a more distinctively Christian tone; lastly, a saying against anxiety for the morrow, a counsel of common wisdom, to which the evangelist has added a clause ("for the morrow will be anxious for itself") which corrects and slightly contradicts the care-free attitude enjoined by the Gospel.

It is likely that, in the common source of Matthew and Luke, the injunction against judging others (vii, 1–5; Luke vi, 37–38, 41–42) followed the lesson on loving one's enemy (v, 44–48; Luke vi, 35–36): a precept of social discipline, rather than of charity, which must have come from Jewish wisdom. The caution against giving holy things to dogs (vii, 6), peculiar to Matthew, is also in the style of a Jewish proverb which Christian tradition found adaptable to its own use and capable of many different applications. The lesson about prayer (vii, 7–11; Luke xi, 9–13) was probably placed in the source next to the Lord's Prayer. In the first revision of the Discourse the command to do unto others as we would be done by, an ancient precept of Jewish morality, must have come between the lesson on loving one's enemy and the caution against judging. The comparison of the two ways (vii, 13–14), familiar in Jewish morality, is an importation into the Discourse, here combined by the Gospel editors with that of the two gates (cf. Luke xiii, 23–24). The warning against false prophets has no sense except as concerning Christian communities already formed. It makes the transition to the figure of the tree and its fruits (vii, 15–20; Luke vi, 43–45), a proverb of easy moral application, placed in the source after the lesson against judging. The declaration as to who will be admitted into the Kingdom of God is composed of two elements: one on the true disciple (vii, 21), a duplicate of that on the true parents (xii, 50), and the other a menace against false disciples (vii, 22–23; Luke xiii, 26–27) who are here false Christian teachers; the whole of it must have been first announced to the community in the name of Jesus. The final comparison of the two houses (vii, 24–27; Luke vi, 47–49) was constructed on a given theme to wind up the Discourse. What we read afterwards about the impression made on the crowd (vii, 28–29) is simply transposed from Mark i, 22.

Taking the Discourse as presented in the canonical version we have before us a treatise on Christian perfection, compiled by the evangelist for the edification of the Churches.

The Ten Miracles supporting the Discourse

To start the series of ten miracles in which Jesus now proceeded to manifest his healing power, the story of the leper (viii, 1–4) has been borrowed from Mark (i, 40–44). In the common source of Matthew and Luke, the Discourse on the Mountain was followed immediately by the story of the centurion (viii, 5–11), as in Luke vii, 1–10: conformably to its symbolic meaning, the saying about the elect who will come from the East and the West has been inserted into it (cf. Luke xiii, 28–29). Thus, while the healed leper represents the elect of Israel, the centurion with his sick servant stands for the elect of the Gentiles. By a free use of editorial discretion the cure of Simon's mother-in-law (viii, 14–15) is next brought in from Mark i, 29–31, along with the numerous miracles of healing which Mark declares were performed on the evening of the same day; in all these our evangelist discovers a fulfilment of prophecy (Isaiah liii, 4). Here he breaks the sequence of stories in Mark, and has Jesus embark on the Sea of Galilee in order to bring on the miracle of the calmed tempest (viii, 18, 23–27; Mark iv, 35–41) and the cure of the demoniacs at Gadara. But before the first of these miracles, he is minded to insert the answers of Jesus to two persons who wished to "follow" him, not in his coming passage of the lake, but as disciples (viii, 19–22; cf. Luke ix, 57–60). Notwithstanding the localization of the two episodes, these doubtless borrowed from the collection of *logia*, the scene hangs in air, nor is it easy to grasp firmly the meaning of the answers attributed to Jesus. At Gadara (instead of Gerasa) Matthew introduces two demoniacs who make in concert the same demonstration as Mark's one demoniac in the synagogue at Capernaum (Mark i, 23–27)—to the great perplexity of commentators. But our evangelist is concerned to retain only the essential features of the miracle, while compensating for his omission of Mark's demoniac at Capernaum by having two at Gadara. (One might suspect him of not being altogether serious in his miracle stories; but the truth is that he is somewhat indifferent to matters of fact.) After this come the cure of the paralytic (ix, 2–7), with the preliminaries of the miracle, as in Mark ii, 1–12, cut down; the calling of the publican (ix, 9; Mark ii, 14), with the saying about associating with sinners (ix, 10–13; Mark ii, 15–17) and the explanation about fasting (ix, 14–17; Mark ii, 18–22). Here the publican, instead of being named Levi, as in Mark, is called Matthew, which has the effect of bringing him into the apostolic college. The conjecture is not too risky that the change of name is connected with the attribution of the Gospel to Matthew, which is not the better guaranteed on that account, the whole being fiction with a purpose (in the apostolic list of x, 2–4 care is taken to accentuate the identification: Matthew the *publican*). The series is concluded by the cure of the woman with the issue of blood and the resurrection of the daughter of Jairus (ix, 18–26) perceptibly abridged from Mark v, 22–43; the cure of two blind men (ix, 27–30), duplicate of the two we shall meet at Jericho (xx, 30–34); and finally by the cure of the deaf-mute demoniac (ix, 32–34), duplicate of the incident (xii, 22–24) which later on will give rise to the dispute about exorcism. The last two miracles may be classed as purely of editorial origin, invented by the evangelist himself to fill up his gallery of prodigies.

Mission of the Twelve

Our Gospel does not relate the calling of the Twelve but presupposes it by inserting, probably from Mark (iii, 13–19), the list of their names in the preamble of the discourse concerning their mission. This preamble (ix, 35–x, 4) draws inspiration from the earlier preamble to the Discourse on the Mountain (iv, 23–v, 2) and also from Mark (vi, 7–13, 30–34), which relate the mission with the preliminaries to the first multiplication of loaves, and are the source of the figure of sheep without a shepherd, associated with the remark about the fewness of the harvestmen. The remark seems to have served, in the common source of the three Scriptures, as exordium to the discourse, and like the discourse itself corresponds, not to the situation of Jesus when preaching in Galilee, but to the time of the first efforts to propagate the Christian religion. If the prohibition to go to the Samaritans and the pagans belongs to the original version, the discourse would be clearly revealed as the work of a Judaizing writer contemporary with the first missions to non-Jews and opposed to them. The missionaries are to operate as exorcists and healers of disease, and they are to announce that the Kingdom of Heaven is at hand (x, 7–8; Luke x, 19; cf. Mark vi, 7; Luke ix, 1–2). The order to carry no money or provisions reflects the conditions of the mission to the Jews. What is said about the house in which the missionary is to lodge, and the care that must be taken not to change it, belongs to a time when the propaganda was carried on, not in public, but privately, to individuals and from house to house. The gesture to be made to mark the reprobation of an inhospitable town is purely Jewish. Woe to the town which repulses the messenger of the Gospel (x, 15; Luke x, 12)! What is said about the likelihood that the apostles will not have gone the round of the Israelite cities before the arrival of the Son of Man (x, 23) was possibly attached, in the source, to these last considerations. The warning: "I send you forth as sheep in the midst of wolves" (x, 16) must originally have introduced the practical instructions, as in Luke x, 3. The conduct prescribed for those who have to confront judges applies to believers of all types and is a later addition to the mission-discourse (cf. Luke xii, 11–12; Mark xiii, 9–13; Luke xxi, 12–17): this feature is later than the trial of Paul and Nero's persecution. Here the evangelist, his mind preoccupied with the persecution, remembers the saying "the disciple is not above his master" and works it into his theme (x, 24–25; cf. Luke vi, 40; John xiii, 16; xv, 20). The next saying, on courageous profession of faith (x, 26–33), was at first an independent lesson (cf. Luke xii, 2–9) in which three elements are to be distinguished: the proverb "nothing is hidden that will not be revealed," with its somewhat forced application to the matter of the Gospel (x, 26–27); the exhortation to fear nothing, since God watches over his own (x, 28–31);

the statement about the witness the Christ will bear before his Father to those who have confessed him before men (x, 32–33). All this is intelligible only as referring to the situation of Christians in the time of the first persecutions. Not more in keeping with the earliest age is what we read about the divisions in families caused by Christian preaching (x, 21; cf. Luke xii, 51–53). The same is true of the call to renunciation (x, 37–39; cf. Luke xiv, 26–27) utilized by Mark (viii, 34–35) as a rectifying complement to Peter's confession; and again of the promise to those who receive the Christ's envoys (x, 40–42; cf. Mark ix, 41; Luke x, 16), a promise here paraphrased into the peroration of the discourse. Putting all this together, what could show more plainly that the discourse was never delivered? What we have before us is a short dissertation on the Christian apostolate composed of elements differing in age and diverse in spirit. It is noteworthy also that "when Jesus had made an end of commanding his disciples" it is not they who go out to preach but Jesus himself who is represented as doing so (xi, 1). The Twelve were never apostles.

Jesus and John the Baptist

Just as in Mark (vi, 14–29), so in Matthew (xi, 2–19) the question of John the Baptist follows after the mission of the Twelve, but with a different sequel, introducing certain fragments from the collection of sayings, thus gathered together in the source, in which John's name makes an appearance. In these passages the earliest Christianity defines its attitude, as well as its apology, with reference to the Baptist sect, from which it was derived, and the statements found in them appear to belong to a layer of catechetical tradition older than the myth of Jesus' baptism by John. The setting of the scene is artificial. John is represented as having heard of Jesus and as sending from his prison to ask him if he is "he who cometh"; Jesus, in answer, unfolds a kind of messianic programme largely founded on texts in Isaiah (xxxv, 5–6) which, it is supposed, John must admit and which Jesus has already fulfilled (xi, 2–3; cf. Luke vii, 18–19, 22–23). It is obvious that the miracles previously recounted in our Gospel have a point to point correspondence with those mentioned in Jesus' answer, and nothing could be more compromising either to the authenticity of the answer or the historicity of the miracles. At least it is evident that the last two of the ten miracles (the two blind men and the deaf-mute) are invented to support the answer as given. In the same way, the finest of Mark's miracles, reproduced in Matthew and Luke, may have been conceived to fit the same programme, though Mark does not mention it. A second fragment (xi, 7–11) is framed in terms so lyrical in praise of John that we may suspect them borrowed from the Baptist's sect; but the text from Malachi (iii, 1), in which the rôle of the Baptist is defined, has been given a Christian turn so as to make John appear as herald of the Christ and not of God only, and the praises accorded to John are cancelled out by the final remark: "But his junior in the Kingdom of Heaven," that is, Jesus "is greater than he." Finally, the relation of John to the Kingdom is defined in terms which suppose the Baptist dead and the Christian Church founded long ago (xi, 12–15; cf. Luke xvi, 16).

In the concluding sentence (xi, 16–19; Luke vii, 31–35) application is made of a popular saying to denounce the incredulity of the Jewish people equally deaf to both God's envoys, John and Jesus. To this our Gospel attaches the invective against the Galilean towns (xi, 20–24; Luke x, 13–15), adapted in the source to the mission-discourse, along with the exclamation of thanksgiving (xi, 25–30; Luke x, 21–22) which in the source was connected with the return of the apostles. Both invective and thanksgiving are oracles of Christian prophets speaking in the name of the immortal Christ and, for the thanksgiving, in the spirit of mystical gnosis.

Jesus in Conflict with the Pharisees

After these instructions the evangelist has decided to exhibit Jesus as a target for the hostility of the Pharisees, who reproach him for allowing his disciples to break the Sabbath and for not observing it himself (xii, 1–14), maliciously attribute the success of his exorcisms to Beelzebub, the prince of the devils (xii, 22–27), and invite him to prove his mission by signs (xii, 38–42). The two sabbath stories are taken from Mark (ii, 23–iii, 6, with the significant omission of ii, 27, "the sabbath was made for man," etc.), and are completed, the one by an argument drawn from the priests' service in the temple and by a quotation from Hosea (vi, 6 already utilized in ix, 13); the other by a comparison (the sheep fallen into a pit) borrowed from the same repertoire as the other arguments directed against the Pharisaic sabbath practice (cf. Luke xiii, 15; xiv, 5). Next, after abridging Mark's indications about the afflux of multitudes and the numerous cures operated by Jesus (which he had already copied for his introduction of the Discourse on the Mountain), our editor has judged it opportune to emphasize the command to the cured persons to keep silence (xii, 16-17), by exhibiting it as the fulfilment of an oracle in Isaiah (xlii, 1-4; xli, 9).

The dispute about the exorcisms (xii, 22-37) comes from Mark (iii, 22-30) and the collection of *logia* (cf. Luke xi, 14-15, 17-23); having been used elsewhere (ix, 32-34 the cure-story which brought on the dispute), the evangelist here adds blindness to the deafness[1] of the demoniac (xii, 22; Luke xi, 14). In the collection of discourses, the two comparisons of the kingdom divided against itself and of the armed man (Mark iii, 23-27) are followed by the saying: "Who is not with me is against me," etc. (xii, 30);[2] these comparisons the evangelist has found already separated by the argument about the Jewish exorcisms (xii, 27-28; cf. Mark iii, 23-27); after the saying about blasphemy against the Spirit (*supra*, p. 79), he has inserted the comparison of the tree and its fruit (already utilized vii, 16-20) and of the treasure within (xii, 34-35; Luke vi, 45), both lessons of common wisdom here adapted to a Christian moral theme, and he has added to them a rider of his own (xii, 36-37); he has transposed the remark about relapse into demoniacal possession after exorcism, and placed it after the answer to those who asked for a sign (xii, 43-45; Luke xi, 24-26) in order that he may interpret it as aimed at the incredulity of the Jews and as a forecast of their destiny. By this interpretation he neutralizes an experience which attests the futility of the results obtained by exorcism and which, in consequence, cannot be attributed to Jesus or to Christian exorcists.

To the Jews who "ask for signs"—that is for miracles giving better proof of a divine mission than that of simple cures—Christian tradition here answers that the only sign the Christ will

---
[1] M. Loisy's translation of κωφός.
[2] In contradiction to Mark ix, 40 and Luke ix, 50, where we read "who is not against me is with me."

give is the miracle of Jonah repeated in his own resurrection (Jonah ii, 1–2), and by denouncing the unbelievers whom the example of the Ninevites and of the Queen of Sheba will confound on the day of judgment (xii, 41–42; Luke xi, 31–32). The saying of the Christ about his true mother and brethren (xii, 46–50) is then brought in from Mark iii, 31–35, but with omission of the motive assigned by Mark for the action of the family, namely their belief that he was out of his mind (Mark iii, 21). The correspondence between the experience of Jonah and the case of Jesus buried and risen from the dead must have been evoked in tradition before the ritual commemoration of the Christ's death and resurrection was attached in common usage to Friday and the following Sunday, with which time-scheme three days and nights of Jonah's experience are incompatible (cf. *supra*, p. 87), and must have made the comparison compromising and best neglected. In all this it is plain enough that our evangelist editors, if not themselves the inventors of much they tell of the Christ's doings and sayings, freely act on their own initiative in the arrangement and interpretation of the materials they employ.

DISCOURSE IN PARABLES

The transition to the discourse in parables (xiii, 1–32) is made by a clumsy formula which might lead us to think that this discourse was delivered on the same day as the preceding instructions. In what follows our evangelist reproduces Mark for the setting of the scene (xiii, 1–2; Mark, iv, 1); for the declaration concerning the aim of parables (xiii, 10–15; Mark iv, 10–13), but bringing forward into it the *dictum* "To him that hath shall be given," etc., otherwise placed by Mark (iv, 25), understood of Christians and Jews, expressly citing the prophecy of Isaiah (vi, 9–10) by which Mark was inspired; then inserting a saying (xiii, 16–17) about the advantage enjoyed by believers in the Christ over believers in the Old Covenant, which in the collection of *logia* was in close proximity to the mission discourse (as in Luke x, 23–24); and, finally, following Mark in his explanation of the sower (xiii, 18–23; Mark iv, 14–20). For the parable of the seed (Mark iv, 26–29) our evangelist substitutes that of the tares (xiii, 24–30), which he has freely developed, if not composed entire, in view of the interpretation he intends to give of it a little further on (xiii, 36–43). To the parable of the mustard seed he adds that of the leaven, borrowed from the collection of discourses which has the same application as the mustard seed. He introduced the concluding words of Mark (iv, 33–34) and illustrates them by a biblical quotation (Psalm lxxviii, 2) in which he imagines he can see a prophecy of Jesus' parables. Amplifying, so to say, Mark's statement (iv, 34) about the Christ's explanations of his parables, given to the disciples in particular, he brings in a commentary on the tares (xiii, 36–43) and then the similes, more or less allegorical, of the hidden treasure (44), of the pearl (45–46), of the net (47–50)—a paraphrase of mystical terms already familiar to Christians, rather than similes. Finally, to wind up the discourse, he puts in the parable of the master of the house, figure of the Christian teacher, who can bring out of his coffers things old and new (51–52). It is to be noted that the parable of the tares refers to the recruiting of members by the Christian communities, intimating that the elimination of the unworthy should be postponed to the final judgment.

Next follows the preaching of Jesus at Nazareth (xiii, 53–58), the evangelist here anticipating the stories which Mark places between the discourse in parables and this anecdote, in which he softens down certain features. After that come the sayings of Herod, considerably abridged, about the Christ (xiv, 1–2; Mark vi, 14–16), the story of John's death (xiv, 3–12; Mark vi, 17–29), the mission of the apostles (Mark vi, 7–13) having been mentioned at an earlier stage. The effect of the transpositions thus effected is that the departure of Jesus for the first multiplication of loaves is occasioned by the death of John; instead of the Twelve coming back to their master after their mission, as in Mark vi, 30, it is now the disciples of John who come to announce his death to Jesus—an indication not without meaning.

Light retouchings are discernible in the story of the multiplied loaves (xiv, 13–21; Mark vi, 31–44). Mark's story of the miraculous walking across the sea (xiv, 22–33; Mark vi, 45–52) is repeated, but adorned with a symbolic episode; that of Peter also walking on the sea to join company with the Christ, a great marvel which, like the main body of the story, must have originally belonged to the resurrection cycle (cf. John xxi, 7). Our evangelist corrects Mark's conclusion by substituting a profession of messianic faith (xiv, 33) for what he says about the blindness of the disciples in presence of a prodigy (Mark vi, 51–52).

He emphasizes the miracles operated in the land of Gennesaret (xiv, 34–36; Mark vi, 53–56); he shortens and retouches the dispute about the washing of hands (xv, 1–20; Mark vii, 1–23) while forcing into it the saying about blind leaders of the blind, to be understood as foretelling the downfall of Pharisaic Judaism. The anecdote of the Canaanite woman (xv, 21–28; Mark vii, 24–30) is somewhat more developed so as to bring out more clearly that the personal ministry of Jesus was confined to Israel. Having spoken twice already of deaf-mutes our author turns Mark's story (vii, 31–37) of another deaf man of the Decapolis into a generalized picture of manifold cures (xv, 29–31). For this story, as for the preceding, he corrects Mark's geography, so as to keep Jesus out of pagan territory.

In the second story of multiplied loaves (xv, 32–39) he follows Mark (viii, 1–9)—without notable variation. The mention of Jonah in the refusal of a sign (xvi, 1–4) recalls the first version (xii, 38–40) of the twice-told incident, which here returns in the form given it by Mark. The strange development that follows about the blindness of the disciples in regard to the leaven of the Pharisees and the leaven of bread has, in like manner, been copied from Mark (viii, 14–21), but Mark's conclusion is here given a turn to make it appear that the disciples understood the lesson that Jesus would have them learn (xvi, 12). As to the blind man at Bethsaida (Mark viii, 22–26), he is clearly a double of the blind man of Jericho, in whom we have already encountered him, antedated in a colourless miracle (ix, 27–31; *supra*, p. 125).

In its account of Peter's confession our Gospel has arranged a kind of verbal antithesis between the Son of Man (xvi, 13) and the Son of God (xvi, 16) which seems to foreshadow the distinction between the two natures of the Christ. But his chief alteration of Mark's account (viii, 27–30) is the insertion of the celebrated address to Peter (xvi, 17–19). "Blessed art thou, Simon son of Jonas," etc., a saying which can only be ascribed to the immortal Christ, and goes far beyond the primitive form of the confession in Mark. There cannot be a doubt that this saying was conceived in the East, in some circle devoted to the memory of Peter, head of the apostles and head of the Church, to counter the claim of the mystical Paul in the Epistles.

For the instructions which follow the Confession (xvi, 20–28)—in which our evangelist seems to be unconscious that Peter's protests against Jesus' announcement of his coming death and resurrection, and the crushing reprimand administered to him (xvi, 22–23) are in flat contradiction with the solemn praise of him as prince of the apostles—for these instructions and for the story of the Transfiguration (xvii, 1–13) Matthew copied Mark almost word for word, adding only a short explanation about Elijah, in regard to which the disciples are credited with intelligence, in substitution for Mark's indication to the contrary a little further back (ix, 10). The incident of the epileptic (xvii, 14–21) is a perceptible abridgment of Mark (ix, 14–29). The lesson on faith forms the epilogue, for the disciples only (xvii, 19–20; Mark ix, 23; Luke xvii, 6). After the second prophecy of the Passion (xvii, 22–23) the disciples are represented as sorrowing instead of not understanding, as in Mark ix, 30–32 and Luke ix, 45. Peculiar to Matthew is the anecdote of the money and the fish (xvii, 24–27) in which an old story is utilized; it answers a question of moment to the Jewish-Christian Churches, even after the destruction of the temple, which question Jesus was supposed to have solved. Contrary to what he is made to say later about tribute to Caesar (xxii, 15–22), he here seems to deny obligation to pay.

The confusion of Mark (ix, 33–50) in his arrangements of the lessons which follow the second prophecy of the Passion is somewhat straightened out and retouched. Instead of disputing as to who among themselves is the greatest (Mark ix, 34) the disciples now ask who is greatest in the Kingdom of Heaven, and Jesus answers by enjoining a childlike spirit, humility and the service of humble believers (xviii, 1–5; Mark ix, 36–37; x, 15). The incident of the stranger whom the disciples had found casting out devils is omitted, together with the saying "he that is not against us is for us." In the warning against "causing to stumble" our Gospel completes Mark from the collection of discourses and arranges a combination, as ingenious as unconvincing, to bring the parable of the lost sheep into his theme (xviii, 12-14; Luke xv, 4-7).

It seems that, in the collection of the discourses, the teaching of forgiveness followed the warning against causing the "little ones to stumble" (xviii, 15-22; Luke xvii, 1-4), and for that reason Matthew gives it in the place of the exhortation to be at peace among themselves (Mark ix, 50). But within it he intercalates a rudimentary scheme of church discipline which enjoins a triple admonition of sinners and excommunication of him who refuses to hear the voice of the community, and includes the power to bind and loose, and the presence of the Christ at the meetings for prayer. Matthew is alone in daring to put oracles expressly concerning "the Church" into the mouth of Jesus (xvi, 18 and xviii, 7). All these were, originally, oracles of the immortal Christ. The parable of the wicked servant and its moral (xviii, 23-35) naturally follow the teaching of forgiveness, but Luke's tradition seems to have been ignorant of this parable.

For his account of the journey into Judea and the preaching at Jerusalem our evangelist follows Mark with the addition of various sayings and parables. In the preamble (xix, 1-2) he substitutes a number of unspecified cures for the unspecified teaching mentioned by Mark (x, 1). In the dispute with the Pharisees over divorce he is careful to introduce the exception for adultery as he did in the Discourse on the Mountain (v, 32) and he adds a lesson, in the mystical style, on continence and voluntary castration (xix, 10-12) in line with the earliest Christian ruling on celibacy and virginity (cf. 1 Corinthians vii, 25-26). The story of the blessing of children (xix, 13-15) is lightened, relatively to Mark x, 16, of matter which would have made it a repetition of the story already told (xviii, 1-5).

In the anecdote of the rich young man (xix, 16-22) the evangelist has clumsily corrected the question as it stands in Mark x, 17 ("Good Master, what shall I do . . . ?") into "Master what good thing shall I do?" and changed the answer ("Why callest thou me good?") into "Why askest thou me about the good?" in order to avoid making Jesus refuse the attribute of goodness which belongs to God. In what is said about the difficulty of salvation for the rich (xix, 16-26) he conforms to Mark. But to Peter's question about the future of the disciples (Mark x, 28)

ANALYSIS OF THE GOSPEL CATECHESIS IN MATTHEW

Jesus first answers (xix, 28-29) by the promise of twelve thrones, which must come from the collection of *logia* and which Mark seems to have omitted deliberately, so as not to have it apply to the Galilean disciples (cf. *supra*, p. 92). The teaching on retribution (xix, 29-30) is completed by the parable of the labourers in the vineyard (xx, 1-16), a theme adopted by Christian tradition and applied to the universality of salvation, but not in very clear agreement with the *dictum* at the head of the parable about the first becoming the last, evangelically interpreted as meaning the reversal of conditions in the Kingdom of Heaven, rather than the bringing of all conditions to an equality.

Jesus in Jerusalem

The confused perspective, obvious in Mark (x, 32-34), before the third prophecy of the coming Passion, is effaced in Matthew's version (xx, 17-19), but the evangelist makes Jesus expressly specify the mode of his death as crucifixion. In order to avoid attributing to the son of Zebedee pretensions disapproved by Jesus, as Mark does (x, 35-45), he brings forward their mother to demand for them the first two thrones in the Kingdom of Heaven (xx, 20-28). We have already seen that he has two blind men at Jericho to compensate for his omission of Mark's blind man at Bethsaida (Mark viii, 22-26). In describing the triumph of the Christ on the Mount of Olives (xxi, 1-9; Mark xi, 1-10) he is at pains to cite Zechariah (ix, 9) and even brings *two* asses on the scene, wrongly thinking that two are mentioned by the prophet. He makes the demonstration last all the way to Jerusalem in order to describe the commotion in the city on the arrival of Jesus (xxi, 10-11). Probably knowing Mark's source he suppresses the interval placed by him (Mark xi, 11) between the Christ's first visit to the temple and the expulsion of the traders. He has also thought well to fuse into one briefer story the two separated fragments on the withered fig-tree in Mark xi, 12-14 and 20-25. After the expulsion of the traders he introduces a collection of miraculous cures, with a new messianic acclamation in fulfilment of prophecy (Psalm viii, 2) and to the confusion of the high priests and doctors of the Law (xxi, 14-16).

Profiting by the mention of John the Baptist in Jesus' answers to the priests' question about his authority, the evangelist inserts the parable of the two sons before that of the wicked husbandmen (xxi, 33–46; Mark xii, 1–12), applying the former to the leaders of Judaism, who had not believed in John, and to the sinners, who had (xxi, 32; Luke vii, 29–30). This application, at first independent of the parable, and fitting rather badly to it, is intended to assimilate the case of John to that of Jesus in presence of Jewish incredulity (cf. xi, 16–19). Both the parable itself and its direct application have the look of being a retrospective assessment, and a justification, of the results obtained by Jesus and by Christian preaching after him in the attempt to convert the Jews. After the parable place is found for that of the marriage feast, borrowed from the collection of discourses (xxii, 1–10; Luke xiv, 16–24), but here enriched with a second conclusion not found in Luke—that of the man who had no wedding garment (xxii, 11–14). This supplement is aimed at bad Christians (cf. the parable of the tares, xiii, 24–30, 36–43); but the *corpus* of the parable is probably based on a theme borrowed from Jewish tradition, and here applied allegorically to questions that arose in the early recruiting of converts.

Of a purely editorial kind are the modifications of Mark in the story of the tribute (xxii, 15–22; Mark xii, 13–17), of the polemic with the Sadducees about the resurrection (xxii, 23–33; Mark xii, 18–27), of the question about the great commandment (xxii, 34–40; Mark xii, 28–34), of the relation of the Messiah to David (xxii, 41–46; Mark xii, 35–37). But the question about the great commandment is regarded as being raised by the Pharisees with a sinister motive, and nothing has been retained of the praise accorded by Jesus to the questioner (Mark xii, 34; cf. Luke x, 25–28). In our Gospel the Pharisees are nothing else than an active source of perdition and the implacable enemies of Jesus. They personify refractory Judaism in its hostility to Christian propaganda.

In the discourse against the Pharisees the indictment of Judaism is carried on throughout from the point of a Christianity already separated from Judaism, and is unintelligible if taken otherwise. We have before us the oracle of a Christian prophet aimed at the people and the city held to have crucified Jesus. The original discourse, imitated from the ancient prophets, contained seven comminatory reproaches,[1] and seems to have been at first presented as the last pronounced in public by the Christ. In Matthew it opens, as an ordinary instruction, with a kind of Judaizing preamble denouncing the hypocrisy of the Pharisees, whose teachings are to be followed, but not their example (xxiii, 2-3). The first two invectives (as in Luke xi, 43-46) are spread out by Matthew into a series of reproaches (xxiii, 4-7) the last of which, their love of being called "master," has been added to make way for a lesson addressed to Christians, who must recognize no master on earth save the Christ, nor claim any dominating power one over another (xxiii, 8-12). To compensate for the two maledictions thus transformed the evangelist inserts two others: the first against the proselytizing activities of the Pharisees, as intemperate in zeal as disastrous in effect (xxiii, 15); the second against their casuistry in the matter of oath-taking (xxiii, 16-22; cf. v, 34-37). Thus the prophet's invective becomes a complete indictment of rabbinic Judaism, which was still powerful and active after the fall of Jerusalem.

Omitting the story of the widow with two mites (Mark xii, 41-44) as of mediocre importance, especially in this place, the great apocalyptic discourse immediately follows. Jesus begins by predicting the ruin of the temple (xxiv, 1-2; Mark xiii, 1-2); then, removing to the Mount of Olives, he addresses to the Twelve (xxiv, 3), and not, as in Mark, to the four leading disciples (Mark xiii, 3-4), his great revelation of the Last Things. Here we find all that Mark has (xiii, 5-37) with the addition of inserted supplements mostly taken from the collection of *logia*: fragments (xxiv, 23-28; perhaps also 36) more abundant than in Mark, of the discourse which Luke reports separately in another connection (Luke xvii, 20-37) and which were intended, in the earliest version, to abate the feverish expectation of the Second Coming; simile of the night-robber (xxiv, 43-44; Luke xii, 39-40), representing an apocalyptic belief of early Christianity rather than a personal teaching of Jesus; parable of the two servants (xxiv, 45-51; Luke xii, 41-48), bearing on the expecta-

[1] As follows: (1) Luke xi, 46; Matthew xxiii, 4. (2) Luke xi, 43; Matthew xxiii, 6. (3) Matthew xxiii, 13; Luke xi, 52. (4) Matthew xxiii, 25-26; Luke xi, 39-40. (5) Matthew xxiii, 26-28; Luke xi, 44. (6) Matthew xxiii, 29-31; Luke xi, 47-48, culminating in (7) the prediction of ruin, Matthew xxiii, 32, 34-39; Luke xi, 49-50; xiii, 34-35—probably a citation from a Jewish apocalypse.

tion of the parousia in the same way as the preceding figure; parable of the ten virgins (xxv, 1–13; cf. Luke xii, 35–36; xiii, 25–27), constructed in Christian tradition as an allegory on the theme of Christ the husband of the Church (cf. 2 Corinthians xi, 2) and bearing on the delay of the parousia in order to bring out the need of positive preparation for the Great Event; parable of the talents (xxv, 14–30; Luke xix, 11–27), a common theme superficially Christianized and adapted, in Christian tradition, to the question of eternal rewards (note in xxv, 29 the insertion of a *dictum* already recorded in xiii, 12); finally the description of the Great Judgment, a piece peculiar to our Gospel, apparently taken from Jewish eschatology and given a Christian turn (xxv, 31–46).

THE PASSION AND THE RESURRECTION

The stories of the Passion and the Resurrection are transcribed from Mark with variants mostly of little importance. Remark, however, that the date indicated by Mark (xiv, 1) is placed by Matthew in the mouth of Jesus and turned into a prophecy of the coming Passion (xxvi, 1–2). Certain characteristic additions have been introduced: the mention by name of the high priest taken from a good source; the thirty pieces of silver given to Judas, to conform with Zechariah xi, 12, and preparing the way for the legend, to come later, of the traitor's death; the designation of him by name during the last meal (xxvi, 25), a detail intended to bring out the clairvoyance of Jesus, but at the expense of probability; the rebuke to the disciple who draws his sword in the Garden of Gethsemane (xxvi, 52–54), from which it appears that Jesus suffers himself to be captured in order to fulfil the Scriptures; the repentance of Judas who returns the thirty pieces to the priests, commits suicide and buys a field, afterwards called "the field of blood" and made into a cemetery for strangers, thereby fulfilling a prophecy in Jeremiah;[1] the message sent by Pilate's wife to the procurator sitting in court, a romantic fiction

---

[1] The strangest element in this fiction is not, perhaps, the astonishing liberty of the interpretation given to the prophetic text, in which a passage in Zechariah (xi, 12–13) is combined with a statement in Jeremiah (xxxii, 6–9), but the indication of the burying-place called Aceldama, of which the name itself, to which the Judas legend has been violently adapted, would seem to imply its use as the common place of burial for suicides and executed criminals, that is, very probably, the place where the dead body of Jesus was disposed of.

intended to bring out the witness to Jesus' innocence borne by highly placed Romans; Pilate washing his hands in order, by a symbolic gesture, to throw back on the Jews a responsibility they hasten to accept (xxvii, 24–25), another fiction which is held to discharge Pilate of the death sentence passed on Jesus, and makes the murderers of the Christ invoke the punishment in store for them; the substitution, again for the fulfilment of prophecy (Psalm lxix, 21), of gall for myrrh in the wine offered to Jesus on arriving at Calvary (xxvii, 34); a supplement to this, taken from Psalm xxii, 7–8, in the insults cried by the chief priests to Jesus on the cross (xxvii, 43); the earthquake, the opening of tombs, the rising of the dead at the very moment when Jesus breathes his last (xxvii, 51–53), miracles easily imagined, but in which the evangelist himself becomes somewhat embarrassed, since he feels constrained to add (53) that the dead did not come forth from their opened tombs till after the Christ had risen from his. But the fact is that this resurrection of the dead was at first conceived in keeping with the original conception of the Christ's resurrection to immortality as taking place, not after death and two days' burial in a tomb, but immediately, at the very instant when he emitted his last breath, the conception of the resurrection found in the Epistle to the Hebrews.

Mark's account of the burial and resurrection of Jesus is filled out by Matthew with the following supplements:

The military guard at the tomb deputed by Pilate at the demand of the chief priests and Pharisees to prevent the theft of the dead body by the disciples (xxvii, 62–66), an apologetic fiction (substituted for Pilate's inquiry of the centurion in Mark xv, 44) the intention of which will appear in its completion further on; the earthquake in the night of the resurrection; the angel descending from heaven among the guard, rolling away the great stone under their eyes, seating himself on the stone and addressing the women on their arrival (xxviii, 2–7), a fiction which xxvii, 62–66 seems to require for completion (and substituted for Mark xvi, 3–5); the apparition of the Christ to the women (xxviii, 9–10) represented as having the duty laid on them to inform the disciples, instead of keeping silence as in Mark xvi, 8; the bargain struck between the chief priests and the guard to deny the resurrection of Jesus and say that the disciples stole the dead body while the sentinels were asleep (xxviii, 11–15), a fiction of late origin invented to answer the theory of Jewish polemists arguing against the first fiction of the empty tomb; finally the scene of the great apparition to the Eleven on the mountain in Galilee (xxviii, 16–20), a scene invented to fill the serious gap which the conclusion of Mark, as it then was, seemed to present, and where our evangelist read no more than what we find there to-day in the oldest manuscripts. Assuredly this scene is admirably drawn and betokens a better and higher inspiration than the invention of a guard at the tomb. Noteworthy is the interpolation into it of the baptismal formula "in the name of the Father, the Son and the Holy Spirit," which was not in use before the second half of the second century. Here is a profession of faith in the immortal Christ and in his watch over the church. The outlook towards the Second Coming has now grown dim; the apostolic legend is fully formed, and the Galilean disciples, who were never apostles, here stand forth as endowed by Jesus with power to convert the world.

The Gospel named after Matthew has great interest for the historian, but his interest is not due to positive information he finds there concerning the life and death of the historical Jesus. What he finds is the gospel legend simplified and developed by the same means which created the first form of it; these were meditation on the ancient Jewish Scripture and imagination in the service of apologetic. Most important among the contents of the first Gospel is the mass of teachings attributed to Jesus, of which the second Gospel offers only a very small part. There, again, what Matthew gives us and Luke, in the main, repeats after him, is something wholly different from a collection of discourses really delivered. But, in Matthew as in Luke, we get a glimpse, between the lines, of the labour by means of which tradition, as it furnished the Christ with a legend, furnished him also with a teaching. Legend and teaching, largely antedated from the eschatological catechesis, were far less the expression of memories about the historical Jesus than of faith aroused by him and founded on him, of a morality practised in his spirit by the earliest Christian communities, and of his mystical presence in the Christian cult. The approximate date of this compilation has been already indicated (p. 69).

Chapter VI

ANALYSIS OF WRITINGS ATTRIBUTED TO LUKE

PERHAPS a day will come when enlightened criticism, on the sole evidence of the prologues which stand at the head of the third Gospel and of Acts, will decide that the author who there addresses himself to Theophilus, and those who arranged the canonical edition of his work, must both be ranked in the same category as the apologists of the second century, who pleaded the cause of Christianity before the Antonines, and that he and they doubtless lived in that age. But as the force of this evidence has not yet got home in current exegesis, we shall now subject these prologues to a new examination and afterwards proceed to analyse the writings they introduce, with a view to ascertaining the true character of the two books.

THE PROLOGUES

Like Justin (*circa* 140), who would impress educated pagans with the importance of the evangelical writings by calling them "Memoirs of the Apostles," so the author of the two books to Theophilus which became, in their canonical edition, the Gospel according to Luke and the Acts of the Apostles, had furnished his bipartite narrative with a double dedication modelled on those which were customary in his time. Who the Theophilus was, to whom this homage is offered, we do not know. He may have been a Christian or a notable catechumen really named Theophilus; or so named rather in adulation or for prudential reasons; or, again, he may be only a typical person representative of what, at this time, was the aristocracy of the Christian religion. Nor do we know any better who was the author of the dedicatory prologues. But tradition, having need of an apostolic name to give authority to the two books, naturally pitched upon Luke, the stories in Acts about the mission of Paul being founded on the notes or journal of one of Paul's companions, whom there is every reason to identify with the physician Lukas mentioned in the Epistles. Nevertheless it is clear that neither the two books in their totality, nor even the prologues, can be attributed to a writer of apostolic time and, consequently, not to Luke. The latter point is important inasmuch as, by examination of the prologues alone, we gain a sufficiently sure base-line for our analysis of the books they introduce.

The prologue to the Gospel introduces the entire work as the original author conceived it. The wording is as follows (Luke i, 1–4):

> Forasmuch as many having undertaken to compose a narrative of the matters established among ourselves, as they transmitted them to us, who from the beginning were witnesses and ministers of the word, I also, who for a long time past have followed everything with care, deemed it a good thing that I should write an orderly account for thee, excellent Theophilus, that thou mayest perceive the certainty of the truths wherein thou hast been taught.

No small difficulty confronts the critics who would have us believe that the person here speaking is Luke, and make out that he wrote his two books before the year 70. Their difficulty will be to explain how, by that time, many writers had already produced an account of the origins of Christianity or even of the career of Jesus. Yet the writer makes it clearly understood that the literary work on which he now embarks is of a kind largely cultivated before his time; and he must have known its products better than we do. A writer who uses language such as this cannot have written before the second century when Christian literature had got into its stride, and by Christian literature we here understand the production of gnosis in every variety that paid homage to Jesus as the Saviour of mankind. The fact that our author is at pains to announce that his work will carry every guarantee shows clearly that he knew of others which, in his view, could make no such claim. What he, for his part, has written, is an account of things established among believers. The "things" in question are also "facts"; but not naked facts; not the raw material of which a chronicle is made; they are facts full of meaning and, we may venture to say, full of faith; they are saving facts; which means exactly, for us, the sacred legend of the origins of Christianity. When our author speaks of "matters established among *ourselves*" he does so because he has the sense of tradition, and because the Christianity of his own day is in line of continuous descent from the age called apostolic. But he lets us see, clearly enough, that the apostolic age is already far behind him.

All this author and his contemporaries could do, and all they did, for the purpose they had in view, was to collect information coming down, when traced to its source, from those who "from the beginning were witnesses (of the 'facts') and afterwards ministers of the word"—the "beginning" in question being understood as the beginning of *the* Gospel, the teaching and salutary work of Jesus. Here the meaning of the "facts" (or "the things") is allowed to slide into that of "the word," because the facts have by this time become the matter of the teaching. Moreover, as the witnessing ministers in question can be no other than the "disciples" whom Christian tradition made into "apostles," we must understand the writer's meaning to be that the men who had been in Jesus' company and eye-witnesses of his beneficent activity, afterwards became "ministers" of the evangelical message which celebrated and perpetuated his saving work. So our author understands the matter. But this mode of understanding it cannot possibly be that of a contemporary with the apostles, but is precisely the point of view found in the Epistle to the Hebrews (ii, 3–4) where mention is made of "a salvation which, having been first proclaimed by the Lord, was confirmed to us his hearers, God joining in their witness by signs and prodigies, by manifold miracles and by distribution of the Spirit according to his will." This is a summary, systematic and idealized, of the beginnings of evangelical and apostolic preaching, a view taken of an object seen far off in the past. We have said already, but cannot too often repeat, that the Galilean disciples were never missionaries, to the world, of faith in Jesus. It was not they who founded the hellenic-Christian Church. Nor were they ever the guarantors of the gospel legend.

Our author "for a long time past" has attentively "followed," not the course of a history of which he has not been a witness, but the *documents* of a tradition he sets out to interpret, the documents, that is, of a legend elaborated before his time even in regard to the so-called apostolic age, though he may well have had very precise information at his disposal for that part of his work which refers to Paul. What he claims to do is to present a well ordered and continuous exposition, conformable to a certain type of received doctrine; briefly, a safe compendium for the believer of what for us is the gospel catechesis, or legend, and the legend of the apostles.

Such was the conception which the writer to Theophilus set out to realize. But his work has not been transmitted to us as it was conceived and realized by him. The prologue to Acts has been added to and mutilated in a way which makes it perfectly clear, before examining the two books in detail, that both the evangelical legend in the third Gospel and the apostolic legend in Acts, as written by our original author, have been re-written and overlaid with secondary work in their canonical version. First, then, let us consider this prologue. Here it is (Acts i, 1–3) in the form given it in the manuscripts commonly judged the best (the Alexandrian text):

> I composed the first book, O Theophilus, on all that Jesus, from the beginning, did and taught, until the day when, *having given command to the apostles, whom he had chosen by the Holy Spirit*, he was taken away. They also it was to whom he presented himself alive after his passion *by many proofs*, etc.

In the recension known as the Western (notably the manuscript *Codex Bezae*) the same text runs as follows:

> I composed the first book, O Theophilus, on all that Jesus, from the beginning, did and taught, until the day when he was taken away, *having given command to the apostles whom he had chosen by the Holy Spirit, and to whom he gave orders to preach the Gospel*. They also it was to whom he presented himself, etc.

It would serve no purpose to discuss the variants in the witnesses to the two texts. What here merits attention is the part common to both versions, which alone is authentic:

> I composed the first book, O Theophilus, on all that Jesus, from the beginning, did and taught, until the day when he was taken away.

We might also translate "until the day when he was assumed." For the reference is not to an *ascension*, or visible passage to the skies, as in the scene described a little later in our version of Acts, but to the *assumption* by the Christ of his heavenly life. This is the proper term which the writer to Theophilus had already used when, to mark the solemnity of Jesus' departure for Jerusalem, he wrote (Luke ix, 51): "Now it came to pass that when the days of his *assumption* were being fulfilled, he stedfastly set his face to go to Jerusalem." The "assumption" is the instant passage of Jesus to God at the moment of his death, as understood in Hebrews x, 12 (cf. *supra*, p. 139).

In the lines quoted above, the writer to Theophilus took up again the thread of his former book. The prudent exegesis of the credal professions may twist his words in all possible ways to get the desired meaning out of them, but it will never succeed in making him say that his first book contained the birth-stories now to be read at the opening of the third Gospel. Quite clearly they imply the contrary and it would be superfluous to argue the point.

It is no less evident that the first part of the prologue to Acts, recalling the object of the former book, necessitates a second part, fellow to the first, in which the object of the second book (Acts) will be described with equal precision. This part has disappeared. It has disappeared because a reviser of the second book, the same reviser who introduced the birth-stories into the first, has suppressed it in order that he may replace it by the infelicitous accretion attached so awkwardly to the part of the original prologue which he has preserved—the accretion italicized above. Both in the Alexandrian and in the Western version this violent surcharge and deliberate interpolation announce themselves as such by the clumsy way in which they are tacked on to the original. What this reviser is aiming at is to bring on, by hook or crook, the account he is about to give of the forty days which the risen Jesus is to spend with his disciples and the instruction he is then to leave with them. We have not to go far to find the reviser's motive for the substitution. The second part of the original prologue had to be suppressed because what it said differed from what he wanted it to say, perhaps announcing certain events on which he intended to keep silence, or excluding fiction which it would suit him to insert. There is not a doubt that the original writer to Theophilus understood the posthumous life of the Christ, and the awakening of the disciples' faith in his resurrection, in a manner quite different from our reviser's presentation. But the point on which attention should be fixed at the moment is the character of the interpolation and its bearing on the character of Acts as a whole. The interpolation is not, as some have tried to make out, a phenomenon limited to the first page of the book; it is the first step in a process of editorial rearrangement and reconstruction which extends, in all probability, to the very end of the book. And the hand which has thus recast the second book to Theophilus has also been at work on the first.

Proof of this is furnished by the first words of the interpolation: "having given command to the *apostles* whom he had *chosen* by the Holy Spirit." Here we have an indisputable reference to the calling of the Twelve in Luke vi, 12–16. There we learn that Jesus, after a night of prayer on the mountain (we are not told its name), "summoned his disciples and *chose* twelve from among them, whom he named *apostles*." Then follows the list of the twelve, which we find reproduced (with the omission of Judas) at the opening of Acts (i, 13). Can we doubt that the hand which wrote all this in Acts is the hand of him who described the choice of the Twelve in the Gospel, and there gave them the name of apostles in readiness for the mission he now gives them in Acts? Once more we have to remind the reader that the Twelve were never apostles even in the proper meaning of the word, least of all in the outstanding and exclusive sense given to that vocable by the writer who recast the two books to Theophilus. The Twelve were the members of the directing committee charged with ordering the affairs of the group of Hebrew believers whom they had recruited by privately conducted propaganda in Jerusalem (cf. *The Birth of the Christian Religion*, 109–112). There is not the least evidence that they were ever itinerant preachers, and never did they regard themselves as commanded to evangelize the world. But, after the lapse of a considerable time, when the need arose to combat the claims of the party which was proclaiming the apostolic pre-eminence of Paul, whose writings it was guarding and amplifying, certain circles of Eastern believers were at pains to exhibit the Twelve as the only true apostles, as the true founders of the Church and the guarantors of tradition, and as instituted for that eminence by the Christ himself. In this picture Peter assumes the rôle of chief while Paul is subordinated to these great apostles who, all things considered, are, in that capacity, nothing more than a

ANALYSIS OF WRITINGS ATTRIBUTED TO LUKE

figment erected into a tradition (cf. *supra*, p. 140). This fiction our editor introduces at the outset of his work because, while it is the first word of his interpolations, it will also be the last word of the interpolated book.

The sequel has other surprises in reserve. First comes information unique in the New Testament, except for a kind of summary indication at the conclusion of the third Gospel. For forty days after his death Jesus is represented as living almost continuously with his disciples "speaking of the Kingdom of God," that is, of the Kingdom about to come—a point not without significance. (It is remarkable that the interpolator of this surprising news has nothing to say of the resurrection on the third day, nor, seemingly, of the two special apparitions related in the third Gospel.) The truth of the matter is that he boldly introduces, at the very beginning of Acts, certain data taken from the eschatological catechesis and closely connected with the Apocalypse of Peter, the forty days terminating with the ascension of the Christ into heaven, localized on the Mount of Olives, as in that apocryphal book. But we are now to see that the instructions here attributed to the Christ are not uniform, and that the eschatological data are broken into by intrusions of mystical theology.

The writer shows Jesus as sharing a common life with his disciples for a *continuous* period, that is, as one not yet risen from earth to heaven, for there is no suggestion of many visions and apparitions that came and went at intervals. He spends the time instructing them about the Reign or Kingdom of God; in other words, about the conditions of the Great Event. "And living with them"—which might also be translated "eating with them," perhaps a reference to the breaking of bread—"he charged them not to go away from Jerusalem but to wait there for the promise of the Father which (he said) you heard from me." According to the words that precede, "the promise of the Father" can only mean the promise of the Great Event; according to the words that follow, something quite different is in question—and brought in most unhappily—namely, the promise of baptism in the Holy Spirit, the miracle of Pentecost, or at least that part of the miracle which concerns the gift of the Spirit: "For John baptized with water but ye shall be baptized in the Spirit a few days hence" (i, 5). To this the "apostles" react as though they had heard only what Jesus had said about the Kingdom (i, 6): "Whereupon they came together and asked him, saying: 'Is it at this time that thou art about to restore the Kingdom to Israel?'" Jesus answers the question in the sense in which it is asked, but refuses to indicate a date (i, 7): "And he said to them, 'It is not for you to know the times and the moments, which the Father has fixed by his authority'": after which the text again runs off the track towards the Holy Spirit (i, 8): "But ye shall receive power, the Holy Spirit coming upon you." Falling again into the general perspective the discourse concludes with the words: "And ye shall be my witnesses at Jerusalem, in all Judea and Samaria and to the end of the earth."

We are on safe ground in thinking (with Turmel, *Histoires des dogmes*, ii, 160–162) that everything in this passage which concerns the Spirit is an afterthought inserted into the context. Note that the same phenomenon occurs at the end of the third Gospel (xxiv, 49*b*) where the promise of the Spirit is surcharged on the instructions of the Christ concerning the fulfilment of the prophecies and preaching the Gospel to all nations. The eschatological teaching is crowned by the story of the Ascension. This is conceived throughout with an outlook towards the Great Event (i, 9–11) and comes to its point at the end when two angels impressively inform the witnesses of the miracle that Jesus will descend from the heavens in like manner as he has ascended into them. Be it remembered that the same story of the Ascension, with some intentional variations, was placed by the same hand at the end of the third Gospel (xxiv, 50–53). May it not be that all this eschatological scenery was called up by way of answer to certain people who had a spiritual conception of the Christ's immortality, and that the writer to Theophilus was, or seemed to be, on that side?

ANALYSIS OF THE THIRD GOSPEL

The third Gospel does not betray a well marked-out plan. After the birth-stories, an accretion on the first book to Theophilus, we may distinguish, in the body of the book, a first section (iii–ix, 50) for which Mark has furnished the setting and the greater part of the matter, all concerning the Galilean ministry; a second (ix, 51–xix, 27) apparently narrating the journey from Galilee into Judea, but into which the revisers of the text have lodged almost everything that is not borrowed from Mark; a third section (xix, 28–xxi) founded entirely on Mark and covering the Jerusalem ministry; finally the stories of the Passion and the Resurrection (xxii–xxiv), of which a considerable part comes from the last editors. Note, however, that the last three sections might be understood as one continuous part, dominated by the outlook towards the death of Jesus, and be counted together as the second part of the book.

The birth-stories are in complete disaccord with Matthew's though more consistent in themselves. The element of marvel is more restrained; they strike a softer note and affect a greater precision of detail. But, just as the gospel legend made a point of annexing John the Baptist to Jesus, as introducing him to his ministry, so here an analogous relation is set up between the Baptist's birth and the Christ's, the one, so to say, preparing the way for the other and enhancing its significance, while the whole is imitated from Old Testament stories of miraculous births with a view to showing that Jesus came into the world under conditions familiar to the most faithful type of Judaism, and not only under the conditions marked out by the prophets.

It would seem, however, that Christian tradition has here taken over and duplicated a legend about John conceived in the Baptists' sect. The first scene (i, 5–25) shows the annunciation of John, who is coming to do what is written of Elijah by the prophet Malachi (iii, 1; iv, 6), with the stage-accessories imitated from the births of Isaac, Samson and Samuel. The second (i, 26–56) gives the annunciation of Jesus and the visit of Mary to Elisabeth; Mary, whom the first Christian version of the legend seems to have attached to the race of Aaron, is at Nazareth, and is cousin to Elisabeth. During her betrothal to Joseph who, on his side, is of the race of David, she receives assurance from the angel Gabriel that she will become the mother of the Messiah. The conversation between the virgin and the angel about the miraculous conception is a surchange made at the last Christian revision. In the earliest arrangement the story (as otherwise attested by an old Latin manuscript) went on at once to Mary's acceptance of the angel's announcement (i, 38) in contrast to the doubt of Zacharias (i, 18) in the first scene, the case of Elisabeth being cited by the angel (i, 36) as a miraculous guarantee that the child about to be born from the coming marriage of Mary with Joseph would be of messianic dignity; in this way the original version found fulfilment of the prophecies relating to the birth of Messiah (including Isaiah vii, 14). This also explains the visit of Mary, now *enceinte*, to Elisabeth, who holds the same relation to Mary as John to Jesus. To complete the balance, the canticle (*Magnificat*, i, 46–55), imitated from Hannah's song (1 Samuel ii, 1–10), and probably added in revision, was at first attributed to Elisabeth, making a counterpart to the canticle of Zacharias in the following scene.

The third scene presents the birth of John (i, 57–80) in close correspondence to his annunciation, the song of Zacharias (*Benedictus*, i, 68–79) being added, like that of Elisabeth. The two songs, imitated from the Old Testament, seem to have existed at first independently of the legend into which they are here incorporated, the *Magnificat* being adapted to it by the addition of a single line (i, 48) in keeping with Elisabeth's condition, and the *Benedictus* by the passage relating to John (i, 76–77).

The fourth scene represents the birth of Jesus at Bethlehem and his presentation in the temple. To get Jesus born at Bethlehem the Christian editor of the book to Theophilus conceived the unfortunate idea of bringing his parents thither to satisfy the census taken by Quirinius, mentioned by Josephus, which took place ten years after the death of Herod (cf. *supra*, p. 20). The scene is set to recall the memory of David, the shepherd ancestor (cf. Psalm lxxviii, 70–71); the intervention of the angelic host and their song (ii, 13–14) is a reviser's addition, as is the remark about Mary (ii, 19); conformably to the Law Jesus is circumcised eight days after birth (ii, 21); on the fortieth day a legal sacrifice, which the narrator seems to confuse with the ransom of the first-born, takes place for the purification of Mary, equally prescribed by the Law (ii, 22–24); two venerable saints, an aged man and an aged woman, salute the infant Christ with prophetic voices (ii, 25–38); here again the story of Simeon is an intromission by the editorial hand, and the same is true of the passage concerning Mary (ii, 34–35). The primitive conclusion of the story is in ii, 33, placed at first after 38. Note the candour with which the author of the primitive story uses the words "his father and his mother."

The anecdote of Jesus at the age of twelve is intended to cover the open gap between the birth-stories and those of the Galilean ministry. Here Jesus assumes the attitude of Son of God, to the great astonishment of his two parents, showing that this story of the child-prodigy was introduced into the Jesus-legend without regard to the miraculous conception. (In ii, 51 the line about Mary's memories has all the look of a postscript.)

Whether the synchronism which stands at the head of the stories relating the ministry of Jesus represents a traditional datum, and, if so, in what measure, cannot be stated with certainty. Only the chief indication, the fifteenth year of Tiberius, is primitive and must originally have referred to the *epiphany* of Jesus, and not to his birth; but the accumulation of time-indications is editorial and probably borrowed from Josephus. The mention of Annas who held the high priesthood from the year 6 to the year 15 is an error, shared, it is important to note, by the third Gospel with the fourth. Joseph, named Caiaphas, was high-priest from 18 to 36. If Jesus was born before the death of Herod, he would be at least thirty-two years old when he began to preach. But these chronological combinations are most uncertain.

The stories of John's preaching, Jesus' baptism and the temptation in the desert (iii, 2–22; iv, 1–13) are built up, like Matthew's, on Mark and the collection of *logia*; in the notice about John (iii, 2–6) the quotation from Isaiah (xl, 3–5) has been extended; the Baptist's teaching, addressed to "the multitudes" (iii, 7–9; Matthew iii, 7–12), is followed by special injunctions given, at their separate request, to the multitudes, the publicans and the soldiers (iii, 10–14)—a free amplification by the editing hand; from the same hand comes the setting in which we find the declaration of John about his mission as forerunner and the distinction of the two baptisms (iii, 16–17); and, similarly, the notice about John's arrest, here antedated, because the editor will avoid reproducing the long story about John's death in Mark vi, 17–29.

The account of the baptism (iii, 21–22) is somewhat abridged from Mark (i, 9–11) but so as to bring into relief the miraculous circumstances of the event, presenting it as a prototype of the baptismal ceremonies in Christian communities. To this a genealogy of the Christ is mechanically attached bringing on a statement as to the age of Jesus at the beginning of his ministry. This genealogy, like Matthew's, was at first intended to establish the Davidic descent of Jesus as a son of Joseph—shown by the clumsy invention "as was believed" in iii, 23—and diverges from Matthew's in a way which betrays them both as artifacts. The constructor of the genealogy going back to Adam "who was the son of God," merely aimed at being complete(!); but the editor of the Gospel had in mind the universality of salvation for the human race.

In the story of the temptation (iv, 1-13), Mark (i, 12-13) is combined with Matthew's source (iv, 1-11), and the order of the last two temptations is reversed because, the first temptation having taken place in the desert, that of the earthly Kingdoms was located between the desert and Jerusalem, and Jesus better placed after the third for bringing him back into Galilee—thereby straightening out the perspective.

For the account of Jesus' entry on his Galilean ministry it is doubtful whether we have to do either with the writer to Theophilus or with an imaginary proto-Luke. The redaction has created a striking scene, like that of Pentecost in the beginning of Acts; Mark's mention of the return to Galilee is there amplified (iv, 14-15) but his summary (i, 14) of the teaching attributed to Jesus is omitted as insignificant; then, after mentioning a successful preaching tour of the synagogues, the Christ is brought to Nazareth, a scene transferred from Mark vi, 1-6 and worked up into a large picture symbolic of the reprobation of the Jews to the profit of the Gentiles (iv, 16-30; for the setting of the scene cf. Acts xiii, 14-16). Various enrichments are here added to Mark's brief narrative; first, a citation from Isaiah lxi, 1-2; lviii, 6) containing the messianic programme (parallel to that of vii, 22 and Matthew xi, 5 but of a more spiritual character) and also the preacher's theme; then a popular saying: "physician heal thyself" with rather forced application to Jesus for failing to repeat at Nazareth the miracles he had performed at Capernaum; this followed up by a commentary attached to the proverb "None is prophet in his own country," illustrated by the widow of Sarepta and Naaman the Syrian, and made to refer to the entry of the Gentiles into salvation (iv, 25–29); lastly, the miraculous escape of Jesus (iv, 28–30), figure of the Christ's triumph over his murderers and of Christianity over persecution.

In order to recover the broken thread of Mark's narrative Jesus is now brought back from Nazareth to the Lake of Tiberias, but first halted at Capernaum. This has the effect of postponing the calling of the disciples till after the events which it precedes in Mark—the preaching in the synagogue and the cure of the demoniac, the cure of Peter's mother-in-law, the miracles of the evening, the secret departure of Jesus and his preaching in the villages of the neighbourhood (iv, 31–44; Mark i, 21–39). The calling of the first four disciples, which contains little of Mark's account, borrows the scene-setting from the Discourse in Parables (Mark iv, 1). By incorporating the miraculous draught of fishes (cf. John xxi, 2–13) the story becomes, like the preaching at Nazareth, largely symbolic, the myth of the institution of the Christian apostolate, which was originally attached to the manifestations of the risen Christ. But our editor, who will localize these manifestations in Jerusalem, has transposed the miraculous draught to the story of the vocation. Of the myth of Peter, as chief apostle of the immortal Christ, there is here more than a bare hint.

The story of the leper (v, 12–14) brings us back to Mark (i, 40–45; Matthew viii, 1–4) and we continue to follow him with that of the paralytic (v, 18–26; Mark ii, 1–12; Matthew ix, 1–8), the calling of Levi and the remarks on associating with sinners, the question of fasting, and the sabbath stories (v, 27–vi, 11; Mark ii, 13–iii, 6; Matthew ix, 9–xii, 14). Next in order the choice of the apostles (vi, 12–16; Mark iii, 13–19; cf. Matthew x, 2–4), in which we have already recognized the hand of the interpolator who mutilated the prologue to Acts, is made to precede the preaching and the miracles by the lake-side (Mark iii, 7–12; cf. Matthew iv, 23–v, 1). This scene, set in a plain, serves as introduction to the Discourse which, in Matthew, is delivered on the mountain.

While Matthew has amplified the Discourse on the mountain, furnished him by the common source, by teachings taken from elsewhere, the redaction of Luke, which has also made some additions, seems to have been more inclined, on the whole, to retrench. Beyond a doubt it has preserved the primitive form of the Beatitudes (vi, 20–23; cf. Matthew v, 3–12). But the artificial counterpart of Maledictions (vi, 24–26) must have been added, the instructions about the love of enemies being very awkwardly placed immediately afterwards (vi, 27–36; Matthew v, 38–48). The antithetic parallel between Gospel and Law, elaborated in Matthew, was out of harmony with the editor's apologetic thesis of the fundamental identity of Judaism and Christianity, which dominates the canonical version of Luke and Acts; the precept of charity, therefore, is all that has been retained of it. Inserted into the lesson on judging and fraternal correction we find the figure of the blind leader of the blind (vi, 39; Matthew xv, 14) and of the master and disciple (vi, 40; Matthew x, 24–25), both of which the source seems to have placed in a different context, as in Matthew. The figure of the trees, valued according to their fruits (vi, 43–45), has been preserved more exactly than in Matthew (vii, 15–20; xii, 33–35), but the warning to those who trust unduly in their personal relations with the Christ has been cut down in order to give the greater part of it in another place (vi, 46; xiii, 26–27; Matthew vii, 21–23). The Discourse ends, as in Matthew, with the simile of the two houses.

Next comes the cure of the centurion's servant at Capernaum (vii, 1–10), a story probably taken from the common source. The intervention of the centurion's friends, who represent believing Gentiles, is to accentuate the symbolism by showing Jesus as not entering into direct relations with the pagan suppliant. The raising of the widow's son (vii, 11–17) is an editorial insertion placed at this point to justify the answer Jesus is about to give to John's messengers. The message of John, the answer of Jesus and the sayings about the Baptist (vii, 18–35) come from the common source. Before giving Jesus' answer the redaction has intercalated a collection of miracles which Jesus performs there and then. (We may recall that this is a practice common to all the evangelists.) The reflection on the relation of John to the coming of the Kingdom in Matthew xi, 12–13 is reserved for another context (xvi, 16) and its place taken by the remark on the respective attitudes of Pharisees and sinners towards John (vii, 29–30; Matthew xxi, 31–32).

The story of the sinful woman (vii, 36–50), framed in with the parable of the two debtors, is peculiar to the redaction of Luke. The inspiration of it comes from the story of the anointing in Mark (xiv, 3–9), with some influence from that of the adulterous woman (John viii, 3–11), or from some account of a woman sinner appended to what Mark tells of Jesus' relations with publicans (Mark ii, 15–17). The adjustment of the parable to the anecdote, brought about by a passage to fill the gap (vii, 44–46), is unsuccessful, the logic of the matter leading to the conclusion, not "her many sins are forgiven, because she loves much," but "she loves much, because her many sins are forgiven." The mention of the women who followed Jesus (viii, 1–3) is inserted with a view to the rôle assigned to them in the discovery of the empty tomb (xxiii, 55–xxiv, 12). Needless to say the names attributed to the women, co-ordinated with the story of the one who was a sinner, have no better historical guarantee than the story itself.

A forced transition introduces the Discourse in Parables (viii, 4–18) which contains the following, taken from Mark (iv, 2–25) with slight abridgment and compression: the sower; the request of the disciples for explanation; the double answer of Jesus; but not the last two parables, the seed (Mark iv, 26–27) being omitted and the mustard seed (Mark iv, 30–32) reserved for another context. Omitted also is Mark's conclusion (iv, 33–34), and replaced by the saying about the true mother and brethren (viii, 19–21, dropping Mark iii, 21 and abridging iii, 31–35; Matthew xii, 46–50).

By another forced transition we come again into the current of Mark (viii, 22–25). Repeated after that Gospel are the following: calming of the tempest; exorcism of devils from the demoniac of Gerasa; cure of the woman with the issue of blood and raising the daughter of Jairus; the mission of the Twelve; talk of the people round Herod about John the Baptist; then, dropping John's death (Mark vi, 17–29), the first miracle of multiplied loaves, which here has no second, is brought on forthwith and followed immediately by the confession of Peter (viii, 22–ix, 17; Mark iv, 35–vi, 44).

A long section of Mark (vi, 45–viii, 26; Matthew xiv, 22–xvi, 12) is thus omitted. Of secondary origin in Mark, this section may have been unknown to the writer who addresses Theophilus.

The editor of his work must have known it, since he uses some of its indications elsewhere, but was not inclined to reproduce the whole, either to avoid using some of it twice over or because some parts of it would have ill-accorded with his apologetic aims. None the less, the confession of Peter (ix, 18–21) comes in without natural connection and hangs in air, as though a gap has been left or a cut made after the miracle of multiplied loaves (cf. *supra*, p. 88).

The account of Peter's confession follows Mark viii, 27–30, but we miss the rebuke administered by Jesus to Peter between the first announcement of the Passion and the lesson of renunciation, together with the saying about the near parousia (ix, 23–27; Mark viii, 34–ix, 1). The Christ's fiery reprimand to Peter (Mark viii, 32–33) has also disappeared. Whether deliberate or not, the omission is significant.

The story of the Transfiguration (ix, 28–36) is lightly retouched, but there is no trace of the statements which follow in Mark ix, 9–13 and Matthew xvii, 9–13, mention being made only of the silence kept by the disciples regarding the miracle. The cure of the epileptic (ix, 37–42) is abridged from Mark but without the conclusion (Mark ix, 28–29; cf. Matthew, xvii, 19–20). The second announcement of the Passion is introduced by a general statement about the incognito which Jesus was resolved to keep henceforth in Galilee, the form of which contradicts that of Mark (ix, 21; Mark viii, 30). Without mentioning his return to Capernaum, note is made of the disciples disputing about the first place (ix, 46–48; Mark ix, 33–37), and of the stranger exorcist "who followeth not us" (ix, 49–50; Mark ix, 38–40). Then Mark is suddenly left aside, the editor showing elsewhere (xiv, 34–35) that he knew his concluding sentences (Mark ix, 49–50).

Mark abandoned and other Sources drawn on

Before returning to the guidance of Mark our editor now proceeds to fill in his story of Jesus' journey from Galilee to Judea with a miscellaneous collection of anecdotes and sayings, which he probably found in his source unfurnished with any indications of time or place, and each originally constructed independently of the others. A chain of connected memories is the last thing they can possibly be.

The solemn formula with which the writer to Theophilus introduced the departure of Jesus for Jerusalem (ix, 51): "As the appointed time drew near for him to be caught up" to heaven (cf. Acts i, 1; *supra*, p. 144) is submerged under an ill-conceived story in which James and John, the two "sons of thunder" (Mark iii, 17), demand the destruction, by lightning, of the Samaritan village which has refused to receive them (ix, 52–56); a fiction invented by the editor, and of importance as figuring the evangelization of the pagans, like the journey into Samaria, which Jesus never made (cf. Matthew x, 5–6). Attached to this anecdote are three answers which Jesus is made to give to people who wished to "follow" him. The first two (ix, 57–60) are found also in Matthew (viii, 19–22); the third (ix, 61–62), like the second, is a popular saying or proverb adapted to the Christian theme of salvation.

The first two answers, in the source, stood in close proximity with the discourse on the apostolic mission, here reported (x, 1–16) as addressed, not to the Twelve, who have had already Mark's abridgment of it (ix, 1–5), but to seventy-two disciples, invented for the occasion, as symbolizing, both by their numbers and the part assigned to them, the evangelization of all the then known peoples of the world. The body of these instructions seems to follow the source more closely than Matthew does (x, 7–16). The invective against the Galilean towns, otherwise placed by Matthew (x, 13–16; Matthew xi, 21–24), has been inserted before the conclusion of the discourse (x, 16; Matthew xi, 1): we may infer from it that Galilee, in the earliest time, was not, in any degree, a centre of Christian propaganda. The success of the seventy-two, and the comments passed on it by Jesus, have no more historical reality than the mission itself, but they have the same symbolic character. In the prayer of thanksgiving (x, 21–22; Matthew xi, 25–26) the last strophe in Matthew's version (xi, 28–30), "come unto me all ye that labour," etc., is replaced by words of congratulation to the disciples on seeing the accomplishment of ancient prophecies (x, 23–24; cf. Matthew xiii, 16–17). By this substitution the editor's apologetic is better served than by the declaration in Matthew, where the cult of Jesus appears as the life and soul of Christianity.

By an editorial device, perceptible both by the awkwardness

of the transition (x, 25) and the embarrassment of the conclusion (x, 37), the parable of the Samaritan is tacked on to the question about the great commandment (x, 25-28). It is the Samaritan who has determined the placing both of the introductory anecdote and the parable which follows (cf. *supra*, p. 96). By itself, the parable should rather be placed in Jerusalem; but, in order to be in keeping with the theme already begun, a Samaritan has been substituted, as a type of charity, for a simple Israelite. The story of the two sisters has likewise been conceived or arranged for symbolism, Martha representing Judaism, or Jewish Christianity, and Mary the Gentile believer.

In the teaching on prayer (xi, 1-4), the Lord's Prayer lacks some of the petitions present in Matthew's version (vi, 9-13); but the pre-canonical reading of the first petition: "May the Holy Spirit come upon us and let it purify us" (confirmed by xi, 13 and apparently Marcion's reading) belongs to a baptismal liturgy not of the first age, in which the bestowal of the Spirit is given particular prominence (cf. *supra*, pp. 36 and 147). Still on the theme of prayer, the parable of the importunate friend next follows, a tale of no moral significance and probably borrowed from a rabbinical tradition. Then come sayings and comparisons relating to the answering of prayer (xi, 9-13 where 12 is the editor's addition), probably derived from the collection of *logia* (cf. Matthew vii, 7-11).

The editor has his own way of combining the dispute about exorcism (xi, 14-15, 17-20; Matthew xii, 22-30, 43-45; Mark iii, 22-27) with the refusal of a sign from heaven (xi, 16, 29-32; Matthew xii, 38-41) which followed in the source. Omitting the sentence about blasphemy against the Holy Spirit, which he keeps for another place, he inserts or constructs a duplicate of the saying about the true mother and brethren (xi, 27-28) previously lodged in viii, 19-21, and places it between the separated parts of the present arrangement. In referring to the sign of Jonah he is careful to avoid the compromising precision of the three days and three nights. The simile of the lamp (xi, 33; already used viii, 16, after Mark) here comes back from the collection of *logia*, linked with that of the eye, light of the body, the evangelist becoming somewhat entangled in a wordy paraphrase (xi, 34-36; Matthew vi, 22-23).

Nothing could be more arbitrary than his conversion of Jesus' lightning invective against the Pharisees (Matthew xxiii, 1–36) into table talk at a dinner party (xi, 37–54). In order to give these terrible threats the appearance of conversation, he cuts them into two series, the first against the Pharisees in general (xi, 39–44), the second against the scribes (xi, 46–52); one part of the citation (49–51) which, in the source, was the peroration of the discourse against the Pharisees (cf. Matthew xxiii, 33–39) is here, as it were, deprived of its sting by inserting it between the second and the third of the woes denounced upon the scribes, while the first threat (Matthew xxiii, 25–26) is watered down into an exordium for what follows. In xi, 52–54 he constructs a transition of vague generalities to the next conglomerate of teachings.

This consists of fragments seemingly drawn haphazard from Mark and the collection of *logia*, and bound together by little tricks of editing. The fragments are as follows:

On the leaven of the Pharisees (xii, 1; Mark viii, 15; Matthew xvi, 6) with the editor's gloss; exhortation to proclaim the Gospel boldly (xii, 2–9; Matthew x, 26–33 in the Mission Discourse); on blasphemy against the Holy Spirit (xii, 10; Matthew xii, 32; Mark iii, 28–29; cf. *supra*, p. 83); promise of the Spirit's help for disciples summoned before Jewish or pagan tribunals (xii, 11–12; Mark xiii, 9–11; Matthew x, 19–20); parable of the rich fool (xii, 16–21), a tale of no originality but easily convertible to the evangelist's aims, with his own introduction (xii, 13–15); warning against preoccupation with things of earth (xii, 22–31; Matthew vi, 25–34); on treasure in heaven (xii, 31–34; Matthew vi, 20–21); on vigilance in expectation of the Judgment (xii, 35–36, an allegory akin to the parable of the virgins, Matthew xxv, 1–13) with the simile of the night-robber (xii, 39–40; Matthew xxiv, 43–44); comparison of the good and the wicked servant (xii, 41–46, but not so well balanced as in Matthew xxiv, 45–51) with a gloss (xii, 47–48) which seems to be inspired by the parable of the talents (Matthew xxv, 14–30); divisions in families produced by the Gospel (xii, 51–53 with an artificial transition 49–50; Matthew x, 34–36); signs of the times not understood by unbelievers (xii, 54–56; cf. Matthew xvi, 2–3); finally, brought in by purely mechanical joining (xii, 57), the figure of the man who exposes himself to condemnation and imprisonment unless he speedily come to terms with his adversary (xii, 58–59; Matthew v, 25–26).

The same preoccupation with the coming end of the world is apparent in the passage which follows (xiii, 1–5) about the slaughtered Galileans and the men of Siloam killed by the falling tower—incidents understood as foreshadowing the ruin in store for the Jewish people. The same preoccupation, again, in the parable of the fig tree (xiii, 6–9), an allegory related on the one hand to the mission of Jesus and, on the other, corresponding in meaning to the cursing of the barren fig tree in Mark xi, 12–14, 20. All the above, in this paragraph and the preceding, must derive, in the last resort, from the eschatological catechesis.

A sabbath story follows (xiii, 10–13), in which, if we read in the light of the context, the cure of the crippled woman may signify the salvation of the Gentiles. The parables of the mustard seed and of the leaven (xiii, 18–21; Matthew xiii, 31–33; Mark iv, 30–32) have been suggested, in their substance, by the rapid progress of Christianity in the Roman world. Then comes an ill-tied parcel containing the following miscellany: allegory of the narrow gate (xiii, 22–24; Matthew vii, 13–14); a sentence inspired by the parable of the virgins (xiii, 25; cf. Matthew xxv, 11–12); a caution to those who think that their personal relations with Jesus will secure them on the Day of Judgment, in which we may perceive the oracle of some Christian prophet against unbelieving Jews (xiii, 26–27); a saying about the elect coming from the four quarters of the world to replace the children of Abraham (xiii, 28–29; Matthew viii, 11–12), another oracle belonging to a time when the evangelization of the pagans, begun in spite of the Jews, was making headway; connected with this, the saying about the first becoming last and the last first (xiii, 30; Matthew xix, 30). The response of Jesus to the threat that Herod Antipas would fain kill him (a threat which has no historical basis, but is imitated from Amos vii, 10–17), contains a repetition (33), in other words, of what has been said just before, perhaps a gloss on the editor himself: it brings on the lament over Jerusalem (xiii, 34–35) which he has detached from the discourse against the Pharisees (Matthew xxiii, 37–39), not daring to mention it in table talk (*supra*, p. 159). All this, again, must be largely bor-

ANALYSIS OF WRITINGS ATTRIBUTED TO LUKE

rowed from the teaching of the Last Things, the eschatological catechesis.

Another incoherent conglomerate: a sabbath story (xiv, 1–6) sketched round an argument (xiv, 3) with no symbolic background; advice about behaviour when invited to a feast (xiv, 7–11) turned at the end into allegory (repeated after the parable of Pharisee and publican, xviii, 14; Matthew xxiii, 12); advice to invite only the unfortunate (xiv, 12–14), derived from the parable that follows in harmony with the ideal extolled in Acts; parable of the great supper (xiv, 15–24) allegorized (while keeping closer to the source than Matthew xxii, 2–10) to signify the salvation of the disinherited, as well as the pagans, in preference to conceited Jews; the lesson of renunciation (xiv, 25–27, this time taken from the collection of *logia* (Matthew x, 37–38; Mark viii, 34–35); similes of the man who would build a tower and the king who would go to war, adapted, but not well, to the lesson of renunciation (xiv, 28–33); finally, the simile of the salt (xiv, 34). All these pieces, which are of very diverse origin, serve the purpose of the evangelist for what they are worth. To discuss the reality of the facts or the authenticity of the sayings would be wasted time and labour. Save for the editor's preoccupations they have no consistency.

The three parables of divine forgiveness, the lost sheep (xv, 3–7), the lost drachma (xv, 8–10, less felicitous and possibly modelled on the preceding), the prodigal son (xv, 11–32) are turned, by the setting of the scene (xv, 1–2), into a defence of Jesus against an attack of the Pharisees. The last of the three combines the theme of the lost son found again with certain features imitated from a fine oriental tale preserved in the Acts of Thomas;[1] towards the end it develops into an allegory of the jealous attitude attributed to the Jews in regard to pagan converts.

The parables of the unfaithful steward (xvi, 1–8) and of the rich man and Lazarus are constructed throughout as a direct attack on the Pharisees. The first is a completely immoral story which some good people have tried to utilize by fitting it with edifying applications which hardly fulfil the requirements of a

---

[1] The story is given in full in the author's *Le Mandéism et les origines chrétiennes*, 126–127. It has points of strong resemblance to the parable of the prodigal son. Burkitt (*Early Eastern Christianity*, 1904) thinks it may be attributed to Bardesanes.

rigorous logic. Following this come a remark on the lack of intelligence among believers in making sure of their eternal welfare (xvi, 8*b*); advice to make friends in heaven by giving money to the poor (xvi, 9); advice to merit spiritual good by a faithful use of temporal riches (xvi, 10–12) and the impossibility of serving God and money (xvi, 13).

The remark on the ill-will of the greedy Pharisees and Jesus' reply (xvi, 14–15; cf. xviii, 9–14) are a literary device for introducing another parcel of sayings, which are not inserted in their proper place: on John and the Kingdom of God (xvi, 16; Matthew xi, 12–13); on the perpetuity of the Law (xvi, 17; Matthew v, 18), doubtless to be taken in a spiritual or typological sense; against divorce (xvi, 18; Matthew v, 31–32); the whole group tending to support the theory of the Gospel as the real fulfilment of the Law, to which the conclusion of the succeeding parable of the rich man and Lazarus is also related (xvi, 19–31).

The main body of this parable (19–26) is the adaptation of a well-worn theme concerning the eternal happiness of the poor and the eternal torment of the rich, but the appendix (27–31) brings out the hardening and reprobation of the Jews incapable of seeing prophecy fulfilled in the Christ. Nor should we dismiss too lightly the question whether the author of the parable may have had in view the resurrection of Lazarus described in the fourth Gospel as a miracle thrown away on the Jews (John xi, 1–46). On that hypothesis, however, we should have to admit that our parable contains a rather free criticism of the Johannine story and that the writing of it cannot be dated very early.

Yet another conglomerate: warning against causing the little ones to stumble (xvii, 1–2; Matthew xviii, 6–7); command to forgive (xvii, 3–4; Matthew xviii, 21–22); the power of faith (xvii, 5–6; Mark xi, 22–23; Matthew xvii, 20; xxi, 21); service of a master and service of God (xvii, 7–10); then, an expansion of Mark i, 40–45, the story of the ten lepers, where the action of the one who "was a Samaritan" puts the Jews to shame.

At the next stage, the editor, after a preamble of the usual type for starting point, brings in an apocalyptic discourse (xvii, 22–37) which Mark has also utilized (xiii, 21) and Matthew more fully (xxiv, 27–28, 37–41). The preamble (xvii, 20–21), a pure literary device, seems intended to replace what Mark says (xiii, 32; cf.

Acts i, 6–7) about the ignorance of the Christ regarding the day of the Second Coming. As to the assertion that "the Kingdom of God is in the midst of you" there is no reason to search, as is the wont of confessional apologetic, for the idea of an inward and individual realization of the divine Kingdom. What probably the evangelist had in mind was the preliminary reality of it in the Christian community (cf. xiii, 18–21); moreover the discourse contradicts the preamble. The parable of the widow and the judge (xviii, 1–5), a story with the same ethical quality as the importunate friend, co-ordinates this discourse with an eschatological application (xviii, 6–8). The parable of the Pharisee and the publican (xviii, 9–14) is conceived in accordance with the evangelical idea of the Pharisee as the type of incredulity and pride and of the publican as humble and believing; it becomes, in application, a prophetic threat to Judaism.

Return to Mark

We come back again to Mark with the story of the babes brought that "he should touch them" (xviii, 15–17; Mark x, 13–16; Matthew xix, 13–15), after which there follow in succession the story of the rich young man and the lessons attached to it (xviii, 18–30; Mark x, 17–30); the final announcement of the Passion (xviii, 31–33; Mark x, 32–34; Matthew xx, 17–19), dropping the greater part of Mark's preamble (x, 32) and the request of the sons of Zebedee for the two best places in glory (Mark x, 35–40). Owing to the latter omission the healing of the blind man at Jericho comes in immediately after the announcement of the Passion (xviii, 35–43). A further difference is that the blind man is healed before Jesus enters the town and not, as in Mark, when he leaves it, thus reserving Jericho as locality for the incident of Zacchaeus; the blind man standing for converts to Jewish Christianity, and Zacchaeus, the double of Levi the publican, for converts to hellenic Christianity, the future course of the Gospel thus falling into the outlook towards the parousia, with which the parable of the talents is supposed to be concerned.

The parable of the talents in the version before us (xix, 11–27), presents a complete transformation of the theme of retribution, as in Matthew's version xxv, 14–30, into an apocalyptic allegory. Nothing could be more tendentious than the preamble which announces this, or than the glosses which effect it. Highly significant, however, are the words of the preamble: "They supposed that the Kingdom of God was immediately to appear." The saying is not easily explained as a conjecture of the evangelist; but to know whence it is derived would be valuable information. In any case it may long have been matter of common memory among the Christians of Palestine and Syria that the first believers expected the coming of Messiah to take place at Jerusalem. The story which follows of the Christ's passing triumph on the Mount of Olives was certainly conceived as a foreshadowing of this final victory (cf. *supra*, p. 93).

Though abridged from Mark (xi, 1–10), the messianic demonstration on the Mount of Olives (xix, 28–38) is enriched by two incidents: protest of the Pharisees against the disciples' acclamations and Jesus' reply (xix, 39–40; cf. Matthew xxi, 15–16), and the prophetic lament of the Christ weeping over Jerusalem (xix, 41–44). It is no matter of chance that this last fragment replaces the symbolic story of the blasted fig tree in Mark. It is followed by a very brief account of the expulsion of the traders from the temple (xix, 45–46; Mark xi, 15–17).

A general statement (xix, 47–48) to be taken up and completed later (xxi, 37–38) replaces Mark's more detailed account of Jesus' comings and goings between Jerusalem and Bethany. Mark is followed in the discussion with the priests about Jesus' authority; in the parable of the murderous vinedressers; in the Sadducees' question about the resurrection; in the saying about the Christ as David's Lord; in the concise warning to the Pharisees (xx, 45–47) and in the widow with two mites (xxi, 1–4; Mark xii, 41–44).

The long apocalyptic discourse (xxi, 5–36) comes also from Mark (xiii, 1–37) with the difference that here the discourse is delivered in public. Some details are retouched: omission of the saying that the Son himself knows not the day of the Great Event (Mark xiii, 32) and complete recasting of the peroration. The final notice, about Jesus' daily habit and the pressure of the crowds to hear him preach, give the finishing touch to the setting of the scene. This notice (xxi, 37–38) seems to have some dependence on the story of the woman taken in adultery, which has disappeared from the synoptic tradition and got inserted, as an interpolation, into the fourth Gospel. It cannot be by mere chance that the wording of it corresponds so closely with the introduction to that story (John vii, 53–viii, 1–2).

The Lucan Story of the Passion

In the story of the Passion the plot of the Jewish magistrates to do away with Jesus and Judas' betrayal of him come together (xxii, 1–6; cf. Mark xiv, 1–2, 10; Matthew xxvi, 1–5, 14–16) as they must have been presented in proto-Mark. The story of the anointing (Mark xiv, 3–9), which the canonical version of Luke anticipates in that of the sinful woman (*supra*, p. 155), must have been unknown by the writer to Theophilus (proto-Luke). The preparations for the paschal meal, in the canonical version, are copied from Mark xiv, 12–16. In the account of the Supper the two elements of the story, the one superimposed on the other, dimly discernible in Mark (xiv 22–25), are clearer in the common text of Luke (xxii, 14–20). But, comparing the variants of the text in the oldest manuscripts, it seems that the second element (the words "given for you" at the end of verse 19 and again in verse 20) is almost entirely interpolated. It is even probable that in proto-Luke—the writing to Theophilus—the last meal was not the paschal meal, but type of the primitive form of the Supper, with the eschatological outlook to the Kingdom, in which Jesus was represented as eating bread and drinking wine with his followers for the last time under the existing conditions of the world, "this Passover" in verses 15 and 16 being a later substitution for "this bread."

Attached to the primitive, or eschatological, account of the Supper, and only explicable as so attached, comes the disciples' dispute about primacy, which brings on the lesson of service, and is combined with the promise of thrones and the intimation of future banquets together in the Kingdom (xxii, 24–30; cf. Mark ix, 34–35; x, 42–45; Matthew xx, 25–28; xix, 28). The apostrophe to Simon is intended to be a promise of his absolute indefectibility in the faith (verse 32 should be translated "and thou, *gathering them together*, strengthen thy brethren") and a prevision of Peter's eminent part as the initiator of faith in Jesus risen from the dead. With this the announcement of his coming denial (xxii, 33–34; Mark xiv, 29–31), and the denial itself, are in contradiction, and stand out clearly as postscripts of the editing hand. To the same source must be attributed the commands addressed to the disciples in prevision of the dangers awaiting them (xxii, 35-38), and introduced as testimony to the Christ's foreknowledge.

The scene in Gethsemane (xxii, 39-46) is more simply constructed than in the canonical version of Mark (xiv, 26, 32-42). Probably founded on proto-Mark, it lacks the hostile thrust at the three principal disciples, surcharged in the canonical version (Mark xiv, 33-34, 37-41). The passage relating the appearance of the angel and the sweat of blood (xxii, 43-44) is omitted in certain manuscripts; whether authentic or not in our Gospel, it represents a secondary development in the formation of the story. The account of the arrest (xxii, 47-53) corrects certain traits in Mark (xiv, 43-49) and introduces, before the speech of Jesus to those who have come to arrest him, a small miracle—restoration of his ear to the high-priest's servant (xxii, 50-51). Not a word is said about the flight of the disciples, the editor having decided to keep them in Jerusalem.

The nocturnal sitting of the Sanhedrim (Mark xiv, 53-64) is omitted, perhaps because the writer to Theophilus had found no trace of it in proto-Mark. To fill the remainder of the night of the arrest the editor has spread out Peter's triple denial (xxii, 54-62; Mark xiv, 53-54, 66-72; Matthew xxvi, 57-68, 69-75; cf. John xviii, 15-18, 25-27), to which he has given a dramatic touch by the presence of Jesus, who awakes the culprit's memory and penitence by a look. The scene of derision in the high-priest's house has also been lifted from Mark (xiv, 65) and in like manner the details of the morning meeting of the Sanhedrim (xxii, 66-71; cf. Mark xv, 1) have been transposed from the nocturnal séance in Mark xiv, 60-64. All these borrowings go to prove the indigence and instability of the tradition. We must not forget, however, that fragments of the original version by the writer to Theophilus may have been suppressed, as they have been in the sequel, the Book of Acts.

In the account of the trial before Pilate the influence of proto-Mark may perhaps be discerned in the fact that the accusation by the Sanhedrim is made to precede the interrogation by Pilate (xxiii, 1-3, 13-25; Mark xv, 1-15; Matthew xxvii, 2, 11-18, 20-25). But immediately after Jesus' avowal that he is King of the Jews, our editor puts a declaration of his innocence into Pilate's mouth. This, at bottom, is an editorial contrivance indispensable for effecting a transition to the appearance before Herod, that complete superfluity, borrowed perhaps from some Gospel then recent, in which responsibility for the Christ's condemnation and death was boldly transferred from Pilate to Herod, as it is in the apocryphal Gospel of Peter. We again pick up the thread of Mark with the incident of Barabbas, round which are grouped repeated assertions of Jesus' innocence (xxiii, 18–25; Mark xv, 6–15; Matthew xxvii, 15-18, 20–26). The incident has the appearance of being another editorial addition (xxiii, 22 repeats 15 which again repeats 4), the idea being that Pilate was compelled to pass sentence of death on Jesus merely to satisfy the hatred of the Jews.

Our Gospel's account of the execution conforms to Mark's in the following: carrying of the cross by Simon of Cyrene; crucifixion between two robbers; division of the garments; mockery by the Jewish magistrates; presentation of vinegar, turned into an act of derision on the part of the soldiers; inscription on the cross; admiring outcry of the centurion, but with a significant attenuation of the formula from "this was the Son of God" to "this was a righteous man."

Turning now to the differences, we recognize the spirit and hand of the editor in many additions: prophetic allocution of Jesus to the women of Jerusalem on the road to Calvary (xxiii, 27–31); prayer of the Crucified for his executioners (xxiii, 34; cf. Stephen's prayer, Acts vii, 60); insults by one of the robbers, prayer of the good robber and Jesus' answer which show Jesus and the robber believing that they will pass at death, not into the tomb, nor into Hades, but "into Paradise" (xxiii, 39–43; cf. xvi, 22–23, the case of Lazarus and Dives carried at death, the one into the bosom of Abraham, and the other into hell); prayer of trustful abandonment to God uttered by Jesus with his dying breath (the words of Psalm xxxi, 5, substituted, as more edifying, for Psalm xxii, 1 in Mark xv, 34); multitude of witnesses present at the death scene and their mourning afterwards, suggested, like the lamentation of the women in xxiii, 27, by a passage in Zechariah (xii, 10–14). A pathetic picture of Jesus' death painted by pious imagination.

Mark's citation of Psalm xxii, 1 in Aramean was eliminated in favour of Psalm xxxi, 5, not because it seemed a cry of despair (for its origin was well known), but because it ran a risk of being imperfectly understood, while for most readers, the Aramean words and the sorry jest they provoked from the soldiers would have no interest. But the chief reason for the change lay in the danger that the words might be taken in the sense of a gnostic doctrine which Mark was thought to favour, the doctrine, namely, that the "aeon" Christ descended on Jesus at his baptism and returned to heaven the moment he expired. This dangerous meaning is contained in the version of the cry given by the Gospel of Peter "My Force, My Force, thou hast left me!"

The author's detention of the disciples in Jerusalem has various consequences. (Observe that every trace of the writer to Theophilus is lost from the moment that Jesus breathes his last.) Our evangelist brings "all his acquaintance" to Calvary together with the Galilean women (without their names, these having been given previously, viii, 2–3): the presence of the women is in conformity with Mark (xv, 40), who is closely followed for the story of the burial by Joseph of Arimathaea; for the rôle of the women as witnesses of the interment; for the discovery of the empty tomb on Sunday morning (xxiii, 50–xxiv, 3; Mark xv, 42–xvi, 7; Matthew xxvii, 57–xxviii, 7). At this point we encounter a piece of verbal jugglery: instead of going on with Mark (xvi, 7) to the coming apparitions of Jesus in Galilee, two angels (cf. Acts i, 10) remind the women of predictions made by him *in Galilee* of his passion and resurrection (xxiv, 6–7); the women then pass on the message to the disciples, who refuse to believe a word of it (xxiv, 8–11; cf. Mark xvi, 8, where the women say "nothing to any man").

The passage describing Peter's visit to the tomb is lacking in several manuscripts, but allusion to the matter of it seems to be made later on (xxiv, 24). If it is authentic the last revision of our Gospel has been influenced by the fourth (cf. John xx, 3–10). We are ignorant of the traditions or sources from which our evangelist has constructed his apparitions of the risen Christ; doubtless he has put a good deal of his own into the stories. The apparition to the two disciples of Emmaus, in which he places in the mouth of Jesus his own (the evangelist's) system of

Christian demonstration by the Scriptures, is finely conceived as an ideal and symbolic story. Nevertheless the conclusion (xxiv, 33–34): "They found the Eleven... who said 'the Lord indeed is risen and hath appeared unto Simon,'" is wholly unintelligible. To balance the story, the Emmaus disciples ought to say to the others: "the Lord indeed is risen and hath appeared unto *us*." Has the passage suffered accidental damage? Or may it be that Simon's name has been brought into it to do justice to Peter's vision (cf. 1 Corinthians xv, 5)?

The story of the apparition to all the disciples which ends with Jesus' ascension into heaven (xxiv, 36–53) is lacking in unity; the incidents are crowded together, they are without connection between themselves and the perspective in which they are placed is of the vaguest. The same theme is resumed at the beginning of Acts with complementary precisions, and certainly by the same editor, or editors. Instead of taking the two accounts as contradictory, on the ground that the Gospel seems to have deliberately placed the Ascension on the night which followed the morning of the Resurrection while Acts put an interval of forty days between the two, the signs rather indicate that we should interpret the one text by the other, the two having been conceived as reciprocal complements and belonging to the same series of fictions. Slight touches in the Gospel narrative suggest interpolation. The ancient authorities which omit Peter's visit to the tomb (xxiv, 12) omit also "Peace be unto you" (36) and further on (40) "when he had said this, he showed them his feet and his hands," two passages which again indicate the influence of John. Finally in the last verses there are two doubtful readings: "he was carried up into heaven" (51) and "when they had worshipped him" (52). In the last two cases omission may have been deliberate to avoid seeming contradiction of the story in Acts with its interval of forty days. We may recall that here, as in the parallel story of Acts, the promise of the Spirit is a postscript (*supra*, p. 147).

The Gospel known as Luke's, in the form in which it has come down to us, is a compilation analogous to that of Matthew. In it we find the first book to Theophilus not only augmented by the birth-legends but substantially remodelled and completed,

THE ORIGINS OF THE NEW TESTAMENT

and the same operations have been carried out on the second book in the Acts of the Apostles. The question of dates is one question for the two writings both in their original and their canonical forms. Enough has been said to entitle us to affirm that the author of the original books to Theophilus wrote in the early years of the second century, at a time when the Christian community in Rome had not entirely rallied to the observance of the Sunday Easter. The subsequent edition presupposes the Sunday observance as completely adopted. Apart from this and supporting it, the dependence of Marcion on the third Gospel (*supra*, p. 71) leads to the conclusion that the traditional text of the Gospel was fixed a little before 140, save perhaps for slight retouchings.

THE SECOND BOOK TO THEOPHILUS CONVERTED INTO THE BOOK OF ACTS

Our analysis of the opening of Acts went no further than the story of the Ascension (i, 9–11). Appended to this story there follow, rather confusedly (12–14), the indication of the disciples' return to Jerusalem, the list of the eleven apostles, which could not be worse fitted to its context, recalling Luke vi, 13–16, where the editorial handiwork has been already noted (p. 146), and mention of the persons who, with the "apostles," are represented as constituting the first group of believers. The particular mention of the women, of the mother and brothers of Jesus, reveals the editing hand. It is that of the editor whose interest in Mary appears in the birth-stories. Mother and brothers now appear as witnesses to the tradition—a bold touch.

Notwithstanding the clumsy insertion into Peter's discourse of a legend about the end of Judas (i, 18–19; cf. Matthew xxvii, 3–10) the account of the choosing of the twelfth apostle (i, 15–26) is all of one piece with, and reflects the chief editor's notions about, the object and meaning of the apostolic witness and its depositaries. The legend of the choice of Matthias and the legend of Judas are directly and avowedly related, making up, in their combination, a single edifying fabrication.

After this artificial introduction come, first, the inauguration of the Christian religion by the miracle of Pentecost, and then, in a double series (iii–iv, 31; and v, 17–42) the conflicts of the apostles with the Jewish authorities in Jerusalem and, in the space between the two passages, a picture of the interior life of the new community and of its progress, helped on by miracles (iv, 32–v, 16). The story is pure invention throughout, but not all of one piece. Peter's discourse is in two parts. The first part, concerning "the gift of tongues" (ii, 14*b*–21 where the outpourings of glossology are confused with the power to speak in different languages), turns on the descent of the Spirit following up certain adventitious elements in the description of the event (ii, 3–4, 6*b*–11, 13). The second part (ii, 22–32, 34–36; ii, 33 and 38*b*, a little further on, being surcharged to keep contact with the first part) corresponds with the fundamental elements of the description. It is obvious that this doubling both in the story and in Peter's discourse is related to a phenomenon we have already observed in the story of the Ascension (*supra*, p. 148). It does not follow that the second editor had the idea of baptism as a purely spiritual act; for it will appear, from other cases where the same interpolator intervenes, that the gift of the Spirit joins on to, and is sacramentally completed by the baptismal immersion in water, which John the Baptist is supposed to have administered to the apostles. Was not this also the case with the typical baptism—that of Jesus?

The scene of Pentecost taken as a whole foreshadows the evangelization of the world, and for that reason is placed as introduction to the story of apostolic preaching, just as the scene of Jesus at Nazareth (Luke iv, 16–30) has been transposed to the opening of the Christ's preaching and arranged as betokening the ulterior fortunes of the Gospel. The conversion in mass of more than three thousand persons(!) follows this fine miracle and solemn discourse and, like miracle and discourse, has no historical foundation. What we go on to read (ii, 42) about the conduct of the converts, their attendance on the apostles' preaching, their coming together to break bread and falling to prayer, may be inspired by the source, but in this place is only edifying padding, as is also the conclusion of the chapter (ii, 43–47) which repeats what has just been said twice (i, 14; ii, 42) and duplicates what will be said further on (iv, 32–35) about the common use of material goods in the apostolic community.

The cure of the paralytic was, in reality, the first public incident to draw attention to the presence in Jerusalem of people who claimed to be followers of Jesus the Nazorean (iii, 1–10). The original account of it has been overlaid in various ways: first by the mention of John at the side of Peter (the surcharge is especially clear in iii, 4, "Peter fixing his eye upon him, *with John*"; the motive for this emphasis of John will appear later on), then by an amplification (8–10) which completely upsets the story; and by a solemn oration of Peter (12–26) substituted for the explanation which the circumstances called for, and which the resumption of the narrative in iv, 1 ("as they talked with the crowd, the priests arrived") supposed to have been actually given. The mention of the Sadducees at this point is intended to indicate that the bitterest form of Jewish opposition to Christianity came from the heresy which denied the common hope of Israel. Now follows a series of fabrications: the arrest of Peter leading on to the appearance of the two offenders before the Sanhedrim next day (iv, 3); the conversion of five thousand men by Peter's oration—particularly outrageous; the scene of the great assembly of persons in authority to consider the matter (5–6); the question (7) then put by the court to the accused which the writer to Theophilus had made the temple police previously address to Peter; and Peter's answer, here paraphrased into a profession of faith, the supposed presence of the cured man in court plainly revealing the hand of its inventor. (It was in the temple and on the spot that Peter, in answer to the police, replied that the paralytic had just been cured by the name of Jesus the Nazorean.) No less fictitious is the sequel to the story; the secret session of the Sanhedrim after clearing the court and the ridiculous embarrassment of the assembly, in which, however, a single echo of the source document may be detected: "they recognized"—i.e. the police recognized on Peter's answering their question "that (he and his companions) had been in the company of Jesus." The bold reply of Peter (and John) is a late insertion, but the natural conclusion of the incident, as the source reported it, seems to be preserved in the threats to which the police confined themselves, not daring to do more than threaten in presence of a crowd which sided with Peter (iv, 21–22). The scene that follows, with the prayer, into which a prophetic quotation (Psalm ii, 1–2) is painfully introduced, and with a little Pentecost for conclusion (iv, 23–31) is an editorial creation from beginning to end.

Of the succeeding *bloc* of stories (iv, 32–v, 16) hardly anything can be retained as historical. Glosses abound in what we are told about the community of goods among the believers (iv, 32–35, at least, is the editor's paraphrase); the same in the notice about Barnabas in which his name, Levitical status and place of origin are all we can retain, the rest being the first step in the process of falsification applied later on to the considerable part played by this great man in the foundation of hellenic Christianity. Whatever may be the source of it, the hair-raising story of Ananias and Sapphira is another invention intended to exalt the prestige of apostolic and ecclesiastical authority. As to the countless miracles performed by the apostles, and especially by Peter (v, 12–16), the only morsel of the tale which a prudent reader can accept as veridical is the mention of the place (the Porch of Solomon) where the believers were accustomed to gather amid the mingled caution and admiration of the lookers-on—signs which show clearly that there was no *public* preaching—with a few words in v, 12*b*–14 about the recruits gained by private propaganda.

Again, the writer gives rein to his imagination in a succession of tales which rather repeat the form of those already told or anticipate others to be developed later on. In v, 17, instead of "and rising up, the high priest," etc., the reading should probably be "Annas the high priest" as in iv, 6 (cf. Luke iii, 2). The imprisonment of all the apostles, v, 17–18, matches that of Peter and John in iv, 3; their miraculous deliverance, v, 19–21, is on the same model as that of Peter's in xii, 6–11; the meeting of the Sanhedrim, v, 27–29, is a replica of iv, 7–12; the secret meeting v, 34–40 a replica of iv, 15–17. The intervention of Gamaliel prepares for the part he will be called upon to play in the legend of Paul, xxii, 3. (The reference to the enrolment, v, 37, betrays the author of Luke ii, 1–3, but the affair of Judas the Galilean and of Theudas, in Gamaliel's speech, 35–39, have been placed in their wrong order by some copyist.) Gamaliel's speech is the high light of the picture and is intended to show what, in the author's opinion, should be the attitude of Jewish authorities to the Christian movement.

The account of the hellenist believers and of the beginning of propaganda to the Gentiles is in four sections: Stephen and the Seven (vi–vii); the dispersion of the group (i.e. of hellenist believers), the exploits of Philip and the conversion of Paul (viii–ix, 31); the apostolic journey and the conversion of Cornelius (ix, 32–xi, 18); the foundation of the Antioch community and the first journey of Barnabas and Paul to Jerusalem (xi, 19–30; xii, 25) with the intercalated account of the persecution under Agrippa I (xii, 1–24).

Stephen and the Seven

The list of the Seven belongs to the same class as the list of the Twelve and is neither more nor less authentic. But the Seven never were deacons acting under the Twelve as edited Acts would have it believed (vi, 1–6); they were the head-men of the *Greek-speaking* group of believers which soon got separated from the original Hebrew group which spoke in Aramean. The statement about the progress of the word (vi, 7) probably replaces the more prosaic information by the writer to Theophilus concerning the activities of the *Greek-speaking* group; the accession of a *few* priests is not impossible. The information about Stephen (vi, 8–15) comes in part from the original work, if not from Luke himself; but instead of loading him with miracles (8) the original would probably note that he was the first to announce *publicly* that Jesus was the Messiah, in the synagogues of the Greek-speaking Jews in Jerusalem. What the suborned witnesses and the popular voice are made to say (vi, 11–12) is a replica and anticipation of what immediately follows (13–14) about his accusation before the Sanhedrim. The base document seems to have described a legal trial by that body; mention of the prisoner's ecstasy (15) comes from the source, perhaps also the high priest's question (vii, 1); but the immediate sequel to this, in the source, was the ecstasist's answer to the question: "I see the heavens open," etc., in vii, 56. Stephen's long speech (vii, 2–53) is an interpolation by the editor between the question and the answer, intended to introduce the reader to the conception of the Jews as the guilty nation before God, proved so by a long history of perpetual infidelity to Divine revelation, guilt which they have now brought to a head in the treatment meted out to Jesus. Except for the words: "they stopped their ears" (vii, 57, where the outcries and popular tumult are an addition) the editor must have suppressed everything in the source which indicated that the death sentence was passed and carried out strictly according to Jewish law. The source stated simply that Stephen was stoned outside the city (58); but the editor, having forced into this passage a reference to the young man Saul, repeats the lapidation (59), and in a like manner having already given (from the source), Stephen's dying words in 59, he has to give him others in 60. The phrase about Saul being a consenting party is to bring on the next topic, that of Saul in the rôle of persecutor.

As imagined by our editor the persecution of believers was indiscriminate, and Saul the chief agent in conducting it (viii, 1, 3; 2, referring to Stephen's burial, is an insertion; 3 seems better placed before ix, 1). The story of Philip's apostolic exploits in Samaria is awkwardly lodged in that of the persecution, the frame of which is wholly fictitious. The only believers who had to flee from Jerusalem were the chief members of the *Greek-speaking* group. In representing the persecution as indiscriminate and as including both groups, Hebrew and Hellenist, the writer would hide the division which existed between them and avoid giving the hellenists the credit, which was really theirs, of carrying the Gospel beyond Judea. By this falsification he becomes involved in all sorts of contradiction. First he represents the entire body of believers, Hebrew and Greek, taking to flight and dispersed "except the apostles" (viii, 1); next, we have Saul entering all their houses when they were no longer there, and haling them to prison. The description of Philip's apostolic work in Samaria (viii, 5-6) is a commonplace of the type in which the editor is wont to indulge his fancy and, whatever it may mean, must clearly be attributed to him.

Exploits of Philip: Simon Magus and the Ethiopian Eunuch

The story of Simon Magus (viii, 9-24) is not all of one piece. There is a first story which represents Simon as amazing the Samaritans by his sorceries (viii, 9-11); amazed in turn by Philip's miracles, he proposes to buy from him the power to do as much. But this conclusion is submerged in another tale (viii,

14–25). The apostles at Jerusalem, informed of what is going on in Samaria, are minded to have Peter and John on the spot, and send them off (the mention of John is here, too, a late postscript as in iii, 1, 3–4, 11). They confer the Holy Spirit on Philip's converts, and it is for having tried to buy the power to do this that Simon gets a cutting reprimand from Peter (viii, 20–23). This proves the existence, at the time it was written, and in some rudimentary form, of the legend which told of a conflict between Peter and Simon the Magician; the writer would here tell how the conflict began. Moreover we here see the Church, through our editor as spokesman putting forth its claim, against the gnostics, to a monopoly of the Spirit (cf. p. 83) and expressing the claim by a special rite, appended to baptism but distinct from it, the rite which confers the Spirit by imposition of hands.

The tale of the Ethiopian Eunuch converted by Philip on the road to Gaza leaves nothing to be desired for naïveté and extravagance (viii, 26–40). The building up of the story on a text from Isaiah (liii, 7–8) repeats the procedure by which nearly all the discourses in Acts are made up, the whole being apparently conceived as the fulfilment of prophecy (Isaiah lvi, 3–7; Psalm lxviii, 31). It is here of little importance whether the tale was invented by the editor or found by him ready made.

Saul—Persecutor and Convert

The legend of Saul, persecutor and convert, now follows (ix, 1–30); the theme of his conversion is treated thrice over (ix, 1–19; xxii, 3–21; xxvi, 4–18) with variations which seem to betray, not the use of different sources, but the extreme licence which the editor allowed himself in exploiting the matter. This legendary tale reposes on information obtained from the Epistles: "Saul, who is Paul" is converted near Damascus in consequence of a vision, after persecuting the believers in Jesus; this upon an erroneous supposition for, at the time in question, the only believers were in Jerusalem, and it is in that city that he should have played the part of persecutor before betaking himself to Damascus, where the vision overcomes him for Jesus. As to the first part of the story, the commission to persecute given to Saul by the high priest is, in the conditions indicated (ix, 1–3), quite inconceivable; the dramatic picture that follows of Saul blinded by the luminous vision is just as unbalanced; the third tale, of Paul's initiation to Christianity by Ananias, under the guidance of two visions, one for the initiator and the other for the candidate (ix, 10–19*a*), is modelled on a well-known type to be met with, for example, in the Mysteries of Isis. Pure invention of the editor is Paul's ministry in the synagogues of Damascus (ix, 19*b*–22), while the circumstances of his flight (ix, 23–25) are partly by the same hand—the plot of the Jews—and partly borrowed from 2 Corinthians xi, 32–33, or from the tradition behind that passage. The impression produced on the Jerusalem believers by Paul's arrival, the intervention of Barnabas, Paul's preaching at Jerusalem, his departure for Caesarea and Tarsus after a new plot against him by the Jews—all these belong to the same class as the foregoing. But it suits the editor's purpose to represent Paul as hurrying away to meet the old apostles and to be associated with their ministry in the holy city—in flat contradiction to Galatians i, 15–17, 21–24.

Fictions about Peter

A stock phrase on the prosperous condition of the churches in Palestine (ix, 31), which at the time in question were not in existence, serves to introduce a number of tales about Peter: two miracles, that of Lydda, imitated from the cure of the paralytic in Luke v, 18–25 and a duplicate of the cure previously performed by Peter himself in the temple (iii, 1–16), and the resurrection of Dorcas at Joppa, imitated from the raising of Jairus' daughter in Luke viii, 41, 42; 49–56, and from the resurrections effected by Elijah and Elisha; next, after localizing these miracles in places that would bring Peter on the way to Caesarea as the right place for the conversion of a Roman officer, comes the conversion of Cornelius, with the usual apparatus of preliminary visions (x, 1–23), the meeting and reciprocal explanations (x, 23–33), Peter's discourse (x, 34–43) making him the announcer, before anybody else, of the principle of universal salvation, and the baptism of Cornelius, all to make it appear that this same Peter was the first to accept a pagan convert without compelling him to be circumcised (x, 44–48). The same motive inspires the apology for his conduct which Peter goes on to offer to "those who were of the circumcision" in Jerusalem (xi, 1–18). All this our editor places before coming to the foundation of the Church in Antioch, by way of putting Peter above Paul and of reserving to Peter the initiative as apostle to the Gentiles.

Foundation of the Church in Antioch

The account of this foundation (xi, 19–26) and of the alms immediately sent to Jerusalem by the new community (xi, 27–30; xii, 25) now follows, but is awkwardly mixed with the story of the persecution by Agrippa I and the death of the persecutor (xii, 1–2, 20–24). The first lines (xi, 19–21) come from the source-document and are continuous with those already given in viii, 1, 4 about the propaganda carried on by the dispersed hellenists after the death of Stephen. But the representation of Barnabas as sent to Antioch by the mother-church in Jerusalem (xi, 22–24) is the writer's fiction, another fragment from the source (xiii, 1) making it clear that Barnabas was one of the fugitives who carried the Gospel to Antioch and were the first to receive pagans into the fold without compelling them to be circumcised: the same motive which inspired the fiction of Peter converting Cornelius here turns Barnabas into a delegate from the Jerusalem believers while the reappearance of Paul (xi, 25–26) is all part of the same scheme. The statement in xi, 26*b* that "the disciples were called Christians first in Antioch" certainly comes from the source.

The next fabrication concerns the prophets who come to Antioch from Jerusalem announcing an approaching famine, in consequence of which the faithful at Antioch make a collection and send it to Jerusalem by the hands of Paul and Barnabas (xi, 27–30). These Jerusalem prophets are replicas of those whom the source-document will presently indicate as already in Antioch (xiii, 1). In like manner the journey of Paul and Barnabas to Jerusalem with the collection in their hands is substituted for that which they made, at the indicated date, for the different purpose of discussing the legal observances. Finally, the collection here mentioned has been substituted for the assessment demanded of the missionaries to the outside world at the Jerusalem meeting over the legal observances (cf. Galatians ii, 10). The famine has been taken by the editor from Josephus (*Antiquities*, xx, 5, 2).

The persecution organized by Agrippa I was doubtless connected with the policy of Claudius to suppress Jewish agitators. The account of it here given comes in the main from the source; but it is probable that the writer to Theophilus recorded in this passage the execution of John as well as of James, the editor sparing John to avoid contradicting the Ephesian legend of his survival, which may also be the reason for the omission from canonical Luke of the incident in Mark x, 35–40 when Jesus predicts the martyrdom of John (cf. *supra*, p. 59). The miracle which procured escape for Peter (xii, 3–19) has the unmistakable look of an invention, but our inventor has avoided mentioning the locality to which Peter betook himself in his flight from Jerusalem (xii, 17) saying only: "he went away to another place." The supposition is irresistible that Peter found his way to Antioch and that the editor avoided mentioning it because he was determined to keep silence about the conflict there between Peter and Paul. But the composer of Acts knew the legend of Simon Magus (*supra*, p. 176) and this creates a possibility that the "other place" so mysteriously designated was meant to be Rome. But did Peter ever find his way to that city?

What became of Peter after his Flight?

The fate of Peter is understood in this passage according to some tale of which the import is not easily measured. At first sight there seems no ground for maintaining that Peter was put to death, along with James and John, in the persecution ordered by Agrippa I. But was not John brought to life again in legend, and did not the composer of Acts intentionally omit the mention of his death and let him live on? May not the same proceeding have been adopted for Peter? Is it entirely natural that the composer of Acts has not a word to say about him after the meeting at Jerusalem? True it is that the Epistle to the Galatians takes him to Antioch after this meeting and shows him there in conflict with Paul (Galatians ii, 11–21). But the story of this conflict is all of a piece with the false account given in the same Epistle (ii, 1–10) of the meeting in Jerusalem. Peter, James and John, who appear there as the "apostles" they never were, and as "pillars," are, in that capacity, figures of legend. May it not be that the story of the Antioch conflict is the first form of the "tradition" which represented Simon Peter and Simon Magus in deadly strife? The matter is shrouded in a little mystery for which an explanation has yet to be found.[1]

The account of Agrippa's death (xii, 20–23), though very different from that given by Josephus (*Antiquities*, xix, 8, 2), cannot be altogether independent of it. Barnabas and Paul, returning to Antioch, are said to take John-Mark along with them, the compiler's reason being that he will need him there later on to explain the separation of Barnabas and Paul (xv, 37–40).

Confused Account of Paul's Journeys

Having made into two the one and only journey to Jerusalem which Barnabas and Paul ever took in company, the compiler is minded to fill the void between them by a great mission which cannot be other than fictitious. Other evidence makes it certain that the debate on the legal observances with the Jerusalem believers was not the sequel to the mission about to be described but to that jointly conceived by Barnabas and Paul in Syria and Cilicia (cf. xv, 23; Galatians i, 21; ii, 1, 9). As to the mission intercalated by the compiler (xiii, 4–xiv), it is clearly made up by combining into one the independent missions undertaken, *after the separation of the two apostles*, by Barnabas into Cyprus (xv, 39) and by Paul into Lycaonia, Pisidia and Galatia (xvi, 1–6). The fragment from the source-document standing at the head of these stories (xiii, 1–2), taken in itself, represents the Antioch congregation as under the teaching of five prophet-instructors, of whom Barnabas is first and Paul last—doubtless because he joined the community after the others. Originally the names of Barnabas and Paul were followed by a short personal note about them—this, changed in form, has been used at an earlier stage. The Spirit commands that these two of the five prophet-teachers are to be appointed for special service, that is, for preaching the Gospel, as their whole-time and continuous occupation, on the spot in Antioch and in the surrounding country (Syria and Cilicia, anticipated in xi, 26). A line of surcharge (xiii, 3) indicating that they were immediately "sent away" adapts the original statement to the story that follows of their felicitous joint mission to Cyprus–Pisidia–Lycaonia.

[1] See the articles "Simon Magus" and "Simon Peter," by P. W. Schmiedel, in the *Encyclopedia Biblica*, vol. iv. *Translator's note*.

It would be wasted labour to discuss the stories about the mission to Cyprus (xiii, 4–12), Sergius Paulus and the two sorcerers, Bar-Jesus and Elymas. They are wholly fictitious. The words "Saul who is Paul" (xiii, 9) must have belonged originally to the enumeration of the five Antioch prophets in the fragment from the source (xiii, 1). Leaving Cyprus, the two missionaries are supposed to make for Perga in Pamphylia, where Paul leads off with a discourse in the synagogue (xiii, 16–41). Observe that from now onwards Paul is brought to the front while Barnabas' name is little more than a *pro forma* insertion—a peculiarity easily explained when we remember that this joint mission never took place. None the less the story of it may contain elements belonging to the mission which Paul, later on, undertook by himself in these countries, and which, in the place assigned to it in Acts, is reduced to little more than a bare itinerary. The preaching scene at Antioch of Pisidia (xiii, 14–15) follows a conventional type (cf. Luke iv, 16–17). The first part of Paul's discourse (xiii, 16–25) is a résumé copy of Stephen's speech; the second (26–41) a variant of Peter's to the Jews in Jerusalem; the whole constructed to convey an idea of Paul's preaching to Jews. Not less artificial is the account of the second Sabbath (42–52). Vague terms are used for the story of Iconium (xiv, 1–7). The miracle at Lystra (xiv, 8–10), modelled on the cure of the temple paralytic in iii, 1–10, brings on, not quite naturally, the mistake of the people of Lystra who conclude that the missionaries are gods (we are in the land of Philemon and Baucis) while the protest of the apostles is a prelude to Paul's coming discourse on the Areopagus. The stoning of Paul by the Jews, here unnaturally brought in (xiv, 19–20), may come from the source-document, where it belonged to Paul's passage through Iconium (cf. xiv, 5; 2 Corinthians xi, 25). All that follows (20–28) is pious padding. In order to bring his travellers back to their starting point at Antioch the compiler returns them through all the towns from which they have just been driven out. Finally, having got them back to Antioch, he makes them say, with a view to introducing the affair of the legal observances, next to follow, that "God had opened a door of faith to the Gentiles"— as if the Antioch community to whom this information was imparted were not itself partly composed of uncircumcised pagans.

The story of the commotion about legal observances (xv, 1–29) opens with a passage from the source-document to Theophilus. Some brethren, come down from Jerusalem, have been making trouble in the Antioch community by putting it abroad that the Law is obligatory on converts from paganism and, in consequence of the disturbance, Barnabas and Paul are delegated to go into the matter with the elders at Jerusalem (xv, 1–2). But fiction immediately breaks out in the triumphant journey through Phoenicia and Samaria and in the scene-setting of the apostolic conference (3–5); in Peter's discourse (7–11) in which the Cornelius affair is called up; in James' discourse in which approval is given to Peter's thesis, with a reminder of certain prohibitions obligatory on pagans in any case. These prohibitions were in force in some of the churches, but the reminder about them in the letter (23–29) addressed to believers in Syria and Cilicia is there a surcharge (28, doubling 25). The message, as reported in the source-document, was sent "by the elders and the brethren," "the apostles" has been added in a surcharge—a point that deserves consideration. In the message as reported by the source the Judaizing agitators were disavowed, the Jerusalem brethren delegating two of their members to carry the letter to the brethren in Antioch and the neighbourhood (in 26 the praise bestowed on Barnabas and Paul should be replaced by that given to the message-bearers, Silas and Judas, in 22). The conclusion of the story (30–33, 35) may come from the source, except the remark about Silas and Judas, "they too being prophets" (32) which connects with the fiction in xi, 27–30 (*supra*, p. 178). The same is true of 34, inserted by the compiler to make a fit with 40.

Exit Peter: Paul now Occupies the Stage

From this point onwards the Book of Acts is exclusively given up to narrating Paul's missions and captivity; for the writer is deliberately silent about his death. The story of the separation of Paul and Barnabas (xv, 36–41), has been imagined to hide the real cause of strife between Paul and the other missionaries, the isolation in which Paul afterwards found himself and the difficulty of his relations with other propagandists and with the Jerusalem elders. Having anticipated the evangelization of the towns in Lycaonia and Pisidia (xiv, 28) the compiler has now nothing new to tell about them (xv, 36–xvi, 10); he stops at Lystra only for the story of Timothy's circumcision, perhaps invented to compensate and neutralize what is said about Titus in Galatians ii, 1–3. What we read about Paul promulgating apostolic decrees in the churches of Lycaonia is a superfluity added for edification. The source-document has furnished the compiler with the itinerary followed by Paul and his companions (Silas and probably Luke himself) from his departure in Phrygia to his arrival in Troas, but Luke's notes of the journey must be greatly abridged.

The circumstances of the departure for Neapolis, of the arrival at Philippi and of the way in which the preaching began there, are all trustworthy indications lifted from the source-document, but only a few echoes from the source are to be heard in the romance constructed by the compiler to crown the mission at Philippi. The incident of the pythoness, "the maid with the spirit of divination," exorcised by Paul (xvi, 16–19) contradicts the charge brought before the magistrates (20–21) which comes from the source, as do also the popular excitement and the flagellation and imprisonment of the accused (22–23); but the earthquake and the wonders to follow can be nothing but an invention added by the editor; similarly, the pardon Paul is made to procure from the magistrates. The truth of the matter must have been that Paul and Silas, under security given by their friends (a detail which seems to have been shifted into the succeeding story, xvii, 9), were set free on condition of their quitting the city without a moment's delay.

The story of the mission at Thessalonica (xvii, 1-9) must be a greatly shortened and altered version of the source-document. The account of how the preaching began in the synagogue conforms to probability, but the Jewish riot which compels the preachers to flee seems to be a shortened repetition of the riot at Philippi. The notice about Berea (10–13), copied from that about Thessalonica, is no less doubtful, especially in its conclusion (14–15 is not an agreement with 1 Thessalonians iii, 1–2, nor even with Acts xviii, 5).

It is a question whether anyth'ng of the source-document survives in the account of Paul's visit to Athens (xvii, 16–34).

His discourse to the Areopagus is the work of the compiler philosophizing in the style of the second century apologists for Christianity a verse from Aratus (28) replacing the quotations from prophecy which adorn the other discourses in Acts. The rest of the story (16–21, 32–34) does little more than provide a frame for his allocution. But the mention of the small number of converts and of two proper names (34) may come from the source.

At the end of the Corinthian ministry (xviii, 1–16), and as a postscript to the account of it, we encounter another Jewish riot which brings Paul into court before the proconsul Gallio (12–17), the object being to make this high magistrate of Rome proclaim that theological disputes between Christians and Jews have no interest for Roman authority and are matters for the disputants to settle between themselves. The wholly concocted story about Sergius Paulus already encountered (xiii, 7, 12) warns us to be careful when Roman officials are brought into the tale. But if there is anything of historical value in the Gallio story, the date of the proconsulate, 51–52, would merit retention.

The true story of the Corinthian mission has not come through without additions and retouches: the mention of the edict of Claudius against the Jews is added to the notice of Aquila and Priscilla (xviii, 2); so, too, what is said at first about Paul's preaching in the synagogue (4). According to the story in the source, Paul, arriving unaccompanied at Corinth after leaving Athens, worked at his trade in Aquila's house (1–3) until the arrival of Silas and Timothy; when "the word took hold on him" (5 which should follow 3). The uproar among the Jews (6) is another contribution, of the familiar type, from the editor's stock-in-trade. Paul, thus inspired, moves from Aquila's house to that of Justus Titius (7) in order to have easier access to the synagogue. After recording the conversion of Crispus, and a great number of other Corinthians, the source went on to describe the serious difficulties that then arose for Paul and of the encouragement he received from a consoling vision (9–10). The account of his difficulties has been dropped, and one has the impression of another gap between the consoling vision and the indication of the time spent by Paul preaching at Corinth (11).

The stories preliminary to that of the mission at Ephesus are remarkable for a confusion which cannot be accidental. From the very outset, Paul's coming pilgrimage to Jerusalem is vexatiously mixed up with the visit he made to the Galatian churches on his departure from Corinth (xviii, 18-23); the mention of his departure (18) is surcharged with a phrase connecting it with the Gallio affair; Syria is noted as the end of the journey (cf. xx, 3), because the compiler's plan is to bring Paul to Jerusalem between the mission to Corinth and that to Ephesus, and for this purpose he splits Paul's last approach to the Jerusalem brethren into two journeys. Thus we are told of a "vow" taken by Paul, a circumstance in keeping with the pilgrimage; but this vow is precisely the "nazirate" which belongs to the last journey to Jerusalem and comes up in xxi, 23-24, 26. In like manner the visit of Paul to the synagogues (19-23a) is an awkward addition to the source. The intention of it all is to hide the true reason why Paul made no stay in Ephesus, namely, that he was in haste to visit the churches of Galatia and Phrygia in order to counter the Judaizing propaganda which had begun in those regions.

The account of Apollos (24-28) may have been taken from Luke's memoirs, but has been touched up by the editor: the restriction "knowing only the baptism of John" (25), and the completion of his Christian education provided by Aquila and Priscilla are not to be strictly taken. It is the compiler again who would have us believe that this man's service to the Corinthian church consisted in his bold and continual refutation of the Jews (28). His aim in all this is to throw a veil over the rôle of Apollos as Christian preacher at Ephesus itself, and the involuntary part he found himself playing in the subsequent divisions at Corinth. The twelve Ephesian disciples whom Paul is said to have baptized (xix, 1-7) are the converts of Apollos, their number probably reduced, whom the editor presents, along with their master, as adepts of an inferior Christianity and recipients of an unspiritual baptism: save as being, in some measure, historical, the case is parallel to the pure fiction of the converts baptized by Philip in Samaria (cf. p. 176) who had not yet received the Holy Spirit.

All that now remains of the authentic story of Paul's Ephesian ministry, which has been mutilated like all the others, is contained in a few lines (xix, 8-10), from which all details are omitted of the success obtained and the difficulties encountered. We are informed instead of cures operated by garments which had touched Paul's body (11–12), matching those of the same compiler's invention, operated by Peter's shadow (v, 15–16), and of Jewish demon-quellers who, on attempting to drive out a demon in the name of Jesus, are turned upon by the demoniac and soundly beaten up—an anecdote picked up from somewhere and made to adorn the history of Paul. Finally we learn of the tremendous impression made by this incident on the believers, who hastened to burn the books of magic in their possession (17–20); another fiction for the edification of Christian readers. Alas for our loss of the record left by the writer to Theophilus, deliberately emptied of its historical substance and the void filled up with this pitiful stuff!

Continued Manipulation of the Source

The last part of Acts is no more solid in construction than the parts preceding it. Paul at the end of his Ephesian ministry planned to revisit Macedonia and Achaia before proceeding to Jerusalem and from thence to Rome (xix, 21). In order to facilitate the accomplishment of this design he sends two of his companions, Timothy and Erastus (22) to prepare the way in Macedonia. So much comes from the source; but the fact is disguised that the business in hand was to gather a collection for Paul to carry to Jerusalem; a veil is thrown over the fearful dangers encountered by Paul in Ephesus and on the incidents which hindered the fulfilment of his plan, notably the divisions which arose in the community at Corinth, the measures that Paul had to take in consequence and the way in which these obstacles were finally overcome. In place of all that, the compiler tells a story of a riot that broke out against Paul in Ephesus (23–40) in which the lines concerning Paul and his friends (29–31, from "having seized Gaius," and 37) are clearly additions made to the story of an anti-Jewish riot which the compiler has here twisted to his own purpose. What we are told of Paul's departure for Macedonia and Hellas is insignificant (xx, 1–3: the compiler avoids the mention of Corinth). But "the three months" which the compiler assigns to his stay in Hellas probably marked, in the source, the time he spent in Corinth before his departure for Jerusalem. The list given of his travelling companions doubtless includes most of the delegates appointed to carry the collection for the "saints" in Jerusalem; but the list is given too early since Tychicus and Trophimus, the Ephesian delegates, were not to join the party till its later arrival at Miletus.

The itinerary comes from the source-document but has been cut up by editorial insertions. The resurrection of Eutychus by Paul at Troas (xx, 7–12) is to match the resurrection of Dorcas by Peter (ix, 36–42). The compiler has used the halt at Miletus to furnish Paul with an oration (18–35) as a model of the pastoral instruction to be given to the church-leaders. The true reason for the halt was that Paul had to avoid Ephesus and that Miletus was the appointed rendezvous where he was awaiting the bearers of the collection from the Asiatic churches. It is noteworthy that the compiler who, as we shall see, will avoid recording the death of Paul, is here careful to make him give a premonitory hint of it in the course of his speech and to say that he will never visit Asia again (25). The source account has evidently been loaded with new matter in the story of the meeting with the brethren at Tyre: the prophetic warning given to Paul (xxi, 4; cf. xx, 23) hangs in air, while the scene of farewell (xxi, 5–6) repeats that of Miletus, just described (xx, 36–38). In the account of the halt at Caesarea, in the house of Philip, the mention of his four prophetically-gifted daughters would naturally be followed by some prediction on their part, but none is forthcoming. Instead of it the compiler has substituted a prediction by Agabus (10–11) whom he has already exploited in an exactly parallel fiction (xi, 28), bringing him from Jerusalem expressly for the purpose. But the conclusion of the incident (12–14), which comes from the source, seems to indicate that Paul's answer followed a prediction given by Philip's prophetic daughters.

Equally derived from the source are the details of the departure from Caesarea (xxi, 15, except the first words "after these days," co-ordinated with xxi, 10); the arrival at Jerusalem and the lodging with Mnason of Cyprus; probably also the visit to James on the day following their arrival; but the compiler has awkwardly inserted a favourable reception by the brethren before the visit to James. In the account of this visit we look in vain for any mention of the collection which was certainly presented and accepted on that occasion. All we are told is that

Paul gave the story of his mission and that the elders praised God for the results (19–20). That done, the elders address Paul in a speech (20–25) which the compiler has done his best to make unintelligible. Paul is informed that thousands and thousands of *believing* Jews are persuaded that he is everywhere turning Jews away from the Law; in order to reassure them he has only to join himself to four brethren who are undergoing a *nazirate* and pay the expenses due on the fulfilment of their vow; as to the Gentile believers, the duties incumbent on them have been already regulated (a lame reference to xv, 28–29). Let those make sense of this rigmarole who can. What is wrong with it all is clear enough. There were no "thousands and thousands" of Judaizing Christians in Jerusalem and all that is needed is to efface the word "believing." The people exasperated by Paul were the Jews in general, and there can have been no question of reassuring *them*, but only of escaping from their wrath. To effect this Paul, who is himself under the nazirate vow (recall that the compiler has anticipated the vow in xviii, 18), is to join the four brethren who are under the same conditions and in this way will have a good chance of not being observed (the reference to xv, 28–29 is obviously by the hand which interpolated the apostolic letter).

It was a wise precaution, but it failed of its purpose. The proceedings of Paul, the character of the riot that arose in the temple when his presence there was discovered, the intervention of the military tribune and of the Roman soldiers (xxi, 26–34) are taken from the source, which is remarkably precise in these details. But, at the point when Paul is about to be taken into the barracks of Antonia, the compiler perpetrates a manifest interpolation, which stands out among all the others for its audacity. He exhibits Paul as delivering a speech to the Jewish people on his merits as a Pharisee, his conversion and vocation, in order that the Jews may appear, on this solemn occasion, as opposed to the salvation of the Gentiles (21–22). The way in which Paul is made to claim his rights as a Roman citizen (24–29) repeats the earlier and fictitious scene in xvi, 35–40 (*supra*, p. 176). There is no doubt that Paul had to make good his status as a Roman citizen, but he did so to escape the vengeance of the Jewish authorities and get his case adjudicated by the procurator.

The meeting of the Sanhedrim, convoked by the procurator to inform him on the case (xxii, 30–xxiii, 10), is fabrication from beginning to end. The compiler would have it believed that the Pharisees were in accord with the Christians in regard to the messianic hope. An element from the source-document probably remains in the account of Paul's vision (xxiii, 11) which ought to have been reported as belonging to the night which followed his arrest, indicating the turmoil of his mind after his capture, and how he was led to base his hope on ever getting to Rome on an appeal to Roman authority. In order to hide Paul's determination to have recourse to Roman authority the compiler imagines a Jewish plot to kill the prisoner, which a nephew of Paul, also invented for the occasion, reveals to the tribune; the consequence being that this officer decides to get Paul out of the way by transferring him to Caesarea (12–22). The general circumstances of his removal from Jerusalem to Caesarea must have been indicated in the source, but the compiler has magnified the size of the military escort (23–24) and himself composed the tribune's report to Lysias, which has no more reality than the meeting of the Sanhedrim to which it refers (25–30). The journey to Caesarea and the delivery of the prisoner to the procurator Felix are from the source (32 is an adjustment to the magnified size of the escort).

The development of the legal proceedings has been deliberately obscured by the compiler. In the scene-setting for the judicial investigation presided over by Felix the naming of the high priest is an error: Ananias was not high priest in Felix' time (xxiv, 1; same error xxiii, 2). The speech of the advocate Tertullus (2–9) and Paul's reply (10–21) are in the compiler's manner. The impression is given that the case was thoroughly investigated, whereas the question then at issue was that of competence to try it. Some influence from the source may be detected in what Paul says about the time elapsed since his arrival in Jerusalem (11) and in the veiled reference to the collection (17). Felix, "knowing all about" Christian propaganda, adjourns the decision (22), though the time for resuming the investigation, "when Lysias shall come," is probably editorial. The measures ordered in regard to the prisoner (23) come from the source. Paul's conversation with Felix and his wife Drusilla (24–26) is a forerunner of the grand affair constructed later on for Agrippa II and Berenice (xxv, 13–xxvi, 32). The intention ascribed to Felix of placating the Jews by not releasing Paul before handing over his powers to Festus (27*b*) has the look of another editorial touch.

The subsequent narration of the resumption of the affair on the arrival of Festus (xxv, 1–5); the sitting of the court (6–8, doubtless a shortened account); the decision of Festus (9); the appeal to Caesar and the granting of the appeal by the procurator (10–12), so far as the substance is concerned, come from the source. The editor has turned the demand of the Sanhedrim for delivery of the prisoner to its jurisdiction into one asking for a "favour" and inserted a Jewish plot (3). By no possibility could Festus remit Paul to the Sanhedrim as an act of benevolence. The very terms of the final sentence make it clear that appeal to the imperial tribunal was the only means left to Paul for saving his life (10–12). It is the compiler who represents Festus as, on the one hand, persuaded of Paul's innocence and, on the other, willing to make a present of his person to the Jews, who would certainly have put him to death. The dialogue between Festus and Agrippa and the story of the meeting organized for the satisfaction of this petty Jewish king are a long piece of editorial padding, though there are signs that it is not by the same hand as the general run of earlier fictions. It is made to rest upon an absurd supposition, namely that Festus had nothing to put into his official report and hoped to get material from the meeting (26). What the compiler is aiming at in all this is to accumulate proofs of Paul's innocence and so discredit in advance the condemnation passed on Paul in Rome, of which when he comes to it, he will say not a word.

The narrative of the journey from Caesarea to Rome (xxvii, 1–xxviii, 16) seems to have been changed only by additions mostly intended to raise Paul's importance. These are easily detected: prophetic warning, unheeded, to winter in Crete instead of at the place called Fair Haven; recall of this warning in the midst of the tempest and prophecy of safety for the ship's company; denunciation of the sailors who would abandon the ship and leave the passengers to perish in it; encouragement by word and example to take food (xxvii, 9–36, "While waiting for day," 33, runs on in the source with "they lightened the ship," 38; 37

should come after 44). In the account of the stay in Malta and of the end of the journey we may suspect the little miracle of Paul and the viper, the cures performed on the Governor and other inhabitants of the island, the stay of seven days at Puteoli, and especially the story of the whole Roman community coming as far as the Appian Forum and Three Taverns to present themselves to Paul (xxviii, 15).

The last "we" of the source-document occurs in the notice of Paul's arrival in Rome and of the permission extended to him to remain in his own lodgings under the continual guard of a soldier (16). This was probably followed in the source by mention (30) of the two years spent by Paul under these conditions to which the compiler has added a gloss (31) to bring out the liberty then enjoyed by the apostle to preach in his own dwelling. The scene, twice repeated, of his interviews with the Jews of Rome (17–28; 29 is a gloss repeating 24–25) stands out among all the other fictions as most clearly the compiler's work. Taken together with the final gloss in 31 it constitutes the conclusion of the book as conceived by the final editor, and symbolically sums up the apologetic thesis he aimed at making good: that Christianity is the true Judaism and, the Jews having rejected it, its true representatives are now the Gentiles; that being so, it has right to the liberty which Roman law allows to the Jewish cult.

Significant Silence of Acts as to the Fate of Paul

We know not, and probably will never know, at what point the writer of the second book to Theophilus brought his story to a close. But there is no denying that the canonical Book of Acts came into being long after the death of Paul; whence it follows that the silence of the compiler regarding it is voluntary and deliberate. He says nothing about it because what he knew and might have said would not have been easily reconciled with his apologetic aims. It may be objected that he could not hide a fact of this kind if it had already happened. The answer is that from one end of the book to the other he is busy in omitting from the facts he knew all those of which he did not wish to speak, and in falsifying at will the shape of those which it suited him to record or which he found it impossible to pass by in silence.

The interest of his apologetic was not the only consideration which governed his proceeding. He is quick to seize any opportunity to leave the way open for the currency of certain legends to which it would have been imprudent to give overt support. After all, his silence about the death of Peter is every whit as surprising as his silence about the death of Paul. We have seen what he leaves us at liberty to infer when, coming to Peter's flight from Jerusalem, he tells us mysteriously that the chief of the Twelve departed "to another place." The document known as the Canon of Muratori may possibly throw some light on the silence of Acts regarding the death of the two apostles. The author of this text observes quite innocently that Luke—whom he supposes to be the author of Acts—"has left aside the passion of Peter and the departure of Paul for Spain," which probably means, "and the passion of Paul after his journey to Spain." This is the Roman legend as completely formed at the end of the second century, which was already in existence, though less sure of itself, when Acts was shaped and elaborated about 130–140. To reproduce the legend at that date was more than the compiler of Acts dared to do; but still less was he disposed to put it out of the question. We may recall how careful he is in the third Gospel and in Acts to avoid contradicting the Ephesian legend about the apostle John.

But then, it will be said, is not the third Gospel, whatever may be said of the others, a book of history along with its sequel the Acts of the Apostles? No: both are for catechetical edification, and we have said enough to prove it. But does not the silence of Acts, explained as above, become an argument against Peter ever coming to Rome? It is quite possible, and we have already hinted that there is need for a new inquiry into the matter (cf. *supra*, p.179).

Chapter VII

THE GOSPEL ACCORDING TO JOHN

WE have already unmasked the audacious literary fiction by means of which the Gospel called John's was introduced to the Asiatic churches among which it was first published and presented as embodying the only perfect type of Gospel catechesis. Such a mode of presenting the book makes it clear that the intention of its authors was not to complete the synoptic catechesis but to supplant it outright, in which, however, this new catechesis did not succeed. It is equally certain that the Johannine Gospel owed much, in its first form, to the Synoptics, and that in order, at a later stage and in regions outside that of its origin, to render it acceptable along with them, various additions were made to it with a view to bringing it more into line with the books in opposition to which it was at first brought out, and giving it a greater resemblance to them. The first publication can hardly have been effected before 135–140; the additions and retouches on synoptic lines will have been introduced soon afterwards when Asiatic Christianity was uniting with that of other churches to make common front against the flood of gnosticism and especially against Marcion. It is none the less true that the fourth Gospel is, essentially, a gnostic document, although its structure-form proclaims it a Christian catechism: moreover it has absorbed a number of gnostic pieces, rhythmic utterances of mystic teaching, originally composed outside the Gospel framework and incorporated with it by methods to be indicated presently, just as the Synoptics have incorporated many a fragment of the earlier eschatological teaching. The result is that the Johannine catechesis is hardly less complex than the synoptic. We cannot claim to untie all its knots. At least let us see what patient analysis of the book will reveal.

Taking it as traditionally constructed we can distinguish in it two principal parts: first, the Epiphany of the Christ, as Logos or incarnate Son of God, in his public ministry (i–xi); second, the preliminaries, teachings and circumstances of his death and resurrection (xii–xxi).

THE PROLOGUE: FIRST PHASE

Dissertation on the prologue to John, its origin, integrity and relation to the body of the book, has been going on for a long time and in many quarters. Here we confine ourselves to a positive statement of what seems to us most probable. Taken as tradition presents it (i, 1–18) the prologue is not a part of the Gospel in the sense of a preface summarizing its theme, but a deeply thought out explanation of what is to follow, and this explanation, thrown into the form of a theological poem, may originally have existed independently of the book to which it is now attached. This prologue, moreover, in the canonical presentation of it, has been glossed and surcharged, as the Gospel itself has also been in every one of its parts.

The first strophe declares the origin, creative activity and life-giving manifestation of the divine Logos (1–5; in 3–4 the logical and rhythmical balance of the strophe requires the cutting of the lines thus: "And without him nothing has come into being. What has come into being, in him was life. And the life," etc.). Our prologue thus announces itself at the outset as, in substance, a piece of high gnosis, and a poem exactly rhythmical in form. But what now follows immediately is not in perfect keeping with this sublime beginning. At this point, and again later on, the sequence is broken by reference to John the Baptist, two interpolations, each striking a false note in the context and dislocating its primitive structure (6–8, 15–16). The object of these intrusions is clearly that of conforming our Gospel to the synoptic tradition freely interpreted in the sense of the Johannine gnosis. But it would be grave error to suppose, as some have done, that the prologue was originally concerned with John the Baptist himself. Whatever may have been said, the Mandean texts furnish not the slightest support to such a conjecture.[1]

It is in concrete terms that the author of the poem describes the manifestation of the divine Logos, made flesh that he may gather around him the children of God, these regenerated by the grace and truth which Jesus Christ procures for his own, as Moses procured Law for the Jews. But the gloss which brings John the Baptist into the poem is not solitary; others have been practised. The line "to those who believe in his name"

---

[1] See *Le Mandéism et les origines chrétiennes* (27–46, 148–155).

(12c) is an explanation co-ordinate to what follows in the traditional text, *"they who are* not born of blood," etc. At first sight one sees no need to say that the children of God are not made such by human generation: but the primitive reading is that known to Irenaeus and Tertullian: "He who was born not of blood, nor of the will of the flesh (nor of the will of man) but of God," the words "nor of the will of a man" having been added to emphasize the miraculous conception of the Christ, the original text simply stating that the Christ was born of God, because the Logos had taken flesh to himself by a mode with which natural generation had nothing whatever to do (cf. Jesus' reply to Mary, ii, 4 and Hebrews vii, 3). After (i, 14): "And the Word was made flesh and dwelt among us" the next words should be "full of grace and truth" continuing with 16–17, and dropping "we beheld his glory, as of the only begotten son from the Father," the last a heavy handed and prosaic gloss. Finally, the verse (i, 18): "No man has seen the Father," etc., is a theological gloss intended to explain how the Word-Son, as the sole master of the mystery and the exegete of God, is able to bring grace and truth into the world.

Restored to its original form the primitive poem would read as follows:[1]

> Au commencement était le Logos,
>> et le Logos était près de Dieu,
>> et le Logos était dieu.
> Il était au commencement près de Dieu:
>> tout par lui s'est fait,
>> et sans lui ne s'est fait rien.
> Ce qui s'est fait en lui fut vie,
>> et la vie était la lumière des hommes;
> Et la lumière dans les ténèbres luit,
>> et les ténèbres ne l'ont point saisie. [   ]
>
> La lumière vraie,
>> qui éclaire tout homme
>> est venue dans le monde,
> Dans le monde Il fut,
>> le monde (qui) par lui a été fait,
>> et le monde ne le connut pas.

---

[1] As translation would destroy the rhythm of the poem as here restored by M. Loisy, his version is presented in the original. The empty brackets indicate the points at which the poem has been glossed or interpolated. *Translator's note.*

Chez lui il est venu,
  et les siens ne le reçurent pas;
Mais, tous ceux qui l'ont reçu,
  il leur a donné pouvoir de devenir enfants de Dieu. [ ]

Lui qui, non des sangs,
  ni du vouloir de la chair, [ ]
  mais de Dieu est né.
Le Logos est devenu chair
  et il a habité parmi nous, [ ]
  plein de grâce et de vérité. [ ]
(Et) de sa plénitude tous nous avons reçu,
  grâce pour grâce,
Parce que la Loi par Moïse a été donnée,
  la grâce et la vérité par Jésus-Christ sont arrivées. [ ]

John the Baptist has been surreptitiously introduced into the prologue by way of preparing for his express testimony to the Christ. This testimony is distributed over two major scenes (i, 19–28, 29–36) which are again subdivided into smaller. The opening scene presents, first, the question of the priests; then, the question of the Pharisees: the second contains, in the first half, John's direct and express witness to "the Lamb of God," whose precursor he declares himself to be; in the second he claims to have seen the Spirit descending upon him who baptizes in the Spirit. "The Lamb" must have been consciously borrowed from the Apocalypse; in the final phase of the Gospel we shall find the mystical relation of the Christ to the paschal lamb clearly indicated. The utmost care is taken to avoid the statement that Jesus was baptized by John, and the general outlines of the scene, in spite of apparent precision in a few details, are wavering and uncertain. The indication of the locality where John was then operating as "Bethany beyond Jordan" has the look of affectation on the part of the narrator. He seems to have known all the places he mentions, but it would be imprudent to conclude that there is any historical warrant for localizing the Baptist at Bethany. Many a marvel which never took place is localized by our narrator quite as minutely as is the incident before us.

Editorial artifice is not less apparent in representing the first disciples of Jesus as sent to him by John; but the transition to the stories (35–37) is unnatural and the indication of the return to Galilee (43) is out of place. The disciples are called up on four occasions (35–39, 40–42, 43, 44–51), all four first conceived as preliminary to the coming manifestation of the Christ in Galilee. The anonymous disciple of the first vocation, discreetly associated with Andrew, and won to the faith before Peter, is probably he who later on will be marked out as "the disciple whom Jesus loved" (xiii, 23). Peter, when his turn comes, is nevertheless allowed a certain prominence, this being the occasion on which Simon receives his surname, but without any indication of its mystic meaning. The Philip, here honoured by a call confined to himself alone (43), is probably the Philip of whom Asiatic Christianity retained some memory. Nathanael, who receives a fuller notice than any of the others, is a person unknown to the synoptic tradition.

Were these stories taken as historical, or even as pretending to be so, they would leave the reader with a hopelessly confused impression. Andrew and his unnamed companion are represented as believing, on the assurance of John the Baptist, that Jesus is "the Lamb of God"; but Andrew's statement to his brother Simon is: "We have found the Messiah" (41) and Philip, speaking in the same sense, says to Nathanael (45): "we have found him of whom Moses in the Law, and the prophets, did write; he is Jesus, son of Joseph, of Nazareth." And Jesus himself, when his gift of second sight has caused Nathanael to recognize him as "Son of God, the King of Israel," declares that he is "Son of Man" (51): "Verily, verily I say unto you, ye shall see the heavens open and the angels of God ascending and descending on the Son of Man" —an assertion not clearly made good in the sequel to the stories. Certainly the writer does not wish it to be understood that Jesus was the real son of Joseph, nor that Nazareth was his real birthplace. He merely accepts the synoptic interpretation of the word "Nazorean." The true definition of the Christ lies in his qualification as Son of God in the transcendent sense established by the prologue; all the rest is intended to convey that the Christ and the Son of Man of the Synoptics are identified with this Son of God.

The sons of Zebedee seem to have been forgotten in our Gospel's account of the calling of the disciples, whence it follows that the anonymous disciple, probably the well-beloved, is not, so far as that goes, identified with the apostle John. On the whole our compiler has not troubled himself to be complete in his account of the vocations, for he seems to suppose, from now on, that Jesus has around him the group of Twelve.

The Miracle at Cana: the First "Sign"

All we have read up to this point is preparation for the epiphany of the Christ, which begins in the miracle at Cana. To the commentators who know exactly where Cana is to be found on the map we would say: enough if we localize it as the place where Jesus first "revealed his glory," so that, from that moment, "his disciples believed in him." The epiphany apparently takes place in a domestic circle; there is a marriage at Cana: the mother of Jesus is there; Jesus arrives with his disciples; they are invited to the feast; but there is no more wine. Jesus orders six urns, placed there for Jewish purification, to be filled with water; the water is changed into wine; and this is the first "sign" given by Jesus. Observe that the miracle is a "sign"; for it is precisely in this that it differs from the same prodigy when performed in the sanctuaries of Dionysus, from which our author has borrowed it. What does the sign signify? The general meaning is that the economy of the Law with its rules of outward purification must now give way to the life-giving economy of faith in the immortal Christ, as symbolized in the Christian sacrament.

Let us pause to consider the feature of this "sign" which, from the earliest time till now, has most disconcerted the commentators. When Jesus and his disciples have taken their places among the guests the wine has given out; the supply for the marriage is exhausted. Jesus' mother then says to him, "there is no more wine." Jesus replies, "Woman, what is there (in common) between me and thee? My hour is not yet come." His mother says to the servants, "do whatever he tells you." Whereupon Jesus orders the urns to be filled and the miracle is effected. What can we make of this? Taken one by one as they stand the statements are incoherent and make up an unintelligible phantasmagory. But not so when we consider the profound meaning of the whole presentation. The mother of Jesus is not mentioned by her proper name; but the person designated is Mary who is, apparently, Jesus' mother, just as Joseph has been previously named as, apparently, his father (i, 45). But this mother stands also for the Judaism which waited for the Kingdom of God, and it is in that character that she is made to declare "there is no more wine." Jesus begins by answering that between him and his putative mother there is nothing in common, because there is nothing earthly in his origin; his hour, which has not yet come, is the hour of his death, on which salvation depends. None the less, he does, there and then, what he has been implicitly asked to do, giving the lesson in the form of a symbol.

Second Sign: Expulsion of the Traders from the Temple

The second "sign" worked by Jesus is the expulsion of the traders from the Temple (ii, 13–17). But before coming to it we are told (12) that Jesus went down to Capernaum, he, his mother, his brothers and disciples. This is the first mention of his brothers, which we might have expected at an earlier stage; but we are beginning to understand that our evangelist is engaged upon something very different from biography. At Capernaum their stay has but a few days' duration because "the Passover of the Jews is at hand" and Jesus will seize the opportunity to manifest himself in Jerusalem. The idea is that the Christ will not preach in Galilee till after he has preached in Jerusalem and in Judea. He is taken to Capernaum only for the purpose of doing a measure of justice to the synoptic tradition (especially Matthew iv, 13), and at the same time arranging a transition to the narrative that follows. From now onwards it is apparent that our gospel editor takes the line of restricting the ministry in Galilee that he may enlarge a ministry in Jerusalem and Judea, which is almost entirely ignored by the synoptic catechesis.

As the author has previously used the expression "the purifications *of the Jews*," so now he speaks of "the Passover *of the Jews*." The reason is that his readers are Gentile Christians unacquainted with Jewish customs, and that he himself looks upon Judaism from the outside as one who himself is not a Jew. Moreover the object of Jesus in coming to Jerusalem at the time of the Feast is, not so much to take part in it, as there and then to "manifest his glory." As the synoptic tradition sees in the expulsion of the traders the first act of the messianic ministry in Jerusalem, so our evangelist attaches it to Jesus' first stay in the holy city. But he interprets it after his own manner, not merely as an act of authority, but as a "sign."

Without pausing over details in the description of the occurrence, let us fix attention on the passage most characteristic both of the spirit of our Gospel and of its chronology (ii, 18–22, already quoted and discussed, p. 60).

The question here ascribed to "the Jews" after the expulsion of the traders is the question which, in the Synoptics, is put to Jesus by the elders of the Sanhedrim (Mark xi, 27–28; Matthew xxi, 23–24; Luke xx, 1–2) combined with the demand for a sign in the same Gospels (Matthew xii, 38; cf. Mark viii, 11; Luke xi, 16). In the Christ's reply as here given a sign is actually offered, but one that would have been wholly unintelligble to his audience, as indeed it has remained for many commentators. This reply is, in effect, an enigmatic combination of Jesus' answer to the demand for a sign in Matthew (xii, 39–40) with the saying of the Christ about the temple, brought up against him in the synoptic account of the trial before Caiaphas (Matthew xxvi, 61; Mark xiv, 58). But here there is a difference in the phrasing. Instead of "I will destroy this temple," he now says "destroy it," as though challenging the Jews to destroy it themselves. For the temple of which he now speaks is his own body. His answer is thus equivalent to the refusal of a sign for the present and, for the future, to the sign of Jonah in the sense given to it by Matthew (*loc. cit.*). To discuss the verisimilitude of the reply would clearly be quite superfluous, and equally so to discuss, from that point of view, what the Jews answer about the forty-six years occupied by the construction of the temple. In the final analysis, what the writer would here convey is his conception of the age of the Christ, forty-six years when he expelled the traders, forty-nine (completed) when he died, so that his jubilee year would be that of his entry on the immortal glory awaiting him on his resurrection (cf. *supra*, p. 61). The disciples themselves are described as unable to find the key to this symbolic riddle till after the resurrection of the Christ (22). We are, then, in presence of a second "sign" parallel to the "sign" of Cana. Like the first, it figures the renewal of the Covenant, substituting Grace for Law, and brought about by the death and resurrection of the incarnate Son of God. Let who will believe that what is here narrated really happened.

The remark on the numerous conversions which Jesus made on this occasion in Jerusalem and on the little value he attached to them, because he knew what was in man (23–25), must be understood as referring to inadequate faith or, rather, to a lower and Judaizing type of faith. This was probably aimed originally at vulgar Messianism and the notion of the Kingdom of God as purely terrestrial and eschatological. So understood the remark links on to the case of Nicodemus and brings on the discourse supposed to have been addressed to him.

Nicodemus

The case of Nicodemus (iii, 1–12) is imagined in order to provide an apparently historical frame for the teaching about spiritual regeneration which the Son, sent from God to save the world and not to judge it, procures for the believer by baptism (5–6, 8, 11–13, 16–18). We find accordingly that this teaching contains an implied criticism of the common eschatology, even that of the Johannine apocalypse. The opening part has been broken by interruptions in accordance with the narrative framework, which almost have the effect of transforming this didactic poem into a dialogue between Jesus and Nicodemus (7, 9–10, 14–15). We shall encounter other applications of the same technique, by means of which interlocutors with Jesus are made to commit blunders, or speak beside the point, in order to bring out the sequent instruction. Nicodemus is a development of the questioner in the Synoptics who asks Jesus what he must do to "inherit eternal life." In the Synoptics Jesus answers the question by laying down the moral conditions for admission to the Kingdom of God; here, the Kingdom is an inward possession of the believer, realized in the Church, to which the believer is initiated by a symbolic act effecting the spiritual regeneration of the individual performing it, and in keeping with the faith in him which the Son, come from God, claims for himself. This lesson on regeneration by water and the Spirit is the first explanation of the spiritual Gospel and comes in most aptly.

We find the lesson completed by a second witness borne by John the Baptist (iii, 26–36); it is the work of an editor, constructed by transposing elements taken from the Synoptics (Matthew xi, 2–19; Luke vii, 18–35). The setting of the scene (22–26), in spite of its geographical precisions, is wholly fanciful. But let the fact be noted that the writer finds it quite in order to represent both Jesus and John as baptizing simultaneously and at no great distance the one from the other. (An unconvincing attempt to put this right is made later on (iv, 2) where we are told that Jesus did not baptize, but only his disciples.) An altercation arising about the matter between John's disciples and *a Jew* (a correction which makes nonsense; the original text was *Jesus*), the disciples come to John to inform him of the proceedings of a rival Baptizer, which they seem to regard as disloyal to him: whereupon John explains himself, recalling his former witness and proclaiming the transcendent superiority of Jesus (note in 28 the figure of the bridegroom and the best man at the wedding, echo of Mark ii, 19–20; Matthew ix, 15; Luke v, 34–35). John's discourse has the same look of planned construction, and of superposition, as the story introducing it.

The Woman of Samaria

From now onwards reference to John is incidental only (v, 33, 36; x, 40–41). Nevertheless the theme of water and the Spirit is not abandoned, but is taken up again in the story of the Samaritan woman, where it will be completed by the theme of the harvest (iv, 5–42). An artificial junction links this episode to the Baptist's testimony (1–4); but the narrative, taken as a whole, is not all of one piece. It looks as if an original story in which Jesus and the woman were the only speakers had been subsequently enlarged by the passages which refer to the disciples (iv, 8, 27, 31, 33, 37–38); there are signs also that, in order to harmonize with the present context, the primitive itinerary which made Jesus pass through Samaria on his way from Galilee to Judea, has been turned round and the whole episode antedated. The setting of the scene is constructed with the same technique which set the scene for Nicodemus, and the conversation proceeds by fits and starts, as these are prompted by the irrelevant replies of the woman to Jesus' remarks. The main purpose is to develop the mystic theme of living water, the gift of the Spirit, which is also the gift of immortality, and, at the same time, to bring out the insignificance of the common eschatology in presence of this mysterious truth: "God is Spirit and it is in Spirit and truth that worshippers must adore him" (24). What is said about the harvest (35–38) is an allegorical paraphrase of a synoptic saying (Matthew ix, 37–38; Luke x, 2) combined with the Sower of the parable; those who "have laboured" are Jesus and the apostolic generation; the reapers are the evangelist's contemporaries. Needless to say, the conversion of the Samaritans and of the Samaritan woman is no fact of history but a symbol of the Gentiles converted to the Christian mystery.

A New Series of "Signs"

After the first miracle at Cana Jesus returns to Jerusalem and appears there as master of the Temple; after the second (revival of the royal officer's son) he returns to the holy city to show himself master of the Sabbath. The first cycle of miracles and discourses concerns the superiority of Christianity, religion of Spirit, over Judaism, religion of ineffectual symbols; the second cycle, which includes the cure of the royal officer's son, the cure of the paralytic at Bethesda and the multiplication of the loaves, together with discourses interpreting the last two (v, 19–46; vi, 22–71), will reveal Jesus as the active principle and sustaining food of the true life. But first it is necessary to bring Jesus from Samaria into Galilee.

This change of place is an editorial device, the departure being explained by the saying: "prophet has no honour in his own country," which comes from the Synoptics (Mark vi, 4; Matthew xiii, 57; Luke iv, 24). But here it receives a particular application which many commentators are slow to observe. Jesus has just been recognized as "Saviour of the World" (42) by the Samaritans; but it is not in the order of Providence that the glory of the Son of God, though revealed in the course of his earthly existence, should be recognized before his death by all men on Israelite territory, the exception of Samaria not destroying the rule.

The new series of "signs" begins at Cana, where Jesus, operating at a distance, cures the royal officer's son (46–54), a transposition to Cana of the synoptic cure of the centurion's son (Matthew viii, 5–13) or servant (Luke vii, 1–10) at Capernaum. Instead of directly prefiguring the conversion of the Gentiles, as in Matthew and Luke, the story here becomes a lesson in the true kind of faith, that which believes on the strength of the uttered word, the characteristic faith of mystical Christianity which ought to characterize the Gentile church, in contrast to the kind which demands miracles.

After curing the officer's son, Jesus leaves Cana and comes to Jerusalem where he cures a paralytic on the Sabbath day (v, 1–18). By this miracle an opening is made for a description of the life-giving work which the Father has sent his Son into the world to accomplish (19–30). While invoking the witness borne to him by the Father, Jesus reproaches the Jews for not hearkening to what John has said of him and for paying no heed to what Moses has written (31–47). All of it is legendary fiction, and cannot indeed be anything else. The evangelist has two reasons for allotting so large a place to the Judean mission; on the one hand, he is working a polemical theme against the Jews objecting that Jerusalem is the true place of the prophets and of the Messiah's epiphany; on the other, he partly dispossesses Capernaum in favour of Cana in order that Jesus may not appear to have preached only in one little corner of Galilee.

The text does not give the name of the feast for which Jesus "went up to Jerusalem," but calls it "the feast of the Jews," their feast *par excellence*, which can only have been the Passover. Irenaeus says that this Passover is the second of three he has counted in the public life of the Christ (*Heresies*, ii, 22, 4), and would hardly have been more positive if he had actually read the word "Passover" in the passage before us; perhaps that is what he did read. The chronological scheme of our Gospel involves a total duration for Jesus' ministry, or epiphany, of three and a half years, the messianic number (cf. *supra*, p. 60). This is why three Passovers are indicated before that which coincides with his death: the first follows the first miracle at Cana (ii, 13); we are now at the second; the third will be mentioned in connection with the multiplication of the loaves (vi, 4). The history of the text shows that, in order to bring John into line with the Synoptics on this point, attempts were made to suppress both the second Passover and the third. It is, however, true that the Johannine chronology is imaginary and symbolic; but so is everything that it encloses. The paralytic miraculously cured at the Pool of Bethesda is the paralytic of Capernaum symbolically interpreted (cf. Mark ii, 9, 11; Matthew ix, 5, 6; Luke v, 22-24) and combined with the synoptic Sabbath story (Mark iii, 1-5; Matthew xii, 9-13; Luke vi, 6-11).

Discourses following the "Signs"

The attitude of the Jews in presence of this violation of the Sabbath corresponds to the conclusion of the Sabbath stories in the first three Gospels (Mark iii, 6; Matthew xii, 14) but with an addition, entirely Johannine in conception (v, 16-18), linked on to the declaration of Jesus about the everlasting joint action of his Father and himself: "for this cause the Jews sought the more to kill him, because he not only brake the Sabbath, but also said that his father was God, making himself equal with God." This brings on the first instruction concerning the working of God, with the Son working in conjunction. To this discourse a few additions have been made for the purpose of somehow adjusting a mystical theory of salvation to the popular conception of the Last Things, which the theory contradicts by suppressing it (v, 22; 28-30, referring to a material resurrection, opening of tombs, etc., are in contradiction with the texts which represent the resurrection as purely spiritual).

The second discourse (31-47), in which the witness of John and of the Scriptures is evoked against the Jews, seems to be entirely of secondary authorship. But it is possible that the passage: "I am come in the name of my Father and you receive me not; if another comes in his own name, him you will receive" is aimed at the false Messiah Barkochba. In the sayings attached to the Feast of Tabernacles (vii) there are some which relate to the cure (v) of the paralytic (vii, 20-24, or rather 15-24, since 25 is exactly in sequence to 14). A transposition has obviously taken place in the text. The fact is that while the fourth Gospel, at one stage of its compilation, was constructed on an orderly plan, there has been considerable dislocation of the plan in subsequent redaction.

The sixth chapter is dominated throughout by the idea of the Christ as bread of life; the multiplication of loaves (1-14) is the symbol of it; the miracle of Jesus walking on the sea (16-21) is an aid to its comprehension; the four discourses that follow (22-40, 41-51, 52-59, 66-71) explain it more fully. The different impressions produced on the Jews by each of these discourses represents the Jewish attitude towards the mystery of salvation, in contrast to the Christian. The general effect is to bring the mystery to summary form in the doctrine of the living and life-giving bread and in the corresponding sacrament.

The Bread of Life

The setting for the multiplication of the loaves is copied from the Synoptics (Matthew xiv, 15; cf. Mark vi, 33) but combined with the scene of the Discourse on the Mountain in Matthew, the miracle itself being constructed so as to symbolize the new faith and the mystery of salvation. The reason for saying "the Passover of the Jews was at hand" is that the multiplication of the loaves, already a figure of the eucharist in the synoptic account, is going to be presented in the same way in the coming discourse on the bread of life, and that a reminder of the Passover is a fitting introduction to the eucharistic symbolism about to be presented. Fundamentally, this is the place at which our Gospel places the institution of the Supper, the eucharist being considered throughout by the evangelist as a mystery which ought not to be offered to his readers in the direct terms used in First Corinthians (xi) and in the Synoptics.

The story of the miracle is also borrowed from the Synoptics but with a few added touches to adapt it to the Johannine conceptions; notable is the personal intervention of Philip and Andrew, whom we know already in the vocation stories (i, 40, 43), and in a conclusion all its own. The crowd, impressed by the miracle, conclude that Jesus is the Messiah and are about to carry him off and make him King: but Jesus gives their enthusiasm no countenance and withdraws out of their reach. In this both Jewish Messianism and the common eschatology of the Christians are implicitly condemned.

In the miracle of the Christ walking on the water we find the same free and symbolic adaptation of what the Synopsis has to tell (Matthew xiv, 22–27, 32–33; Mark vi, 45–52). The lesson is that the immortal Christ will never abandon his own, all appearances to the contrary notwithstanding.

By an obviously forced transition the crowd, which had been the witness and beneficiary of the multiplied loaves, is brought back to Jesus, on the following day, to hear his discourse on the bread of life (vi, 22–58). In its original form the discourse is a didactic poem, like the discourse to Nicodemus, and quite as easy to reconstruct if we eliminate the interplay of dialogue, which breaks the poem at several points (28–31, 34, 41–42, 51a–52), and omit a special instruction on predestination which someone has tried to incorporate into the main discourse, an interpolation made in order to affirm the resurrection of the dead (end of verses 39, 40, 44). Moreover it is clear enough that the last strophe of the poem (to be extracted from 53–58, dropping "I will raise him up at the last day" in 54 and 58b) has been added to introduce the sacramental system taken by the synoptic tradition from First Corinthians (xi, 24–25), the symbolism, namely, of the bread-body and the wine-blood of the Christ.

Like the end of the discussion, the end of the story which frames it (59–71) is also editorial work. The intentions behind it are various; to soften down the hardest sayings of the discourse, in the last strophe, by an explanation which emphasizes their spiritual character (61, 63);[1] to create the opportunity for Peter's confession, imitated from the Synoptics but with a Johannine interpolation (Matthew xvi, 16; Mark viii, 29; Luke ix, 20), and to make room for the first denunciation of the traitor Judas (64–65, 70). The whole is intended to bring out the blindness of the Jews and of certain Judaizing Christians in presence of the mystery just explained. Even Judas is not, as some would have us think, an individual traitor on whom the apostle John vents his spite. He personifies the Jews' hatred of Jesus and of Christianity.

SECOND PHASE

The scene for the second phase of the Christ's combat with the Jewish enemy is laid exclusively in Jerusalem and covers the last year of Jesus' ministry. The events and discourses of chapter vi having been dated with reference to the Passover at the beginning of this final year, those which fill the five chapters to follow, and end at the great Passover coincident with the Passion, fall into two groups attached for their placing to two intermediate festivals, that of Tabernacles and that of the Dedication. De-

[1] Verse 62, asserting the bodily ascension of the "Son of Man" is a gloss.

pendent on the first are some polemic discourses and the cure of the man born blind, with the discourse that follows it (x, 1–21), the whole dominated by the idea of the Christ as light of the world. The second group marks the definite breach between the Christ and the Jews (x, 22–42). Before the last Easter will come the raising of Lazarus, symbol of the Christ-life and greatest "sign" of all.

The preamble (vii, 1–13) introducing this second series of doings and teachings is deeply confused. Jesus abstains from going about in Judea because the Jews are resolved to kill him and confines himself to Galilee; the Feast of Tabernacles coming round, his brothers, who however do not believe in him, urge him to go to Jerusalem and reveal himself there as what he pretends to be; Jesus refuses, alleging that his hour is not yet come; his brothers then depart for the Feast; he follows them *incognito*; goes up to the temple in the midst of the solemnities and begins to teach. The opening of the preamble is based on the cure of the paralytic at the Pool of Bethesda (cf. v, 16–18), but the dialogue with the brothers, parallel to the remarks exchanged between Jesus and his mother at Cana, suggests that Jesus is about to show himself at Jerusalem for the first time. His brothers, moreover, personify incredulous Judaism. Instead of vainly speculating on the meaning of it all, we are content to remark once more that our Gospel must have been worked over more than once before assuming its final form. Let it be remembered also that the first words of the preaching attributed to Jesus in vii, 15–24 need to be placed at the end of the story of the paralytic in v.

The preamble analysed in the last paragraph introduces the discussion, which is placed further on (vii, 25–36), concerning the origin of Jesus, where an answer is given to an objection from the Jews. Their objection is that everybody knows where Jesus comes from, whereas, when Messiah shall appear, nobody will know his place of origin. Jesus answers that the Jews are under a great illusion in thinking they know that he comes from Nazareth and is the son of Joseph; he alone knows whence he came and who sent him. (A certain kind of critical benevolence must be applied to the matter if we are to overlook the plain contradiction of the birth stories in Matthew and Luke conveyed by these statements.) Duplicates are not wanting in these chapters (vii and viii): for example, the discussion on the presumed origin of the Christ, the Jews maintaining that he was not to come from Galilee but from Bethlehem in Judea and would belong to the race of David (vii, 40–52), which takes us over the same ground as vii, 26–38 and implicitly repeats the contradiction of the birth stories in the Synoptics; and, again, the repetition of the attempts to take Jesus prisoner, and each time with no success (vii, 30, 44; viii, 20, 59). Found anywhere else than in a book we are accustomed to venerate, and is truly worthy of veneration in many parts of it, these wranglings about the origin of the Christ would impress us as a rather tiresome academic exercise. They are the echoes of ancient controversies between Christians and Jews.

An editorial hand has inserted into the text a passage (vii, 37–39) which it is important to note, not only on account of its correspondence with another insertion into the story of the Passion (xix, 31–37), but also because it is seldom rightly understood. The passage should read as follows:

> Now on the last, the great day of the feast, Jesus stood forth, and cried, saying:
>
>> If any man is athirst, let him come to me,
>> and let him drink, him who believes in me,
>> According as Scripture has spoken,
>> *Rivers of living water shall flow out of his belly.*

In applying this quotation (Zechariah xiii, 1; xiv, 8) to the believer, the writer introduces a gross and incongruous image. And the more incongruous inasmuch as Jesus alone, and not the believer, can be thought of as the source of the water of life. The writer is referring to the water that burst from the side of Jesus at the stroke of the soldier's lance, and accordingly takes pains to tell us (39) that the living water is the Spirit, to be given to believers when Jesus has entered into his glory.[1]

Another interpolation which has no connection whatever with the evolution of the written Gospel is the section known as the story of the woman taken in adultery. It belongs to the late history of the Greek text and falls outside the scope of our present

---

[1] For the full discussion of this passage, which has many important bearings, see *Le Quatrième Evangile*, 270–273.

inquiry. Deliberately banished from the synoptic tradition, of which the story is a lost fragment, it has got itself, by the strangest of accidents, here tacked on to the Johannine Gospel (vii, 53–viii, 11).[1]

Immediately following this intrusion, Jesus' controversy with the Pharisees resumes its broken course. He now answers the last objections raised in vii, 41, 52, although, if strict regard be paid to the everchanging *mise en scène*, it would seem that he cannot have heard them. After declaring himself "the light of the world," he defies his adversaries, telling them that he alone knows whence he comes and whither he goes, while they know nothing of either. By this he means that he comes from God and returns to God. Declarations of this kind afford a sure starting point for determining the conditions of his epiphany as the Christ, both as to its opening and its close; it will be seen that they exclude both an earthly existence before epiphany and a corporeal resurrection after death. Needless to say his auditors understood not a word of it (viii, 12–29).

Close attention should be paid to the following (viii, 28–29):

> When ye have lifted up the Son of Man,
>   then shall ye know what I am,
> And that of myself I do nothing,
>   but even as the Father has taught me,
>   so speak I;
> And he who sent me is with me;
>   He forsakes me not,
>   because what is pleasing to him, that do I.

This seems to be an intentional contradiction of the saying —a quotation from Psalm xxii, 1—which Mark (xv, 34) makes into the dying outcry of Jesus, and which might easily be misunderstood (cf. *supra*, p. 168). Whence we may infer that the passage is a late development in the text.

In the final phase of this dispute (viii, 20–59) a discourse on Jesus' Father, who is God, and the Jews' father, who is the Devil (viii, 26, 38, 42–47, 54–55), seems to have been broken up by the compiler and the interstices filled with an unrelated argument about Abraham (30–37, 39–41, 48–53, 56–58). In connection with Abraham comes the indication about the age of Jesus (57):

---

[1] See *op. cit.*, 278–286.

"Thou art not yet fifty years old, and thou hast seen Abraham!" (An ancient variant reads: "Abraham has seen thee.") The fact is not without significance that this indication of Jesus' age is found in an editor's addition and not in a fundamental document.

The Light of the World

On leaving the temple, where the Jews had tried to stone him, Jesus reveals himself as "light of the world" by curing a man born blind, a "sign" which brings out the spiritual blindness of the Jews (ix). The interrogation of the man's parents is possibly interpolated into the original story of the miracle (ix, 18–23). A man *born* blind makes a suitable figure of humanity ignorant of the blessings of revelation, but the Johannine story aims primarily at intensifying the cure of blind men localized by the Synoptics in Galilee and at Jericho; moreover this evangelist times the miracle on a Sabbath day. The Pharisees, spiritually blind, as usual represent Judaism in its unbelief of the Christian gospel. But the last lines "for judgment I came into this world," etc., are the compiler's addition. There has been nothing to raise the question of "judgment" in the proper sense of the word; but in any case the Christ, as we have already been told, did *not* come "to judge the world, but to save it" (iii, 17–18).

The Good Shepherd

The poem of the Good Shepherd (x, 1–18) must at first have existed independently and without connection with the story of the blind man. Verse 6, to the effect that the audience did not understand what Jesus was saying, is a compiler's invention together with verse 7, which takes up the broken thread of the poem: other additions are the lines about the Christ as the Door (9: the original must have been: "I am the *shepherd* of the sheep"); and the verses on the sheep outside the fold who must be brought into the flock (16). The question has often been raised as to the identity of the false shepherds who came "before" Jesus and are here stigmatized as "thieves and brigands" (8). Is the reference to Moses and the Prophets? If so, would it here be said "that the sheep heeded them not at all"? Nothing is gained by the omission, found in certain texts, of the words "before me"; that only leaves the assertion vaguer than before and does nothing to answer the question. The Jewish teachers, then; or the false Messiahs? More probably the reference is to the spiritual powers which have hitherto taken part in governing human affairs but have not succeeded in seducing the children of God. And is there no connection with the mystical shepherd—allegory in Zechariah xi, 4–17; xiii, 7–9? The question remains. A piece of narrative is added (19–21) to complete the framework intended to link these events and discourses with the Feast of Tabernacles.

Three months afterwards comes the Feast of Dedication, and Jesus is in the midst of the solemnities. After defining once more his rôle of saviour of all predestined to salvation he is again threatened with stoning (22–31). He explains why he has the right to call himself the Son of God, and then evades further persecution by retiring beyond Jordan (40–42). What we are told as occurring at the Feast of Dedication forms the conclusion of the controversies that have gone before: the preamble (22–24) is certainly the compiler's work, and Jesus' words about the sheep who give heed to his voice and will never perish seem to have been originally the last strophe of the allegorical poem of the Good Shepherd (x, 25; starting from "the works that I do" but without "I and the Father are one," (30) added to make transition to the attempt at stoning).

The argument by which Jesus is made to justify his claim to divinity is the compiler's argument. Its defence of the saying "I and the Father are one" is remarkable rather for subtilty than for exactitude (31–39). It ends in another attempt of the Jews upon Jesus' person and by another escape from their clutches (39).

The account of Jesus' retreat into Perea (40–42) may be part of the frame within which the story of the resurrection of Lazarus was originally enclosed, but it has been glossed by the lines which refer to John and to the numerous conversions effected by Jesus. These believers beyond the river are another figure, after their kind, of the diffusion of the Gospel beyond the borders of Israel. When the writer of this passage makes the Jews say "John gave no sign," it is because he found no miracle of John's described in the Synoptics. But he has overlooked the passage where we are told that the tetrarch Antipas, on hearing about the miracles of Jesus, immediately made the comment: "Here is John risen from the dead," which leaves no doubt that miracles analogous to those of Jesus were attributed to John. It would indeed be surprising if it were not so.

The Raising of Lazarus

And now, at last, the greatest of all the miracles recorded in the Gospels, the resurrection of Lazarus, supreme revelation of the Christ who is life (xi, 1–14), encounters the full intensity of Jewish unbelief and brings on the final catastrophe. The high priests and the Pharisees—such, according to our Gospel, is the composition of the Sanhedrim—resolve to put Jesus to death as the only way to prevent the conversion of the people; and Jesus, whose hour is not yet come, goes into hiding, awaiting the time of the Passover, the hour decreed by Providence as the termination of his existence on earth (xi, 1–57).

It need hardly be said that this distinctively Johannine "sign" is charged with the maximum of symbolic meaning, attained by concentrating and intensifying the resurrection of Jairus' daughter and of the young man at Nain (Mark v, 35–42; Luke vii, 11–17). Our Lazarus has a resemblance to Simon the Leper (Mark xiv, 3); but we have already seen (*supra*, p.162) that the Lazarus of Luke's parable (xvi, 19–31) is rather dependent upon him. The two sisters in Luke (Martha and Mary, x, 38–42) are turned by the compiler into sisters of Lazarus; Mary, as a further improvement, is substituted for the sinful woman of Luke (vii, 37–38) and for the woman of the anointing in Mark and Matthew. But these combinations, which have sorely taxed the ingenuity of commentators, were not all effected at a single stroke. At the very outset (xi, 1–2) the text is visibly glossed by the notice about the sisters, whose rôle in the story is largely superadded to the original.

The original version seems to have contained the message of "the sister" announcing the sickness of Lazarus (xi, 3); Jesus' comment on the sickness (4); the announcement that he would go to Judea, with the disciples' objection and the Christ's reply (7–10); the dialogue between Jesus and "the dead man's sister" (21–27), Jesus having arrived not four days after the interment, but at the moment when the funeral was just over; Jesus weeping with the other mourners (33, omitting his indignant groan); the visit to the tomb and the order to remove the stone (34–39, again omitting the repeated indignation and Martha's remark about the condition of the corpse); the removal of the stone; Jesus' prayer and the resurrection of the dead man (41–44). The later additions aggrandize the miracle, but give it the mechanical turn characteristic of supernatural magic.

The essence of the matter lies, not in the miracle as such, but in the truth it offers to belief, truth which the miracle is intended to drive home and make good. Nothing else really counts. The work of raising a dead body to life is but the guarantee of a work with importance of another and higher kind, the universal and final work of raising humanity to life in the Spirit. The resurrection of Lazarus, as it was originally conceived, was not intended either to announce or prefigure the bodily revival of all the dead, but as symbolic testimony to the *spiritual* resurrection, the eternal life of all who believe. Observe that not a word is said as to what became of Lazarus after he was loosed from his grave clothes and "let go" (44). The reason is, that in this miracle, as indeed in many another already encountered, the reader is invited to carry his vision beyond earthly contingencies and find in higher truth the conclusion of which the story itself seems to stop short. And what is the conclusion here? It is that whosoever believes in Jesus is in present possession of eternal life; he has escaped from a house of death to which he will never return; he is "let go" for unceasing advance, in light and life, to God, heaven and everlasting glory; and humanity, regenerated in like manner by the ever-living Christ, and so made the true Jerusalem of earth, begins to mingle with that eternal Jerusalem into which it will be wholly merged at the end.

Sequel to the Great Miracle

What we read of the effect of the miracle and the information laid before the Pharisees (46) may come from the source (omitting "which came to Mary" in 45), together with the notice of the Pharisees laying plans to put Jesus to death (53). But the deliberations of the Sanhedrim and the unwitting prophecy of Caiaphas (47–52) are editorial supplements. So, too, are the words "high priest for that year" which suppose that the Jewish high-priesthood was an annual office, like that of the Asiatic bishops, and involves an error about the conditions under which Caiaphas held the pontificate (cf. *supra*, p. 151). The retreat of the Christ to the town called Ephraim (?) and the conversations of the Jews waiting for his arrival at the Passover duplicate his previous retreat into Perea after curing the man born blind (x, 40–41), and the remarks of the Jews who waited for him at the Feast of Tabernacles. It would seem that the source-account placed a very short interval between the resurrection of Lazarus and the Passover, and that it kept Jesus at Bethany, because the Passover was approaching and his hour at hand.

The anointing in the house at Bethany is a symbolic prelude to the death of the Christ (xii, 1–8); the triumphal entry into Jerusalem (9–19) prefigures the glorious issue of his departure from the visible world; his last discourses forecast its results—the conversion of the Gentiles (20–36) and the reprobation of the Jews (37–50). The accounts of the anointing and of the triumph are fragments of the synoptic tradition, here transposed and turned in the Johannine sense by the same hand which added its supplements to the raising of Lazarus. Mark (xiv, 1; cf. Matthew xxvi, 2) places the anointing two days before the Passover; this writer says "six days before," doubtless for some symbolic reason; the sixth evening before the Passover would be that of the Sabbath before the Passion in correspondence with the Sabbath of interment, the triumphal entry next day (9 Nizan) thus anticipating the triumphal resurrection of the following Sunday. The accusation of theft lodged against Judas (4–6) replaces the betrayal for money in the Synoptics; when the hour comes for Jesus to suffer himself to be arrested, there is no bargain between the Jewish priests and the traitor, as in the Synoptics, but Satan informs them by the mouth of Judas where they can find and capture him. The qualification of Judas as a robber indicates the length to which the writer is willing to go in utilizing the synoptic tradition about him; but his putting Judas in charge of the alms-bag, in analogy with a practice of the early Christian communities, must surely be an anachronism. Notwithstanding the efforts made to bring the messianic triumph somehow into sequence with the raising of Lazarus, it is doubtful whether this piece of the synoptic catechesis (the triumph) belonged to the original economy of our Gospel.

Of secondary authorship also is the discourse in the temple

which Jesus is made to deliver about the Greeks, or Gentiles, who ask to see him (20–36). Noteworthy features are the artificiality of the preamble, in which Philip and Andrew again appear, and the curious transposition into the middle of the discourse (27–30) of a sublime equivalent for the synoptic scene in Gethsemane. In this equivalent the Christ's prayer is transformed from the synoptic version, in which he prays to be saved from the fate awaiting him, into a distinct refusal so to pray; instead of so praying he calls upon God to glorify his name. This better befits the Johannine conception of the Christ. After that, in place of the consoling angel in Luke (xxii, 43), comes a voice from heaven echoing the voices of the baptism and the transfiguration in the Synoptics. This miraculous interlude is not for the encouragement of the Christ, who is above all such needs, nor for the crowd who are pictured as not understanding it, but for the education of the Christian reader. The last discourse to the Jews is symbolic throughout. It is followed by a last disappearance of Jesus into hiding (36). In manner like to his disappearance, the light of the Gospel, offered to the Jews, will pass away from them into Gentile possession. Such is the design of Providence, and the Jews are powerless to hinder it.

A yet later and, if possible, a more unreal addition is the afterthought conclusion of the Jerusalem ministry (37–50), in which the compiler makes Jesus deliver a new discourse (44–50), after the Christ has been finally withdrawn from his incredulous audience. This discourse (to which 24–25, 31–32, 35–36 in the previous discourse seem originally to have belonged) may have been found ready-made and here utilized by the same editor who applies the text from Isaiah (vi, 9–10) to the reprobation of the Jews at the moment when the Christ's ministry among them comes to an end (39–41). The same use of this text is made by the Synoptics in connection with parables (Mark iv, 12; Matthew xiii, 14–15; Luke viii, 10) and the compiler of Acts gives it the same application at the end of his book (xxviii, 26–27. For the quotation in xii, 38 of Isaiah liii, 1, cf. Romans x, 16).

So ends the Johannine account of Jesus' ministry. Everything in it is governed by symbolism which all the circumstances are constructed to suit without regard to the consistency of the narrative. The discourses, moreover, are surcharged with repetitions revealing the anti-Jewish bias which so often inspires the editorial elaboration of the source. The original miracle stories all betoken the spiritual work of Jesus which the original discourses proceed to explain. The editors, elaborating the original, have striven to show that the Jews understood nothing of the mystery of salvation and the spirituality of the Gospel: accordingly they kill a Messiah whose greatness is beyond them, and whom the death they inflict upon him renders back to the eternal glory whence he came, and so makes him the saviour of the world.

THE CYCLE OF THE PASSION

The second part of our Gospel presents the Christ's rôle of Saviour, the conditions in which he is to exercise it and those which he laid down as the foundation of the Christian community. The conversations at the last supper reveal to the disciples how salvation is ordered and the glory to come, together with the law of love by which they are bound for ever to the immortal Christ. This law is first illustrated by washing the disciple's feet (xiii, 1–17); it is there expressly promulgated (31–35) and placed between two predictions; the first declaring the treachery of Judas and pointing out the beloved disciple (23–26); the second announcing Peter's denial (36–38). The Christ proceeds to exhort his faithful ones, promising them a place in his Father's house, assuring them of his continued presence, even of his and the Father's immanence in them (xiv, 1–14, 18–24, 27–28). In the midst of it all he breaks in with a double promise of the Holy Spirit which the Father, in his name, will send them (15–17, 25–26). The preamble to the washing of feet (xiii, 1–3) appears to have been retouched and surcharged. What is this supper, "after" which the washing takes place? The original author probably gave at this point an account of the last meal; this has been suppressed, because a second writer, under the influence of the Synoptics, had introduced it already (xii, 1–8) in the story of the anointing. Doubless the original account, which we are bound to believe underlies all this, seemed too unorthodox to be retained. The washing of feet, so ill-placed that its character as a surcharge can hardly be mistaken,[1] must belong to an intermediate account into which interpolations have later been introduced, this version being related by its principle idea and the subtilty of its symbolism to those parts of the first Johannine Epistle which speak of purification from sin by the blood of the Christ (1 John ii, 2; iii, 5; iv). Thus the washing of feet, in its character as memorial of the Christ as a servant, living and dying with those who were his own, must have been substituted in an earlier version for the symbolic distribution of bread and wine, that is, for the eucharistic symbols. For that reason the washing is said to be a repetitive completion of the essential purification realized once for all in baptism (6–10).

There are details in the story which would be quite unintelligible if we failed to take account of the profound meaning which attaches to the scene as it is described, not only as a whole, but in the details also. In reality the "service" which the Christ is rendering to his own is that of *his death*, of which the eucharistic love-feast is a figure; and for that reason Peter's opposition to the act which Jesus would perform (6–7) is the equivalent of the attitude assigned him by the Synoptics at the first announcement of the Passion (Mark viii, 32–33; Matthew xvi, 22–23). In like manner the reply of Jesus, "if I wash thee not, thou hast no part in me," is a defiance of all probability unless we understand the symbolism of it. Is Peter, then, to be damned because he has refused to have his feet washed by Jesus? The words refer directly to the Christian mysteries, baptism and the eucharist, both regarded as necessary for salvation, both inseparable from the unique symbol of life-giving water and from the unique idea of salvation procured by Jesus in the death by which he became alive for ever. There is no question here of overcoming the personal repugnance of Peter to having his feet washed by Jesus. The matter in hand is to combat the Jewish Messianism in the words attributed to Peter, which imply that he would not have Jesus lower himself to the service of a life-giving death; to which Jesus replies that by this service the sanctifying rites which

---

[1] Normally ablutions of this kind took place *before* the meal. But from the moment that the washing was made into an eucharistic symbol, it had to be presented as a pendant to the meal or, better, *after* it. Some manuscripts read "a meal taking place," others "a meal *having taken* place"; the first reading, seemingly a correction to avoid contradicting what follows in xiii, 21–30 where the meal is still in progress.

unite the Christian to the source of life are guaranteed as permanently efficacious. Already, in earlier passages of our Gospel, baptism and the eucharist have been proclaimed as necessary to salvation (vi, 53); so far is the Johannine Christ from being indifferent to these sacred and efficacious symbols. His interest in them is entirely natural. He is himself, by the definition given of him, a kind of living and ever-active sacrament and, along with this, a Master of Mystery and a God to be worshipped.

The following sayings, attributed to Jesus either during the meal or after it, and all of high mystic significance, may be considered as coming from the fundamental account:

xiii, 31–32, God is about to glorify his Son; xiv, 1–3, the Son goes to prepare for his own a place near the Father; 6–7, he himself is way, truth and life; whoso knows him knows the Father and has seen him; 10–13 (after "the words which I speak unto you") his works are the Father's works and whoso believes in him will do the same, and yet greater works, because the Son goes to the Father and will do all that is asked of him; 19–21, 23–24, soon the world will see the Son no more, but those who love him and keep his commandments will see him; the Father and the Son will make their abode in them, for the word of the Son is that of the Father.

These instructions are, at the outset, twice interrupted by compilers' additions regarding the treachery of Judas in xiii, 10–11 (after the words "and you are clean") and in 18–19. It might seem that the betrayal is here brought in for the purpose only of maintaining the atmosphere of darkness and death which envelops the last meal of the Christ with those who loved him; that may be so, but the writer will not lose the opportunity to recall that Jesus knew all that was in store for him; moreover the felony of Judas had been foretold in prophecy, and Jesus must cite the Scripture which announces it (Psalm xli, 9). Of secondary origin also are the sentences (xiii, 12–17, 20) borrowed from the synoptic tradition (cf. Matthew x, 24, 40; Luke vi, 40), the connection of which with the mystic example of the washing is not very obvious, to say nothing of their connection with the predictions of Judas' treachery.

An editor of our Gospel, perhaps the last, has given a Johannine turn to the direct announcement of the betrayal (xiii, 21–30), in which the Christ is made to reveal the traitor's identity to the beloved disciple; a somewhat childish piece of imagination, notwithstanding the symbolism in the "sop" (mouthful) given by Jesus to Judas (26–27). This is the first occasion on which the beloved disciple is brought into prominence, and it is in his honour that our editor exploits the denunciation of the traitor in the Synoptics (cf. Mark xiv, 19; Matthew xxvi, 22; Luke xxii, 23). In the perspective of the story the disciple in question can only be one of the Twelve, but his anonymity has the immediate effect of suggesting that he is a symbolic figure, type of the true disciple, even though his introducer intended him to be identified with an historical person to whom the composition of the Gospel might thereafter be attributed. The place assigned him at the Christ's side makes not only a relation of personal friendship with Jesus, but complete partnership of the well-beloved in the spiritual riches which are to overflow mankind from the breast of Jesus (cf. vii, 38; *supra*, p. 209). It is to this disciple that Peter turns to find out who is to be the traitor, and it should be noted that an analogous relation, in which the beloved disciple takes the lead, exists between the two every time they appear on the scene in company (xviii, 16; xx, 4–8; and again xxi, 7, 20–22)—a plain indication of the superiority claimed by the Johannine to the common apostolic tradition. The incident of the sop given to Judas must be secondary in relation to the preamble. In the preamble (xiii, 2), the devil has already entered into Judas before the meal began; here he is delivered to Satan after eating the sop, which he eats to his damnation (cf. 1 Corinthians xi, 29; Luke xxii, 3).

The exhortation to mutual love, conceived in the spirit and style of the first Johannine Epistle (cf. 1 John ii, 7–10; iii, 23) is a surcharge on the announcement of Peter's denial, which has already been borrowed from the synoptic tradition as it stands in Mark, Matthew and Luke. One feature not derived from that source is the veiled allusion to the later martyrdom of Peter, in the symbolic words "thou shalt follow me afterwards." This mysterious prediction, we must add, is far from being an indication that the passage which contains it is either primitive or of high antiquity.

The mystic allocution flows on from xiii into xiv, unmindful of the inserted conversation between Peter and Jesus. Similarly intercalated into its continuation are the following:

The naïve question by Thomas about the locality to which Jesus says he is about to go (4–5); the no less naïve demand of Philip, "show us the Father," and the words in which Jesus expresses his astonishment (8–10a); the promise of another Helper, the Spirit of Truth (15–17, 25–26); and the question of Jude (22).

The Spirit appears in our Gospel mainly as the continuator of the revelation inaugurated by the Christ, and its action is partly merged into that of the Christian sacrament. Thus, in a sense, the Spirit is a substitute for Jesus. We may recall at this point that in the Acts of the Apostles the reign of the Spirit is brought in by the miracle of Pentecost which takes place ten days after the Ascension. In the mind of the Gospel editor there can have been no thought of a *human* substitute, Marcion, Montanus or any other, since it is expressly stated that the Helper will "be with you for ever" (xiv, 16). In any case the discourses, in their original form, rule out the possibility of a substitute for the immortal Christ, who abides continuously in those who love him (cf. 1 John ii, 1 where the Christ is himself the Paraclete, the Helper). Finally, it is evident that the reflections (27–31) which follow the reiterated promise of the Paraclete, and end with the words "Arise let us go hence," were imagined by the compiler of the preceding instruction with a view to proceeding immediately with the story of the Passion. But another compilation, three chapters in extent (xv–xvii), has been inserted between this point and the opening of the Passion story (xviii, 1).

Last Instructions of the Christ

No introduction is arranged for this new collection, the reader apparently being invited to take it as the continuation of the preceding discourse. The subjects treated in it are, moreover, the same as those in its predecessor, as follows:

Allegory of the vine (xv, 1–10) urging the disciples to remain united in the Christ, the source of eternal life, and direct exhortation to abide in the love of Jesus (11–17). Condemnation of a world gone astray which will hate the disciples as it has hated their Master (18–25 and perhaps xvi, 1–4). New promises concerning the Spirit which will support the disciples in persecution and condemn the world (26-27; xvi, 5-16). New announcement of persecutions to come, but the sorrow of the persecuted will be changed into joy, and the Christ himself will visit his own (xvi, 16-24). All this Jesus has spoken in plain terms, because he is about to depart; let the faithful, in the hour of persecution, be at peace in him (25-33). Finally the Christ, to crown his exhortations, offers to his Father a long prayer that all believers, present and to come, may be preserved in mystic union with himself (xvii).

Like those that precede them these last instructions of the Christ are presented as though he were giving them to his disciples while still among them but with death immediately before him; in reality they are addressed, by the immortal Christ, to his Church. But though in a manner complementary to what has gone before, they are not all to be regarded, either separately or together, as pieces of secondary composition.

The allegory of the vine, with the exhortation attached to it (xv, 1-17), may be considered as a primitive document self-contained and independent of the compilation in which it now finds a place. The allegory has an orderly development in the style of the prophets (cf. Isaiah v, 1-7; Jeremiah ii, 21; Ezechiel xv, 1-6; Psalm lxxx, 8-16). The suggestion of it comes from passages in the Synoptics where mention is made of the vine and its fruit, chiefly from what is said about wine in their account of the eucharistic institution (Mark xiv, 25; Matthew xxvi, 29; Luke xxii, 18). The first words, then, are enough to show that this new course of instruction has the same close connection with the eucharist as the two preceding chapters, always linked to the eucharist, as they are, by the conception of that highest form of love which is willing to die for the sake of the beloved. Considered from another point of view, the allegory of the vine which, in some parts, makes a fellow to that of the Good Shepherd (x, 1-18), is the less well-balanced of the two, the author pressing hard on disparate images, that of the gardener who tends the vine and that of the necessity for the branch to remain united to the main stem. As supporting the application made of them to the Christ and to the disciples, the two images are ill-matched.

While love is the relation between the Christ and his own,

the world, on its side, is characterized by the hate it bears to both of them. The theme has already been indicated in vii, 7; cf. 1 John iii, 13–16 where the hatred-theme is also treated in connection with the love-theme. But here the brief discourse on the world as the enemy (18–25) comes in awkwardly. Its secondary character appears in its making a back reference (20) to a statement, lacking in originality, already made in the text (xiii, 16).

In like manner, the new dissertation on the "Helper" (the Paraclete) is of feebler inspiration (xv, 26–xvi, 15). What is said there about the judgment to be passed on the world (xvi, 8–11) is a confused rigmarole which recalls the least impressive passages in the first Johannine Epistle. One interesting statement, however, stands out from the rest: "the Paraclete shall declare unto you the things that are to come." To what else can this refer than to the Johannine Apocalypse? If that be admitted, the inference will follow that all the passages about the Helper were added by the compilers of the Johannine collection of books, and that these additions were made at the time when they were engaged in the attempt to obtain acceptance, under the same apostolic name, of the Apocalypse, the fourth Gospel and the three Epistles. Another important point to be noted is the saying in xvi, 4: "these things I said not unto you at the beginning *because I was with you.*" These words sound strangely as coming from the Christ. Without intending to do so the author has given away the secret that the speaker has long quitted this world and that, while seemingly addressing his first disciples, he is really speaking to the Church of the second century.

The final Consolation (xvi, 20–24, 26–28, 32–33), given in view of the coming persecutions, was possibly at first an independent composition. A preamble has here been constructed for it (16–19) which might be understood as referring to the Christ's resurrection, his apparition and even his second coming; but the Consolation to which it leads on has a different theme; it is a hymn of the mystic union, spiritual and perpetual, with the ever-living Christ, a hymn of his return in that sense. An interruption by the disciples has been introduced into the Consolation itself (29–31, to which 25 is co-ordinate). Intercalated in also the remark on the parabolic, i.e. allegorical and symbolic, character of the teaching in all these discourses. But the disciples' interruption has been inserted by an editor who wished to emphasize their lack of intelligence and to give a character of formal prophecy to the allusion made in the discourse to their abandonment of Jesus in the Passion (32).

Let it be noted that, on this point, the Synoptics in their canonical form, do not say so much, and that the Johannine account of the Passion gives it flat contradiction. With this the Gospel of Peter, which probably depends on John, is in agreement, and the version very possibly retains a primitive datum. Contrasting with the disciples' abandonment of their Master comes the saying: "but I am not left alone, because my Father is with me" which we have already encountered (viii, 16, 29). It has the same bearing here as before (*supra*, p. 210).

"In the world ye shall have suffering; but be of good cheer; I have vanquished the world." So the Consolation ends, in language which expresses confidence in victory to come; but the voice which speaks is, before all else, that of the Christ in glory, the Christ of the Eucharist, imparting courage to Christians everywhere. In the very act of dying, the Christ, now in glory, overthrew the world and the prince who ruled it (cf. xii, 31). Those who love him and whom he loves, his own, will conquer the world in their turn, nor will they fall into the hand of its prince when they, too, come to die.

The final prayer of the Christ (xvii) is not only the crowning utterance to the lessons taught, but the eucharistic keynote of the Last Supper, conceived as the first Love Feast (Agape). We may regard it as the first act of solemn thanksgiving, the first eucharist, a supreme utterance of Christian charity appropriate to the occasion. Jesus begins by asking that he may be glorified, because his work is done (1-8). Then he commends his loved ones, whom he is leaving in the world, to the care of the Father (9-19). Finally he prays that God, the Christ and the loved ones may all be one in love (20-26). His prayer is a lyric, constructed rhythmically and with balance of the parts.[1] Although apparently uttered in particular circumstances, it may, originally, have had no place in a Gospel story. We may take it as a type of eucharistic prayer, placed in the mouth of Jesus as master of the mystery;

---

[1] For the prayer with which the hymn concludes, as restored by M. Loisy, see Appendix to this chapter. Translator's note.

perhaps the oracle of some Christian prophet first recited to the community at the Easter celebration, not as the common thanksgiving but as the prophet's own. The same may be true of other passages in our Gospel, especially of the discourses after the Supper, of which the analysis is now concluded.

Two small additions may be detected in the final prayer: the profession of faith in verse 3, impersonal both in form and tone, out of keeping with the context and with nothing in it specifically Johannine; and verse 12 "except the son of perdition, that the Scripture might be fulfilled" evidently added to correspond with xiii, 18, 21–30, but equally out of place with the foregoing.

THE JOHANNINE ACCOUNT OF THE PASSION

The arrangement of the Passion and the Resurrection stories in our Gospel has, to all appearance, an almost systematic ordering; the Christ is now returning to his Father; he goes by the way of death; he arrives by resurrection. The scenes of his arrest; of his appearance before the high-priest, with Peter's denial of him; of Pilate passing judgment; of the crucifixion; of the burial; of the resurrection—all these follow in an order and develop in a manner that furnishes a worthy conclusion to the revelation of glory, which has pursued its course from the beginning of the book. But the story is far from being all of one piece.

It may be said that the Johannine Christ himself controls the conditions of his arrest. He dispatches Judas on his errand, commanding him to do quickly what he has to do (xiii, 27). When the hour strikes, he repairs with his disciples to the place where the traitor will come to take him, a garden beyond Kedron (xviii, 1; note that the name Gethsemane is omitted). Judas, on his side, calls up the Roman cohort and the tribune in garrison at the tower of Antonia, and with them the service-men of the Sanhedrim; this last to enhance the importance of the scene about to be enacted; for we may be very sure that if the armed forces of the procurator took any part in the affair there would have been no need either of the temple police or of Judas himself; nor would Jesus have been taken before the high-priest. When the force arrives at the garden, Jesus advances to meet it, demands its business, and receiving the answer that they are looking for Jesus the Nazorean, speaks a word that throws them all backward to the ground. Then he gives himself up, ordering his captors to let his companions go.

Introduced into a scene of such dignity, the sword-stroke that cut off the ear of the high-priest's servant is clearly out of place and keeping. But the compiler who mentions the incident knows that the servant was called Malchus; that his right ear was the one cut off; that the disciple who struck the blow was no other than Peter, and that Jesus rebuked him: "return thy sword to the sheath. The cup my Father has given me, shall I not drink it?" (10-11). This, surely, is the cup of Gethsemane which Jesus in the Synoptics prays the Father to remove from him. Peter's sword-stroke takes the place of the protest he raises in Mark (viii, 32) and Matthew (xvi, 22) at the first announcement of the Passion; and the rebuke he now receives is the Johannine equivalent of the terrible apostrophe: "get thee gone, Satan." From instances such as this, of which there are many in our Gospel, we may learn how to interpret its dependence on the Synoptics, and judge at the same time in what kind of relation to theirs is the treatment of Peter's prestige by the editors of John. Here, as in Mark, Peter is the man to whom the mystery of salvation is at first wholly unintelligible, and who, in his ill informed zeal, would prevent its realization. Of the remaining traits in the story of the arrest, the omission of Judas' kiss is not less significant than these additions.

The story continues (xviii, 12): "Then the cohort, the tribune and the Jews' servants laid hold of Jesus and led him to Annas." This follows on naturally after the order given by the Christ to leave his disciples at liberty,[1] and marks as a secondary addition the intervening incident of Peter's outbreak and the severed ear. But the account of Jesus before the high-priest is loaded with postscripts to a degree which has baffled interpreters from the first; even the textual history of the passage shows that it has been revised again and again, in the vain attempt to find a satisfactory reading, and the same is true of like attempts made by modern critics. The confusion arises from the fact that the primitive account knew of only one high-priest, Annas (Hanan); it knew nothing of Caiaphas as concerned in the matter, and, equally,

---

[1] xviii, 9 is a lame reference to xvii, 12.

nothing of Peter's denial. Caiaphas has been joined to Annas to make some sort of agreement with Matthew xxvi, 57, when it is to Caiaphas and not, as here, to Annas that his captors take Jesus; this is done by making him son-in-law to Annas, on the ground that several sons of Annas had become high-priests and that Caiaphas was presumably one of the family. His antecedents are also recalled (xviii, 13a–14; cf. xi, 49–50; *supra*, p. 214).

Peter's denial, imported from the Synoptics, we find divided into two parts (xviii, 15–18; 25–27) for the editorial convenience of finding a rôle for a certain unnamed disciple who is said to have been an acquaintance of the high-priest's, and can be no other than the well-beloved. This disciple introduces Peter to the high-priest's court, where he has the unpleasant surprise of encountering a kinsman of the Malchus whose ear he had cut off. All these precisions reveal the compiler of our Gospel as a man of lively invention. It is abundantly clear that in the original account not one of his disciples followed Jesus after his arrest (xviii, 8; xvi, 32).

The author of the foundation-story who knew Christianity as the religion of a sect, reduces the whole trial before the high-priest to an enquiry about Jesus' disciples and teaching (19). Jesus answers that he has always spoken openly to the world, either in the synagogues (Galilee)[1] or in the temple (Jerusalem); let the question of his teaching be asked of those who heard it. (In reality the author is replying to the Jews and pagans of his own age, who alleged that Jesus had preached only in a lost corner of Palestine and converted a few ignorant Galileans.) At this answer one of the court officials, judging it an impertinence, strikes Jesus with his hand: this is all that the author chooses to retain of the ignominious scene described in the Synoptics (Mark xiv, 65; Matthew xxvi, 67–68; Luke xxii, 63–65). Jesus answers with great dignity (23), so great indeed that the answer would be too solemn for so mean an insult were it not that the insulter stands for the unbelieving Jews, murderers of the Christ and persecutors of his followers. Thereupon the inquiry closes, and Jesus is taken away from the quarters of the high-priest (Annas in the original story, Caiaphas in the altered text) to Pilate's praetorium.

[1] It is, however, the fact that only one case of this is reported in our Gospel (vi, 59).

The author is careful to note that this happened on the morning of the day in the evening of which the paschal lamb was sacrificed. This timing is more important to him than the imagined consequence in the development of the scene. For it results from the date indicated that Jesus died on the day and at the hour of the paschal sacrifice; in this way our Gospel represents the Christ's passion as confirming the Easter usage of the quartodecimans. This, for him, was the essential matter; but it leads him on to imagine that the Jews must have abstained from entering the praetorium from fear of contracting legal impurity (28); nevertheless he makes Jesus go in. The tribunal is in front of the palace, a kind of open space where a crowd of Jews awaits the result of the proceedings inside, an unnatural arrangement constructed with the object of introducing a private conversation between Pilate and his prisoner, when Jesus will utter some lofty sayings which the writer will not allow him to utter in the presence of Jews. In consequence of this arrangement, the judgment scene falls into two parts, as Pilate goes away from the Jews, who are outside the building, to Jesus, who is inside, and then comes back from Jesus to the Jews.

The trial now proceeds as follows. First, the procurator receives the accusation which "the Jews" (the Jewish magistrates) refuse to withdraw and deal with themselves, on the ground (29–31) that they have no right to pronounce sentence of death (which was true at the time the evangelist was writing, but not in the time of Jesus). This happened, remarks the author (32), in order that Jesus might be *crucified*, as he had predicted,[1] crucifixion being a punishment which Roman authority alone could inflict. Pilate then goes inside to interrogate the accused who, on receiving the blunt question "art thou the King of the Jews?" makes the mystic answer that his "kingdom is not of this world" and is not defended by armed force; he is King "that he may bear witness to the truth." These sublime declarations are beyond Pilate's comprehension, but he concludes that there can be no harm in a king of truth, and accordingly goes back to the Jews to inform them that he finds no crime in the prisoner (38). At this the Jews break out into protest, declaring that the accused falls under the stroke of the Law for

[1] iii, 14; viii, 28; xii, 32–33.

saying he is the Son of God (this is the charge of blasphemy, which in the synoptic account,[1] is ground of condemnation by the Sanhedrim; but here "Son of God" is taken in the Johannine sense). Troubled by this, Pilate now goes back to Jesus and asks him whence he comes. No answer. Pilate insists and impresses on the prisoner that he has power to release him or to put him to death on the cross; Jesus replies that he would have no such power had not Providence conferred it upon him; so much the heavier is the guilt of Satan who has prompted Judas and the Jews to deliver him to Roman justice (xix, 7–11). Reassured on that side, Pilate makes a new effort to get the accusation withdrawn, only to meet with fresh protest from the Jews, who cry out that a pretender to kingship is Caesar's enemy, thus returning to the political charge with which they had begun. This brings Pilate to the end of his resistance. Yielding to the necessity of the situation (needless to scrutinize his psychology) he has Jesus brought out and makes him sit down on the judgment seat. The right translation here is "made him sit down," as the Gospel of Peter and Justin (*Apology*, 35) both understand it. If we suppose that Pilate himself sat down, the common translation, the whole scene loses the significance intended by the evangelist, who imagines it as the presentation of a king to his subjects only to be rejected instead of acclaimed. This is the meaning of Pilate's announcement to the Jews "behold your King!", of the clamour that immediately breaks out for the crucifixion of the man offered them, and of the declaration that they will have no king but Caesar. Faced with this blind obstinacy Pilate, we are to suppose, is now powerless to refuse sentence of death, and has no alternative but to hand Jesus over to them for crucifixion (13–16). It is the doing of the Jews, then, that the King of Truth is condemned to death as the King of Israel.

The picture before us, remote as it is from all reality, even from verisimilitude, is nevertheless grand in conception and in the profound irony with which, from the height of a sublime mysticism, the Jews are exhibited. To conform with the Synoptics there have been wedged into it the incident of Barabbas (xviii, 39–40) and the mockery in the praetorium (xix, 1–3), the latter symbolically dramatized and corrected as the presentation of

[1] Mark xiv, 61–64; Matthew xxvi, 63–66; Luke xxii, 66–70.

"the man" (4–6). But this added presentation repeats in advance the presentation of "the King" (14) and greatly diminishes its effect. Note how, at the end of xix, 6, we are back at the point where we left off at the end of xviii, 38. Note also that in xviii, 40 the Jews are made to "cry out *again*" though our Gospel has not mentioned any previous cry. This is a slip of the interpolator: by inadvertence he here follows Mark xv, 13, whereas for the whole of the Barabbas incident he has been following Luke xxiii, 16–19.

The Crucifixion

Having obtained the sentence they demanded the Jews lead the condemned to the place of punishment, Jesus himself carrying his cross (16b–17; in contradiction to Luke xxiii, 26). The sequel, however, shows clearly (23) that the execution is carried out by Roman soldiers, Pilate himself controlling the details (19–22). The contradiction of the Synoptics on the point of Simon of Cyrene carrying the cross is deliberate, the set purpose of the evangelist being to bring out the Christ's free and sovereign control in the preliminaries of his death and in death itself. Perhaps also there was an intention to combat certain gnostics who, like Basilides, maintained that Simon was crucified in the Christ's place. They bring Jesus "to a place called the Skull, Golgotha in the Hebrew"—the synoptic designation—"where they crucified him, and two others with him, one on either side, and Jesus in the midst" (18). The author refrains from saying that these two companions were thieves; this by way of suppressing the suggestion of infamy.

The inscription on the cross gives occasion to a symbolic incident (19–22): despite the opposition of the chief priests, Pilate maintains the wording of it, "Jesus the Nazorean, the King of the Jews." Thus Jesus keeps his Kingship and Christhood, let Jewish incredulity protest as it will. The three languages betoken the universal sovereignty of the Son of God.

In the incidents that follow, up to the original conclusion of the book (xx, 30–31), it is not easy to distinguish what belongs to the fundamental document from the secondary additions. What we are told about the division of the garments may be secondary: it is the forced interpretation of a prophetic text (Psalm xxii, 18) the fulfilment of which had to be marked, the "garments" and the "vesture" meaning the same object. Doubtless more was intended than to mark the fulfilment of a prophecy, the robe without seam suggesting an allegory in which some of the Fathers recognized the Church. Such a symbolism, however, is not in the same current as that of the "signs" encountered at an earlier stage, such as those of the man born blind and the raising of Lazarus.

The latter symbolism returns in the incident that follows, the words spoken by the Christ to his mother and the beloved disciple (25–27). As this incident concerns only the mother and the disciple, it may be assumed that the other women whose names are given (25) have been added to achieve some sort of agreement with the Synoptics. Here again, as in the story of Cana (ii, 4), Jesus addresses his mother as "Woman"; but this time he does not repudiate her. The meaning of the incident seems to be that converted Jews must accept hellenic Christianity as the legitimate offspring of the old Covenant, while the same Christianity, on its side, must regard as its mother the Jewish-Christian Church with its Old Testament tradition.

The last incident preceding the death of the Christ is the offer of vinegar; it marks a simple fulfilment of the prophecy in Psalm lxix, 21. But a touch of symbolism is not wanting, for the vinegar is offered with a bunch of hyssop, in allusion to the paschal ritual (Exodus xii, 22) which prescribed the use of hyssop to splash the house-doors with the blood of the lamb. The symbolism is somewhat far-fetched. Its presentation as a fulfilment of Scripture has the look of being a surcharge. The beginning of the verse (28a) is in contradiction with the end of it, which brings in another Scripture still to be fulfilled. We should read as follows: "Jesus, knowing that all was accomplished"—his rôle completely finished according to providential designs, whether expressed in Scripture or not—"in order that the Scripture might be fulfilled, said, I thirst." The natural sequel to "knowing that all was now accomplished" comes after the presentation and reception of the vinegar (30): "he said, it is finished. And bending down his head, he poured out the spirit."

This peaceful and willing death is the Johannine substitute for the scene in the first two Gospels, in which a great cry escapes from Jesus at the moment when he expires (Mark xv, 37; Matthew xxvii, 50). It figures the gift of the spirit which Jesus, with bent head, breathes forth in his last breath on the beloved group gathered round the foot of the cross; they symbolize his Church. The death of the Johannine Christ provides no scene of agony, ignominy and darkness, for it is nothing else than the resurrection of Jesus to his glorious and blessed eternity; his death and his resurrection are coincident. We must bear that in mind if we are to understand the meaning attached to Easter by the quartodeciman Christians of Asia.

Their Easter, coinciding with the Jewish Passover, might fall on any one of the seven days of the week, but it is a fact to be noted that up to this point our Gospel had not told us on which day the Christ's death took place. We are now going to be told, and to see how the Johannine Easter was made to fit in, by one means or another, to the synoptic framework in which Easter is celebrated on Sunday. The very first incident to follow the death of Jesus in the Johannine account informs us that Jesus died on the evening of a Friday and that he had to be buried before the Sabbath of next day. In its basic form the passage (xix, 31–37) informing us of the finishing blow administered to the victims and the prompt removal of the three bodies for common burial (31) is quite independent of the Synoptics and may well represent an important tradition, inasmuch as this tradition would contradict not only the stories of the Christ's burial in the Synoptics but those which, under synoptic influence, are now to follow in the Gospel before us. But, in the traditional form in which it comes down to us, there are features in the paragraph which class it among the latest additions to be found in our Gospel; these are, first, the symbolism of the water and the blood betokening the Christian sacraments, and, second, the calling up of a text from Exodus (xii, 46), "not a bone of his body shall be broken," which symbolically identifies the Christ with the paschal lamb, and another from Zechariah (xii, 10), surcharged upon the former, and made to predict the lance-thrust of the Roman soldier. The passage referring to the incident in the first Johannine Epistle (1 John v, 6–7) is also an interpolation in that Epistle, but stands there as the authorized interpretation of the Gospel passage now before us, the two possibly coming from the same writer. According to this interpretation we are to understand the Spirit which John the Baptist saw descending on Jesus and which Jesus, with his last breath, poured out upon his own, as connected with water and blood, the water of baptism and the blood of Calvary figured in the Eucharist, the two together bearing one inseparable witness to the immortal Christ.

There is something more in the passage as it has come down to us. The Gospel compilers attest the prodigy on the testimony of the beloved disciple who was present when Jesus died. But who are the compilers who allege this testimony? They are the same persons as those who would have it believed that the Apocalypse, the Gospel and the three Epistles are all the work of one author, and that author the apostle John (cf. xxi, 24). We may conclude that the scene in our Gospel, the witness of the beloved disciple and the attribution of the book to the apostle John are integral parts in a single fiction of late invention.

Burial, Resurrection and Apparitions

The story of the burial by Joseph of Arimathea is borrowed from the synoptic tradition. To him has been added Nicodemus who brings with him a great weight of spices to furnish the Christ with a princely embalmment. (The compiler forgets that the utmost haste was necessary to get the body buried before the Sabbath began, and that an embalmment on this scale would be a very lengthy operation.) Needless to say the "garden" in which the sepulchre is situated has a mystic meaning: it is the new garden of God where the Church, the new Eve, will be drawn from the side of the new Adam; the new sepulchre and the spices belong to the same current. But it may well be doubted whether the author of the Gospel in its original form, who understood everything in a spiritual sense, and the resurrection most emphatically so, was concerned to this extent with the dead body of Jesus, or that he is responsible for the stories in our present fourth Gospel which turn the resurrection into a miracle of the physical order, attested by material proofs.

To find a clear path through the events described in chapter xx is no easy task. The descriptions show signs of successive retouchings, and elements belonging to the fundamental document are but dimly discernible. Three apparitions of the Christ follow without a break; the first to Mary of Magdala (1–18) on the morning of the resurrection; the second to the assembled disciples on the evening of the same day (19–23); the third, again to the disciples, now including the sceptical Thomas, on the Sunday following (24–29).

The first apparition is surcharged with the news carried by Mary to Peter and the beloved disciple (1–2, after the words "she saw the stone had been turned aside from the sepulchre"); by the visit of the two disciples to the tomb, where it becomes clear that this addition, as well as the foregoing, has been imagined to the greater glory of the beloved disciple, who must be the first to believe in the resurrection of Jesus, contrary to what the primitive tradition tells of Peter; finally, by the appearance of angels to Mary (11–14, after "as she wept, she stooped")—this to make agreement with the synoptic introduction of angels, but a meaningless repetition of the apparition of Jesus himself. In this, the message to the disciples entrusted to Mary has a solemn dignity: she is charged to inform the "brethren" that Jesus has reascended to God. But the attempt to determine exactly the original meaning of this first apparition is a vain one. The story of it must have been modified profoundly, doubtless because it differed too obviously from the other Gospels.[1]

Brief as it is, the account of the second apparition has been overlaid at several points. In the general arrangement it resembles the account in the third Gospel (Luke xxiv, 36–40, 45–49). We are inclined to think that, to the original creator of the scene, this was the one and only sensible apparition of Jesus after his resurrection, expressed in the simple statement that, the disciples being assembled and the doors closed, Jesus appeared in their midst and said: "Peace be unto you." Immediately after there is a surcharge, intended to prepare the way for the coming apparition to Thomas, of which that story, when it comes later, has no knowledge—"and saying this, he showed them his hands and his side" (xx, 20*a*), the reference to the soldier's lance-thrust probably due to the compiler who has inserted that episode in the story of the Passion. As though there were nothing surprising in the apparition, the only sentiment attributed to the disciples is that of joy (20*b*). After which Jesus repeats his salutation and

---

[1] On the ancient writers who substitute the mother of Jesus for the Magdalene, see *Le quatrième Évangile*, 504.

gives them their mission (21; cf. xvii, 18 and Matthew xxviii, 19–20). Although the repeated salutation (21) may be a surcharge, added to prevent the discourse of Jesus being only the announcement of a mission, it is probable that the words which follow, about the power to remit sins, also come from the original author, omitting those which refer to the insufflation of the Spirit.

The third apparition (24–29), made for convincing Thomas, is an appendix to the second, and due to some reviser who was concerned to demonstrate the reality of the Christ's bodily resurrection; the remarks of Thomas, "if I see not the mark of the nails," etc., makes that clear enough. Nevertheless the moral of the story is to the effect that normal faith has no need of such proofs. It is possible that the anecdote was added to combat Docetism, but what it directly contradicts is the doctrine of the original evangelist, which taught the spiritual immortality of the Christ, but not the material resurrection of his dead body. It remains to note that this third apparition is conceived by the author as definitely the last to occur. After the words "blessed are they who, not having seen, believe" any further apparition stories would be worse than superfluous.

The concluding lines (30–31), concerning the object of the book, come from the writer whom we may call the first editor of the Gospel. They give no sign that he wished to be regarded as an apostolic person. Moreover he bids farewell to his readers with the unmistakable air of having finished his work and completed the mystic instruction of the Christian. After this the chapter that follows is clearly marked as an accretion, of which the effect is to derange the primitive economy of the whole book.

The Supplementary Apparition

This supplementary chapter has the threefold object of relating an apparition of the risen Christ to Peter and six of the disciples by the Lake of Tiberias (xxi, 1–14); the rehabilitation, by a triple profession of love, of Simon-Peter to whom the Christ confides the care of his sheep (15–17); predictions of Jesus about the martyrdom of Peter and the future of the beloved disciple (20–23), an editorial invention, relatively late, and connected with the attribution of the Gospel to this disciple in the epilogue (24–25).

To the same editor belong, without counting retouches and the arrangement of the material he is working on, the formula of introduction (1); the rôle of the beloved disciple in the miraculous draught, where the disciple is before Peter in recognizing Jesus (7); the statement about the number of fish and the resistance of the net, symbolic touches in the editor's usual vein; finally the number in the series assigned to the apparition (14). The whole is composed of borrowings from the synoptic tradition of apparitions in Galilee, and from the third Gospel. The general intention of it all is, beyond doubt, to make the Johannine Gospel acceptable in the churches at large, the prominence given to Peter being certain to win the approval in particular of the church in Rome. But the conglomerate of material here collected from various sources is as far as possible from holding together. It breaks up on analysis into the following borrowed elements: the miraculous draught of fishes, which is a myth of the institution of Christian propaganda, anticipated in Luke v, 1-11 (the introduction just here of this, the primordial, meaning of the miracle, is somewhat strange); the incident of Peter plunging from the boat into the sea in order to be with Jesus again, which recalls a similar incident in Matthew (xiv, 25-33, the antedating of a resurrection story); the meal of bread and fish, recalling the miraculous multiplication of the loaves (vi, 5-13), the meal with the pilgrims of Emmaus, and especially the peculiar feature of the broiled fish in the apparition to all the disciples recorded by the same Gospel (Luke xxiv, 41-43).

The solemn colloquy of the Christ with Peter (15-17), in which the primacy of the apostle is consecrated, has been consciously moulded into an equivalent of what we read in Matthew xvi, 17-19, which it imitates even to the form, and in Luke xxii, 32, though it was at first conceived independently of this Gospel. It is a safe conjecture that the prediction of Peter's martyrdom (18-19, echoing xiii, 36) was worded with an eye on the Apocalypse of Peter (*supra*, p. 53). All this, for better or worse, and for worse rather than better, is crowded into the same perspective.

The last sayings about the beloved disciple (20-23) are of the feeblest invention, but are intended to prepare the way for the conclusion of the chapter (24-25), which is also to be the conclusion of the book. The object aimed at is to present the Elder,

John the Old, a well-known figure long resident in Asia, as author of the Gospel and to convey a hint—no more than a hint is given—that he is the same person as the apostle John, son of Zebedee. Who are the "we" who guarantee his testimony (24)? They are "the Elders" who had known this John and brought out under his name the collection of Johannine books. We thus see that this supplement to the Gospel, intended to make it acceptable to all the Churches, was also intended to give it apostolic authority and value.

Such, then, is the sublime but inconsistent book whose destiny it was to dominate Christian theology and to fix its form. How did it originate?

Towards the end of the first century or the beginning of the second there lived a mystic prophet, a master of gnosis rather than an apostle of the faith, from whom came forth the hymns and symbolic visions on which the fourth Gospel is founded. A little later, towards 135–140, his sublime meditations were collected and framed in a Gospel story, to be used as a manual of initiation into the Christian faith, like other books of similar form already in circulation among the churches. The chronological framework was probably fixed at the same time and a part of the borrowings made from the synoptic tradition. At this stage and in this form the book had no auther's name attached to it and its diffusion was limited, or nearly so, to the province of Asia. Some fifteen or twenty years later, towards 150–160, the Marcionite heresy having broken out, this Asiatic book was amended, completed and more or less worked over, not only by the addition of chapter xxi, but by other retouches and additions in the main body; it was then boldly presented as the work of an apostle. But everything was welcome that gave satisfaction to faith, and the result just described was accepted by those whose will-to-believe found the truth in it. Thus it came to pass that, when the Montanist controversy broke out, the adversaries of these pretended writings of the apostle John found nobody to listen to them. When later, towards 190, the great controversy arose about the keeping of Easter, the Roman Church failed to perceive, or pretended not to perceive that, while the Synoptics supported the ritual tradition of Rome and of most other Christian churches, the fourth Gospel supported the different tradition followed by the churches of Asia.

APPENDIX

The concluding Prayer in Chapter xvii.[1]

> Holy Father, keep them in thy name,
> > those thou hast given me,
> > > that they may be one as we are . . .
> I ask thee not to take them out of the world,
> > but to guard them from the Evil One . . .
> For them I sanctify myself,
> > that they also may be sanctified in truth . . .
> And the glory thou gavest to me, yea to me,
> > I gave to them,
> That they may be one
> > as we are one,
> I in them
> > and thou in me
> > > that they may be perfect in unity,
> > That the world may know
> > > that thou hast sent me
> > And that thou hast loved them
> > > as thou hast loved me.
> Father, those whom thou hast given me,
> > I would that where I am
> > > They too may be with me,
> > That they may see my glory,
> > > which thou hast given me,
> For thou hast loved me
> > before the foundation of the world.
> Righteous Father, the world has known thee not,
> > but I, I knew thee;
> And they too have known
> > that thou hast sent me.
> And to them have I made known thy name,
> > and will make it known,
> That the love wherewith thou lovest me may be
> > in them and I in them.

[1] See *The Birth of the Christian Religion*, p. 241. (Appended here by the translator.)

Chapter VIII

THE EPISTLES AND THE CATECHESIS

WE have already seen how the epistolary method of instruction was employed in the early times of Christianity as a complement to the catechesis properly so called. This service was rendered in various ways; sometimes by genuinely authentic letters; sometimes by recourse to literary fiction, which might consist in amplifying the apostolic letters by interpolations, as happened to certain letters of Paul, or in publishing apocryphal letters under apostolic names, as in the case of those put out under the names of Peter, John, James and Jude, as well as of some ascribed to Paul. These letters, whether authentic or not, are samples of Christian teaching in the earliest times. As we follow the evolution of the catechesis we shall find that this epistolary literature reveals three stages, or forms, of its teaching. At its point of departure it is eschatological, concerned, that is, with the coming Kingdom; at the second stage it becomes penetrated by gnosis and begins introducing gnostic themes into both the eschatological and the evangelical teaching; finally, when gnosticism has got out of hand and is producing a flood of heresies, it turns against them, becomes anti-gnostic, and gives the catechesis a turn in that direction.

THE FIRST STAGE—ESCHATOLOGICAL

When Paul set out as an independent missionary, about the year 44–45, he went about the world founding church after church, without fixing his abode anywhere, except when imprisonment immobilized him. In such conditions epistolary relations were the only means by which control could be maintained between the churches and their founder; without them these newly formed communities would have run the risk of dissolution. External difficulties attended the propaganda and internal difficulties were almost inevitable; in addition to which the very peculiar situation of Paul in regard to the other missionaries gave rise to a campaign of abuse against which he had to defend himself. It is a probability as near as possible to certainty that not all his writings have come down to us; and the same is true of the letters written under somewhat different conditions by the other missionaries, by Barnabas for example, which are irrecoverably lost. The surviving letters and notes of Paul are not correspondence of the ordinary kind; they are all concerned more or less with his apostolic labours, and their interest for us lies precisely in that.

1 *Thessalonians*

The oldest of these letters subsists in the first Epistle to the Thessalonians.[1] The Christian group at Thessalonica had been recruited by Paul, accompanied by Silas and Timothy, in 48–49, and the letter was written from Corinth about 50–51. It is addressed in the name of Paul and his two auxiliaries "to the community of Thessalonica (which is) in God and the Lord Jesus Christ (i, 1)." But the writer, or dictater, of the letter is evidently Paul himself. The believing group forms a spiritual unity, an *ecclesia*, in God and in Christ. The beginning of the letter (i, 2–10) contains praises which may seem exaggerated, but are really encouragement. The point to be retained is the important indication it gives of the object of the Christian catechesis at this stage:

> People tell of you what a reception you gave us, and how you were converted from idols to God, to serve the God who is living and true, and to await the coming from heaven of his Son, whom he raised from the dead, Jesus, who saves us from the approaching wrath.

Paul seems to have wished greatly to revisit his converts that he might assure himself of their perseverance; but he can do no more than send Timothy from Athens. Timothy on returning finds him at Corinth and gives a most favourable report on his mission, at which Paul is greatly consoled; so let them continue to advance on the good way (ii, 17–iii, 2a, 5b–13). The passage ends thus:

> The Lord make you to grow and abound in love among yourselves and towards all men, as ours towards you, to strengthen your hearts, (rendering them) irreproachable in holiness at the coming of our Lord Jesus with all his saints.

[1] For a critical analysis of this document see our *Remarques sur la litétrature épistolaire du Nouveau Testament* (1935), pp. 85–89.

The dominating feature in the apostle's outlook is, clearly, the Coming. This it is which gives added urgency to the moral precepts, first and foremost to those concerned with conjugal chastity (iv, 2–8):

> For you know what teaching we gave you in the Lord Jesus; that you abstain from unchastity: that each of you learns to possess his own vessel in sanctity and honour, not with passionate lust, *like Gentiles who know not God* (Psalm lxxix, 6); not to deceive his brother nor do him injury in his own affair, because the Lord is the avenger of all that, as we told you and proved before . . . It follows that he who pays no heed to this, it is not to man he pays no heed, but to God.

This has nothing to do with commercial relations; "his own vessel" is his wife, and the affair by which he may receive injury is adultery. This advice on sexual morality, which touches the heart of the existing situation, should be compared with the studied casuistry of I Corinthians vii, where the same matter is dealt with. The same may be said of the counsels that follow (iv, 9–12) on the practice of fraternal love to all men, with this application:

> Make it a point of honour to lead quiet lives, to do manual work, as we advised you to do, and to deal honourably with those outside, that you may be dependent on nobody. The Great Event will come as a surprise for everybody, but those who conform to these counsels have nothing to be afraid of. Till the Coming there will be no time for sitting with arms crossed, gazing at the sky (iv, 11, 12; v, 2, 4, 6).

Corinthians

The letters to the Corinthians are, in one respect, of less importance to our present inquiry; they deal less with the Christian catechesis and more with the divisions that arose in the community, the difficulties Paul had to face and the means he took to overcome them. The first letter, written about the year 55, when Paul was on the point of leaving Ephesus, was occasioned by divisions that had recently broken out and which the apostle believed he could allay by his message and by sending Timothy. In the letter he entitles himself as "called to be an apostle of Christ Jesus by the will of God," perhaps because his standing as an apostle was being challenged. In writing to Thessalonica he had claimed no title. The faithful at Corinth, like those at Thessalonica are "waiting for the manifestation of our Lord Jesus Christ," that is, for his second coming in his "day"—the day when the Kingdom of God will appear. But, while there is agreement in this matter, there are divisions in another:

> I beseech you, brethren, in the name of our Lord Jesus Christ, that you all make the same profession, and that there be no divisions among you, but that you be all united in the same feeling and the same thinking. For it has been reported to me of you, my brethren, by Chloe's people, that there are disputes among you. I mean this: one of you says "I am Paul's man"; another, "I am for Apollos"; another, "I am for Cephas." Is Christ then divided? was it Paul who was crucified for you? or was Paul the name in which you were baptized?

We have already seen in what circumstances Apollos won his position among the Corinthians (*supra*, p. 185). If there was also a party for Cephas, it had not been created by Peter's presence in Corinth, but by people who had doubtless come from Syria with the story that the only genuine apostles were those of the Jerusalem communion. Paul has sent Timothy to Corinth to restore order. Moreover he will soon come himself and, if need be, will apply the rod to those who think too highly of themselves (iv, 17–21). He has heard of a horrible scandal; there is among them a man "living with his father's wife; let this incestuous person be expelled from the community" (v, 1–2, 6–7*a*). As to the collection for the saints at Jerusalem, they must arrange the matter as Paul has already done in Galatia, so that he may find the money ready when he arrives from Macedonia, and if the amount is important he will take their delegates with him to Jerusalem after himself spending some time among them (xvi, 1–9).

In the Second to Corinthians two short letters are embedded which concern this collection, both lodged in the very middle of the Epistle, and it may be said in passing that they are enough to prove it a relatively late compilation; for, plainly, they were not written at the same time. Moreover each letter has its own subject clearly defined and was probably at first written without connection with any other message; finally, the place they occupy shows that they were originally attached to the group of chapters i–vii and later, in order to simplify the transcriber's work and get more reading substance, the group x–xiii was attached to the group i–ix, the two being apparently addressed to the same destination. The older of the letters (ix) has inadvertently been placed second.

In the older letter Paul encourages the Corinthians by saying that he has held them up as a model to the Macedonians. "In experiencing this service of yours" the saints at Jerusalem "will praise God for the submission which led you to confess the Gospel of the Christ and for the generosity of your contribution to them and to all" (ix, 13). The collection does, in fact, prove that a real fraternity was established between these young Christian communities and, further, that the "saints" of the mother-church were held by them in respect. The second letter (viii, omitting the mystic gloss of verse 9) states that the collection in Macedonia is now completed and that the Macedonians have shown themselves generous givers; let the Corinthians, then, whose goodwill was expressed when the affair began, lose no time in giving a fitting completion to this fraternal and beneficent work, and let them respond to the efforts of Titus and of the other brethren who are gone with him to Corinth to see the business through.

Titus had first visited Corinth as peacemaker to the quarrelsome community and been successful. "You won his heart," wrote Paul (vii, 15) in a letter earlier than this second note about the collection "and the more completely when he called to mind how teachable you all were, and how you received him with fear and trembling." The fact of the matter is that Titus played the rôle of mediator, not only between Paul and the Corinthians, but also between Paul and the Jerusalem elders, and that his interest in the collection for their necessities was not unconnected with his mediating work in regard to them.

Perhaps a reminder will here be in place as to who these "saints" were and how it came to pass that they were poor. They were the men of the primitive faith, the original believers, the dauntless heroes of the Great Hope, abiding in Jerusalem and there expecting the coming of the Christ on the clouds with the Kingdom of God in his train. They were poor because they were wholly preoccupied in expectation, in waiting and waiting always. Paul himself would never have thought of bidding them, as he wrote to the Thessalonians, to work for their living and be a charge to nobody.

The First to the Corinthians has told us that there were divisions in the community. Some elements of a second letter, sad and severe in tone, written after Paul had made an attempt at Corinth to allay the mischief, which had only further inflamed it, are preserved in chapters x–xiii of our Second Epistle (x, 1*a*, *c*, 2*a*, 9–11):[1]

> I, Paul, who am humble when present with you, am bold when away from you, beg you that when I come I may not have to be bold, that I may not seem to be frightening you with letters. For his letters, they say, are severe and strong, but his bodily presence is weak and his speech of no account. Let him who says that, ponder thus: that as I speak in my letters when absent, so I will act when I come to you.

Paul goes on to defend himself against lack of sincerity in his dealings with the Corinthians. The only fault they could find with him is that of having asked them for nothing and of living among them on help sent him from Macedonia: this charge, if charge it be, he will continue to incur (xi, 6*b*–12*a*; xii, 13–15). The reproach of trickery recurs further on (xii, 16) but his reply to it has been suppressed (we need not ask why) and replaced by a reference to the collection (17–18). The author of the substitution, to whom the whole completion is also due, here makes Paul refer to what is written in our chapter ix, without perceiving that he commits an anachronism, the present letter being earlier than that which deals with the mission of Titus. Paul is now ready to come to Corinth for the third time, but fears that he will find there the same controversies and quarrels as before, and that he will have to groan over many who have been sinning of late and have not repented in the least of the unchastity, shamelessness and debauchery they have engaged in (evidently something quite different from the case of incest referred to in the first letter). He repeats that when he comes he will not mince matters, and warns his correspondents of what they may expect, in the hope that it will save him from having to go to extremes (xii, 19–xiii, 2, 10*a*). Taken realistically this evidence helps us to understand the moral situation, which seems to have improved later, though

[1] See *Remarques*, 54–57.

much less through Paul's message than by the subsequent intervention of Titus.

The letter of reconciliation, the third written by Paul to the Corinthians, may be extracted from the first *bloc* of the compilation (i–vii). It was written in the name of Paul and Timothy (i, 1–2). The apostle begins by describing the extreme despondency he has experienced in Asia—impossible for us to say whether it was due to some external peril or to the grief which had overwhelmed him at the thought of the condition in which he had found and left the Corinth group. But God had been pleased to deliver him from that affliction. If he has not kept the promise he made to the Corinthians to visit them again, the reason is that he was unwilling to be twice among them in a state of distress; now he is pleased with what they have decided about the man who had offended; but he waited impatiently at Troas for the return of Titus whom he had sent to Corinth on his behalf; passing through Macedonia he met Titus who told him the happy result of his mission, the sorrow of the Corinthians and their zeal for their apostle. "I rejoice," he concludes, "that in all things I can rely on you." The message is deeply impressive, though many of its details are dark to us (i, 8–11, 15–20, 23; ii, 1–13; vii, 6–16). But at least it enables us to recognize the authentic accent of Paul when it is his own voice that speaks to us. But if we are helped thereby to understand the personality of the catechist, we have to look elsewhere for the light on his catechism.

Galatians

On this point, the Epistle to the Galatians, of which the first version goes back to 55–56, will give us a little information. At least we may learn from it something of Paul's method in defending his doctrine and practice against the Judaizing emissaries who had more or less got the upper hand among his Galatian converts. He broaches the matter as follows (i, 6–7):

> I am astonished that you so quickly desert him who called you by grace, for another Gospel, which is no Gospel at all; I refer to the people who are upsetting you and trying to overthrow the Gospel of the Christ.

The people to whom he refers retain the promise of the Kingdom and profess that Jesus is the Christ, but they disturb the conscience of the believers by changing the real conditions under which the promise of the Kingdom was given. And here are the conditions (iii, 6–9, 11, 14*a*, 15–18, 19*b*):

> *Abraham believed in God, and that was counted to him as righteousness* (Genesis xv, 6). Understand, then, that men of faith are the very sons of Abraham. Scripture, foreseeing that God would deem the Gentiles righteous in virtue of their faith, predicted it to Abraham: *in thee shall all the Gentiles be blessed* (Genesis xviii, 18). So then, men of faith are blessed along with faithful Abraham[1] [ ]. That no man is deemed righteous before God by the Law is evident, *since the righteous shall live by faith* (Habakkuk ii, 4). Now the Law is not based on faith, but *who does that, by that shall he live* (Leviticus xviii, 5) [ ] so that the blessing comes at last to the Gentiles. But then, I speak in terms of human affairs: it is ever the rule that nobody treats a man's will as of no account or makes additions to it. Now it was to Abraham that the promises were made and to his posterity. God did not say to *posterities* in the plural, but to his *posterity* (Genesis xii, 7; xxii, 18) which is the Christ. Now I say this: a disposition previously ratified by God cannot be invalidated by the Law which came four hundred years later, so as to cancel the promise. For if the heritage depend on the Law it ceases to depend on the promise. Now it was in promise that God made a gift of the heritage to Abraham, until the *posterity* should arrive which the promise was concerned with[ ]. For you are all one in Christ Jesus. But if you are in Christ then are you the posterity of Abraham, heirs in virtue of the promise.

After recalling the circumstances in which he had evangelized the Galatians and saying how much he wished he were with them to enlighten them (iv, 11–20), he resumes his theme as follows (iv, 21–23, 28–31):

> Tell me, you that want to be under the Law, pay you no attention to the Law? For it is written (Genesis xvi, 15; xxi, 2, 9) that Abraham had two sons, one by a bond and the other by a free woman; but the son of the bond was born according to the flesh, but the son of the free in virtue of the promise [ ]. Now you, brethren are, like Isaac, children of the promise. But just as then the one born of flesh persecuted the other born according to Spirit, so it is to-day. But what says the Scripture? *Drive away the bondwoman and her son; for the son of the bond shall not inherit with the son of the free* (Genesis xxi, 10). Therefore, brethren, we are not children of the bond woman but of the free woman.

---

[1] The empty brackets to indicate that an interpolated passage is being omitted.

Then follows an exhortation to forsake error and return to rightmindedness.

Resumption of the Theme in the Epistle to the Romans and extraction from it of the Primitive Message

The theme is resumed, but with better logical order, in Paul's letter to the Christians in Rome, written at the beginning of the year 56, at the moment when the apostle was making his arrangements to leave Corinth for Jerusalem, whence he intended to journey to Rome. Note that the letter to the Thessalonians is addressed to "the community of the Thessalonians which is in God," etc.; those to the Corinthians "to the community of God which is at Corinth"; that to the Galatians "to the communities of Galatia"; whereas the letter to the Romans is destined "for all the beloved of God in Rome" (i, 7). Doubtless there were several Christian groups in Rome, which, without being rivals, were not yet united into a single church. In the preamble (i, 8–17) Paul states his intention and defines the theme which he desires his letter to make good:

> So, as much as in me is, I am anxious to preach the Gospel to you who are in Rome; for I am not ashamed of the Gospel. For it is the power of God for the salvation of every believer, to the Jew first, but also to the Greek. For God's righteousness is revealed in it by faith and for faith, as it is written, *whoso is righteous by faith*, shall live (Habakkuk, ii, 4).

And here is how he makes this thesis good (iii, 28–iv, 14, 16–24; iii, 27 adjusts the argument to the interpolated context; cf. ii, 17).

> We hold that a man is made completely righteous by faith without any works of the Law. Is God the God only of the Jews? Is he not also God of the Gentiles! To be sure he is God of the Gentiles, for there is only one God, who will make the circumcised righteous by faith and the uncircumcised by means of it. Are we then abolishing the Law by faith? Not in the least. We are giving the Law a firm basis.
> What, then, was it that Abraham, our ancestor according to the flesh, discovered for himself? For if Abraham became righteous by doing the works of the Law, he had something to be proud of, but not before God. For what says the Scripture? *Abraham had faith in God and that was imputed to him for righteousness* (Genesis xv, 6). Now the wages of a workman are not considered as a favour but as his due,

while to him who does no works, but has faith in him who makes the ungodly righteous, his faith is imputed to him for righteousness. In like manner David describes the blessedness of the man whom God counts as righteous without works on his part. [Here follows the citation of Psalm xxxii, 1–2.]

Was this blessedness promised to the circumcised, or to the uncircumcised as well? Again I say: *His faith was imputed to Abraham for righteousness.* How then was it imputed? To Abraham as a circumcised man? No, but when he was still uncircumcised. And he afterwards received the sign of circumcision as seal of the righteousness of faith, a righteousness won by him in his uncircumcised condition, to the end that he might be the father of the uncircumcised believers, to whom righteousness would be imputed in like manner, and father also to the circumcised, who follow in the steps of our father Abraham's faith.

The promise made to Abraham that he should inherit the world does not hold in virtue of the Law, but in virtue of the righteousness of faith. For if the followers of the Law are the heirs, their faith is of no account, and the promise given to it comes to nothing [   ]. That is why faith is the one thing that matters, so that all proceeds by favour, and the promise made secure for all posterity, not only for that which follows the Law but for that which is in the faith of Abraham, who is the father of us all, even as it is written *I have made thee father of many nations*—all this in the presence of God who makes the dead alive and calls the non-existent into being, and in whom he had faith. From his despair of posterity he passed to hoping in faith that he would become the father of *many nations*, even as God assured him, *thy offspring shall be numberless* (Genesis xiii, 16). He knew that his body was virtually dead, for he was nearly a hundred years old, and that Sarah's womb was also dead, but that did not weaken his faith in God's promise. On the contrary his faith asserted itself the more, and he was fully convinced that God was able to give him the promised posterity. And that is why it was *imputed to him for righteousness*. Now the words "imputed to him" were not written for him alone, but for us as well, according as we have faith in him who raised Jesus from the dead.

The subtilty of the argument is entirely in the Rabbinic style. But what becomes of Israel in all this? Is not Israel after all God's chosen people? Paul has his answer to the objection, and in the answer he explains the economy of salvation (ix, 1–5*a*, 6–13, 30–x, 21; xv, 8–12):

I speak the truth in Christ, I lie not; my conscience bearing me witness in the Holy Spirit that my sadness is great and my heartache incessant: I could wish myself under the curse of Christ for the sake of my brothers, my kinsmen in the flesh who are Israelites; theirs is the sonship, the glory, the tables of Law, the rite of worship and the promises; of them is the Christ an issue according to the flesh [   ].

Now it is not possible for the word of God to become obsolete. For Israel is not the totality of Israel's descendants; all are not children who are descended from Abraham. No; it is *through Isaac that thy posterity shall be reckoned* (Genesis xxi, 12). I mean that all children of the flesh are not children of God; only the children of the promise are counted as posterity. . . .

The case of Rebecca's twin sons is then cited. Although both were Isaac's offspring it is yet written of them: "Jacob have I loved, but Esau have I hated" (Malachi i, 2-3). Comment is as follows:

What shall we say then? We say that the Gentiles, who were aiming at righteousness, attained it, the righteousness that comes of faith; whereas Israel, who were aiming at a law of righteousness, failed to reach that law. And why? Because they sought it, not by the way of faith, but by conduct, and ran into the stone that makes men stumble, according as it is written. [Here follows citation of Isaiah viii, 14; xxviii, 16. The letter continues (x, 1).]

Brethren, my heart's desire and my prayer to God are for their salvation. I can bear witness to their zeal for God; but not a zeal enlightened by knowledge; for, in their ignorance of the righteousness of God, they failed to submit to it and sought rather to establish their own. For the end of the Law is the Christ, that everyone who believes in him may thereby become righteous. For Moses wrote of the righteousness which comes by the Law, *whoso practises that, by that shall he live* (Leviticus xviii, 5); but the righteousness which comes of faith speaks differently (Deuteronomy xxx, 12-14): *Say not in your heart: Who will go up to heaven?*—to bring the Christ down—or: *Who will go down into the abyss?*—to bring the Christ up from among the dead. No, what faith-righteousness says is this (Deuteronomy xxx, 14): *very close to thee is the word in thy mouth and in thy heart*—meaning the word "faith" which we preach. Mouth and heart mark you. For if you confess with your mouth that Jesus is Lord, and believe in your heart that God has raised him from the dead, saved you shall be. For with the heart we believe to be made righteous, and with the mouth we confess to be saved. For the Scripture says (Isaiah xxviii, 16): *Whosoever believes in him shall never be put to confusion*. There is no difference here between Jew and Greek, seeing that all have one and the same Lord, who is full of bounty to them that call on him, *for everyone who calls on him shall be saved* (Joel ii, 32). But how shall they call on a Lord in whom they have no belief? And how believe in a Lord of whom they have never heard? And how shall they hear of him without a preacher? And how shall we preach him unless we are called?—even as Isaiah

writes (lii, 7): *how beautiful are the feet of him who brings good tidings.*
But not all have yielded to the Gospel, even as Isaiah says (liii, 1):
Lord, who has believed our report? So then, faith comes from preaching,
and preaching by the word of the Christ. But, say I, have they not
heard it? Yes, they have: *their voice has gone all over the earth and their
words to the end of the world* (Psalm xix, 4). Then, I ask, have they not
understood? Moses was the first to say it: *I will make you jealous of a
nation that is no nation; I will provoke your pity for a nation with no
understanding* (Deuteronomy xxxii, 21). Then Isaiah boldly says: *I
have been found by those who did not seek me; I have revealed myself to
those who question me not* (lxv, 1). And to Israel he cries: *I have held out
my hands all day long to a disobedient and contradictory people* (lxv, 2).

Now I tell you [continuing with xv, 8] that the Christ has been ready
to serve the circumcision by showing them God's veracity in confirming the promises made to the patriarchs and that the Gentiles glorify
God by his mercy, according as it is written (Psalm xviii, 49): *Therefore I will exalt thee among the Gentiles and sing praises to thy Name.*
And again he says (Deuteronomy xxxii, 43): *Rejoice, ye Gentiles,
with his People.* And again (Psalm cxvii, 1): *Praise the Lord, all ye
Gentiles, and let all peoples extol him.* And Isaiah once more (xi, 10):
*there shall be a shoot of Jesse springing forth to rule the Gentiles: in him
shall the Gentiles hope.*

At this point the fundamental thesis of the letter written by
Paul to the Roman Christians comes to its natural close. The
letter is no skeleton outline, but a complete exposition, well
balanced and well developed, of what Paul, in the given circumstances, had to say to these Christians. The complementary
matter, added by other hands to the original document, is entirely superfluous. Least of all does it need the juxtaposition[1] of a
gnosis, which contradicts it at every point of its structure, nor
the emollient paraphrases which try to make the gnosis fit in
with the primitive teaching here revealed by Paul; nor the
violent outbreak against pagans and Jewish sectaries in the
opening chapters (i, 18–iii, 26); nor the moral counsels (xii–xv, 7)
which are wholly foreign to its theme. We have now to
examine the original conclusion of the document (xv, 14–xvi, 16,
19a, 20–24).

Paul declares himself persuaded that the recipients of his letter
have no need of his exhortations; but, as minister of the Christ
among the Gentiles, he simply desires to fortify their good dis-

---

[1] We say "juxtaposition" in opposition to certain expositors who, without taking the trouble to probe the matter, make it a case of *fusion*—the fusion of two doctrines.

positions. The truth is that the results of his ministry have been such as to justify him in a certain boldness before God and in a measure of pride in the Christ Jesus. Has he not carried the preaching of the Gospel, starting from Jerusalem, throughout the entire circuit of the Eastern Mediterranean—the statement is somewhat summary, but this was not the moment for entering into detail—and has he not done this while holding to it, "as a point of honour, to preach the Gospel only in places where the Christ's name was unknown, so as not to build on another man's foundation"? All the same, he would have come to Rome long ago, had he not been prevented. These statements should not be taken too literally; none the less there is one thing that may be deduced from them for a certainty: while the Christians of Rome were in considerable numbers, it is clear that they had not been recruited there by renowned propagandists of the new faith, nor by any one of them. They had drifted into the imperial city from various quarters, and such propaganda as they could carry on would be a private affair among individuals. Hence Paul could look upon Rome as new ground. So his intention is to establish himself in Rome for some time with a view to going later into Spain, doubtless with the idea of carrying his message to the furthest point of Western civilization. We should be in error in supposing this to mean that he thought it his mission to convert the then known world. He meant simply that he hoped to carry the name of the Christ, and the announcement that the Kingdom was at hand, to the furthest point he could reach—a simple programme joined with a great simplicity of outlook. The teaching we have just considered fits in with it perfectly.

He goes on to say that before visiting Rome, he must go to Jerusalem to deliver a collection gathered up from the believers in Macedonia and Achaia, and he asks his friends in Rome to help him with their prayers that "he may not fall into the hands of Jewish unbelievers" and that his "service for Jerusalem may prove acceptable to the saints there." Of the two conditions only the second seems to have been fulfilled.

There has been much discussion on the long list of salutations at the end of the Epistle, some critics holding, gratuitously enough, that Paul cannot have had so many personal acquaintances in Rome, and supposing, still more gratuitously, that the list refers to believers in Ephesus: as if, with Ephesus in view, Paul would not have had to salute a formed community, instead of the listed individuals such as he here cites by name. The personal salutations are satisfactorily explained as addressed to believers who belonged to groups scattered over a wide region. The conclusion of the list implies that these persons had now found their way to Rome. This conclusion should be reconstructed as follows (xvi, 16, 19a, 20–23):

> Salute each other with a holy kiss. All the churches of the Christ salute you [ ]. For your obedience has come to the knowledge of all [ ]. The God of peace will soon crush Satan under your feet, etc.

Why all the churches should salute certain Ephesian believers by the mouth of Paul is by no means clear, but that Paul should pass on to the Roman Christians the greetings of all the churches he had founded in the East is intelligible enough. Moreover what is said about the common knowledge of their obedience to faith in the Christ is in keeping with what Paul has written in the preamble of his letter (i, 8): "your faith is celebrated throughout the world." The praise bestowed by the two passages clearly concerns the same persons.

We conclude that Paul's original letter to the Romans is an unimpeachable document from which we may learn with certainty the precise form of the eschatological catechesis—the primitive teaching of the End of the World. In substance it was as follows:

> *Jesus, risen from the dead as Christ and Lord, is at God's right hand; to him and to those who believe in him belongs the "heritage of the world"; he will establish the Kingdom of God over the whole earth and annihilate the powers which have so long made it the Kingdom of Satan.*

SECOND STAGE IN THE EVOLUTION OF THE CATECHESIS

The transformation of the primitive catechesis of the Kingdom, which we have just considered, into the evangelical catechesis of salvation, followed in the steps of the transformation which changed the Christ of the imminent Coming into a divine redeemer, whose terrestrial career, a mystic epiphany more or less substituted for his lately expected epiphany on the clouds, was so conceived as to make him author of the mystery of salvation. The catechesis of Mark, the catecheses of Matthew and Luke, the catechesis of John show, in that order, the advancing steps of the transformation. But, just as it is impossible to assign a precise date to each new element, as revisers introduced it into the catechesis represented by the four canonical Gospels, so it is equally impossible to fix the dates of those gnostic and anti-gnostic elements which were interpolated into the Epistles named after Paul and into the other Epistles of the New Testament canon.

On what principles these added elements are to be distinguished from the original matter, and their significance explained, may be gathered from our former work *Remarques sur la littérature épistolaire du Nouveau Testament* (1935). In the present book, therefore, it would be superfluous to demonstrate at length what we have proved in its predecessor, namely, that if Paul be the author of the teaching we have just studied, so far as it is developed in the Epistle to the Romans, it is impossible that he be, at the same time, the author of the gnostic system interpolated between the broken fragments of that teaching, and flatly contradicting it while pretending to give it a firmer standing. Had the two expositions been lodged in the same brain they would have been fused into one, instead of appearing, as they do, at cross purposes and dislocating the Epistle. That is a psychologic and literary fact against which sentiment and theology are powerless. Let the official apologists of Catholicism repeat *ad libitum* their charge, if they can do so with straight faces, that we have misunderstood the intimate harmony of the Great Apostle's thought and are incapable of placing ourselves at its centre, since we lack the faith that was Paul's. We, on our part, know that these are words without meaning. We know also at what centre these champions of authenticity have taken *their* stand. It is the centre of accepted convention and of orders received from the Pontifical Commission on Biblical Study.

The Superadded Gnosis, not Paul's, in the Epistle to the Romans

We now proceed to examine the gnosis in Romans, taking account of variations and additions made to it in Galatians and Corinthians. The gnoses in Philippians, Colossians, Ephesians and Hebrews demand separate consideration as presented under different conditions.

In the gnosis of Romans, Israel and Abraham drop out of view, nor is the theme any longer concerned with the promises made to them, nor with the Christ who is to come, nor with faith in the Christ risen from the dead as the sole condition of admission to the approaching Kingdom of God. It is now a question of the *whole human race*, in bondage from its beginnings to sin and death, which the Christ, descended straight from heaven, has ransomed by his own death, and is now ready to share his divine immortality with all those who mystically unite themselves to his death and resurrection in the rites of Christian initiation. The essentials of this gnosis have nothing to do with promises contained in the Scriptures; they are concerned with the revelation of the mystery hidden in God till now revealed, which mystery, when occasion demands it, is expressly distinguished from the eschatological catechesis with its foundation in Scripture. Moreover, the two catecheses present marked differences of style as well as of subject-matter. While the eschatological thesis is developed almost in the language of every day, and as though the author were augmentatively conversing with his readers, not as a philosopher, but as a rabbi making good his case with a grand array of subtly interpreted Scripture texts—while this is the way of Paul's catechesis, the gnostic theme on the other hand, with its point of departure in the biblical myth of the first sin, takes form as a system of doctrine, a theory of moral philosophy with a certain measure of logical appeal. In this presentation the argument does not need a Scripture text to support each step of its advance, but bids for acceptance on its own merits in a way which suggests that the system was originally constructed independently of the Epistle into which it has been inserted. Needless to say that with this difference of subject and style there goes a different vocabulary. This will be obvious at once to anyone who will take the pains to compare the two.

Here, to begin with, is the preamble to the gnosis very cleverly inserted before the development of Paul's eschatological theme (iii, 21–24, where it will be noted 21 seems to have been first written to make sequences with i, 16–18, the whole of i, 19–iii, 20 being added later):

> But the righteousness of God has now been revealed without the Law [   ]. It is a divine righteousness; but all men can win it by believing in Jesus Christ. For there is no distinction among men in this respect, since all men have sinned and fallen short of the divine glory. This righteousness is bestowed on men as a free gift of grace, thanks to the redemption effected by the Christ Jesus, whom God appointed propitiatory victim [   ] to demonstrate his righteousness, after passing over sins committed under his forbearance, and in view of the revelation of his righteousness due to come in this present time and to make it plain that he is, himself, righteous and that he deems every man who has faith in Jesus to be a righteous man.

The making of men righteous by their faith (justification of faith) is still the theme; but it is neither the righteousness, nor the faith that we encountered before. In this new presentation righteousness means liberation from the sin which has ruled the world since Adam, while faith is unwavering confidence in the redemption effected by the death of the Christ in his quality of propitiatory victim for the whole of mankind. The thesis recurs further on in passages now separated but originally forming a single *bloc*—v, 1–8, 10–vii, 6; viii, 1–9a, 10, 12–13, 23b–25, 28–35, 37–39; iv, 25 makes a forced transition.

We are first told that our hope is grounded on the fact that, while we were yet sinners, God revealed his love for us, the Christ dying on our behalf; reconciled to God by the death of his Son we too are rendered immortal by communion in the death and resurrection of the Son whom God has raised from death. This has providentially come to pass, and the way of it is as follows:

> The explanation is that sin came into the world by one man, and death by sin, and that thus all men were doomed to death because all have sinned. For there was sin in the world before the Law was given, but it was not reckoned as sin because there was as yet no Law. But death had dominion from Adam to Moses, even on those who had not sinned after the manner of Adam's transgression, and Adam is a figure of him who was to come.

In this statement there are some enormous absurdities which neither philosophers nor historians need spend time in discussing. Let us rather take up the doctrine of the two Adams, the two heads of the human race—the man, Adam the sinner who stands as the antitype of the other man, Adam the Saviour Jesus Christ.

First Corinthians (xv, 21–22, 45–47) will tell us that, of the two men, "the first is terrestrial, the second celestial"; the first, "living animal"; the second, "life-giving Spirit." The exposition goes on:

> But it is not the case that the trespass committed and the grace bestowed are in equal measure; for while all other men die in consequence of one man's trespass, the grace of God and the free gift by the grace of the one man [ ] Jesus Christ, overflowed in far greater measure to all those others. Nor is the effect on them of this free gift on an equality with the effect which followed the sin of the first sinner. For while the judgment on the one sin was a sentence of condemnation, the free gift after many sins is a sentence of acquittal. For while by one man's sin, death reigned over all mankind through him alone, all who receive the abundant gift of grace and righteousness shall reign in life by that One who is Jesus-Christ—which is a far greater thing. Go to, then: as all mankind was condemned for a single act of sin, so, by a single righteous act, justification for life became available to all. For, as by the disobedience of one man all the other men in the world were made sinners, so by the obedience of One, they are all made righteous. The Law was introduced in order that sin might abound; but where sin abounded grace abounded still more, so that, just as sin formerly reigned by death, grace now reigned by righteousness to eternal life by Jesus Christ our Lord.

If anyone choose to believe that this wholly abstract, scholastic and false conception of the Law was imagined and professed by a man who had long lived in obedience to the Law, we shall not pause to argue with him. The writer continues:

> What are we to infer from this? Shall we remain in sin that grace may abound? ... Have you forgotten that all of us have been baptized into Christ and, in that, are baptized into his *death*. This means that we have been buried with him by baptism unto death, so that, just as Christ was raised from death by the glory of the Father, we also are to walk in newness of life. For, if we are associated in his death by this symbol, we are equally associated in his resurrection, knowing, as we do, that our old man has been crucified with him, that the sinful body might be destroyed. ...

In the same sense the Epistle to the Galatians understands the Christian as a "new creation" (vi, 15); the Second to Corinthians has a like conception (v, 17). The writer proceeds:

> Thus there is no condemnation now for those who are in Christ Jesus, for the law of spirit of life in Christ Jesus has delivered thee from the law of sin and death. For God [ ] having sent his own

Son in the semblance of sinful flesh, and because of sin, has condemned sin in the flesh, so that the righteousness of the Law is fulfilled in us who walk not according to flesh but according to spirit....

For I reckon that the sufferings of the present time are not to be compared with the glory due to be revealed in us. For the eager creation longs for the manifestation of the sons of God. For futility has been imposed on the creation, not of its own will, but by the will of him who imposed it, with the hope that the creation itself, as well as ourselves, will be delivered from slavery to corruption, that it too may share the liberty of the glory of the children of God. For we know that the whole creation is united in suffering and cries of pain till now; and not the creation only but [ ] we ourselves inwardly cry with pain as we wait for filiation, for deliverance from our body; for it is in hope that we are saved....

But we know that to those who love God everything converges to good, to those called according to plan, because those whom he foresaw, them he predestined to be conformed to the image of his Son, that he might be first born among many brothers. Now, whom he predestined, them also he called. Whom he called, them also he deemed righteous, whom he deemed righteous them also he glorified. What, then, shall we say to that? If God is for us, who will be against us?... Who shall separate us from the love of Christ? For I am persuaded that neither life nor death, nor angels, nor principalities, nor present, nor future, nor powers, nor any other created thing can separate us from the love of God which is in Christ Jesus, our Lord.

A noble theory, conceived by an impassioned soul. And something more. We have here a gnosis sketched in grand outline, but an outline that needs to be filled. For the part played by the Law is strangely lowered. Opposed to the triad Law—sin—death stands the triad grace—righteousness—immortality. What can the Law be, then, but the auxiliary of sin? Moreover, one sacrament only is thrown into relief—baptism. But palliations are introduced, notably the short dissertation on the inner conflict that arises between the consciousness of duty and the carnal lusts; by this the opposition between the Law and grace, shifted from the ground of abstract theology to the ground of moral philosophy, becomes the opposition of natural desire and spirit, the Law itself becoming "the oldness of the letter" which gives place to "the newness of spirit."

The Gnosis Developed in Second Corinthians

The same point of view, in which the Law regains a significant and positive rôle in the scheme of salvation, is resumed and developed at length by the author of certain mystical passages in Second Corinthians (ii, 14–vi, 13). In the extracts we propose to give from this Epistle, Paul the mystic, who is effaced behind his subject in Romans, advances into the foreground:

> Our ability comes from God, who himself has made us able ministers of the new covenant, not of the letter, but of the spirit. For the letter kills, but the spirit makes alive.

The letter is the Law, and the letter kills if we remain confined within it; rightly understood, then, the ministry of the Law is here, in Second Corinthians, a ministry of death, as we find it in Romans. None the less the Law can lead on to the spiritual gnosis, to the true Gospel of the Christ, playing the part of "pedagogue" (Galatians iii, 21–25). We take up the sequence of our text (2 Corinthians iii, 7):

> Now if the ministry of death, in letters graven on stones, shone with such splendour that the children of Israel could not look on Moses' face on account of the passing splendour of it, how much more glorious will be the ministration of the spirit! For if the ministration was glorious when it condemned to death, the ministration which justifies vastly excels it in splendour. Indeed the former splendour was no splendour at all compared with this higher. For, if that which was passing away shone with splendour, how much more glorious shall that shine which will never pass away.
>
> Having such a hope in me, I use no disguises; I am not like Moses, who veiled his face that the children of Israel might not see the passing splendour on it. Ah, but their intelligence was blinded; for, indeed, to this very day the same veil hangs unlifted over the reading out of the Old Covenant, for the Christ alone can take it away; yes, to this very day, when Moses is read, the veil falls on their hearts. *But the veil is lifted from the moment they turn to the Lord* (Exodus xxxiv, 34).

The author repeats himself a little, unless the phrases headed by the words "to this very day" are textual variants. But, whichever hypothesis we prefer, the meaning remains the same. We may well ask whether the recruits Paul had gathered in Corinth would have understood a single word of these subtleties. It is true that here the Mosaic revelation counts for something as having a figurative sense; but to what a distance are we now come from Paul's eschatology with its climax in the second coming of the Lord! However, a great advance has been made by admitting the co-ordination of the two Covenants, of which the gnosis in the Epistle to the Romans gives no sign. But here is the conclusion of our passage:

> Now the Lord is the spirit, and where the spirit of the Lord is, there is liberty. And all of us, with faces uncovered, reflecting the splendour of the Lord, are ourselves transformed into the same image from one splendour to another, the splendour that comes from the Lord, from the spirit.

Ancient Scripture, then, is a figurative enigma, in which the gnostic Christian may read his participation in the splendour of the Christ-Spirit. A kind of mystic vision in which the initiate into a Mystery finally sees himself clothed with the splendour of his God.

The ministry of him whose mission it is to proclaim such a Gospel is unique:

> By manifestation of the truth I commend myself to every man's conscience before God. And what if my Gospel is veiled? Veiled it may be, but only among the lost, there where the god of this age has blinded the minds of the unbelieving, that they see not the light of the Gospel of the splendour of the Christ, who is the image of God.

"The god of this age" is the chief archon who presides, with such indifferent success, over the destiny of our world and the present age (compare "the princes of this age" in 1 Corinthians ii, 8; "the prince of this world" in John xii, 31; xiv, 30; xvi, 11). He may be Satan, but certainly not Marcion's demiurge. As to "the lost" and "the unbelieving," they are not unbelievers in the general doctrines of theology, but those whom the mystic Paul regards as the adversaries of his own doctrine, and whom he treats as Judaizers.

> It is not myself that I preach, but Christ Jesus and myself your servant for Jesus.

Following this (iv, 7–15) comes a dithyrambic eulogy of the special apostolate claimed by this mystic Paul, who has also much to say about himself in the Epistle to the Galatians (see our *Remarques sur la littérature épistolaire*, 33–45, 50–57). We do not propose to repeat here what we have said in that work about the inconceivable pretensions there put forward by the mystic Paul, nor to discuss again the accusations brought by this Paul, Paul only in name, against his straw-made Judaizers, the question seeming to us sufficiently elucidated in the former discussion. To proceed:

> Though my outward man is wearing out, my inner man is renewing itself from day to day; for my light affliction of the moment is preparing me for a plenitude of eternal splendour beyond all conceiving, my gaze being turned not to things visible, but to things invisible; for the visible pass away, but the invisible are for eternity. Indeed know I well that, if the earthly tent I dwell in were to melt away, I have a home from God, a house not made with hands, eternal, in the heavens.... Being, then, of good heart, and knowing that while at home in the body I am an exile from the Lord—for I walk by faith in him, not by sight of him—I have no fears, and would rather be an exile from the body and at home with the Lord.

The purely spiritual idea of the resurrection contained in this passage is unmistakable and needs no insistence. How near it brings us to the Song of Love in 1 Corinthians xiii! But how far it takes us from the eschatological catechesis of the real Paul!

> Love of the Christ holds me, my conviction being this: that One having died on behalf of all, all are then dead; and he died for all, that the living should live no more for themselves, but for him who died on their behalf and rose from death. The result is that from henceforth I, for my part, know no man according to the flesh. Even had I known the Christ according to the flesh, I would not now know him in that way. To tell the truth, if any one is in the Christ, he is a new creature; old things have passed away; see, they have become new!

We can hardly hide from ourselves that this mystic notion of salvation was conceived with the eschatological catechesis in mind, perhaps even with an eye to the evangelical catechesis, as the Synopsis presents it in substance. Nor can we fail to see that, on this theory, the Christ of flesh in his human life counts for very little, or even for nothing at all, in comparison with the Christ-Spirit in his immortality. That the intention of it all is to depreciate the Christ of the so-called Judaizers, that is the Christ of the common tradition, is almost equally evident. But what prevailed in the long run was not this uncompromising mysticism. The author goes on:

> But all this comes from God, who has reconciled me to himself through the Christ and given me the ministry of reconciliation. Because God was in the Christ, reconciling the world to

> himself, not holding men guilty of their transgressions, and implanting in men the message of reconciliation. So, then, I am an ambassador for the Christ, as if God were preaching with my voice. Be reconciled to God! On behalf of Christ I so entreat you! Him who knew not sin, he made to be sin on our behalf, that we poor men may become God's own righteousness in him. Following his leading in all that, I thus exhort you not to receive the grace of God in vain.

Here we come back into the current of the mystic doctrine already encountered in the Epistle to the Romans, but with a marked difference in the emphasis now laid on the unique rôle attributed to Paul in the economy of salvation, in which he is represented as the accredited ambassador of God to the human race. A purely theoretic conception, if ever there was one, and formed at a great distance from the first Christian age; the more plainly so as the system of gnosis here presented is visibly of later date than even the gnosis in Romans, of which, in certain respects, it offers an attenuation.

The Eucharist Finds its Place in the Mystery

In all we have had under review no sign has appeared that the eucharistic Supper had any place in the mystery of salvation. Perhaps its place was not defined as early as that of baptism. Or is it not more likely that it was held secret? Does not the fourth Gospel strictly avoid speaking of it in direct language, and is there not a like reserve in the Epistle to the Hebrews? We find it, however, in certain secondary parts of the gnosis presented in First Corinthians; and first of all in the account of the normal course of the Supper (xi, 17, 20–34. See *Remarques*, 60–64):

> For I myself have had it passed on to me from the Lord, and have passed it on to you, that the Lord Jesus, in the night when he was betrayed, took bread and, after thanksgiving, broke it and said: "This is my body, which is given for you. Do this in remembrance of me." Likewise, after the meal, the cup, saying: "This cup is the new Covenant in my blood. Do this, whenever you shall drink it, in remembrance of me." For every time you eat this bread and drink this cup you proclaim the death of the Lord, until the time when he comes.

The first point to be noticed in the above passage is that the author has the evangelical catechesis in mind and that he intends his mystic doctrine of the Supper to be set in a frame which by this time had become traditional, that, namely, of the early eschatological view of the Supper, which conceived it as a memorial meal symbolic of the Christ to come, and as a foretaste of the banquet of the elect in the Kingdom of God. In this way the meaning of the concluding formula, "you proclaim the death of the Lord, till the time when he comes," is explained. In like manner we can understand the double meaning involved in the mode of presentation, which exhibits the author as having received from the Lord himself a "tradition" either ignored or forgotten by the Corinthians. He presents the Supper as a tradition, which it really was from its origin, and at the same time fixes the meaning he desires it to have as a mystery, while affecting merely to recall it. Doubtless he found both the bread and the cup, with another commentary, in the story he is here exploiting, and the mention of the Great Coming, is also taken from that source. There is ground for saying, then, that by a kind of compromise between later gnosis and primitive eschatology he has introduced his mystic interpretation of Jesus' last meal into the earlier frame of the eschatological view of the Supper. It follows that this compromise is less ancient than the gnosis we have just considered. It seems, however, to be earlier than Marcion; and the testimony of Justin, who found this very compromise introduced into the synoptic Gospels, attests its relative antiquity (compare our analysis of the story in Mark, *supra*, p. 100).

Another fragment of First Corinthians is presented under similar conditions—the instruction on eating meat sacrificed to idols (x, 1–22), in which the sacraments of Christian initiation are both mentioned. The author appeals to the sacraments of the desert as a type of the Christian sacraments. The chief interest for us of this curious passage lies in its making of baptism and the eucharist the two parts of one sacrament, so connected that they can be found combined in the Old Testament, which is the last place in the world where one would expect to find them; for the rest, the homiletical character of the passage is made obvious in the moral lesson it is chiefly intended to convey. The comparison would also suggest a form of the sacrament in which water was used instead of wine; but we have discussed that elsewhere (see *The Birth of the Christian Religion*, p. 238, and *Remarques*, 65, n. 2). Let us rather consider the relations which the passage institutes between the Christian Supper and the pagan sacrifice:

> The cup of blessing which we bless, is not that communion in the blood of the Christ? The bread which we break, is not that communion in the body of the Christ? Because, though we are many, there is only one bread, only one body; for we all partake of the one bread.

This communion with the Christ is pronounced incompatible with participation in the sacrifices of the pagan religions, even though the meat offered to idols is only meat and the idols themselves nothing at all. But, behind the meat which is only meat and the idol which is nothing, there are the demons, and they are to be reckoned with:

> What the pagans sacrifice, to the demons they sacrifice it and not to God; and I would not have you in communion with demons. You cannot drink the cup of the Lord and the cup of demons; you cannot share the Lord's table and the demons' table. What! shall we provoke the Lord to jealousy? Are we stronger than he?

The Christian has communion with his Lord in the Supper because the Supper mystically realizes the death of Jesus and brings it into spiritual operation. In this we get a clear perception of the idea which the Christian mystery formed of its Christ and see, at the same time, the fundamental affinity between the Christian and the pagan mysteries in their conception of eternal salvation. Another passage of the same Epistle (viii, 4–6) on the question of idol-meat puts the matter beyond all doubt:

> About the eating of idol-meats, we know that no idol exists in the world and that there is no God but ours. There may be so-called gods either in heaven or on earth, but, for us, there is only one God, the Father, the source of everything and for whom we exist, and our Lord, Jesus Christ by whom all exists and we exist.

So, then, there is only one God and one Lord, but the universe harbours lesser powers, more or less dangerous, against whose influence we need to protect ourselves. The fundamental

The Christological Gnosis in Philippians, Colossians and Hebrews

ideas of this Christian gnosis are not far removed from those of pagan mysticism current at the same time.

More precise definition of the Christological gnosis is to be found in the short poem picked up by the Epistle to the Philippians (ii, 6–11); in the Epistle to the Colossians (i, 15–20) and in the Epistle to the Hebrews (i, 1–4). On this we confine ourselves to summarizing the conclusions reached in our *Remarques*.

The poem inserted into the gnostic-moral part of Philippians (see *Remarques*, 91–95) is the oracle of some Christian prophet, a Christian gnosis earlier than its context in the Epistle, certainly earlier than the gnosis in Hebrews, but probably not earlier than the mystic gnosis of the great Epistles. It conveys the following information.

There existed a being in godlike form, not God himself but a sharer in the divine splendour and under the orders of the Deity. Merit is ascribed to him for not affecting equality with God—which implies that other beings of the same order had the insolence to put themselves forward as gods and to get themselves worshipped as such. The being in question put off his godlike form to take human form and, in that form, to submit to death in obedience to God; in recompense for that obedience he has been elevated to God's right hand, where he is worshipped as *Lord* and carries that name. Behind this profession of faith in one only God, and in the kind of shared divinity bestowed on Jesus, there lies a cosmology, a world-economy, a doctrine of salvation, consisting in the restoration of the cosmic and human economy which has been thrown into disorder by the backsliding of mankind and by the fall or failure in duty of certain powers. This background of the poem is purely gnostic. We see it only in glimpses; enough to conjecture its general form but not to reconstitute in all its parts.

A christological poem has been similarly inserted into the Epistle to the Colossians. This, too, is the oracle of a Christian prophet inserted as an afterthought into the Epistle, which is in no sense whatever the work of Paul (see *Remarques*, 95–101). The cosmogony is different from that in Philippians, and there is another conception of the divine mediator, a deeper gnosis and probably of later date. Here he is the image of God, living and active, in whom and by whom (so says the second strophe of the poem) the universal balance is to be restored after an overthrow of which we are not told the circumstances. The soteriology is less clearly outlined than in the poem of Philippians. Nevertheless it is made clear that "the first born of all creation" has now become "the first born of the dead"; he has become so by making himself man, undergoing death as man, and by rising from the dead as the first born of the risen: by the power of this saving death the divine order, "the Pleroma," which has been shattered, will be restored. We are told in the body of the Epistle (ii, 14–15) that the Christ has "brought us all to life with him, having wiped out the writing against us (the Law), with the clauses that condemned us; he has taken them away by nailing them to the cross; having despoiled the Principalities and the Powers, he has put them to shame, triumphing over them by his own might." The "Pleroma" is a gnostic term which should be taken here in the sense given it by the gnosis, that is, as the totality of all divine emanations and creations. The restoration of this Pleroma in the Christ implies reconciliation with God. As to the "body" of this divine redeemer, we are told further on (ii, 9) that "the entire Pleroma of Divinity resides *bodily* (that is, in the manner of body) in the Christ; thus the "body" and "the Church" are not confined to the believing part of humanity and to the church on earth, but comprise the body of the now balanced universe and the Church whose members are worlds, as the author of the Epistle to the Ephesians (i, 19–23) also understands them. With this meaning we are told (Colossians ii, 10) that the faithful are "pleromed"[1] in the Christ. All that is pure gnosis, if gnosis is to be found anywhere; but not the same gnosis as that of the poem in Philippians. As regards the diversity of gnoses which have found their way into the Epistles, the writer of the present book is altogether innocent; he is not their inventor; he merely endeavours to understand them, but without attributing them, in spite of their manifest diversity, to Paul as the sole author of them all.

---

[1] "Complete in him" (A.V.); "made full" (R.V.); "reach your full life" (Moffatt); *pleromés* in the French. *Translator's note.*

The Christ-gnosis in Hebrews

Another gnostic definition of the Christ is given in the Epistle to the Hebrews. This gnosis is more deeply studied than the preceding and the author takes greater pains to exhibit the Christian revelation as the consummation of those which God made "to the fathers by the prophets." But here also the Son is an image, an imprint of Divinity, an agent in creation by whom God made "the worlds." The text says "the aeons," which are neither "the age" nor "the worlds," but the series of existences in their harmonious hierarchy and time-order (cf. xi, 3). The author insists that the Son of God is higher than the angels in name, status and nature, the reason for his insistence being that he knows of people who class, or seem to class, the pre-existent Christ in one category with the celestial spirits called angels; is not that pretty much the case with the good Hermas? And might we not, with no great difficulty, interpret the christological poem of Philippians in the same sense? For the rest, the body of the Epistle is mainly occupied in explaining how "purification from sin" is effected, the Son of God having come to earth in order to accomplish, by his death and the offering of his blood, an act of priestly expiation, of which Melchizedek of old was the type.

The author understands the statement about Melchizedek (Genesis xiv, 17–20) in a way of his own (see *Remarques*, 108–109). The Christ, besides being the true "king of justice" and the true "king of peace," is an eternal priest after the order of Melchizedek. He has come into the world to accomplish a priestly and redeeming work; he is "without father" and "without mother"; therefore "without genealogy" and so "without beginning of days," for he pre-existed his earthly manifestation; nor has his life an ending, because his death began his immortality without any waiting in the tomb, or rising of his body, for he entered the heavenly sanctuary at once and for all "through the veil, that is, through his flesh" (x, 20). Thus he would have us understand the miracle of the rent veil in the synoptic tradition of Mark, Matthew and Luke. This again is gnosis, embroidered on a groundwork of Biblical texts, but genuine gnosis, though linked with the revelations of the Old Covenant.

Moreover, the author himself is at pains to inform us that we are in the realm of gnosis, and the point merits consideration (v, 11–vi, 2). The doctrine he expounds belongs, he says, to the order of "perfection," that is, of gnostic initiation, and this he distinguishes from what he calls "the elementary theme of the Christ," meaning the common catechesis of his time and place. This catechesis, as we have already shown (p. 43), was still almost entirely eschatological in its teaching.

The comparison of his readers to little children, whose normal nourishment was the milk of this elementary doctrine, shows that he knew the analogous remark of the mystic "Paul" who in First Corinthians (iii, 1–3) employs this same comparison, informing his readers that, because they are incapable of receiving it, he has withheld from them the wisdom which, in the self-same context, he nevertheless expounds for their instruction. In both cases the contradiction arises in the same way. It comes from the fact that the primitive catechesis, under the lapse of time and the evolution of ideas, had come to seem more or less obsolete and that pains were being taken by new teachers to comment and correct it in the light of a teaching with another character. So strange a perspective allows no other explanation, though many commentators, even critics, are still loth to perceive it.

The Gnosis in the First Epistle of Timothy and the First of Peter

The short Christological creed, rhythmically formulated, in 1 Timothy iii, 16 must here be mentioned: it is perceptibly older than its context (see *Remarques* 118–119):

> He was manifested in the flesh,
>   he was vindicated in the spirit;
> He was seen by the angels,
>   he was preached among the Gentiles;
> He was believed on in the world,
>   he was taken up into glory.

This poem has the same character as those in the Epistles to the Philippians, Colossians and Hebrews, and the same spiritual idea of the resurrection, by which the Christ is "vindicated," the glory of his immortality making good the ignominy of his death.

The First Epistle of Peter is inspired by an analogous doctrine, but the author adds to it on his own responsibility a descent into hell, in which the mystic gnosis is coloured by a touch of pagan mythology (iii, 18–22; iv, 6; see *Remarques*, 120–131). Both gnosis and style begin to show signs of decay; both are derivative in their relation to most of the gnoses previously considered.

The romance of the descent into hell is borrowed from the Book of Enoch and mediately from old Eastern mythologies. The "spirits that were in prison" are the fallen angels who, mating with women, produced the giants and provoked the punishment of the Deluge. To these fallen spirits the Christ-Spirit goes with the good news; they are the first to submit to the immortal Christ, the other celestial powers being conquered by his ascent into heaven, as these others are by his descent into hell. The preaching of the Gospel to the general mass of the dead was accomplished by the Christ himself on the occasion of his instructing the fallen angels. Thus all who lived on earth before the coming of the Christ have had their chance of salvation; condemned to death as "men of the flesh" and as punishment for their sins, the grace of God has enabled them to live again in spiritual glory. It would seem, then, that this author knew only of a spiritual resurrection, whether for the Christ himself or for the human believer.

Moral Teaching in the Epistles

All our Epistles are more or less weighted with moral teaching. The earlier Gospel catechesis had its own, as the preaching of Jesus had, and that from the very first. "*Repent*, for the Kingdom of God is at hand" is an urgent appeal for a change of life. But it will be more in keeping with our present purpose to point out briefly how the interest taken by the mystic teaching of the Epistles in the moralization of life extends progressively over wider fields in proportion as excitement about the Second Coming passed into decline, and even, with many, to the point of extinction. Hence the insistence with which the moral renewal, implied in the spiritual and mystic rebirth of the believer, is brought to the front; hence, too, the production of short codes of religious morality, clearly such, for the individual, for the family and for social relationships. The last chapters of the Epistle to the Romans are thus occupied (xii–xv, 7), in which we may note especially the surcharge, out of relation to its context, recommending obedience to established powers, because they come from God (xiii, 1–7)—certainly this proclamation of the divine origin of the imperial powers does not belong to the first Christian age (see *Remarques*, 30–31). Some parts of First Corinthians are short treatises on moral discipline, or even of casuistry, such as the instructions about marriage and virginity (vii). The teaching on spiritual gifts (charismata), which concern the right ordering of Christian assemblies (xii, xiv) appears under like conditions, but with this striking difference, that the interpolation in its midst of the Song of Love (xiii) is on an infinitely higher level than the disciplinary matter which the singer of it had before him and into which he or somebody else thought the hymn might be fittingly inserted (see *Remarques*, 69–74). The instructions on the control of "speaking with tongues" (glossolaly) may be placed side by side with the queer little dissertation on the veiling of women (xi, 5–16) while praying or prophesying, and we may recall the more recent interpolations which forbid them to speak at all (xiv, 34a–35; cf. 1 Timothy ii, 8–15).

The Epistle to the Galatians contains instruction in mystic morality conceived in the same spirit as the distinctively gnostic passages (v, 13–26; vi, 7–10, 12–16). The Epistle to the Colossians, taken, as a whole, is a moralizing gnosis, but it includes special precepts for wives, husbands, children, fathers, slaves and masters. The Epistle to the Ephesians is in the same case, except that it waters down the moralities of Colossians. Finally, the First of Peter is a mystico-moral homily with special applications; respect for established authority (probably imitated from Romans xiii, 1–7); advice to slaves, wives, husbands, and encouragement to martyrs. In the last we are told that to suffer for the name of Christ and as a good Christian is a thing of little moment, provided one has not to suffer for crime of the common order (iv, 12–19). But the counsels which the author addresses to the leaders of the Christian flock, where the Christ is characterized as the chief shepherd, place him in the time of the Pastoral Epistles, although, unlike them, he makes no allusion to the gnostic peril.

DELAY OF THE SECOND COMING: ANXIETY AND APPEASEMENT

Would Christianity have survived if it had not been supported by faith in the imminent coming of God's Kingdom and the parousia of the Lord Jesus? The question is idle in view of what happened. There is no doubt that the minds of thoughtful Christians were early preoccupied, as was natural, with the delay of the Lord's Second Coming. Reasons for the delay were found; but the fact is that, in the end, such reasons ceased to be sought for, because, without dismissing the Christian hope in its primitive form, it became modified and softened down in a way to render the delay no longer tormenting. But that was the work of long centuries which lie outside the scope of the present history. What does lie within our scope is to show how the expectation of the Second Coming was soon reduced, from its first fever-heat, by faith in the invisible presence and help, here and now, of the immortal Christ. Moreover, a consciousness more intimate and more profoundly mystical was soon grafted on to this. It was the consciousness of everlasting union, begun in the present life, with the Christ of the mystery. The sensitive consciousness of Christ's life in his Church and in each soul that belonged to him had the effect, in the end, of virtually neutralizing the anxious expectancy in which the first believers waited for the resurrection of the dead and the coming of the Kingdom, but without destroying belief in either.

The Second Epistle to the Thessalonians gives the impression of a real disquietude about the matter. The chief object of this Epistle is the short dissertation (ii, 1–12) on the delay of the Lord's arrival and the manifestation of a person whom we may call Antichrist, though in reality he was a false Jewish Messiah, probably Barkochba (see *Remarques*, 89–91). The delay in the fulfilment of prophecy was to be of brief duration and the Lord would arrive in the very near future. But although the prophecy remained unfulfilled this apocryphal Epistle was not compromised on that account: Marcion himself kept a place for it in his collection, and that very shortly after it appeared. It should not be overlooked that the author, who seems to have been a man full of common sense, gives his readers some excellent advice on the necessity of daily work, imitated from an authentic part of the First Epistle (iv, 11, 12). We may conclude, then, that while faith was apt to grow anxious about the Second Coming, there was no great difficulty in reassuring it, even at this early date.

A broader explanation of the delay is offered in a secondary fragment of the Epistle to the Romans (xi) where the question is discussed whether the reprobation of the Jews is final or temporary. Their reprobation is declared to be provisional, the hardening of the Israelite majority having been providentially arranged to give time for the accession of the pagans. That achieved, Israel will be reconciled and the resurrection of the dead, the Great Event, will follow. And here the author of the explanation breaks out in admiration of the "depth" of the divine wisdom. Note the perceptible intercalation of the same idea in the synoptic apocalypse (Mark xiii, 10; Matthew xxiv, 14 where it is added "and then will come the end"; Luke xxi, 24 touching "the times of the Gentiles" represents a different idea).

The conflict, more or less open, between the mystical conception of salvation and the teaching on the coming End is clearly portrayed in the gnostic Epistles attributed to Paul, where eschatological Christianity is directly attacked as Judaizing error; on the other side, the letters of the Christ to the Seven Churches in the Book of Revelation denounce the disciples of the gnostic Paul as false Christians and a danger to the true faith (see *Remarques*, 141–146). The conflict ended in a compromise, but not till after much wrangling.

The substitution of mystical Christianity for its eschatological predecessor might be described as discreetly effected by the mystical "Paul" of the Epistles and the author of Hebrews; but the change was not effected in the faith of the churches as the two writers conceived it. The First Epistle of Peter would belong to the same category, except that the author is not fully conscious of his gnosticism. Nevertheless certain exaggerated forms of the gnosis, so outrageous that they had to be treated as heretical, had the effect of producing some reaction to the eschatological cause. The place of some of the Epistles in the evolution of this conflict and its final solution is not otherwise easily determined.

The Epistle of James is a strange specimen of moral teaching combined with the minimum, not of gnosis only, but of eschatology. The author devotes a free, but not violent criticism to the theory of salvation by faith without works, which he refutes by exegetical means similar to that employed by Paul in constructing the doctrine. There is nothing to show that he was referring to the other, the mystical, theory of salvation to be found in the Epistle to the Romans as it has come down to us. While he was not ignorant in the matter, his incomprehension of it is such as to be equivalent to radical hostility. What is most interesting in his case is the cavalier way in which he criticizes the doctrine, as though it were a mischievous opinion of no great importance, the mere mention of which was enough to condemn it. In the history of Christian literature this Epistle belongs to the precanonical age of the New Testament when the writings attributed to Paul were not considered as in any sense authoritative, or worthy to be placed on the same level as the Scriptures of the Old Covenant.

The Pastoral Epistles to Timothy and to Peter

The three Epistles known as Pastoral have all the same object—the institution of a system of government which will put the churches in a posture for effective resistance to the attacks of dangerous innovators.

To understand this effort of resistance it will be helpful to go back at this point to a passage in Acts (xx, 18–35) which has the same object; we refer to the discourse which Paul is supposed to have addressed to the elders of Ephesus whom he had summoned to Miletus apparently to receive his final instructions, and which commentators have described as a model of pastoral theology. And indeed, the discourse, though apocryphal, is an outstandingly fine piece of its kind and for us highly instructive, since it was composed in full view of the gnostic crisis in the second quarter of the second century, and in the same spirit as our three Pastoral Epistles. The Apostle begins by recalling his own devoted activity, more or less in imitation of the gnostic "Paul." He foresees the fate in store for him at the end of his journey to Jerusalem and declares himself ready to sacrifice his life. Here are his admonitions:

> Take heed to yourselves and to all the flock in which the holy Spirit has made you bishops to feed the Lord's church, which he has purchased with his blood.

This carries us forward to a time much later than Paul's meeting with the elders who came to bring him a collection

THE EPISTLES AND THE CATECHESIS

made in Asia for the Jerusalem saints. The churches have their appointed heads, elders or supervisors, priests or bishops, placed by God's will and the Christ's in authority over the flock now threatened by destructive propaganda:

> I know well that after my departure grievous wolves will come, not sparing the flock, and that even from among yourselves men will arise with perverse speech in their mouths, to draw away disciples after them. Therefore watch, remembering that for three years, night and day, I ceased not to exhort every one with tears....

He concludes by recalling the virtues in which he has set them an example. Who were the heretics here aimed at in particular? Gnostics, surely, in the second quarter of the second century. But which? And where was this discourse composed? If in Asia, who would be the heretics whom the author describes as rising up "even from among yourselves" of the Asiatic churches? And of these who was more dangerous between 130 and 140 than Marcion? At all events we here come into contact with the very theme with which the writers of pseudo-apostolic letters, and the Pastorals in the first place, were continually occupied about the same time.

Our three Pastoral Epistles are so closely related that a common origin is quite possible and, were their literary composition homogeneous, their date would be easily determined. A glance at the conclusion of the First to Timothy (vi, 20-21), where the *Antitheses* of Marcion are aimed at under their proper name, would be enough to settle the matter. Moreover, Marcion knew only ten Epistles of Paul's; had the Pastorals in 140 figured in the collection of the Apostle's letters Marcion would certainly have retained them. But the first draft of the Epistles may be contemporary with the outburst of Marcionism.

Having made elsewhere a detailed analysis of these documents (*Remarques*, 114-126) we shall here confine ourselves to two points in the First to Timothy: the instruction to pray for persons in authority and for the emperor in particular (ii, 1-3) and, yet more important, the regulations laid down for the choice of bishops and deacons (iii, 1-6).

The episcopal function is regarded as of great importance (iii, 1-7). The qualities enumerated in detail as requisite for the office are, in one part, such as would be demanded in a high functionary of the temporal order. This gives a clue to the date, and the fact that the bishop is spoken of in the singular is to the same effect. To be sure, he is not expressly distinguished from the priest (elder), but it is pretty plain that, while the episcopate is not yet fully monarchical, it is nearly so. And the rules laid down are not solely for the man to be elected; they are equally for his electors. The same is true of what is said about deacons, who are mentioned in the plural, since their number is to be proportioned to the size and the needs of the church. The deacons, or "ministers" (iii, 8–13), whose business is concerned with external order and material needs, must possess qualities analogous to those demanded in a bishop. Care is taken to specify the virtues needed in their wives, and it is obvious that these same virtues are indispensable, and for stronger reasons, in the wife of the bishop. There is also a discipline for widows of whom a certain number, wisely selected, are well fitted to serve the community (v, 3, 5–7, 15; it would seem that v, 4, 8–14, 16 is a complementary surcharge).

The advice given to Timothy presumably implies that he is a kind of archbishop presiding over the organization of all the churches (iii, 14–15; iv, 6; v, 1–2; vi, 3–5, 8–14, 16). Note how in these instructions, which belong to the first draft of the letter, the obligation is stressed to guard the words of faith and good doctrine, to turn a deaf ear to "impious fables and old wives' tales" and to reprove the man "who teaches a strange doctrine and is not devoted to the wholesome words of our Lord Jesus Christ; conceited sect-makers who delight in vain arguments and see in religion a means of making money." (He would be indeed a bold man who maintained that such a sample of gnosis came from Paul.) Have done with novelties; there is a fixed deposit; a doctrine of faith; an orthodoxy; so we must have a rule of faith, a discipline for conduct, and there must be men in authority to compel the observance of what is prescribed. There is no getting away from the fact that the spiritual atmosphere of all this is wholly different from that of the oldest Epistles. Nascent orthodoxy, indeed, is already summed up in a profession of faith (ii, 5–6; v, 21). The brevity of v, 21 is highly significant: "I adjure thee before God, Christ Jesus and the elect angels"—note this trinity—"to obey the rules without prejudice, doing nothing in partiality." With this goes violent denunciation of indiscipline, gnostic or otherwise. The denunciation, however, is made here in terms too general to permit our identifying the persons aimed at.

A more precise denunciation, but surely of later date, is that which some reviser has joined on to the short Christological poem quoted above ("he was manifest in the flesh," etc. (iv, 1–5), see p. 267). The denunciation is given as a revelation of the Spirit (iv, 1). The formula of introduction, "the Spirit says," may strike us at first as strange, but is unquestionably in the same class as that found in the Apocalypse (ii, 7, 11, 17, 29; iii, 6, 13, 22): "He that has an ear let him hear what the Spirit says to the churches." The Spirit and the Christ are two names for the same (cf. 2 Thessalonians ii, 2 and especially 2 Corinthians iii, 17). The Christian prophets, as they uttered their oracles at the bidding of the Spirit, were speaking in the name of the immortal Christ. Now there can be no doubt that in the passage before us the Spirit is aiming at Marcion and his adepts, who prohibited marriage and abstained from certain foods precisely as here described, while they attributed the creation of the visible world, not to the supreme God, but to an inferior deity. The text before us thus falls into line with the explicit denunciation of Marcion's *Antitheses* at the end of the Epistle (vi, 20–21). To the same chronological level (*circa* 140) belongs the advice to Timothy to drink a little wine (v, 23). But the interest of him who gives the advice is not really in the condition of Timothy's "stomach." This is his way of implicitly condemning the abstinence of the encratites, and in particular of Marcion, who would not allow the use of wine even for the Holy Supper.

The same remarks apply to the solemn adjuration addressed to Timothy towards the end of the Epistle (vi, 13–16). This has the sound of a formal profession of faith; and that indeed is what it is. The commandment to be guarded is the "deposit" spoken of in the concluding injunction (vi, 20–21; *supra*, p. 273). The deposit is a "precept," that is, the Christ's teaching as deposited in the Gospel books. In like manner, the "good confession" of the martyred Christ is an echo of the Gospels; but they are not the source from which the mention of Pontius Pilate has been taken; that comes from a profession of Christian faith already officially adopted. Nevertheless, the background of this creed is the Gospel scheme of the Passion, and it is significant that the final utterance, on the invisible God, whom no man has seen or can see, is closely related to the fourth Gospel (John i, 18; vi, 46; cf. Matthew xi, 27). This suggests the question whether the Pastorals are also of Asiatic origin. The question is reasonable. But what we have to be clear about, first and foremost, is that this profession of faith, in which the eschatological and the Gospel catecheses seem to meet, is anti-Marcionite in its essential aim. It is against Marcion that the author so impressively affirms the identity of the one eternal God, master of all things, with God, the creator of the world and Father of Jesus Christ. We are here in the full current of the anti-Marcionite reaction between 150 and 170.

The Second to Timothy gives less space than the First to questions of Church discipline, but while affecting to enter into personal details (discussed in *Remarques*, 122–125) it presents Paul as the type which Timothy—that is, the leading churchman—must make his model (cf. Acts xx, 18–35, *supra*, p. 272). The apostle, represented as a prisoner in Rome, orders Timothy, who is at Ephesus, to come to him, and at the same time gives him instructions which, if they were authentically Paul's, would have been no more needed and no more appropriate than those of the first Epistle. It is worth noting that the author seems to be acquainted with the Book of Acts in its traditional form, iii, 11 being apparently a reference to the fictitious stories in Acts xiii–xiv, 20 (cf. *supra*, p. 181); further, that he combats an advanced form of gnosis and that, in some secondary additions, the Epistle expressly repudiates it, and Marcion in particular.

Paul is represented as rejoicing in the memory of Timothy's affection for him and in the sincerity of his faith; let him revive the gift of God which he received by the imposition of Paul's hands (in 1 Timothy iv, 14 Timothy has been ordained by the Elders; but the difference is not of essential import and the two indications are compatible). Let him be strong and unashamed of his captive master, nor discouraged from bearing testimony to the Gospel, which Paul, spite of his sufferings, continues to preach in full confidence; let him guard the instructions received from the apostle, that "good deposit"; let him pass on the teaching he has kept to safe men, and fight on like a good soldier of the Christ. If we wish to reign with the Christ, we must die with him and for him, as Paul himself has died: this is the doctrine to be preached, paying no heed to disputes that lead to nothing, silly questionings and arguings, but always using gentleness in dealing with the enemies, if perchance God will bring them to conversion and grant them escape from the snares of the demon. Timothy knows what Paul has suffered; all who would live in the Christ are thus persecuted, while the impostors go from bad to worse, "seducers and seduced." So let Timothy preach on like a brave man; yes, even though the time be come when men are running after teachers who pander to their passions. As for Paul, he has had his day, finished his course, kept the faith, and he knows that God has a crown ready for him; and it will soon be his. All this makes a homogeneous whole, in which the modernists of that day were duly branded, but not without an effort to bring them over to the true faith.

Emphasis should be laid on the injunction to Timothy to avoid the "impious babblings" of those who declare that the resurrection has already taken place (ii, 16–18). The surcharged passage ii, 19–26 (which joins on to 14–15) may be aimed at the Marcionites. The attack on the seducers of women (iii, 6–9) is directed against the licentious gnostic sects, such as that of Marcos, the disciple of Valentinus. The praise of the ancient Scriptures (iii, 15–16), a sudden intrusion in the context, is also a counterblow at the gnostics who rejected the Old Testament, and to Marcion as the chief of them.

The Epistle to Titus

The Epistle to Titus seems to be founded on the false supposition that Titus was a disciple of Paul on the same level as Timothy. So far as we can judge from the authentic text he was nothing of the kind (see *Remarques*, 125–126). Equally in substance as in form the Epistle to Titus has a closer resemblance to the First to Timothy than to the Second, and might even be considered a duplicate of the First; just as Paul is supposed to have left Timothy at Ephesus in the quality of chief bishop, so he is made to leave Titus in Crete to carry out the organization of the churches founded in that island. In all the towns Titus is to institute "elders" (priests) as bishops (i, 5–9); the bishop is to possess such and such qualities, substantially as in the First to Timothy (iii, 1–4), with more insistence laid on the need for his being a master in doctrine. For there seem to have been in Crete many circumcised heretics fond of Jewish fables; but the quoted saying of Epimenides on the vices of the Cretans is a mere literary ornament and gives no clue to the sectaries the author has in mind (i, 10–16). They are certainly the same persons who, towards the end of the letter, are said to busy themselves with "fools' questions, genealogies, disputes about the Law." Perhaps Crete is not the region where they were really to be found. It is not impossible that certain heirs of the Pauline tradition kept up the strife against Paul's adversaries, representatives of common Christianity, and treated them as Judaizers. While not impossible it is not very probable, and the artificiality of the whole composition makes it useless to search for precise applications.

Titus is to preach sound doctrine and to give specified counsels, some to old men, some to old women, some to young people, some to slaves (ii, 1–11). The series is parallel to that found in other Epistles notably in 1 Timothy. This must have been the common theme of catechism (cf. 1 Peter ii, 13–iii, 7).

The grace of God has appeared to men that they may follow the laws of the good life, in expectation of the manifestation in splendour of our great God and Saviour Jesus Christ. Here we have the identification of the Christ with God which is also to be met with in both Epistles to Timothy. This, as we have remarked elsewhere, is not a feature of Marcionism but of modalism (see *Remarques*, 116).

In giving this teaching Titus is to speak with authority and to enforce respect for his office (cf. 1 Timothy iv, 12). He will command obedience to magistrates (cf. 1 Timothy ii, 1–2; Romans xiii, 1–7; 1 Peter ii, 13–14); he will enjoin the practice of benevolence to all men and bid Christians remember that they were formerly as mad as other people, until God in his pity was pleased to save them by the bath of regeneration (passage about the effusion of the Spirit, iii, 6–7, seems to have been added); let every man, then, apply himself to good works and keep away from vain disputes; let the man who foments faction by those means be thrust out, if he fails to mend his ways after due warning (iii, 11). All this makes a kind of summary of the more diffuse synthesis, or compilation, represented by 1 Timothy; it has a studied conciseness and lays greater emphasis on the exclusion of incorrigible modernists; it is also free from surcharges directly aimed at the Marcionites.

The first draft of the Pastorals seems to have been anti-gnostic but not expressly anti-Marcionite; the canonized edition is formally anti-gnostic with some new matter added directly against Marcion; thus we may infer that the first draft was earlier than the explosion of Marcionism and the canonical later. Books of this kind were the more eagerly received by the Church into her apostolic collection at a time when she was setting up the New Testament as a barrier against the inundation of gnosis; they openly condemned the gnostic heresies, and represented the first effort to stem the flood in the name of a tradition deemed to be apostolic, embodied and guarded by bishops regularly appointed to rule the churches. Henceforth the function of teaching is to be in the hands of these bishops, and the prophets are no longer to have a place at their side. In 1 Timothy i, 18 and iv, 14 there are indications that the prophets took part in what we might call Timothy's episcopal consecration; but once consecrated, the rôle of teacher is the bishop's exclusive privilege. The formula "The Spirit says," in 1 Timothy iv, 1 (*supra*, p. 275) is a conventional cliché introducing an oracle deemed to be traditional.

The Epistle of Jude

With an apostolic title, and an opening and conclusion appropriate to a letter, the Epistle of Jude is, in the body of it, an anti-gnostic fulmination, or rather a fragment of diatribe set in the frame of an Epistle. The title-address (1–2), visibly marking a distinction from that given to the Epistle of James (i, 1) presents the author as one of those whom the Gospel calls "brothers" of Jesus (Mark vi, 3; Matthew xiii, 55). But, as James modestly calls himself "servant of God and of the Lord Jesus Christ," so Jude not less modestly calls himself "servant of Jesus Christ and brother of James." The doxology (24–25) which serves as colophon, shows some signs of modalism, resembling the preamble in that respect. In this intervening space (3–23) we find a series of object lessons; first, of the Israelites rescued from Egypt, of whom large numbers were destroyed for their unbelief; next, of the disloyal angels, who deserted their posts and are now in prison (these are the imprisoned angels, to whom the Christ preached in hell, mentioned in 1 Peter iii, 19–20; see *supra*, p. 267); finally, the men of Sodom and Gomorrah whom God exterminated for their filthiness. The sectaries whom the author is denouncing have revived all these abominations, although the example of the archangel Michael when he disputed with the Devil over the body of Moses ought to teach them better manners towards the Celestial Powers (this refers to an incident related in the apocryphal book called *Assumption of Moses*). These impious scoundrels repeat the crimes of others who stand accused—Cain, Balaam, Korah, of whom Enoch wrote; and a quotation follows which can be found at the beginning of the Book of Enoch (Ethiopean version). The false teachers are finally characterized as drivelling critics, pompous orators and flatterers with an eye to the main chance.

> As to you, beloved, remember the words of prediction spoken by the apostles of our Lord Jesus Christ, which told you: "At the end of the time mockers will appear who go the way of their impious lusts." These are they who make schism, psychics, not having the spirit, etc. (17–19).

We note, but without lingering on the point, the equivocal phrasing peculiar to this outlook, phrasing which always recurs in parallel cases, for example, in 2 Peter iii, 2–3. Here, plainly, the innovators aimed at boast of being "spiritual" (which they are not) and treat as "psychics" (which they are themselves) the common run of Christians. Compare what the mystic "Paul" is made to say, in 1 Corinthians iii, 1–4, about "spirituals" and "carnals."

In spite of its quotations from apocryphal books, which for us constitutes its originality, there is no disguising the fact that this diatribe against gnosis is a feeble composition, and as violent as feeble. Nevertheless, the author, so far as we can understand him, enjoins his readers at the end to save those who are perishing while avoiding defilement by too close contact. What makes the composition an apostolic letter is nothing more than the address in the preamble and the doxology of the colophon. As the Second of Peter is inspired by the diatribe which forms the *corpus* of the composition, and derives nothing from its epistolary form, it is possible that pseudo-Peter did not know it as an Epistle, but knew and used only the document, afterwards furnished with a framework of epistolary form at the beginning and the end. Hypothetically therefore we may place the diatribe between the years 130 and 140, and its conversion into the pretended Epistle of Jude about 150.

The Second Epistle of Peter

Pseudo-Peter has made full use of Jude's diatribe, but has omitted his quotations from apocryphal books, which perhaps were beginning to come under suspicion in pseudo-Peter's circle. While the Second of Peter already depends for its central part (ii) on the diatribe which constitutes the substance of Jude, its first part (i, 3–21), in which he exalts the testimony of the prince of the apostles, is as clearly dependent on the apocalypse of Peter—the capital point for the understanding of this falsely attributed Epistle (see *Remarques*, 131–137). The third part (iii) is the author's direct refutation of the gnostic sect which was pouring mockery on the delay of the Second Coming. Peter's pretension to the universal apostolate is announced in the superscription (i, 1–2) which has the strong look of a form in regular use.

An easy transition introduces the second part of the Epistle (ii). As there were false prophets in olden time, so now there will arise, among "believers," false teachers who pervert the truth. This is followed by a denunciation of gnostics in general, especially those with immoral tendencies, all in better logical order than the corresponding part of Jude. There is no mention of the unbelieving Jews, so ill-placed in Jude at the head of his list of reprobates: after recalling the disloyal angels, the people drowned in the Deluge are next brought in, as they must have been in the source (cf. 1 Peter iii, 19–20; iv, 6); what follows is a paraphrase of this common source. For himself, when not following his source, the writer is much preoccupied by jests that are being made in certain quarters about the delay of the parousia (iii, 1–13). The pain he has taken to keep his instruction in line with the

First to Peter is significant, notwithstanding the difference in dates between the two. Some of the surcharges in the first Epistle, such as iii, 19-20; iv, 6, can hardly be much earlier than the Second. Our author answers the mockers as best he can; the world, he remarks, has already perished by water in Noah's flood, and the present world is going to perish by fire. God, in his pity, is delaying the event in order that all of us may have time to repent; but a thousand years are to him as but one day. Nevertheless, the day of the Lord will come like a thief (cf. 1 Thessalonians v, 2; Matthew xxiv, 43-44; Luke xii, 39-40). In that day the heavens will disappear in roaring flame; the elements will become white hot and melt and the whole earth with everything in it will be consumed to ashes.

With this prospect before him let every man keep himself unspotted and undefiled, making the most of the respite (iii, 14-18) "as our dear brother Paul, according to the wisdom given him has also written to you," etc. The warranty here given by Peter to Paul provides the critic with a valuable clue. It is clear that, by the time these words were written, Peter and Paul, in spite of what the Epistles make the latter say, had become definitely reconciled in the current tradition concerning them: and, further, that Paul's Epistles were held to be Scripture, though certain heretics, with Marcion certainly in the first rank, were strangely perverting them. This could not have been written before the year 170. But one would gladly know what Epistles the writer had in view. Was it the original collection of ten? Or that of thirteen; or that of fourteen, with Hebrews included? This last is possible, if the writer were of Alexandria.

The Three Epistles of John

The three Epistles named after John keep more or less closely to the Fourth Gospel, and it is not surprising that the satellites present the critic with the same problems as the parent orb. Not that their origin presents even the shadow of doubt; all three come from the same workshop, if the term may be used, as the Gospel, not so much completing as convoying it, and helping to promote its diffusion and its credit. The first Epistle especially, which has the form not of a letter but of a homily, and is not all of one piece, seems to have been compiled in the closest possible connection with the Gospel book. The fact that certain passages are written in regular rhythm has given rise to the conjecture that the formless instructions are the paraphrase of a didactic poem analogous to the chief discourses in the fourth Gospel. But there is no other proof of the hypothesis.

A solemn prologue, in heavy-handed imitation of the prologue to the Gospel, reveals the general intention of the book (i, 1–4):

> That which was from the beginning, that which we have heard, that which we have seen with our eyes, that which we have gazed upon and our hands have touched concerning the Word of life (life has been manifested, and we have seen, we testify and declare unto you the eternal life that was with the Father and has been revealed to us); that, I say, which we have seen and heard we announce unto you, to the end that you may have communion with us; verily our communion is with the Father and with his Son, Jesus Christ. And this we write that your joy may be complete.

This opening is enough to give the character of the whole: a watery paraphrase of the ideas which form the base of the Gospel, tiresome in its repetitions—life, light, love, union with God and in God. We leave the matter there and proceed to point out some notable peculiarities of the compilation. We read (ii, 1*b*–2):

> If anyone sin, he has a *defender* with the Father, Jesus Christ the righteous. He is, himself, propitiation for our sins, but not for ours alone; for the sins also of the whole world.

When those words were written the fourth Gospel had not yet spoken of *"another* Defender, the Spirit of the Truth," the *Paraclete,* who would fill the place of the Christ, now gone back to God, in helping the faithful (John xiv, 16–17; xv, 26; xvi, 13; cf. *supra,* p. 221–223).

The author knows the Apocalypse and on two occasions speaks of the Antichrist, but for the purpose of explaining—very freely it must be confessed—that Antichrist is already come in the person of divers heretical teachers. On the first occasion these heretics are denounced for denying that Jesus is the Christ (ii, 18–22). On the second occasion we are told that the spirits must be proved, "because many false prophets are come into the world"; and the test is this: "every spirit that confesses Jesus Christ come in the flesh is of God," and whosoever does not confess Jesus "is of Antichrist, of whom you have heard say that he is coming and who now is already in the world." This second denunciation aims at Docetism and, very probably, at Marcion. In the first case the author—if he weighed his words, which is not certain—is not thinking of the Docetists but of people who distingush the heavenly *aeon*, which was the Christ, from the man Jesus; this would be the error attributed by tradition to Cerinthus who maintained that the *aeon* Christ was united only for a time with the man Jesus, a doctrine which might be adjusted with a little forcing to the Gospel catechesis of Mark. Whatever be their precise application the two denunciations presuppose an outbreak of gnostic heresies in the Asiatic circles to which the Epistle belongs, the probability being that the two denunciations are not concerned with the same heresy, since they are not by the same writer. We shall presently see, moreover, that the second Epistle is in line with the second denunciation, which would thus be the later of the two.

Towards the end of the Epistle we come upon a remarkable surcharge clearly aimed at Docetism, the relation of which to a surcharge to the same effect in the fourth Gospel cannot be fortuitous. The author is in course of proving that whosoever believes in Jesus and obeys the law of love is born of God and is, by his faith, victorious over the world (v, 1–5). The faith in question is based on the witness that God has rendered to his Son, the witness being that God has given us the eternal life which is in his Son (v, 9–12). At this point the author, intentionally picking up the original conclusion of the Fourth Gospel (John xx, 31), proceeds to write: "I have written this to you that you may know you have eternal life, you who believe in the name of the Son of God." But some reviser of the Epistle, before introducing the testimony thus rendered by God to his Son, has thought fit to insert the following gloss (v, 6–7. Verse 5 is a late interpolation, which does not here concern us) about the Christ and the witness rendered to him.

> This is he who comes by water and by blood, Jesus Christ,
> not with water only,
> but with water and with blood;

THE EPISTLES AND THE CATECHESIS

> And he who bears witness is the Spirit
> because the Spirit is the truth.
> So there are three that bear witness;
> Spirit, water, blood;
> and the three make one.

We have already pointed out the relation between this parenthesis and the incident of the lance-thrust in the story of the Passion (pp. 209, 232), and the inference to be drawn from that relation for the common history of the Gospel and the Epistles.

The two short Epistles that follow have more resemblance to letters; but they were never addressed to anybody. Both are explicitly attributed to the Elder, that is to the person whom the fourth Gospel invests with authority as the beloved disciple and the author of the Gospel itself.

The first is written for a church whom it names Lady Elect. Her children are bidden to practise charity and be on their guard against seducers who, denying that Jesus is come in the flesh, are Antichrist and people not to be received into houses nor saluted in the street (4-11). This discloses the purpose of our short letter—to support the denunciation of Docetic gnosis in the first Epistle.

The third letter is supposedly written to a believer in the church to which the former was addressed. This time the object is to commend the travelling brethren who carry the good doctrine—i.e. the Johannine writings—to the care of friends, and to discredit the church leaders who, like the conceited Diotrephes, refuse to receive the Elder and his books. The reference is to the bishops who would have nothing to do with the new fourth Gospel and drove out its supporters.

To sum up. The Epistles called after John contain religious and moral doctrine co-ordinated to that of the fourth Gospel, denunciation of certain gnostic heresies, and highly forced reasons for accepting the testimony supposed to guarantee the apostolic character of those doctrines and of the writings that contain them. The two short Epistles and the canonical edition of the first go back to the neighbourhood of 150-160 and the first version of the first Epistle to 135-140.

Chapter IX

CONCLUSIONS

WHAT we now proceed to gather up is not a heap of certitudes, but a sheaf of hypotheses which we endeavour to bind together, according to their degree of probability or verisimilitude, in order that we may reconstruct the history of which we directly see the outcome only. The outcome is that, towards the end of the second century, there existed a collection of writings called the New Testament, in use among the congregations of the Church called catholic, and sharply distinguished from the sects which had broken off from it, or formed on its frontiers, this collection being placed side by side with another which the said Church had inherited from Judaism and called Scriptures of the Old Testament. It must be added, however, that the Church's collection of the Old Testament was not completely identical with the official Scriptures of Judaism, for it included certain writings, or fragments of writings, held in honour among the hellenizing Jews of Egypt. Nor was the New Testament collection identically the same in all the churches of the Mediterranean world. There was general agreement on the four Gospels, the Acts of the Apostles, thirteen Epistles of Paul (the Epistle to the Hebrews attributed to Paul in the East was not recognized as apostolic in the West), the First of Peter and the First of John. But the Epistles of James and of Jude, the Second of Peter and the two short Johannine Epistles were not universally accepted, and the Apocalypse of John was long under discredit, in the East, after the beginning of the third century. Indeed there was a group, attacked by Irenaeus, which rejected all the writings attributed to John as apocryphal, and this opposition was active in Rome about the year 200. On the other hand, writings, such as the Epistle of Clement to the Corinthians and the Pastor of Hermas, were long read as public lessons in many of the churches.

As to the origins of the New Testament writings and to their collection, they are, as we have seen, very imperfectly documented. Only by faith can the four Gospels, the Acts of the Apostles, Paul's Epistles, the catholic Epistles and the Book of

CONCLUSIONS

Revelation be accepted as apostolic and integrally authentic. The verdict of criticism is otherwise (cf. *supra*, p. 10).

THE PROPHET JESUS AND HIS ORACLE

Jesus, who lived in the time of Tiberius, when Pontius Pilatus was procurator of Judea, was not formally recognized as Messiah or Christ till after his death, when his disciples proclaimed him as the immortal Christ at the right hand of God, whence he would presently come to establish on the earth, more precisely at Jerusalem, that Reign of God whose speedy arrival he had himself announced in his lifetime. The historical existence of Jesus is postulated and implied throughout the entire history of the Christian religion. That is why we abstain from proving it. Such a proof is no business of ours, save in so far as the history of the New Testament origins depends on him who was historically, if not the founder of the Christian religion, at least the initiator of the Christian movement. Moreover the hypotheses of the mythologues, who have recently denied that Jesus ever existed, do not require refutation, seeing that they are all built on air, no positive proof being forthcoming that the particular myths ever existed which, according to these conjectures, are the foundation of the Christian religion. And even if this were the time for criticism of such theories, this is not the place for it.

Our sole business, in our present undertaking, is to determine, by reference to the New Testament literature, what the conditions were under which this human life was lived, a life on which, from the historical point of view, our information is most imperfect; and that for a double reason; first, because the Gospels never were and never pretended to be historical documents for the earthly life of Jesus, but were manuals, in short books, of instruction in the cult of the Lord Jesus Christ; and, second, because these books, which were not otherwise concerned in gathering exact information about Jesus, are later by three-quarters of a century to the time when Jesus, after a very brief period of teaching in Galilee and Jerusalem, ending in his death by crucifixion under sentence of Pontius Pilatus, was proclaimed as alive for ever with God and in readiness to come with God's Kingdom. Nor does the rest of the New Testament tell us any more of the matter than do the Gospels, since all these writings presuppose the faith as already acquired and give no direct information as to how the faith first came into being. One thing, however, is clearly evident: the name of Jesus and the speedy arrival of God's Kingdom were indissolubly bound together from the furthest point to which Christian memory went back. That is very far from being a fact of no account. But it does not inform us how Jesus himself brought into being the faith of which he soon became the object.

That the time when Jesus made his appearance in history, and faith in Jesus-Messiah was born, was a time of great religious and national excitement is another indisputable fact. The Jewish rising in the year 66 which ended in the fall of Jerusalem and the destruction of the temple in the year 70, was, in all strictness, a messianic movement, founded on the essential principle of the Jewish national hope, to wit, that Israel owed obedience to one master only, to God, the establishment of whose Kingdom would involve the complete overthrow of foreign rule. So far as we are able to judge, the Galilean prophet Jesus whom his contemporaries called Jesus the Nazorean[1] was possessed by the same idea. According to him, the arrival of the Great Kingdom, the rule of justice and salvation, was on the point of realization; God would erect it on the ruins of the idolatrous government, and repentance was the necessary preparation for that sweeping revolution. A certain John, named the Baptizer, of whom it would seem that Jesus was originally a disciple, had proclaimed the same message before him, baptismal immersion being the sacrament of repentance, of purification and of the right to be admitted to God's Kingdom. From the very beginning Christianity was the religion of a baptist sect, for Jesus himself had not only received baptism after John's manner but sanctioned it in that form. Those who would make out that Jesus repudiated John's baptism are breaking a perceptible link between Jesus and the religious conditions of his time; and such links are rare.

So far as Jesus can be said, in strictness of speech, to have *taught*, the speedy arrival of God in his Kingdom was the substance of his teaching. Unlike the Zealots, who advocated armed

---

[1] A personal qualification, with no mythological significance, *Nazorean* being, so far as we can ascertain, a sect-name which could be applied to individuals.

revolution,[1] Jesus expected that the liberation of his people would be the work of God alone, the firm simplicity of his faith saving him from the fanatical blindness of the hot-heads who imagined that by armed revolt against Rome they would come to the help of God, or force his hand. Nevertheless it was the same faith as theirs that rendered him blind to the inevitable danger of his advance on Jerusalem, where he was certain to find himself immediately confronted with the power whose destruction he was announcing, at least by implication.

It may be affirmed with the minimum risk of error that he was the prophet of a single oracle only, as John the Baptist seems to have been before him. That he speculated at length on the part reserved for him in the coming Kingdom is improbable; nevertheless the place assigned him by his disciples after his death rather suggests that he did not expect that his rôle in it would be that of an ordinary participant. That his public activity included the part of a healing exorcist is rendered highly probable by the fact that his disciples played the same part after him; indeed the character of a man of God could hardly be conceived, in his time and place, without including that function. When, further, we have admitted the profound and humanely moral character of his message as the dominating feature of its form and nature, we have said all that the historian is able to say about his activity without overpassing the limits of safety.

The above statement is made only as justifying the following conclusion, which concerns the proper subject of our study: Jesus was a prophet rather than a teacher of doctrine; he did not regard himself as the founder of a new religion; something of his prophetic and humane spirit survived in the sect which claimed him as its head; but he has left on the literature of the New Testament only a faint impression of his personality and the memory of his death. His cult-legend is widely different from a direct and faithful image reflected in a mirror.

Jesus was dead, and almost immediately the belief arose among his followers that he was the Messiah about to return. Their faith in his message of the swiftly coming Kingdom did not change its ground to the extent to which the Gospel stories might

---

[1] Though the name of a Zealot figures in the list of the Twelve (cf. Luke vi, 15; Acts i, 13. Note also that *zealot* is the exact translation of the epithet *Canaanite* applied to the same disciple in Mark iii, 18 and Matthew x, 4).

lead us to suppose; they are stories of much too late invention, and too systematically worked out to represent the travail in the soul of his followers when Jesus' fate overtook him. In the Gospel stories they are presented as receiving material proofs of his resurrection, proofs never received, for they were impossible, and would have been superfluous in any case, because they are without appeal to a mentality such as theirs was at the time. For them, Jesus was not raised from the dead in the gross, almost brutal, manner in which tradition told the story at a later date. Jesus had passed on to God *at death* in full possession of his selfhood—so said the spirit that was in them. To the fate of his dead body they gave not a thought and asked not a question about it. Him whom God had sent was now with the God who sent him; there he was, alive and glorious at God's right hand, and thence, in life and glory, as the Christ, he would soon be coming to establish the Reign of God upon the earth. Such was their faith; but it was born without a literature, for not a line had yet been written about it in any Christian book.

It would be a mistake to expect from the New Testament authentic information about the catastrophe which ended the earthly life of Jesus, or about the new direction into which his disciples' faith was turned by the catastrophe, though we know very well who was the chief agent in giving it that turn. He was Simon, called Peter. But the third Gospel seems to have retained some traces of the state of mind in which Jesus and his following of Galilean enthusiasts brought the proclamation of the Kingdom to Jerusalem at the stage immediately *before* the catastrophe fell.

We read in that Gospel that Jesus, after the halt at Jericho, delivered a parable "because he was near to Jerusalem" and because "*they all believed* that the Kingdom of God was on the point of appearing" (Luke xix, 11). This was not a feature imagined after the event, and to be immediately refuted in the sequel. It is a datum of genuine tradition which the evangelist could not wholly eliminate, but which he only thought he would correct by fitting on to it the parable of the talents (12–27), which has no relation to it whatever, though touches added to give it a relation throw a little light on the mentality of Jesus and on the Christian mentality at the time when the Gospel legend was beginning to take shape. These touches are the following: "A man of noble birth went away into a far country to be made a king and to return"—meaning that Jesus, already dead, has gone to heaven to receive messianic royalty. (All that follows about the money distributed among the prince's officers would be out of keeping with the opening were it not that the Christ is conceived as already appointed the judge of mankind as well as Messiah.) But the final touch (27) corresponds with the opening: "As to these my enemies, who would not that I rule over them, bring them hither and slay them in my presence." Such is the crime which has brought destruction on the Jewish people; him whom God had made Christ in heaven, him whose speedy coming the Christian preachers are announcing, they had refused to recognize. In this way the parable furnishes a sketch, rudimentary enough, of the primitive faith, although it was not put into writing till after the year 70, if not till after 135.

Equally illuminating is the saying, about which Christian tradition became so confused, "I will destroy this temple and rebuild it in three days"—attenuated in Matthew (xxvi, 61) "I *can* destroy," etc.; corrected in Mark (xiv, 58) "I will destroy this temple *made with hands*, and in three days build another *not made with hands*"; while Acts (vi, 14) make it appear as a charge against Stephen. This may well have been really alleged against Jesus in the trial before Pilate, as a proof of messianic pretensions. If so, it would indicate a highly exalted state of mind in him who pronounced it, combined with a reforming zeal afraid of nothing—this at the very least.

As to Peter's initial vision, it may be said that, while it is everywhere spoken of in the New Testament, it is nowhere described. The reason is that it was not of the same order, and could not be made to fit, with the imaginary experiences by which at a much later date it was sought to prove the resurrection of Jesus as a fact materially verified and verifiable. The message of Jesus was not, in substance, of the kind which lends itself to argumentative polemic or needs long discourses for its delivery, and the same may be said of the message which the Galilean disciples carried back to Jerusalem after his death. Peter's faith is fairly well summed up in the formula given to it by Acts (ii, 36): "Let all the house of Israel, then, know for a certainty that God has made this Jesus whom you crucified into Lord and

Christ"—except perhaps that Peter and his companions clothed it with rather less solemnity. As to the supporting arguments drawn from the Old Testament, they were only gradually discovered as the need arose for them, and by persons more learned than Peter and his band.

Who was the first preacher of the new faith to carry the name of Jesus into the Jewish synagogues and publicly argue for his faith? Exegetes cannot be reminded too often that this preacher was Stephen, a *hellenist* convert of great daring and enterprise, and doubtless the most learned in that category. To those who consider the matter calmly and without prejudice it will be clear that this critical step could not have been taken otherwise.

It is obvious that our information as to the particulars of Stephen's preaching is extremely imperfect. We can only say with confidence that he was filled with the spirit of his group, the group which was soon to admit uncircumcised pagans into the community of believers, and that his trial implies that his preaching had the appearance of being more or less subversive of the Law —for example, that certain rules, held to have been laid down by Moses, would be abrogated in the Kingdom of God. For with Stephen, as with the others, the one question on which everything turned was the coming Kingdom which the Christ would establish at his speedy return. The same holds true of Stephen's former companions who escaped to Antioch, and there founded the first Christian community which admitted Gentiles to the messianic hope without imposing on them the rite of circumcision.

The conditions being such as we now see them to have been, there is no room for astonishment that Paul has nothing whatever to say about the earthly existence of Jesus nor of his characteristic teachings. Paul, like the other believers, knew Jesus as the founder of the Christian hope, as the Messiah to come, but not as Messiah already come and revealer of the Christian mystery. If we consider Paul to be the real author of everything written in the Epistles, and Jesus as the real author of every teaching ascribed to him in the Gospels, even in the Synoptics, Paul's relation to Jesus, as we might gather it from the Epistles, then becomes not only passing strange and at bottom indefinable, but essentially unintelligible. But, in the light we have now gained upon the matter, the relation of Paul to Jesus drops its former character of an unreadable enigma and an insoluble problem. Paul did not teach everything ascribed to him in the Epistles, nor Jesus everything ascribed in the Gospels. With that in mind Paul's eschatological preaching becomes perfectly clear. What, then, was it?

The Real Teaching of Paul

When Paul wrote to the Thessalonians (i, 9–10): "You have been converted from idols to God, to serve the true and living God and to await his Son from heaven, whom he has raised from the dead, Jesus, who saves us from the wrath to come," it is certain that he was not recalling any particular teaching of Jesus; he is proclaiming Jesus as the Christ to come, not as the Christ already come; he is declaring that the conversion of the pagans consists in recognizing the one and only God and Jesus, his Son, who will rescue believers in the day of "the wrath." Paul's catechesis thus implies both moral and eschatological teaching combined with Jewish monotheism and the conception of Jesus raised from death to become the living Christ. In like manner he writes to the Romans (x, 9): "If thou confessest with thy mouth that Jesus is Lord, and if thou believest in thy heart that God has raised him from the dead, thou shalt be rescued." Fundamentally it is the same doctrine as in Thessalonians, and in neither case is there the faintest reference to anything Jesus did or taught before he came to die. But let not the mythologues suppose for one moment that this pleads in favour of their thesis that Jesus never existed. In the same Epistle Paul states explicitly (ix, 5) that the Christ, like the patriarchs, is of Israel's seed; and Paul was a contemporary of Jesus.

Elsewhere, the argumentation by which Paul proves the universality of the messianic rescue is worked out without the slightest dependence on what we are in the habit of calling Gospel tradition. He abstains, for a good reason, from quoting any teaching of Jesus in support of his argument. The story of the centurion of Capernaum and the universalist propositions which the Christ is made to emit on that occasion (Matthew viii, 5–13; Luke vii, 9–10; xiii, 28–29) are entirely ignored by him, and the personality of his Christ derives its significance solely from the Great Event in store for the world. For proof of his thesis he goes indeed to the Scriptures, but the only Scripture he knows and reveres as divine are the Jewish Scriptures which he submits to a wholly irresponsible exegesis, following methods practised by the Rabbis of his time.

It is in these Scriptures that he finds the universal principle laid down of justification by faith, and he not only finds it there but proves it by juggling with words. In the Book of Habakkuk (ii, 4) it is written: "the pious man finds the assurance of his existence in his fidelity to God"; this Paul understood as meaning that by faith alone in God and his Christ any man may become qualified for the messianic rescue from the "wrath" (salvation) without any works of the Law being needed for his qualification; and he pursues the demonstration by bringing forward other texts, although he has begun by announcing, as though it were some trifling commonplace, a principle of plain common sense, namely (Romans iii, 29–31) that God is the God of all men and not only of Jews, to recognize which is not to abolish the Law, but the contrary. But on that he does not dwell; he is only concerned to prove how the scheme of universal salvation by faith was instituted in Abraham, father of all the Jews according to the flesh, father of all believers according to the spirit. The proof is that Abraham was as yet an uncircumcised man when his faith was imputed to him for righteousness—and so on. The imperturbable logic of the apostle, advancing from one absurdity to another, finally comes to this conclusion: that not only to Abraham was faith imputed for righteousness "but also to us who believe in him who raised Jesus our Lord from the dead."

As the argument proceeds we learn what it was that God promised to Abraham and to his posterity. This was not exactly eternal life, the "blessed immortality" of the theologians, but "the heritage of the world" (iv, 13), Genesis having said (xxii, 17) "thy posterity shall inherit the enemies' cities," which Paul understands as promising universal domination over the people of the earth. This shows us that, in the mind of the apostle, the idea of the Kingdom of God and his Christ had not taken the spiritual form. It was still the triumph of God over all nations as predicted by the prophets. Thus the Gospel is still, as it previously was, the proclamation of the coming Reign of God on earth, except for the clause which now offers salvation to pagans who adhere to the saving faith.

Paul added nothing to that belief beyond moral counsels, administered as a cooling draught to the fever of expectation. We have already heard him exhorting the Thessalonians, and that severely, to practise conjugal chastity (iv, 1–8; *supra*, p. 241), and again charging them (iv, 11–12) not to sit idly with crossed arms waiting for the parousia, but "study to be quiet and do your own business and work with your hands . . . that ye may walk honestly towards outsiders and may have need of no man."

The motives which led the apostle to charge his Thessalonian converts to earn their own living and be a burden to nobody becomes clear when we consider the collection he organized for the poor "saints" in Jerusalem. On this affair Paul explains himself rather cautiously in Romans xv, 26–27: "Macedonia and Achaia," he says, "have decided to make a contribution for the poor among the saints at Jerusalem; sharing their spiritual blessings, they ought to help them with material blessings." It is not correct to give the Christians of Hellas the credit of initiating the matter, for we know that Paul had organized the collection at Galatia before calling upon Macedonia and Achaia to put it into effect. The truth must have been that the missionaries to the countries of the dispersion pledged themselves to make the collection when they were at Jerusalem about the year 43–44 on the question of the legal observances.

The question has sometimes been asked whether "the saints" at Jerusalem were really so poor, and, if so, why? The answer is that the saints in question were probably remnants of the little group of earliest Galilean believers which returned with Peter to Jerusalem when the faith that Jesus had risen from death as the Christ was first established and affirmed. We know that they gathered a few recruits, but we know also that their dominant interest was not in propaganda; they had come to Jerusalem to await the second coming of the Lord and to be on the spot where it was due to take place immediately. Their resources were of the scantiest and, the parousia not arriving, were soon exhausted. Thus our saints, whose professed occupation was waiting for the expected event, were really "poor." Their mere existence reveals what faith in the Christ was in its very earliest form. There could be no greater misconception of their mentality than that which takes them to have been the first depositaries and witnesses of what is commonly called the gospel tradition. They were on the watch for the coming of the Lord Jesus and had no other care.

CONTRIBUTIONS OF THE CHRISTIAN PROPHETS TO THE GOSPEL STORY

Eschatological teaching could not remain, and did not remain for long, confined to the simple terms professed by the apostle Paul, although it had already received some enlargement from the activity of the hellenist converts and of Paul himself, who together had adapted it to the conversion of uncircumcised pagans. But all these acquisitions became crystallized, so to say, round the original theme of the coming Kingdom. Meanwhile, under the influence of the gnoses which sprang up spontaneously among the recruits to the new faith, the notion of a divine Christ, Saviour of mankind in virtue of his death, in whom the mystery was at once typified and revealed in the course of his earthly career, was gradually leading on to the transformation of the eschatological into the Gospel form of teaching.

Let us note at the outset and never lose sight of the fact that this evolution, from beginning to end, and especially in the early stages, was effected in an atmosphere of superheated mysticism in which there was little room for reflection and none at all for criticism. Christianity was born under the rule of vision and prophecy. Jesus himself, so far as we are able to estimate him, was an ardent visionary, although the worse than meagre information we have about it is hardly sufficient to fix the character of his visions. But what we do know is that he *saw* the Kingdom of God preparing to come by his ministry, and that after him his disciples *saw* the Kingdom ready to come by his act, and himself now living with God as anointed Lord and Christ. These visionaries were of necessity prophets also. We might conjecture as much even if we were not plainly informed of it. Moreover, it is *a priori* certain that these Christian prophets delivered oracles, if not always in Jesus' name, at least about him, and as animated by his spirit.

A few examples of contributions by Christian prophets will

suffice to show how their insertion was effected. What we are about to say is independent of the credit unquestionably due to the statement in Acts xiii, 1 about the five prophet-teachers who presided over the Antioch community before two of them, Barnabas and Paul, were chosen for regular missionary work in that region. We simply assume as a fact beyond question that at an early hour these prophet-teachers, or masters in prophecy, made their appearance in the Christian communities and that they played a great part in the enrichment of the gospel catechesis.

As a type of this teaching-prophecy we choose first the short apocalypse, or allegory of the eschatological Christ, now inserted in Mark xii, 1–11, where it is presented as a specimen of the teaching given by Jesus at Jerusalem, but which, as we have already seen (p. 95), he never gave there, nor could have given.

> A man had planted a vineyard; he had surrounded it with a hedge; he had dug a cellar there for his winepress and built a tower; he leased it to vine-dressers, and went out of the country.

The description of the vineyard is borrowed from Isaiah v, 1–2; the vineyard is Israel and the owner of it is God. The great simplicity of the imagery is remarkable: after miraculously establishing his people in their home, God returns to his.

> And in due season he sent a servant to the vine-dressers to receive part of the produce of the vineyard; but they seized him, beat him and sent him back empty-handed. Thereupon he sent them another servant; to him they gave insults and beat him on the head. He sent them yet another, and this one they killed; and so with many others, of whom some they flogged and some they killed.

Obviously this refers to the sending of the prophets, to whom Israel is supposed to have turned a deaf ear.

> He had still somebody else to send, a well beloved son; he sent him last of all saying "they will respect my son."

Observe that this "son" arrives under the same conditions as the servants; he, no more than they, comes direct from heaven, and he is called "son" in his quality of the Messiah promised to Israel.

> But these vine-dressers said one to another: " 'Tis the heir! Up, let us kill him and ours will be the heritage."

Jesus is "the heir," as having authority to set up the reign of God in the holy land.

> And laying hands on him they killed him and threw his body out of the vineyard.[1] What then will the master of the vineyard do? He will come and destroy the vine-dressers and will give the vineyard to others.

It is obvious that, when this was conceived and put into form, Jerusalem was destroyed and the Gospel preached outside of Palestine, and it is to these believers beyond its borders that "the heritage" will revert; to them will the Kingdom belong, when Christ appears.

> Have you not read this Scripture (Psalm cxviii, 22–23):
>
> The stone which the builders threw aside has become the corner stone. It is the Lord who has made it so, and the stone is a wonder to gaze upon.

The Son, killed by the Jews, is none the less the Lord Jesus Christ. Plainly this short prophetic allegory is a fragment of anti-Jewish polemic drawn up towards the end of the first Christian century by way of complement to the eschatological catechesis. Thrown back into the earthly life of Jesus it was at first intended to serve as his last discourse at Jerusalem, to be received later into the gospel catechesis. Later still it has been thrown back a stage in Mark's catechesis and placed after the question of the priests about his authority (xi, 27–33) where it stands with nothing logically leading up to it. The other two Synoptics found it there and borrowed it from Mark (Matthew xxi, 33–43;[2] Luke xx, 9–18). But the pushing back of our allegory in Mark's catechesis from its first intended position as the last discourse of Jesus was brought about by the intercalation of a more considerable piece of eschatology, to wit the great apocalypse of the Synoptics, which first came into existence as teaching delivered by the risen Jesus, that is as the utterance of a Christian prophet speaking on his behalf and in his name.

We have already seen that the history of this apocalyptic document is older than that of the allegory of the wicked husbandmen in Mark; but the case requires closer study for its

---

[1] Hardly in keeping with the story of an honourable burial.
[2] Where Jesus, after the final citation from Psalm cxviii, is made to add: "Therefore I say unto you, the Kingdom of Heaven shall be taken from you and given to a nation that will produce the fruits of it."

bearings on the evolution of the Christian catechesis. The kernel of it, as we have remarked above (p. 97) is a short Jewish apocalypse, earlier than the capture of Jerusalem by Titus in the year 70. But the adaptation of it to Christian teaching is later than that event. Moreover it seems clear that the first draft of Mark was ignorant of it as an element of Christian teaching. This conclusion results, not only from the use made of the allegory of the wicked husbandmen in the conditions we have just described, but also from the fact that Mark represents Jesus as delivering the Great Apocalypse almost in secret before the four principal disciples. Mark has the prophecy delivered on the Mount of Olives, the reason being that the source from which he drew it presents it as delivered there by the risen Christ when about to ascend into heaven, that is to say, in the exact condition in which the Apocalypse of Peter presents an analogous revelation. We have equal ground for believing that the artificial introduction to the Book of Acts contains the rudiments of a similar discourse with the scene set exactly as in the Apocalypse of Peter.

Thus our hypotheses are not groundless imaginations; they are inductions as solid as the matter permits of, and based upon texts whose form was under continual alteration until finally fixed in the canonical edition of the New Testament books.

Another point needing careful consideration and easily established, though this is not the place to enter into details, lies in the fact that the revelations about the End in the synoptic apocalypse are accompanied by moral precepts concerning the right attitude, not only in presence of the final catastrophe, but also in meeting the persecutions in store for believers. These precepts are to be found, expressed in almost exactly the same terms, in the instructions given in earlier passages to preachers of the Gospel. The truth is that both the moral instructions and the commission of the apostles were conceived with an outlook to the Second Coming and originally formed part of the teaching about the end of the world. They, also, are instructions given by the risen and immortal Christ. Before the death of Jesus no *apostles* were in existence to receive commission. Strictly speaking apostolic activity did not come into being until the great outbreak of propaganda was let loose by the hellenist believers. All this advice to apostles and victims of persecution, when closely studied, will be seen to have no *raison d"être* in the personal message of Jesus. Most assuredly it does not come from him. It is an utterance of Christian prophecy spoken after Jesus' death in the name of the immortal Christ and with an outlook strictly eschatological.

The Apocalypse of John—a typical Christian Prophecy

That is not all. There is one whole book to attest the long persistence of the view which interpreted the providential mission of Jesus with predominant reference to the coming Reign of God. It is the Apocalypse of John (*circa* A.D. 90). This Apocalypse has only a faint and fugitive allusion (xi, 8) to the crucifixion of Jesus at Jerusalem and refers to nothing else in his earthly career. From beginning to end the figure on which attention is focussed is the Christ-about-to-come; and this whether he speaks himself or by the mouth of his prophet. In the first part of the book the Christ writes to the churches, addressing them directly as the true head of them all; in the body of it he makes his prophet write a kind of eschatological summary concluding with his own triumph. Though doubtless he is mystically the sacrificed Lamb, he never ceases to be the One-who-is-coming. In telling the myth of his own birth (xii) he makes his birth of one piece with the myth of his final exaltation, inasmuch that, for him, being born and being carried up to God, preparatory to his coming triumph over the Beast and Satan, are virtually the same event (xii, 5). In plain truth the author of the Apocalypse would seem to be totally ignorant of the gospel presentation. Is not that significant?

The Mystery of the Lamb

Though the Apocalypse is wholly eschatological in substance, it must not be forgotten that a well-characterized mystery pervades it throughout and brings it into close contact with those whom it attacks so bitterly in the letters to the seven churches. This is the mystery of the Lamb, a Jewish figure. The eschatological character of the book also comes in part from its sources and these, in the body of the work, are purely Jewish, the Christian elements being an added embroidery.

In the letters to the seven churches, written in imitation of the

CONCLUSIONS

Epistles, the reward promised to the faithful Christian is as follows: "to eat of the tree of life, which is in the paradise of God" (ii, 7); to be untouched by "the second death," that is, to escape the eternal fire (ii, 11); to eat "the hidden manna" and to possess "a white stone, on which a new name is engraved, known only to him who receives it"—a feature in the mysteries borrowed from paganism (ii, 17); to have the Gentiles in his power "shepherding them with an iron flail and shattering them like a potter's jars" ... and to possess "the morning star"—this last a feature of astrological magic (ii, 26–29); to be "clothed in white raiments," symbol of purity and of immortality (iii, 5); to be "a pillar in God's temple" and to have inscribed on him "God's name, the name of the new Jerusalem and the new name" (of the Christ)—all features of mystery cults (iii, 12); "to sit with" the Christ "on his throne" as the Christ "sits with his Father on his throne"—a strange enlargement in the perspective of the believer's reward, and hardly in keeping with the idea of the new Jerusalem as coming down to earth (iii, 21). Parallel to this conception of the Christ as enthroned with God is the conception of him as pre-existent, in the preamble to the same letter, where he is entitled "the beginning of the creation of God," which is what the Old Testament says of the Divine Wisdom (Proverbs viii, 23) and is not far removed from "the Logos of God," the name given later on to the conquering Christ (xix, 13). However, it is not impossible that this transcendent mysticism was introduced into the book at the time when the Apocalypse was edited for inclusion in the canon. None the less true is it that the Apocalypse in its earliest form was strongly coloured by astral mysticism.

But here there is another mysticism which is not astral, and has nothing to do with the Ram of the Zodiac. This is the Christ-Lamb, early substituted, as we know, for the Jewish paschal lamb in the quartodeciman Easter, observed to the second century by the Christians of Asia and consecrated by the Johannine Gospel. The Lamb appears as the chief figure in the vision of the book with the seven seals, the book of destiny, which the Lamb only may open. He is first announced (v, 5) as "the lion of Judah" and "stock of David" (Isaiah xi, 1–10)—which reveals the gospel catechesis, at least in process of formation. The description then follows:

And I saw in the midst of God's throne a *lamb* standing upright as *with a cut throat* (Isaiah liii, 7) . . . and he came and laid hold on the book . . . and when he had taken the book, the four Living Ones and the four-score Aged Ones fell down before the Lamb, chanting a new canticle, saying:
> Thou art worthy
> to take the book and break its seals,
> because thou hast been cut with the knife
> And by thy blood thou hast ransomed for God
> men of every tribe, tongue, people and nation,
> And hast made them a Kingdom and priests for God,
> and they shall be rulers over the earth.

In this passage we have before us a myth of salvation by the Lamb as the redeeming victim. But this is not the mystic gnosis of the Epistle to the Romans. It is a myth of the Christ as the paschal lamb, attached, for consistency with prophecy, to the description of the suffering servant in Isaiah. This Christ-Lamb opens and explains the Book of Destiny, all that is due to happen before the end of the age. The revelation is closely framed in the primitive eschatology, redemption and the revealing of salvation coming to pass by this Kingdom of priests, who are to rule *over the earth*. It is true that, later on, the elect are represented as standing in heaven "before the throne and before the Lamb" (vii, 14–17); but that description refers to a provisional stage of the glorified martyrs before the final triumph to be realized on the regenerated earth.

Elsewhere (xiii, 8) the reprobates, worshippers of the Beast, are described as "those whose names are not written in the book of *the sacrificed Lamb*, since the foundation of the world." The book of the Lamb is the book of the elect, which has existed since the beginning of all things. But this does not mean that the Lamb has been *immolated* since the world's foundation (cf. 1 Peter i, 18–21, written in the same spiritual atmosphere as our passage).

Further on (xiv, 1–5) we next find the Lamb on Mount Sion, with the hundred and forty-four thousand of the elect (from vii). They are those "who have been ransomed from the earth" and "have not defiled themselves with women"; they "follow the Lamb whithersoever he goes." We are again told that the kings who fight for the Beast "will fight against the Lamb, and he will overthrow them" (xvii, 12–14). "The marriage of the Lamb" is announced to follow the destruction of the Beast (xix, 7); but the wife of the Lamb does not appear till after the last judgment. She is the Church of the Blessed (xxi, 2, 9–10), new Jerusalem, where will be the throne of God and of the Lamb (xxii, 1, 3); God and the Lamb will be its temple and its light (xxi, 22–23; xxii, 5). Conclusion (xxii, 16):

> I, Jesus, have sent my angel,
> > to give you this testimony in the churches.
> I am the stock and the offspring of David,
> > the bright star of the morning.

This can hardly be the star which Balaam predicted would rise out of Jacob (Numbers xxiv, 17). Far more probably it is the planet Venus in her character of a great astral power, so that here, in the concluding note, the element of astral mythology is still present, complicating the Jewish eschatology. On the other hand, the insistence on the Davidic descent of the Christ turns us towards the gospel catechesis, which we must suppose to be now sufficiently developed to make the forms and influence of the gnoses revealed in Gospels and Epistles sensibly felt in the Apocalypse also.

In dating the Apocalypse back to the reign of Domitian (81–96), Irenaeus must have placed it somewhat too early, a consequence of the thesis which attributes its authorship to the apostle John. The last retouching of the book may well be not much earlier than 140. The allusion to "the twelve apostles of the Lamb" (xxi, 14) not only proves that the author cannot himself have been one of the Twelve, but further, and above all, that the myth of Twelve Apostles, founders of the universal Church, and preachers of the Gospel to the whole world, was completely formed at the time this allusion was made. This confirms the remark just made regarding the relatively late date of the Apocalypse.

The Apocalypse of Peter: another Christian Prophecy

Coming now to the Apocalypse of Peter we recall that while, like the Apocalypse of John, it is a revelation delivered by the Risen Christ, it is not dominated to the same extent by pre-occupation with the approaching parousia. After giving instruction parallel to that of the synoptic apocalypse, which seems to prolong the perspective to the time of Barkochba, it describes at length the pains in store for the damned and the blessedness of the elect, coming to an end in the exaltation of the Christ carried up to heaven. This Apocalypse, like most of the others, is a compilation. In the first part it gives us eschatological instruction by the Risen Christ parallel to that of the synoptic apocalypse, of which it reproduces certain elements, and also parallel to the brief summary found at the end of Luke and in the beginning of Acts. But it has certain peculiarities of its own, such as the eschatological explanation of the allegory of the barren fig-tree, of a kind which turns this part of the book into confirmation of our thesis that teachings originally attributed to the Risen Christ speaking through Christian prophets have been transposed into the Gospel story, and there presented as given by Jesus before his death, when preaching in Galilee or at Jerusalem. Another peculiarity is that our Apocalypse, in the last part, and especially in its account of the pains of the damned and the bliss of the elect, describes them as going on in the actual present, as though the fate of men were decided immediately after death by a judgment which classed them for ever as lost or saved. This indicates a point of view entirely different from that of either Jewish or Christian eschatology, but is rather in line with the pagan mysteries, Orphic and Egyptian, in which there was no *general* resurrection.

As to the appearance of Moses and Elijah and the assumption of the Christ to heaven in their company, it is quite clear that our Apocalypse is the original source of the scene which, thrown back into the earthly life of the Christ, became the miracle of the Transfiguration. This explains why the miracle, narrated only in the Synoptics, is said to have been witnessed only by three leading disciples and the injunction laid upon them, according to Mark (ix, 9) and Matthew (xvii, 9), to say nothing about it until the Son of Man be risen from the dead, while, according to Luke, they did keep silence at the time. This is tantamount to saying that the transposition is avowed by the evangelists themselves.

From all this it follows that the gospel legend, as well as the gospel teaching of Jesus, were constructed, in important parts, by a process of transposition and anticipation of elements

CONCLUSIONS

borrowed from the eschatological catechesis. The fact is significant and by no means lacking in importance. Nor is it in the least surprising, because, however it be explained, it only shows that the teachings of the catechesis, mystic doctrine or seeming narrative, were not dominated by historical considerations but by its own catechetical aim. And this aim, through all its manipulations of the material utilized, which seem so irresponsible to us, was ever one and the same—to exalt the Christ in such manner as to draw men of goodwill to worship him. Had the Gospels been offered as historical tradition one would have to say that those who fixed the form of it were audaciously making sport both of the tradition and of those to whom they would transmit their work.

ESCHATOLOGY FULLY TRANSFORMED INTO GOSPEL LEGEND

Viewing the New Testament literature in its totality, we have now seen how the Christian catechesis, at first eschatological, took the form, in the Epistles regarded as apostolic, of a mystical gnosis *before* it assumed, in the Gospels, the form of a sacred legend by means of which the eager catechumen was initiated into the Christian cult. We have now to consider a little more closely the fortunes of this gnosis before it passed into legend.

For example, we have seen how, in the Epistle to the Romans, a mystical gnosis was hitched on, so to say, to the eschatological theory of salvation expounded by Paul in his original letter to the Christians of Rome. Not only are the two theses (setting aside a few glosses) developed in mutual independence, but each is complete in itself and in contradiction with the other. If, instead of being thus independent and contradictory, the final text presented them as reconciled and fused into one, the mind of the author having thus fused them, then indeed we should have to maintain that this arrangement of the two doctrines was the outcome of spiritual forces at work in Paul himself. But this is not a case of fusion but of juxtaposition, in other words of editorial combination, as anyone who is willing to see what is under his eyes will discover at once on literary analysis of the text.

This is also the right place to recall the further fact that the duality of these two doctrines, the eschatological and the gnostic, is admitted, in principle, by the Epistles themselves. When Paul, that is the pretended Paul, is made to write (1 Corinthians iii, 1–2): "As for me, brethren, I could not address you as spiritual, but as carnal, as babes in Christ; I have given you milk to drink, not solid food; for you were not able to bear it"—when he writes thus about milk and solid food, "milk" can only mean some teaching regarded as elementary, to wit, the eschatological catechesis, while "solid food" is the gnosis of salvation which the author himself is actually in process of addressing to his readers, after having artificially hitched it on to what the real Paul has said about the baptism conferred by him on certain Corinthians (i, 14–16). Now the fact is that the "wisdom" which the mystic or pseudo-Paul declares to be reserved "for them that are perfect," for the fully initiated, wisdom which he teaches "in mystery," because it is "hidden" and which even "the rulers of the world have not known, because if they had known it they would not have crucified the Lord of glory" (ii, 6–9)—the fact is that we have here the very doctrine which he proceeds to expound to the very people whom he declares incapable of understanding it. It would be impossible to avoid the most absurd of contradictions if we remained blind to the double perspective created by this pretended Paul, who now expounds a gnosis in regard to which the teaching formerly given by the real Paul, to wit, the eschatological catechesis, is described as only milk for babes. Whoso is willing to understand, let him understand!

The case of the author of the Epistle to the Hebrews is exactly the same, except that this author gives us explicit information about the elementary catechesis to which he claims that his own gnosis is superior. We have already studied the text which establishes the distinction between the two (vi, 1–2) and made our commentary (*supra*, p. 34). What the author calls "the initial theme of the Christ" is the common catechesis of his time; what he calls "perfection" is gnostic initiation; "the foundation of repentance" is the moral teaching which urges the catechumen to be sorry for the sins of which he will be cleansed by baptism. What is this but the eschatological catechesis, and in a form in which not the least place can be found for the evangelical catechesis of the Gospel story? But, in making this distinction between his own mysticism and the elementary catechism of

Christianity, the author professes the very principle of gnosis and, in proceeding to impart his mystical poetry to people whom he declares to be incapable of understanding it, he falls into the same contradiction as the gnostic who introduces his doctrine into First Corinthians. The sole difference between the two is that the author of Hebrews avows the contradiction. If he really intended to pass himself off as Paul, that is, if it was he who wrote xiii, 19, 23–24, the position of the two gnostics would be exactly the same. In any case, that is the position of the writer who, at the end of the Epistle, speaks in the name of Paul.

The great gnosis developed in the middle part of the Epistle to the Romans (v–viii; see *supra*, p. 253) may have been conceived with no reference to the eschatological theory, and the author does not *himself* pretend to be Paul. But, by incorporation with the Epistle, it is presented as coming from the apostle, and whoever so incorporated it intended it to confront the eschatological Christianity as a higher fulfilment and rectification of its eschatology, just as it is presented in First Corinthians and as the author to the Hebrews presents the gnosis peculiar to his Epistle. The same holds true of the gnostic parts of the Epistle to the Galatians and of Second Corinthians where pretended Paul, Paul the mystic, is represented as the unique depositary of a gospel uniquely true, this gospel being no other than the salvation gnosis preached by him. In the Epistle to the Galatians he prides himself on owing nothing to those who were apostles before him, meaning by that the Elders at Jerusalem. But how often must we repeat that the Twelve, in their lifetime, were never *apostles* and that the real Paul never knew them as such? He also prides himself on having, in a revelation given to himself in particular, received the gospel which he preaches among the Gentiles, to wit, the salvation gnosis summarily taught in the Epistle to the Galatians and, with all the amplitude it merits, in that to the Romans. In Second Corinthians our pseudo-Paul goes as far as to say that since the Christ died "that the living should live no more for themselves but for him who died for them and rose again, henceforth he knew no man after the flesh, and if ever he had known the Christ after the flesh, now he knew him no more." Commentators have been much embarrassed in their attempt to understand what our author means by "the Christ after the flesh." Certainly it was not precisely the Christ of history—for that conception was not in existence at the time. It can only have been the Christ-man of the eschatological catechesis announced by those whom pseudo-Paul condemns as Judaizers—Jesus made Christ by his death and Lord in his immortality. The Christ of Paul the mystic, on the other hand, is the spiritual Man, made flesh to effect redemption by his death and live again as the Lord of his mystery. In this conception, that of the Epistle to the Romans, the revelation of the mystic Christ stands as clearly opposed to the primitive eschatology as in First Corinthians and Hebrews.

Many Forms of Gnosis in the Epistles

Though "the gnosis of Paul" is a phrase freely used, it would be more exact to speak of the gnoses that have been put out under his name. For it is far from true that one and the same gnostic system is professed in all the Epistles, or in all parts of the same Epistle, which have their origin in gnostic mysticism. While there is no ground for making all these gnoses into reflections of Marcion's system, no less unfounded is the fault found with the author of *The Birth of the Christian Religion* for representing them as distinct, since that is precisely what they are when interpreted in the sense conveyed by their own language.

What, for example, is the meaning of the gnostic poem inserted into the Epistle to the Philippians (ii, 6–11; *supra*, p. 264)? Is it not the odyssey of a divine Being, a panegyric of the spiritual Christ, lodged in a moral exhortation penetrated by gnosis, and conceived in complete independence both of the gospel catechesis and the eschatological?

What, again, is the gnostic poem which has got itself enshrined and paraphrased in the Epistle to the Colossians (i, 15–20; cf. *supra*, p. 265) but another definition of the mystery of salvation, analogous to that elaborated in Hebrews as well as to that which underlies the fourth Gospel and, like the foregoing, independent of both catecheses, and perhaps used in the Epistle to counter a pagan mystery with a Jewish colour (ii, 16–23; cf. *The Birth of the Christian Religion*, p. 265).

And is there not yet another gnosis in the Epistle to the Hebrews? And is not this one of the most original, and not the less so because its author presents it as the climax of the revelations made to Israel, apparently lodging it in the frame of the primitive catechesis and giving us a glimpse, through some of its features, of the gospel catechesis in process of formation (cf. *supra*, p, 266).

Finally, we have the brief gnostic poem in the First to Timothy (iii, 16), there offered as a definition of "the mystery of godliness," in which we find a proclamation of the very principle of the gospel catechesis, to wit, "the appearance of the Christ in the flesh." Though of later date than the preceding, does it not seem, in saying that the Christ was "justified in spirit," to retain the original conception of the resurrection as purely spiritual, which is certainly not that of the gospel story in its canonical forms?

In addition to all this, we know how the epistolary teaching made acquisitions of many kinds; how it was not only a depositary for various gnoses, with or without adaptation to the primitive eschatology, but became charged with doctrinal enlargements and compromises, and especially with moral teaching and exhortation, even with rules of church discipline, all this being done by those who believed they had the right to make the apostles give answers on these points whenever conditions in the churches suggested that a ruling was called for.

But, first and foremost, we have only to confront the Epistles attributed to Paul with the seven letters which the Christ of the Apocalypse addresses to the churches of Asia by his prophet-spokesman to satisfy ourselves that in these churches, and chiefly at Ephesus, there were Christian groups which claimed Paul's authority and ascribed it to those whom we may call his literary successors. To such circles as these we owe the creation of the fictitious gnostic Paul who, especially in the Epistle to the Galatians and in Second Corinthians, puts forth the altogether preposterous claim to be, by the special choice and revelation of the Christ, the unique depositary of a unique Gospel, to wit, the revelation of the mystery, under the diverse forms or definitions it assumes in the great epistles and in the lesser. Opposing this fictitious Paul stands the fiction of the Twelve Apostles and that of Peter, the pretended source, original and also unique, of the Christian apostolate. And, combined with this in Asia, we have the fiction of the beloved disciple who, like Paul, is author of a small library, Apocalypse, Gospel and three Epistles. All this in preparation for the final stage when these more or less contradictory theses will be brought to a synthesis, and their divergences somewhat smoothed over and apparently reconciled in the gospel catechesis and the canonical collection of the New Testament.

The Real Paul and the Fictitious

We have now reached what is, perhaps, the most important result of this part of our study. This consists in the radical dissimilation of the Paul who really spoke and the Paul who was represented as speaking. The first, the historic Paul, was the preacher of the primitive eschatological catechesis, enlarging it only, as it had already been enlarged by the Antioch missionaries, with a view to bringing pagans into the fold by sparing them the constraint of the legal observances. The second was Paul the mystic, with his audacious pretensions, his perpetual and tiresome boastfulness, his gross abuse of the old disciples whom he makes out to be Judaizers. As a personality having a place in primitive Christian history this second Paul would be wholly inexplicable, but is intelligible enough as the mouthpiece of Christian groups which believed themselves heirs of the Pauline tradition. They it was who, in reality, brought into the tradition, not indeed the principle of universal salvation by faith in the risen Christ—from the beginning there had been not great difficulty in admitting that—but the mystery of salvation by mystic union with a Saviour who had come down from heaven and returned to it in glory—a Saviour to whom the ardent believer was united, not only by knowledge of the mystery, but in an intimate communion effected by sacraments, with their ritual of probation, participation and final vision. This point is reached in the baptismal hymn quoted in the Epistle to the Ephesians (v, 14) and by Clement of Alexandria:[1]

> Awake, thou sleeper,
> rise up from among dead men,
> And Christ the Lord shall enlighten thee,
> the sun of the resurrection,
> Begotten before the morning star (Psalm cx, 3)
> giving life by his beams.

[1] *Protrepticos*, viii, 84, 1, 2. See *The Birth of the Christian Religion*, p. 228.

CONCLUSIONS

As, on the one hand, the mystery retained in substance the ethic of the primitive eschatology and even tended, in certain parts, to improve upon it; as, on the other, it had its own way of understanding the Last Things as the inward and spiritual Reign of God, so it was inevitable that the mystic Paul would be made to deliver oracles on the problems thrown up by the state of the churches and the course of events, and also, when the mounting extravagances of the gnostic Christians made it necessary, on the compromises and the discipline needed to prevent the Church dissolving in a fermentation of sects. Our analysis has already shown the place in the evolution of nascent Christianity which belongs to the documents pretending to be Epistles, and we shall not repeat the exposition here. It is easy enough to understand why Paul was made to deliver oracles on marriage and virginity, on joining pagans in their sacrifices, on the ordering of the Supper, on spiritual gifts, on faith in the resurrection. All that was done spontaneously and under the pressure of circumstances. This it is that explains the differences we encounter in regard both to doctrine and practice, to be found among these lucubrations which, in the view of their authors, seemed required by the needs of the moment.

What could throw a more revealing light on this matter than the intrusion of the Song of Love in 1 Corinthians xiii? If there is one point in the criticism of the Epistles that admits of no doubt, it is that the Song of Love in its primitive form[1] is nothing else than the spontaneous reaction of some highly gifted mystic, of a Christian mind that soared aloft beyond the gnoses and the vulgar eschatology, in presence of the poor display of "spiritual gifts" spread before him in the preceding chapter. We can see how this noble poem got slipped into the Pauline dossier: some scribe or editor, finding it to hand, undertook to place it there as best he could. He has not placed it very happily, but his interpolation has saved it for us, and Christians have good reasons for the profoundest gratitude to its author, who has here bequeathed to us the true "essence of Christianity." How is it that our critics are not impressed by this evident interpolation? The answer is only too plain: if they allowed themselves to recognize it our cause would be won all along the line. The respectable

---

[1] See *Remarques*, 69-74.

limitations of their approach to these questions will long prevent them making that admission.

The authoritative pronouncement on the Resurrection in 1 Corinthians xv[1] reveals an attempt to adapt eschatology to gnosis, the material idea of the resurrection to the spiritual, the historic Paul and the mystical Paul to the conventional Paul, who already has almost become the Paul of orthodoxy, full of respect for the Twelve, like the Paul of Acts, and willing to accept the subordinate position imposed upon him by the interest of the Christian communities then in process of unification as the Catholic Church. Here we shall not repeat the detail of what we have said elsewhere on the small retouches and late interpolations this chapter has undergone.

The Remaining Epistles

We have already named the various stages of the Christian movement to which the Pastoral Epistles, the Epistle of James, the two of Peter, Jude's and the three of John, severally correspond. The whole of this literature is as completely fictitious, from the literary point of view, as any writings could be; none of it goes back to the apostolic age; every part of it originated at a moment when it seemed required for the service of a Christianity now established or in process of establishment. The catechesis attributed to James shows that a well-intentioned believer had come to the conclusion that the doctrine of salvation by faith alone, as it had been announced in certain pages of the Pauline *dossier*, might have results reprehensible from the moral point of view. The Pastorals, confronting the gnostic crisis, are concerned with the organization of government in the churches and the crystallization of the traditional deposit of faith. The First of Peter does not look so far ahead; its main interest is in the gnosis which the author finds in the Pauline *dossier* and in the moral consequences it seems to involve, and this is the case of all the other Epistles occasioned or penetrated by gnostic influence. For example, at a given moment between the years 110 and 130 the duty of submission to the established powers became a commonplace with these moralists. The Epistle of Jude betrays a horror of gnostic excesses. The Second of Peter, boldly taking its stand

[1] *Op. cit.*, 74-84.

on the last products of eschatological teaching, also denounces the gnostic peril, but seems mainly preoccupied in presenting a total debâcle of the primitive catechesis by explaining that the delay of the End is a breathing-space of which profitable use should be made, and, strangely enough, points to Paul's Epistles as likely to lead, unless care be taken, to wrong conclusions in this matter. But this pretended Epistle of Peter proves, by the allusion just named, that there existed at the time it was written a collection of letters attributed to Paul, and that these formed part of a body of Scripture, and that it was then possible to speak of a New Testament Canon. As to the Johannine Espistles we have already seen that they shared the fortune of the major writings in that category, the Apocalypse and the Gospel, especially the latter, to which they were intended to serve as convoy. And this leads us to summarize our conclusions regarding the gospel catechesis of which we have already seen glimpses but await a full view.

THE GOSPEL CATECHESIS IN FULL VIEW

We make no apology for repeating, what cannot be repeated too often—that the Gospels were not originally understood as a history of Jesus, of which the material had been furnished by those who had known the Christ in the course of his existence on earth. The primitive catechesis turned on the Last Things; it was eschatological and looked on Jesus not as the Messiah, the Christ, who *had come* (in which case it would have been led to interpret his earthly career as a messianic epiphany), but believed in him solely as the Messiah *about to come*, the effect being to withdraw his earlier existence from the realm of mystical interest and leave the first believers indifferent to it. In consequence, all the interest attaching to the name of Jesus then lay, not in his earthly career, but in his approaching parousia. This in sum was the essential object, if not the unique object, of faith. The Jesus on whom this faith centred was not Jesus as he *had lived* on earth, but Jesus as the Christ *now living* with God, and the conditions needed to make sure of a place in the Great Kingdom he would soon bring in. All the teaching of Jesus known to this catechesis on the Last Things, to this eschatological catechesis, was attributed by it to the immortal Christ in heaven; and we have already seen that it was only at a later period that this teaching was antedated and thrown back into the life of the Christ on earth, and how his exaltation as Messiah was treated in exactly the same manner.

Whence it results that the messianic interpretation of the earthly life of Jesus is not primordial, is not an experience of the age called apostolic; in all strictness of truth it is a *product* of the new faith. It was not with a view to retrieving a forgotten story that the gospel catechesis was drawn up. That was bound to happen, and did happen under a kind of inward necessity resulting, not precisely from the theories of salvation—for mystical speculation was first directed to the death of Jesus as the condition of his exaltation to Messiahship—but from the establishment of the Christian mystery as a *cult* to which initiation was necessary. Of this cult Jesus became, for the faith, not only the divine object, but the founder and master of the mystery, himself the prototype of the salvation which, if we may say so, he had achieved in himself, that he might make it a reality for all who were his. In this way catechesis was transformed into Gospel, into Good News, inasmuch as it showed forth the epiphany of a Saviour, Jesus the Christ. The gospel form of the catechesis, the story form, was non-existent in the first Christian age and cannot go, and does not go, so far back.

This also explains the relative but incontestible poverty of the gospel legend and the perpetual artifice of its construction. Many of our exegetes still speak of it as a selection made from abounding memories. In point of fact, as we have said already and repeat with assurance, neither memory nor selection has anything to do with the matter. The elements of the legend have been taken from various sources; much, and not the least important, has been borrowed, as we have seen, from the eschatological catechesis; and all of it has been adapted, as best might be, to the main object in view, that of setting forth the Christian mystery. The dependence of Matthew and Luke, even of John, on Mark is certainly no indication that a great wealth of material was available; for it is obvious that the Marcan sketch became the base of the other books simply for want of anything better. The workings over and the additions this sketch has undergone, both in Mark's Gospel itself and in the other evangelical writings, have far more the effect upon us of accentuating the artificial character of the story than of disguising it. On a wide view, the first Gospel and the third are a fusion of the sacred legend, sketched in by Mark, with a mass of teaching, mostly moral, whose original place was the eschatological catechesis, while the fourth Gospel is constructed on the model of the other three.

In like manner the documents which exegetes are wont to call "sources" of the Gospels lack the qualities of historical documents, of which use could be made for a biography of Jesus. But that does not prevent the names of places from belonging to a real geography nor the names of persons being those of men who were once alive on earth. Jesus the Nazorean, John the Baptizer, Pontius Pilate belong to the history of their time; but among the actors in this sacred tragedy it may well be that Pontius Pilate is the one about whom history has the most certain, or the least uncertain, information. When human history goes deep into its subject, it finds the rôle played by official persons easier to define than that of others which are often more real and of greater influence on the course of events. But we must not enlarge upon that.

The Catechesis of Mark

Mark's formless sketch is not all of a piece and certainly has been worked over more than once. Memories of Peter? The idea is out of the question. In Mark's Gospel Peter is not a source of information but an object of almost constant abuse. It would seem that the original draft of the Gospel had none of the preliminaries concerning John the Baptist; it began by placing Jesus at Capernaum for the calling of the first disciples, and finished with the exclamation of the centurion on hearing the last outcry of Jesus on the cross: "Verily this man was the Son of God"; at that moment Jesus was deemed to enter upon his eternal life and the tale of his Passion was ended. What follows reflects the relatively late idea of a material resurrection the third day after death, co-ordinated with the Christian celebration of Easter on Sunday. To search for the lost end of Mark is waste of labour, since all endings beyond the centurion's exclamation are only postscripts. The preliminaries of the Gospel, the mission of the Baptist and the baptism of Jesus, are additions borrowed from the source used by Matthew and Luke for the purpose of fixing

John's position as that of forerunner of the Christ, John's rôle, in the messianic epiphany (antedated, as we have seen, to the earthly life of Jesus) being the rôle which the primitive catechesis gave him in regard to the coming Kingdom of God. Then, too, the baptism of Jesus, conceived as the prototype of Christian baptism, served as opening to the catechism of the Christian initiate, and this beginning was the preface to various teachings on the economy of the Christian mystery and its differentiation from Judaism, or what was considered as a Judaizing conception of salvation. For the second part of the Gospel, which begins with Peter's confession at Caesarea Philippi, turns on the mystery of the redeeming death, memorialized in the mystic celebration of the Eucharist.

In one current of this mystic gnosis a point was made of emphasizing Peter's complete lack of understanding in presence of the revealed mystery, to the extent that it was thought fitting to make the Christ characterize him as Satan. His incomprehension is not less complete in presence of the Transfiguration, nor at Gethsemane. It was even thought to be a known fact that, at the trial of Jesus, he had found occasion to deny his master thrice. In presence of the third prediction of the Passion, the sons of Zebedee are not less unintelligent than he; their only response to the prophecy is to ask for the two chief thrones right and left of the Christ's in his Kingdom! But we must not forget that the messianic confession of Peter is the throw-back of what was originally a post-resurrection episode; that the miracle of the Transfiguration is another, and that the whole conception of the mystery in like manner anticipates a later stage in the evolution of early Christian thought. The same may be said of the calling of the fishermen whom Jesus is represented as making into apostles on the spot; of everything, also, that is said about the character of the Son of Man, which, in the gospel tradition, is the definition of the Christ dying for the salvation of mankind. This is the mystery in presence of which the disciples, who knew it not, are said to have shown themselves unintelligent with a perseverance that nothing could overcome. Care also has been taken to inform us that they understood nothing at the two miracles of multiplied loaves (vi, 35–44; viii, 14–21). This also is most sign ficant. For the story of these two miracles is nothing else than the myth of the eucharistic institution at an early stage in the evolution of the mystery at which, without being expressly the symbol of Jesus' saving death, the Supper had come to signify communion in the truth and immortality given by the Christ to his own. This conception has now acquired its mystic character and is no longer purely eschatological.

Lastly we have a feature characteristic of Mark's catechesis and at the same time a revealing light on the general antedating by the Gospels of the divine epiphany: it is as follows.

In the view of the evangelists Jesus is revealed as the Messiah by his miracles, by his own discourses and even by the remarks addressed to him by others. On such occasions the order is given to all to keep silence about what has happened, as if a secret were being violated which ought not to be disclosed until Jesus is dead and risen. Thus we find the demons never fail to cry out that Jesus is the Son of God while Jesus, who continues to drive them out, never fails to bid them hold their peace. The same order is expressly given to the disciples after Peter's confession, and is repeated after the Transfiguration. Nothing could show more clearly that the whole display of messianic signs belongs to a secondary stage in the Christian faith, at which Jesus was consciously invested during his earthly life with a glory originally belonging to him as the Risen Christ.

We conclude, then, that Mark's Gospel, considered as it stands, has a long and complex history. It is impossible to assign precise dates to all the elements it contains. There are details in the compilation which prove a plurality of stages in the drafting of the document. One of these is the note, quite early in Mark (iii, 6), which terminates the series of Jesus' quarrels with the Pharisees, especially those about the Sabbath: "The Pharisees, having departed, took counsel with the Herodians against him how they might destroy him." This half opens the door on the perspective of the Passion, the story of which it may have originally served to introduce.

The facility of the gospel narrator in improvising miracles—and the remark holds good for all the Gospels, and not only for Mark—for no other purpose than to emphasize his exposition and make the point of it clearer, may well cause us some surprise. But it would be a mistake to think that these writers or editors enjoy the invention of the marvellous for its own sake and indulge in it as a pastime or, which would be more serious, that they are boldly taking advantage of the credulous age to which their writings were addressed. The truth is that the stories they tell are, for them, true stories in virtue of the meaning they imply in regard to the spiritual work of the Christ. Unless we take account of this we may be tempted to rank their authors as barefaced purveyors of falsehood. There can be no doubt, however, that they regarded their inventions as justified for the above reason, and we have to take the stories accordingly, attaching more importance to the spirit than to the letter.

Taking the book as a whole, the Gospel according to Mark can hardly have assumed its final form before 130–140, the date at which we find the good Papias acquainted with it. The first drafts of it may go back to the beginning of the second century, the period when the conception of the Christian mystery took definite shape, and the need began to be felt for a catechesis in narrative form embodying the mystery. At an indeterminate stage of its compilation the Gospel must have fallen into the hands of some mystic group in which Peter and the Galilean disciples were no better treated than in certain Epistles attributed to Paul. There is nothing extraordinary in this, but we do well to bear it in mind.

We may accept it as probable that whoever slipped into the Gospel the arrangement of the resurrection stories that authorize the Sunday Easter did so in the interest of that arrangement at a time when the Sunday observance had been accepted by all the groups of the Roman Church; for Mark seems to have been mainly elaborated as a Roman Gospel. It is obvious that the book had no other usage in view than that of public reading in the assembled congregation. Those who think it possible to maintain that the book was written as a chronicle and for private edification are under a radical illusion as to the nature of such literature and the objects for which it was written.

To be sure, no attempt was made to incorporate into Mark the mass of moral instructions more or less closely bound up with the eschatological catechesis. This is what the compilers of Matthew and Luke set themselves to do, for the greater enrichment and efficiency of Christian teaching. The two Gospels, in their traditional form, bear witness to equal concern in a direction opposite to that in which the teaching on the Last Things was turned—that of going *back* to the terrestrial birth of the Christ. This Mark's Gospel had not dared to attempt, the integration it presents of the public life of Jesus with his messianic epiphany being already more than enough to characterize the Gospel as innovating. Preoccupation with this subject would first show itself in Judaizing circles, which had to answer awkward Jewish questions about the person of their pretended Messiah who had no visible claim to be descended from David, as the Messiah must needs be. By some believers this objection had been met by denying that Davidic descent was an essential qualification of the Messiah, quoting Psalm cx as their authority, in which David was said to address the Christ as his "Lord." Mark, Matthew and Luke all record this way of meeting the objection. But the compilers of Matthew and Luke seem to have overlooked the fact that, in this denial of the necessity of Davidic descent recorded by both of them, the genealogies they produce to prove it are rendered superfluous. The compiler who inserted the denial in Mark (xii, 35–37) may have thought it was enough that the Christ should be Son of God. Two genealogies were then invented, both fictitious, and contradictory, as we have seen, to the point of being quite worthless, were it not for the light they throw on other things. Moreover they have not come through without being neutralized and put out of court by the myth of Virgin Conception, from which it would follow that Jesus was only the putative descendant of David by Joseph, who was not his real father, as intermediary. In addition to this, the birth-stories in Matthew are built up on the Virgin Conception, whereas in Luke the Virgin Conception has been interpolated and surcharged (i, 34–35). This divergence, as we have pointed out, is far from furnishing an argument for the priority of Matthew.

The Catechesis in Matthew

The first Gospel may well be of less ancient date than is commonly supposed, not only because its birth-stories are dominated by the Virgin Conception, but also because it has been constructed on Mark in the form given to that Gospel by the oldest manuscripts, and must therefore be later than the literary work which produced the second Gospel. At certain points it may be, and doubtless is, later than Luke, though certainly not dependent on it. Some of the materials collected in it have a Judaizing tendency, though that is not true of its general spirit. Its liking for Old Testament prophecy, of which it never tires of showing the fulfilment, is evidence that this form of argument was of present force with the audience for which it was intended; indeed, the critics are agreed that this Gospel was composed in the East—to be more precise, in Syria. Its dependence on Mark is the more significant on that account; so, too, is the facility with which it has absorbed all that Mark adduces to the discredit of Peter and the Galilean disciples. The reason doubtless is that this part of the story had already taken the form of an accepted tradition.

The remarkable fact remains to be noted that in the solemn episode of the messianic confession the compilers of the Gospel have exalted Peter beyond anything to be read about him elsewhere in the New Testament. To the question propounded by Jesus (xvi, 15): "Who say ye that I am?" Peter not only replies as in Mark (viii, 29): "Thou art the Christ," but "Thou art the Christ, son of the living God." To which Jesus makes answer:

> Blessed art thou, Simon son of Jona,
>   because flesh and blood have not revealed it to thee,
>   but my father who is in heaven.
> But I also say to thee, thou art *Peter*,
>   and on this *rock* I will build my church,
>   and hell's gates shall not prevail against it.
> I will give thee the keys of the Kingdom of Heaven,
>   and what thou shalt bind on earth shall be bound in heaven,
>   and what thou shalt loose on earth shall be loosed in heaven.

Placed beside the "Back, Satan!" etc., by which Peter is crushed in xvi, 23, copied from Mark (viii, 33), these words are simply stupefying. We are told that the play of words on Kepha, "Peter," is possible only in Aramean. That is so; these magnificent propositions were born in the East. Moreover, they are aimed at the mystic Paul with an eye to Galatians i, 11, 15–17: "The Gospel I announce is not according to man . . . I *received it by revelation of Jesus Christ* . . . When it pleased God to reveal his Son in me, *without regard to flesh and blood*, without going to Jerusalem to those who were apostles before me," etc. In our text, he who receives the revelation of Jesus Christ is Peter; he who owes it not to any man is Peter; he who has been appointed foundation of the Church is Peter. But this solemn declaration is no invention of the gospel compiler; he found it complete and ready to his hand. The piece is only the more precious to us for that, but not more authentic nor more ancient. Briefly, it corresponds to the position attributed to Peter in the Book of Acts, and found its way into the first Gospel about the year 140. It would be superfluous to repeat at this point the evidence which forbids us to assign a much earlier date to the *canonical* edition of the whole Gospel, though it was known to Papias along with Mark.

The Catechesis in Luke and Acts

The case of the third Gospel and of the Acts of the Apostles is more complicated than that of Matthew, seeing that the two original books addressed to Theophilus have undergone a process of elaboration of which our two canonical books are the result. It is certain that the writer to Theophilus, like Matthew, knew Mark without further ending than the discovery of the empty tomb by the Galilean women, if indeed he knew it thus, for in that case it could only be the canonical edition of the Gospel. But it is neither certain nor probable that he knew the section of Mark comprised, in the canonical version, between the two miracles of multiplied loaves (vi, 45–viii, 26). In all probability he had no story to tell about the birth of Jesus and began his gospel narrative with the account of John's baptizing. He seems to have known Mark at a stage when it lacked the symbolism of the mystic Supper and of the bread-body and wine-blood of the Christ. Similarly, in the second book (Acts) he seems to have known nothing of the Ascension and its preliminaries nor of the miraculous descent of the Spirit on the first believers at Pentecost. We may infer from this that a long time elapsed between the original composition of the two books and their canonical edition in the form they now have, with its contrivances in favour of the Ephesian legend about John, its set purpose of subordinating Paul to the Galilean apostles (falsely called apostles) and especially to Peter, its grossly material conception of the resurrection and its deliberate reticence about

Simon the Magician, about what happened to Peter after his flight from Jerusalem and, at the end the book, about the fate of Paul.

If we assume that the two books to Theophilus, in their original form as they came from the writer's hand, were earlier than canonical Mark, we might then place their compilation in the first quarter of the second century, between 110 and 120. It is true that the writer to Theophilus supposes that many writings analogous to his own were already in existence. But we must not conclude from this that numerous bipartite expositions of the catechesis, like his, were then in circulation; enough that there were many and varied specimens whether of the eschatological type, which was not yet out of date, and concerned in substance with the origins of the faith and of Christian propaganda, or of sketches more or less rudimentary of the gospel catechesis, such as that which we may continue to call proto-Mark.

As to the date of the canonical edition of the third Gospel and of Acts we may (as indicated above, p. 192) fix it between 135 and 140, with this reservation, that while the third Gospel had, to all seeming, acquired its final form before Marcion, who must have known the *corpus* of the Gospel almost in the form it now has, we have not the same evidence for the date of Acts, though it is certain that one and the same editor gave the two books their characteristic form of apologies for Christianity as the authentic heir of Judaism and the messianic fulfilment predicted in Jewish scripture. It is certain also that features peculiar to the third Gospel and Acts were acquired before Marcion; these features are the symbolic anticipation of Jesus' preaching at Nazareth and of the miraculous draught in the vocation story; the symbolic mission of the seventy or seventy-two forerunners; the representation of the Twelve and chiefly of Peter as the depositaries and authentic apostles of Christian truth. Moreover, Marcion seems to have held that Luke was not free from Jewish contamination. It remains to add that the first edition of this Gospel, like the first of Mark, was adapted to the quartodeciman Easter, and the final edition to the Sunday observance, as was also the final edition of Mark. It would be of great value to the historian if the date could be ascertained when the devices were practised which altered the chronology of the Passion so as to make it support the Roman observance on Sunday; the documentary evidence is lacking that would enable us to fix it with precision (cf. *supra*, p. 75). We know only that between 150 and 160 the Roman bishop Anicetus pretended to authorize the Sunday observance of Easter by citing the practice of his predecessors. We must be resigned, at least provisionally, to be ignorant about certain matters on which our documents were not intended to enlighten us, but rather to keep us in the dark.

The Catechesis in the Fourth Gospel

We have already discussed the origin of the fourth Gospel and seen that the documents on which it rests expound a mystic doctrine which, strictly speaking, is not a gospel doctrine in the sense of the synoptic catechesis, nor strictly eschatological in the sense of the primitive teaching; pieces of gnosis rather, in keeping with the idea of the Christ's continual presence in those who are his own and their participation in his immortal life. The adaptation of it to gospel type sprang from the desire to accommodate mystic gnosis to the teaching pattern of the synoptic catechesis, which was also mystico-gnostic in its own way, though not in its literary form. Nevertheless, the Johannine adaptation remained in keeping with the Easter observance known as quartodeciman, and sublimated into mystic gnosis, as was everything that its catechesis had to borrow from the earlier Gospels, not for the purpose of completing their account, but with a view to displacing them and becoming their substitutes. We have already studied in chapter iii the grandiose and daring fiction that was constructed to invest the new Gospel with the apostolic authority of John. But it arrived too late to supplant the others completely. In the beginning it seems to have had no acceptance beyond the frontiers of the Asiatic province where it saw the light, and where, doubtless, it was at first not unopposed from the side of those who still clung to the synoptic catechesis previously known.

The development of the gnostic crisis seems to have had a great influence in determining the modifications that were soon introduced into this Asiatic Gospel. They were mainly as follows: account was taken of John the Baptist, and even a large use made of his personality; the attempt was made to conform the document to the general framework of the Synoptics, while retaining its own chronology; due respect was paid to the traditional eschatology, which the fundamental doctrine of the book seemed rather to exclude; lastly, without abandoning the fiction of Johannine authorship nor the somewhat equivocal personality of the beloved disciple, considerable prerogative was accorded to Peter, the same that he receives in Matthew and in Acts, to wit, the charge and function of chief shepherd of Christ's flock. It follows that, if we date the first writing of the Gospel at approximately 135, the last working over of its catechesis may certainly be placed between 150 and 160, that is to say, at the time when we have good grounds for supposing that the negotiations took place between the chief Christian churches with a view to fixing the canon of authorized Gospels as a defence against the dangers of the oncoming gnostic tide.

MARCION'S CATECHESIS

It is generally known, or ought to be, that the first author of a New Testament canon was none other than the heretic Marcion. Appealing mainly to the authority of the mystic Paul he sets himself to prove that the Jewish scriptures, made much of in the common tradition of Christians—and the more so because they had no recognized scriptures of their own to which appeal could be made—set himself to prove that this Jewish revelation, together with our bad terrestrial world, were the work of a hard-hearted and incompetent demiurge, while the Gospel of the good, transcendent God, who had been unknown to the world till the epiphany of Jesus, had nowhere been preserved in its purity. Nowhere; for the gospel books used in the churches had been contaminated by the Judaizing influences openly denounced by Paul in his Epistles. This was the state of things which Marcion claimed to have demonstrated in his *Antitheses*. In his great solicitude for the salvation of all men of goodwill, he had determined to publish Christian scriptures, cleansed by him of Jewish poison; to which end he put forth, first, *the* Gospel (*Evangelion*) which was our Luke *minus* the birth stories, with such omissions or retouchings as respect for the true doctrine demanded; and, second, the *Apostolicon*, the collected ten Epistles then attributed to Paul, their text purified by the same methods and to the same end as that of *the* Gospel.

The Canon becomes a Necessity to the Survival of the Church

It was a great innovation, but one which the Church itself also was bound sooner or later to undertake—meaning by the Church the totality of the Christian communities, then scattered about the Mediterranean world, which continued to await the Reign of God and the coming of the Christ Jesus, while continually exalting their Christ in the direction of the Godhead. It was not only in the Church that the production of Gospels went on apace; many gnostic sects had Gospels of their own; Bastilides had one; Valentinus had another. Nor was Marcion alone in rejecting the Old Testament. Argument about the interpretation of Old Testament texts no longer yielded any profit except against the Jews, not indeed by converting them, but by meeting their objections. An armament was needed against the uncontrolled insurgence of gnostic heresies, and this could only be found in the documents of the faith, which the Church already had in its hands. It remained only to sift them and bring them to a point. This was done. Towards the year 180 the collection of the four Gospels was definitely constituted. To be convinced of that we have only to read Irenaeus.

How the operation was carried through nobody knows and we can only offer conjectures. We are bound to suppose that certain of the leading churches came to an understanding about the Gospels that were to be received to the exclusion of all the many others; failing this, the anarchy which had reigned in the production of Gospels, up to the middle of the second century, might have continued indefinitely. In particular, and chiefly, Asia had to make her own Gospel of John accceptable to the other churches, and in return to give equal consideration to the synoptic catechesis as represented by the Gospels according to Mark, Matthew and Luke respectively. It was an association of members that leaned different ways, in spite of the various retouchings effected to create a sort of harmony, apparent rather than real, between the fourth Gospel and the other three. The mere fact, therefore, that the four were brought together proves that the fourth was introduced into the group as the result of a positive agreement between the churches of Asia, which would never abandon their pretended Gospel of John, with the other churches who held to one or more of the three forms of synoptic catechesis.

The solution that would have been most advantageous, had it been practicable, was to publish a single Gospel containing a synthesis of the four. But this, doubtless, could not be thought of. It is easy to understand, in the urgent need for a rule in the matter, how impossible it would have been to bring the various churches to the point of renouncing the particular Gospel used in their liturgical worship in favour of a revised version of the Gospel to which none of them was accustomed. Tatian might succeed in this, on new and limited ground, with his *Diatessaron*, of which a fragment in the original Greek has lately been discovered at Doura.[1] But an enterprise of that kind for all the churches scattered throughout the Roman empire was quite impossible. The probability is, therefore, that the canon of the four Gospels was fixed, as far as it could be, by positive agreement between the Asiatic church and the Roman.

But when? If we search in the history of the time for an occasion when such transactions may have been set on foot, or the ground prepared for them, the most natural would be that of the conversations which took place in Rome about 150–160 between Polycarp of Smyrna and the bishop Anicetus of Rome. Perhaps we may be permitted to remind apologists of a certain type that Polycarp's journey to Rome was anything but a pious pilgrimage *ad limina*, and that the four Gospels deemed apostolic were not canonized by the sole fact that their supposed authors, apostles or disciples of apostles, themselves made a present of them to the churches and so secured their acceptance as sacred writings. None of the Gospels is apostolic in this rigorous sense, and none was imposed on church usage in the conditions supposed. At a given moment these catechisms were stamped with the authority of an apostolic name to justify the credit they already enjoyed; but neither their origin nor their text was guaranteed by the names chosen to adorn them. Challenged by the gnostic movement, and especially by Marcion's proceedings, the Church found herself summoned to oppose her

[1] Discovered March 5, 1933. See Lagrange, *Revue Biblique*, July, 1933, pp. 326–327.

own texts to those of the heretic. The canon was her answer. It is unlikely, one might even say morally impossible, that in the conversations between the Asiatic and the Roman bishops, when the question of Easter observance was carefully avoided, the two being immovably fixed in their respective practice, that the question of the Gospels to be authorized was not discussed. The hypothesis should not be dismissed as altogether groundless, but the question is, in essence, accessory (cf. *The Birth of the Christian Religion*, p. 342).

The canonization of the four Gospels most in use must have contributed to promote their regular employment in liturgical exercise throughout all the churches, as well as to determine their authority as Scripture by the side of the Old Testament. That is not to say that hitherto they had been regarded as ordinary books and that they were considered as works of the Spirit only in retrospect. All our catecheses had been accepted as works of the Spirit, in this sense, that from the very beginning their content was regarded as animated by the Christ-Spirit. But, for all that, they were not yet official Scriptures in the full and absolute sense in which the term was applied to the sacred books inherited from Judaism. All documents of Christian teaching shared, more or less, in the Spirit. This explains why the writings of certain churchmen, which had found enough credit in the churches to be employed for public reading, enjoyed in their time a sort of provisional canonicity, but lost it when the decision was taken to make apostolicity an indispensable condition for inclusion in the New Testament canon. The Epistle of Clement to the Corinthians and the Pastor of Hermas are cases in point. Certainly these writings were not less worthy of veneration than the Epistles falsely attributed to Peter and to other apostles. But they had no apostolic label, and the door to canonicity was promptly closed against them.

We cannot say what the conditions were under which Alexandria accepted what was soon known as the tetramorphic Gospel. The fact is that she herself made no contribution to the canonical collection and seems to have had no part in the negotiations which prepared it. Nevertheless Clement of Alexandria, who freely quotes the Gospel of the Egyptians, knew the canon of the four Gospels commonly received (cf. *Stromata*, iii, 92–

93), and the Gospel of the Egyptians soon fell into the complete discredit in store for the writings to be henceforth known as apocryphal. As far as we can judge by the known fragments this Gospel was deeply penetrated by gnosticism, of which Alexandria seems to have been a hot-bed in the second century. A more exact description of the situation there would be that there were in Alexandria at this time, not a single church more or less organized, but, as formerly in Rome, various Christian groups without central attachment, of which some were deep in gnosis. Not till after the lapse of considerable time was there unification in Alexandria of the more or less traditionalist groups, and clear differentiation of these from the others which fell into heresy. In the third century it was catholic Alexandria that delivered a damaging blow in the East to the fortunes of the Johannine Apocalypse, the true character of which it had clearly perceived. Later, in the Byzantine Church, the Apocalypse regained the confidence in which it was still held by the more massive faith of the West.

The Catholic Epistles

St. Jerome expresses himself rather freely on some of the catholic Epistles. On James he writes as follows (*De Viris*, 2):

> He wrote only one Epistle, which is one of the seven Catholics. It is said that this letter was written by another under his name, although it gradually gained authority with the lapse of time.

This is the best that could be said. On Jude he wrote (*De Viris*, 4):

> Jude, brother of James, has left a short Epistle, which is of the seven Catholics; and because he brings in a quotation from the book of Enoch, which is apocryphal, the letter had been rejected by most people; notwithstanding, it deserved credit by its antiquity and by usage, and was counted among the Holy Scriptures.

On Peter he writes (*De Viris*, 1):

> He wrote two Epistles, which are called Catholic: the majority deny that the second is from him, in view of the difference in style when compared with the first.

These objections soon fell asleep, and the Canon of the New Testament became as solid brass till the time of the Reformation.

But we might almost say of every piece that entered into its composition that it won credit "by antiquity and by usage," not by the real apostolic authorship of its content.

THE FUTURE OF CHRISTIANITY

Putting aside all considerations of supernatural magic, and paying no heed to the narrow prejudice of rationalism, which leads to the denial of all human value in whatever is mingled with historical or literary fiction, dismissing all this, it still remains true that the collection of the New Testament, incomplete and incoherent as it may be in many respects, is the ever-living witness, to those who have ears to hear, of an extraordinary spiritual movement.[1] That movement was the Christian religion in its early youth.

As to the future, we may rest assured that the vitality of this movement, so stagnant at certain stages, so despised and rejected at others, is far from being exhausted. Of the two parties it is hard to say which falls into the deeper error, that which supposes Christianity to be perfect at every point, miraculous and divinely true both in its beginning and in its development to our own day—a theological myth, a dogmatic puerility, old legends converted into absolute dogmas—or that which thinks itself in the way to destroy Christianity and that soon it will be no more—another myth which fancies itself the last word of science and, from the human point of view, is no less childish, no less sterilizing than the other. The distance between mystic illusion and human truth is not as great as such people imagine.

Nothing in nature, so they tell us, ever perishes. Doubtless the same is true in the life of humanity. In the future remaining to man, a future whose end is yet far off, the food on which humanity will live will be, for the better part, the food on which it has lived hitherto. That which happened in "the fifteenth year of Tiberius Caesar," and in the first hundred and fifty obscure and tumultuous years of Christian history, will be matter of consequence to the human race to the last day of its existence on earth, because, while man lives not only upon bread, neither does he live only on science. Before all else he lives on the dynamism

[1] The same is true of the Old Testament.

of the spirit, on the moral electricity of devoted love. Therein lies the true fulfilment of his destiny.

Little does the bare letter matter of what Jesus, Peter, Paul or John, and their interpreters, have had to say on that topic. What matters is the fire they kindled, and it is a fire that will never die till mankind is no more. Men pass away, but humanity remains; religions die, but religion shines for ever. Man would have perished long ago, victim of his own folly, had not the religious ideal of humanity rescued him from the edge of the abyss. May he mend his ways and himself establish this law of his progress on an ever firmer foundation!

INDEX

Acts of the Apostles, Luke and, 11, 13, 170f., 321–3
Alexandria, centre of gnosticism, 328
Anicetus of Rome, 326
Antedating, 54–5
Antioch, foundation of the church at, 178–9
Antitheses of Marcion, 71, 273, 275, 324
Apocalypse. *See* Revelation, Book of
Assumption of Moses, 280

Baptism, rite of, 33–4, 36
Barkochba, 270, 304
Basilides, 70, 325
Birth stories, of Christ, 19f., 319; in Matthew, 113–6; in Luke, 149, 150

Cerinthus, 284
Clement, Epistle of, 70, 286, 327
Clement of Alexandria, 310
Codex Bezae, 144
Colossians, Epistle to the, 264–5, 269
Corinthians, first Epistle to the, 241–5, 269, 306, 307; second Epistle, 257–61, 307
Couchoud, P. L., 71n.
Cyprian, St., 61

Diatessaron, Tatian's, 326
Didache, the, 43–7
Domitrain, 303

Easter Observances, 98–9, 232, 237, 322, 323
Ecclesiastical History. *See* Eusebius
Egyptians, Gospel of the, 327, 328
Ephesians, Epistle to the, 269
Eucharist, the, 261–4
Eusebius, 63, 69

Galatians, Epistle to the, 245–7, 269
Galileo, 11
Glaucias, 70
Genesis, 11
Gnosis, forms of, in the Epistles, 308–10

Hebrews, Epistle to the, 43–4, 264–5, 266–7, 306
Heresies. *See* Irenaeus
Hermas, Pastor of, 51, 286, 327

Isaiah, 12–13
Ignatius, 70
Irenaeus, 56–62, 71, 195, 204, 286, 325

James, Epistle of, 271–2
Jerome, St., 328
John, Epistle of, 282–5
John, St., Gospel according to, 25–7, 193f., 323–4
John the Baptist: and Jesus, 33–40; Mark's presentation of, 78–9, 85; Matthew's, 116–18, 127–8; Luke's, 149, 159; St. John's, 196, 202, 323; and the establishment of the Kingdom, 288
Jude, Epistle of, 279–81
Justin, 71, 141

Lazarus, 213–4
Luke, St.: and the writer of Acts, 13–14, 141–8, 321–3; gospel according to, 70–6, 148f.; dependence on Mark, 148–56, 163–9

Magic, element of in the O.T., 15–19 in the N.T., 19–23
Marcion, 70, 71, 72, 75, 193, 221, 270, 273, 275, 276, 279, 284, 308, 322, 324–5
Marcos, 277
Mark, the gospel according to, 77f. 297, 298, 299, 315–9
Matthew, the gospel according to, 111f., 319–21
Montanus, 221
Montibus Sina et Sion, de, 61
Moses, and authorship of Pentateuch, 12
Muratori, Canon of, 192

Nicodemus, 201

Papias, 56, 63–70, 71, 72–3, 75, 318
Passion and Resurrection: in Mark, 99f.; in Matthew, 138–40; in Luke, 165–9; in John, 217f.
Pastoral Epistles, 272–9, 312
Paul, St.: the real and fictitious, 14, 310–12; summary of primitive teaching, 41–3; and Acts, 176–7, 180f.; epistles of, 239f.; pastoral epistles of, 272–9; real teaching of, 293–6; pseudo-Paul, 305–8
Peter, St., 177–8, 179–80, 192, 197, 290, 315, 316, 320, 321
Peter, Apocalypse of, 52–4, 303–5
Peter, first Epistle of, 267–8, 269, 271; second Epistle of, 281–2
Philip, 175–6
Philippians, Epistle to the, 264–5
Polycarp of Smyrna, 70, 326

Resurrection. *See* Passion

Revelation, Book of, 11, 15, 49–52, 300–3
Romans, Epistle to the, 247f., 268, 307

Simon Magus, 175–6
Stephen, 174–5, 291, 292

Tatian, 326
Teaching of the Apostles, The. See Didache
Tertullian, 195
Theodas, 70
Theophorus, 70
Thessalonians, first Epistle to the, 240–1; second Epistle, 270
Timothy, first Epistle to, 267–8; Epistles to, 272–7
Titus, Epistle to, 277–9
Turmel, 57–8

Valentinus, 70, 325

www.ingramcontent.com/pod-product-compliance
Lightning Source LLC
Chambersburg PA
CBHW071652160426
43195CB00012B/1443